DUDLEY W. ADAMS.

Master of the National Grange.

THE GROUNDSWELL.

A HISTORY

OF THE

ORIGIN, AIMS, AND PROGRESS

OF THE

FARMERS' MOVEMENT:

EMBRACING

AN AUTHORITATIVE ACCOUNT OF FARMERS' CLUBS, GRANGES, ETC.; A FULL DISCUSSION OF THE TRANSPORTATION QUESTION AND OTHER GRIEVANCES; AND A HISTORY OF INDUSTRIAL EDUCATION IN THE UNITED STATES;

TOGETHER WITH

SKETCHES OF THE LIVES OF PROMINENT LEADERS,

Etc., Etc., Etc.

BY

HON. JONATHAN PERIAM,

Editor Western Rural; First Recording Secretary of Board of Trustees and Superintendent of Agriculture, Illinois Industrial University; Vice President Illinois State Board of Agriculture; Secretary Northern Illinois Horticultural Society for 1872; First President Chicago Agricultural and Horticultural Society, organized 1857; etc.

Over One Hundred Illustrations.

CINCINNATI: E. HANNAFORD & COMPANY. | CHICAGO: HANNAFORD & THOMPSON.

1874.

ELECTROTYPED AT FRANK-
LIN TYPE FOUNDRY, CIN.

TO

The Producing Classes of America,

THIS VOLUME,

(BACK OF WHICH LIES THIRTY YEARS' PRACTICE WITH PLOW AND PEN)

IS RESPECTFULLY DEDICATED BY

THE AUTHOR.

PREFACE.

Notwithstanding the somewhat unusual facilities which my editorial and other relations had furnished me for the collection of data, etc., it is quite probable that I should have regretted yielding to the solicitations of my present publishers to prepare a history of the origin, aims, and progress of the FARMERS' MOVEMENT, had I not been so fortunate as to secure the co-operation of a number of gentlemen, whose assistance has been valuable to both the reader and myself in the highest degree. I desire here to return my thanks to my fellow-laborer on the "Western Rural," Mr. Avern Pardoe, without whose aid it would have been extremely difficult, if not impossible, for me to have responded to this extra demand upon my time. Grateful acknowledgments are also due to my friends Hon. W. C. Flagg and Mr. J. W. Midgley for the papers on Transportation and Railroads which are given in Chapters XXXIV to XXXVII of this work. No apology can be needed for the admission of the "Railroad side," so strongly presented by Mr. Midgley. Intelligent and practically useful discussion of the farmers' undoubted grievances in respect to railroads will be greatly facilitated by a true understanding and careful sifting of the arguments presented by the opposing interest. I also desire to return thanks to many other friends, East, West, and South, who have favored me with valuable information and advice; and to bear testimony to the kind and often painstaking courtesy extended to me by the secretaries and other officers of the Granges, Clubs, and other societies organized in the interest of agriculture.

Want of space has compelled the omission of considerable matter which it was my original intention to embody in this volume—among which are, a list of the Clubs, Granges, etc., in the United States and Canadas; extracts from such of the leading agricultural and other journals of the country as have taken a prominent part in the discussion of the Farmers' Movement; and an admirable paper by my friend Rufus K. Slosson, of Morris, Ill.

In the following pages the endeavor has been made to present history with accuracy and impartiality. When my own opinions have been expressed upon the great and still growing power of monopolizing capital, it has been sought to do so without prejudice or bitterness; and, in fact, on many points I have expressed myself far less strongly than I have really felt. The breach between the Farmers and the Railroads, though wide, by no means seems to me past all healing. It has been perniciously widened by hot-headed enthusiasts and designing demagogues upon both sides. Time and again, with vituperation and invective without stint, it has been declared that the railroad companies would never be satisfied until they had "wrung the last drop of blood from the people." Simultaneously, and with equal lack both of judgment and truth, the railroad organs have denounced the farmers as having no just grounds of complaint; and said they merely seek a pretext for the repudiation of their bonds and the confiscation of railroad property, and even (as a prominent railroad official has lately asserted) that they are really casting about for a method of establishing a sort of commune!

As long as this spirit prevails, a peaceful solution of the matters at issue lies in the future. The railroads will yield nothing unless compelled, while believing, or at least professing to believe, that a concession would be but the occasion for further demands; and the farmers will not abate one jot or tittle of their claims for redress, while insulted by the transparent falsehood that they have no just cause for complaint. Among a people who profess to be self-governed, it ought to be possible to remedy all such grievances without an appeal to regulatory legislation; and the writer, for one, would yet gladly see delegations appointed in behalf of the contending parties, empowered to confer and arrange the basis for an amicable compromise, reasonable, practicable, and just to all parties.

Whatever may be the issue of the pending war between the producers and transporters, however, it is clear that from the Farmers' Movement, as a whole, great good must result. It has opened the eyes of the masses to gigantic frauds in other directions. Even if this were not the case, the increased interest which the members of Farmers' Clubs, Patrons of Husbandry, and like Associations, have manifested in our social and public affairs must be productive of great good to the masses, in the proper education of the present and rising generations in their duties as individuals and citizens. It is through this great quickening of the toiling masses, and their stimulation to higher endeavor, that either the renovation or overthrow of the effete and corrupt political parties of the day is to be effected.

J. P.

CHICAGO, ILL., 19th January, 1874.

CONTENTS.

CHAPTER I.

PAGE.

INTRODUCTORY.—A Groundswell—The origin of Groundswells—Some modern Groundswells—The Groundswell of to-day—Types and anti-types. 21

CHAPTER II.

AGRICULTURE AND ITS SUBDIVISIONS.—What Agriculture embraces—Effect of Science on Agriculture—The fathers of modern Agriculture—Scientific Experiments in the United States—Status of Agriculture in ancient times—The true definition of Agriculture—Co-operation the panacea. 30

CHAPTER III.

RELATION OF AGRICULTURE TO HORTICULTURE.—Education the key-note to progress—Advanced state of horticultural science—Gardening of old and its progress—The future influence of Horticulture—Why are farmers behind horticulturists?—A little knowledge a dangerous thing. 41

CHAPTER IV.

FARMERS' CLUBS IN GREAT BRITAIN.—In Scotland and Ireland—The first Farmers' Club in England—The Royal Agricultural Society and present organizations of England—Conditions of English farmers—The farm laborers of England—English farmers agitating—A good time coming. 51

CHAPTER V.

AMERICAN FARMERS' CLUBS.—At the time of the Revolution—Clubs in Pennsylvania—Clubs in the South—Clubs in New York—"American

PAGE.
Institute Farmers' Club "—Clubs in Massachusetts—The spread of Agricultural Societies—The present want and future duty. . . . 62

CHAPTER VI.

POWER OF THE FARMERS.—Why farmers do not wield political power—Our defective educational system—Farmers must arouse themselves—Numerical strength of the farmers—Representation of the farmers—United, earnest action demanded—Union of Clubs and Granges necessary. 73

CHAPTER VII.

CO-OPERATION AMONG THE INDUSTRIES.—What organization may accomplish—Superior organization of other industries—The penalty paid for past negligence—The agricultural press a trusty counselor—The power of the moneyed classes consolidated—How panics are generated—Combine, consolidate, concentrate. 84

CHAPTER VIII.

CONSTITUTION AND BUSINESS OF FARMERS' CLUBS.—Preliminary steps in organization—After workings—Model for a Constitution—Standing committees, order of business, etc.—Co-operation of Clubs—Form of Illinois Farmers' Clubs' Constitution—State organization—Constitution of the Tennessee Farmers' Association. 94

CHAPTER IX.

INNER WORKINGS OF FARMERS' CLUBS.—Farmers' Clubs must be social—Clubs must collect facts—Subject for debate in Clubs, etc.—Horticulturists better organized than farmers—Organized pleasure taking—Co-operative buying and selling—The advantage of mutual assistance. 104

CHAPTER X.

THE ORDER OF PATRONS OF HUSBANDRY.—What is a Grange?—Degrees of the Order symbolized—Higher stages of progress—Objects and advantages of the Granges—What a Grange is not. 115

CHAPTER XI.

THE ORIGIN OF THE ORDER.—How it came about—The germ-idea—Maturing plans—Forming the first degree of the Order—The founders of the Order—Selecting a name—Organizing the "National Grange." 125

CHAPTER XII.

PAGE.

EARLY STRUGGLES AND THEIR FRUITION.—Testing the work already done—Carrying the work forward—The first four dispensations issued—Discouragement, but not despair—Working against difficulties—The Headquarters of the Order—Wonderful growth of the Order—Strength of the Order. 134

CHAPTER XIII.

AIMS AND OBJECTS OF THE ORDER.—Salient features of the Order—Educating the intellects—The business feature—A thirst for knowledge—The secret nature of the Order—The secret feature exaggerated and misapprehended—The real character of the Order. 146

CHAPTER XIV.

OTHER PROMINENT FEATURES OF THE ORDER.—Woman's mission in the Grange—Women as keepers of secrets—How the Patrons prevent lawsuits—The colored brother as a Patron—No Granges speaking foreign languages—The Illinois "Staats-Zeitung" on the Granges—Some of the unjust charges against the Granges—Some gains of the Granges—A case in point—Co-operation of independent organizations necessary to ultimate success. 155

CHAPTER XV.

LAWS AND BY-LAWS OF THE ORDER.—Officers and Constitution of the National Grange—Constitution of State Granges—County Councils, Constitution, etc.—Constitution of Subordinate Granges. 168

CHAPTER XVI.

THE MOVEMENT TOWARD CO-OPERATION.—What are the farmers' grievances?—Farmers' troubles of modern growth—Operations of railroad rings—Where the blame originally lies—The village merchant as an extortioner—Growth of grievances—Building of the first railroad and its effects—The Centralia, Illinois, Convention. 196

CHAPTER XVII.

THE NATIONAL AGRICULTURAL CONGRESS OF 1872.—Revival of Clubs at the South—The Tennessee Farmers' Association—The first National Agricultural Congress. 207

CHAPTER XVIII.

PAGE

THE FIRST BLOOMINGTON (ILLINOIS) CONVENTION.—Effect of the war on Agriculture—The end of endurance—The bugle-call—Gov. Palmer's letter—General business of the Convention—Only a partial success, and why. 222

CHAPTER XIX.

THE KEWANEE (ILLINOIS) CONVENTION.—Origin of the Convention—The delegates, and their difficulties—Business of the meeting—Speeches and poetry—Results of the discussion. 232

CHAPTER XX.

THE SECOND BLOOMINGTON (ILLINOIS) CONVENTION.—The storm gathering—The call for the Convention—Opening for business—The Railroad abuses—Farmers in council—Railway legislation and railway reform—Charters and contracts—Rights of the people *versus* railroads—Formation of the Illinois State Farmers' Association—The resolutions. 242

CHAPTER XXI.

THE PATRONS OF IOWA, AND THEIR WORK.—Two meetings of the State Grange—Railroads, land grants, salaries, and Grange Agents—Speech of Worthy Master A. B. Smedley. 263

CHAPTER XXII.

THE KANSAS FARMERS' CO-OPERATIVE ASSOCIATION.—The State Convention at Topeka—Resolutions, and debate thereon—Constitution, By-Laws, and Officers—Local organizations, etc. 271

CHAPTER XXIII.

THE SPRINGFIELD (ILLINOIS) CONVENTION.—Growth of the movement, and call of the Convention—Gov. Beveridge on the Movement—Gov. Palmer on Railway Monopolies—The resolutions—Divided counsels—Concerning reconsideration. 280

CHAPTER XXIV.

PAGE

THE TEST CASE ON THE UNCONSTITUTIONAL ILLINOIS RAILROAD LAW.—The McLean County test case—Judge Tipton's decision—The three-cent-a-mile war—The argument on the appeal—Decision of the Supreme Court; the law unconstitutional. 292

CHAPTER XXV.

THE NEW ILLINOIS RAILROAD LAW, AND ITS WORKINGS.—The Railroad Commission squabble—The new Railroad Law—Working of the new law 302

CHAPTER XXVI.

THE ILLINOIS JUDICIAL ELECTIONS.—The first charge along the line—The Princeton Convention—The result at the polls—The result of the election misconstrued. 312

CHAPTER XXVII.

THE AMERICAN CHEAP TRANSPORTATION ASSOCIATION.—The Grain Growers' Transportation and Loan Association—The Farmers' and Producers' Convention—The resolutions—President Quincy's call for the Washington Convention. 317

CHAPTER XXVIII.

THE NATIONAL AGRICULTURAL CONGRESS OF 1873.—Opening formalities, etc.—Financial, horticultural, and entomological—Exhaustive report on the transportation question—Report on the railway system—The Agricultural College land grand bill—Pro and con—The election of officers, etc. 327

CHAPTER XXIX.

THE NORTHWESTERN FARMERS CONVENTION AT CHICAGO.—The call, attendance, and organization—Tho question of governmental aid—Hon. W. C. Flagg's address on the regulation of Railroads—Mr. Hooten on Railroad abuses—The resolutions, and their consideration—Pork to be held for a rise—Report on the Illinois Railroad Law. . . . 342

CHAPTER XXX.

PAGE

BIOGRAPHICAL SKETCH OF WM. SAUNDERS.—One of the fathers of the Patrons of Husbandry—Early career—Literary labors—Connection ith the Agricultural Department—Future projects. 363

CHAPTER XXXI.

BIOGRAPHICAL SKETCH OF GEN. JACKSON.—Early life—At West Point and in the army—War breaks out—His part in the war—After the war—The warrior as a farmer 369

CHAPTER XXXII.

BIOGRAPHICAL SKETCH OF JOHN DAVIS.—Early pioneer life—Grinding at the horse-mill—Getting an education, and start in life—"Westward Ho"—Present prominence and labors. 377

CHAPTER XXXIII.

BIOGRAPHICAL SKETCH OF HON. W. C. FLAGG.—Parentage and education—Connection with Illinois Horticultural Society—Legislative career—Agricultural education from a scholar's stand point—Editorial connections and further honors. 383

CHAPTER XXXIV.

(*By Hon. W. C. Flagg, President Illinois State Farmers' Association.*)

THE PEOPLE *versus* RAILWAY MONOPOLIES.—A great public danger—Private corporations governing States—Railway corporations defiant—Facts and figures—Highways of transportation should be controlled by the public authorities—Actual cost of carrying passengers—Transportation rates in Europe and the United States—What freights cost, and what is charged—Western experience—Excessive charges in Tennessee and Iowa—Self-interest the railway rule of action—Evils of unjust discrimination—Railway interference with legislation—The beginning of the end. 389

CHAPTER XXXV.

PAGE

(*By J. W. Midgley, Esq., Chicago, President's Secretary, Northwestern Railway.*)

RAILWAY LEGISLATION AT HOME AND ABROAD. 406

CHAPTER XXXVI.

(*Continuation of Mr. Midgley's Article.*)

CONCERNING RATES AND GOVERNMENTAL RAILWAYS. 427

CHAPTER XXXVII.

(*Conclusion of Mr. Midgley's Article.*)

THE BENEFITS CONFERRED BY RAILROADS. 436

CHAPTER XXXVIII.

TRANSPORTATION AND THE MONEY-KINGS.—The question from antagonistic stand-points—Legislation not the panacea for all evils—We must strike at the root, corruption—One way of robbing the West—How the great railroad corporations corrupt public morals—Vanderbilt as a phlebotomist—The communism of capital. 452

CHAPTER XXXIX.

MONOPOLIES AND SPECIAL PRIVILEGES.—What are monopolies?—The communism of protected industries—Examples of odious protection—Railroads as protected monopolies—Vested rights and politicians—Special privileges dangerous to the people at large—The farmers not inimical to railroads. 464

CHAPTER XL.

CREDITS MOBILIER, FAST FREIGHTS, ETC.—"Credit Mobilier" defined—The great Credit Mobilier—Smaller Credit Mobilier associations—Wheels within wheels—Watered stock. 474

CHAPTER XLI.

PAGE

GOVERNMENTAL OWNERSHIP OF RAILWAYS.—Its corrupting power—The cost of railroads in the United States—Watered stock; New York Central—Central Pacific Stock—Government purchase of railroads a fallacy. 484

CHAPTER XLII.

BIOGRAPHICAL SKETCH OF COL. A. B. SMEDLEY.—Outline of a useful career—As a Patron of Husbandry. 493

CHAPTER XLIII.

BIOGRAPHICAL SKETCH OF DUDLEY W. ADAMS.—Youth and emigration westward—Services in behalf of Agriculture—Early struggles and public services—Services in the Order of Patrons of Husbandry. . 495

CHAPTER XLIV.

INDUSTRIAL EDUCATION.—Importance of the subject—Where shall our children learn?—How shall we begin?—Farmers as craftsmen—Experience as a thorough teacher—The classics and Agriculture . . 501

CHAPTER XLV.

POPULAR AGITATION ON INDUSTRIAL EDUCATION.—A want long felt—Industrial League and further agitation—Memorial to the Illinois Legislature—The legislative resolutions—Leading utterances of twenty years ago—The Albany (N. Y.) convention on Industrial Education—The voice of Agriculture 510

CHAPTER XLVI.

CONGRESSIONAL ACTION ON INDUSTRIAL EDUCATION.—How the Agricultural College bill became a law—Text of the Act of Congress—The Amendment to the Act—Distribution of the lands to the several States 524

CHAPTER XLVII.

PAGE

AGRICULTURAL COLLEGE EDUCATION.—Its scope and aim—One great mistake—Practical education to Agriculture—The study of chemistry, physiology, and other specialities—Practical education need not be restricted or sordid—"In the sweat of thy brow"—The future of Industrial Education. 532

CHAPTER XLVIII.

BIOGRAPHICAL SKETCH OF PROF. J. B. TURNER.—Early struggles—Professor at Illinois College—Introducer of Osage Orange as a hedge plant—The educator as an inventor—Contributions to science—Championship of education to the industries—Advocacy of a National Bureau of Agriculture, etc.—Personal simplicity, and greatness of his work. . 544

CHAPTER XLIX.

WHAT THE GROUNDSWELL HAS ACCOMPLISHED.—The good work in California—In other Western States—Action of the Iowa State Grange, December, 1873—What the Illinois State Grange Believes—Action of the Illinois State Farmers' Association. 555

CHAPTER L.

THE ORDER OF PATRONS OF INDUSTRY.—Its organization and rapid growth—Aims, advantages, and methods of the order—Officers, degrees, etc.—Constitution and by-laws of the Order—The Order law-abiding, and benevolent in its designs. 566

LIST OF ILLUSTRATIONS.

PAGE

Dudley W. Adams, Esq.—Portrait—frontispiece.
A Groundswell, ... 23
"Thou, too, sail on!" 26
"Watch 'em!" 28
Vignette, ... 30
English Farm Scene, ... 32
Great Seal of the United States, ... 35
Agriculture Speaking English, ... 41
The Wealth of Orchards, etc., ... 43
Fruit Piece, etc., ... 45
The Cabin of the Peaceful Pioneer, ... 47
Coat-of-Arms of Great Britain, ... 53
Shall we Emigrate? 56
One of the Grievances of English Farmers, ... 59
A Pennsylvania Barn-yard, ... 63
When Cotton was King, ... 65
1620—The Genius of History, ... 69
The Old South—Negro Quarters, ... 70
Brought to the Bar at last, ... 76
The Motto for Farmers, ... 81
Some of the Classes that should Co-operate, embracing:
The Farmer, ... 87
The Machinist, ... 87
The Miner, ... 87
The Seamstress, ... 87
The Blacksmith, ... 87
The Builder, ... 87
Fidelity, ... 93
Going to the Club Meeting, ... 95
State Seal of Illinois, ... 99
State Seal of Tennessee, ... 101
Not to be Trusted—The Farmer *versus* the Politician, . . 107
Brawn and Brains, ... 109
Neighborly Help, ... 113

PAGE

What the "Granger" is Not—The Opinions of Some to the Contrary Notwithstanding—embracing:
- Owl, ... 123
- Bear, ... 123
- Frog, ... 123
- Sheep, ... 123
- Crawfish, ... 123

William Saunders, Esq.—Portrait, ... 129
O. H. Kelley, Esq.—Portrait, ... 137
What the Order is Not, ... 143
A Farm Scene, ... 150
The Matron at Home, ... 157
Justice, ... 158
Cotton Plant, ... 160
"What shall We do with Him?"—The "Granger's" Advent among the Politicians, ... 175
State Seal of Missouri, ... 176
In Union there is Strength, ... 205
A Virginia Tobacco Barn, ... 208
All forgotten save the Nation's Unity, ... 222
The Monopolists' Mistake--Not the Type of the Farmer, . . 224
Steamboat and Railway Cars, ... 235
"For them the Bobolink sang not," 239
The Demand of the Industries, ... 243
Life on a Prairie Farm--Receiving Reports at Evening, . . 245
Railway Train, ... 252
State Seal of Iowa, ... 264
"Through Trial, Toil, and Blood," 266
Danger! 267
State Seal of Kansas, ... 272
"Other Interests also," 282
A Model Monopolist, ... 285
The Highway of Civilization, ... 295
Obsolete Method of Transportation in the Tobacco Country, . 305
A Princeton Convention Man, ... 314
3,000 Majority for Craig, ... 316
Constituents of the S. P. C. A., for whose Transportation Congress has already Legislated, ... 318
Loading a Steamboat on the Mississippi, ... 322
A Farm in Indiana, ... 329
Busy Bees, ... 344

PAGE
Harvest Scene, ... 353
At Three Cents a Pound, ... 356
"Pay as you go." Live in the Old House till the Farm is all paid for, ... 358
Held for $5.00 per 100, ... 361
General W. H. Jackson—Portrait, ... 371
John Davis, Esq.—Portrait, ... 379
Colonel A. B. Smedley—Portrait, ... 379
Hon. Willard C. Flagg—Portrait, ... 391
Homestead on the River, ... 419
"Speed, Comfort, Safety." 428
The Rural Toilers of Forty Years Ago, ... 437
Before the Era of Railroads, ... 445
The Old Bird Fairly Aroused, ... 455
State Seal of New York, ... 459
Interior of Farm-house in the Olden Time, ... 465
"We 're going to have a Railroad!" 471
The Stalking-horse of Swindlers, ... 475
The Water-Sprite—Farmer's Daughter, ... 480
Farm Scene—The First Snow, ... 487
The Capitol at Washington, ... , . 491
Off to School, ... 503
What has made Industrial Education possible, ... 504
Pegging Away, ... , . . 512
The Farmer's Boys, ... 521
The Rural Home, ... 525
The Stock-Breeder's Museum, ... 536
Feeding the Lamb, ... 537
"Nature's Miracles on Every Side," 538
Prof. J. B. Turner—Portrait, ... 545
Bird, ... 558
Saturday Afternoon, ... 563
A Page for the Little Folks, embracing
Lots of Fun, ... 567
Picking Apples, ... 567
One of the Pets, ... 567
Back of the Barn, ... 567
Nooning in the Shade, ... 567
A Sly Little Customer, ... 567
Finis, ... 576

THE GROUNDSWELL.

CHAPTER I.

INTRODUCTORY.

A GROUNDSWELL.

"Ahoy!" "Bear a hand!" "Cut that painter!" "Cast loose!" A score of such cries, with sundry incoherent yells, broke suddenly upon the repose of a small fishing hamlet nestling in a cave that opened out upon the wide Atlantic.

There had been almost a dead calm. The sea, stretching far in the distance, rocked in gentle undulations, like a child in its cradle, and clear as a mirror curled gently up on the shore. The sough of the waters, as they lazily rose and fell, was varied only by a soft, long-continued "*swi-i-sh*," as the ever-recurring, ever-advancing wave of the incoming tide rolled over the shells and pebbles, with a tinkle murmurous and musical. Nothing suggested the resistless power of this calm blue water when lashed into fury by Old Boreas; nothing in the state of the weather indicated aught but a long-continued calm; for the tranquillity which reigned over all seemed the result of a settled determination upon the weather's part to remain serene, and was not, by any means, the ominous, oppressive stillness which precedes a storm. All was beauty and peace.

The boats belonging to the village were drawn up on the beach, in orderly array, the sails of some hanging listlessly, and those of others stowed carefully away or lashed trimly to the masts. Of the sturdy fishermen lolling about on the beach, the younger ones were chatting gayly, or lazily smoking their short pipes, evidently enjoying their enforced idleness; others, more restless, and chafing under their inactivity, strolled to and fro, ever and anon casting an eye, now seaward, and now toward the line of cliffs shutting in the broad sandy beach. But not a sign did they discern of the much desired change of the monotonously fine weather. The longed-for breeze which was to take them to their fishing grounds gave no token yet of its appearance. Even the older salts, whom a life of constant watchfulness had rendered wary as cats, had relaxed some of their accustomed vigilance, and, gathered in little groups, were smoking and discussing old times.

Suddenly, almost instantaneously, the scene changed as if by magic, and the beach became a spectacle of bustling confusion and activity. The sun still shone with grateful warmth, and the same dead calm continued; but, far in the distance, there was a sudden upheaval of the waters, innocent in the depths of the ocean, but terrible in its force against the shore. One of the veterans who had been watching the sea, from force of habit rather than any thought of danger, saw it, and suddenly leaped up. "A swell! A groundswell!" he shouted; "Quick! Quick!" And, motioning to his two mates, he rushed, as with the vigor of youth, to where his boat lay with the others upon the beach. In an instant the craft was launched, and he and his comrades were rowing out to sea, as if for life.

Scarcely had their boat got well out from shore, before the waters swiftly receded, only to be suddenly brought back by a huge wave, swelling in resistless majesty as it advanced. As its base touched the bottom of the shoaling water, the top curled into a gigantic comb, and, as it fell forward, the mighty mass was thrown with deafening roar upon the beach. The boats still lying at their moorings were caught up like feathers, and hurled yards farther inland. With the same terrific dignity which marked their incoming,

A Groundswell.

the waters rolled back, leaving the little fleet in indescribable confusion—bottom up, or end up, or on their sides, some piled two or three together, others stove in, and not a few wrecked irreparably. Around their boats quickly swarmed the now thoroughly aroused fishermen. Each crew seizing their craft, if happily it could be got at, ran it up the beach still higher, out of the reach of the waves which experience had taught them were yet to come, and higher than before.

Not half the work was done, when a very mountain of water buried the recedence of the first wave out of sight, advanced as before, picked up a number of the unfortunate boats, and dashed their luckless owners, half-strangled, bruised and dripping, high up the beach. Recovering their feet as the water left them, these returned bravely to the rescue of their crafts, and by dint of tugging and hauling, when the third and greatest wave rolled thundering on the beach, most of them were safe, high and dry.

Soon the ocean settled down into its accustomed quiet, and the inspection of damages commenced. The sides of Jack's boat were stove in, Bill's thwarts torn out, and Rob's mast, oars, and tackle all lost, while Steve's craft was an entire wreck. Hardly a boat had saved its mast and rigging unharmed, saving alone the one which got out to sea before the first swell came in.

THE ORIGIN OF GROUNDSWELLS.

Such is a groundswell—a mighty upheaving of the waters, grand, resistless, terrible, its power never to be withstood, and to be eluded only by the utmost watchfulness and skill. It is born of a struggle for mastery between the winds and waters, perhaps hundreds of miles away, or it may be even in mid-ocean. Cast a stone into a pond, and it produces ripples, at first large and well defined, then gradually fading out, but not dying away entirely until they have broken upon the shore, be it never so faintly. So a tornado or a submarine earthquake in mid-ocean stirs the mass of living waters, and transmits its mighty undulations to the utmost shores. When least expected, when the knowing ones and weather-wise predict a continuance of fine weather, when there is no appearance of a commotion among the elements, near or remote, the far-reaching effects of a distant storm may catch the unwary coaster in his fancied security, and dash him high on the beach, crippled for life, or a dead and sightless corpse.

As the effects of a groundswell are proportionate to the violence of the storm or disturbance which occasioned it, so in the bodies politic and social we observe a similar proportion in the strength of periodic agitations resulting from mal-administration, or other grievances which have grown up in the lapse of years and become strong and odious.

SOME MODERN GROUNDSWELLS.

Modern history records many popular upheavals which may well be termed groundswells, some of them actually marking epochs in the life of the human race upon the earth.

Such was the convulsion, which, after centuries of misrule and corruption, shook English society to its center, in the days of the first Charles, and ended only after that monarch, more sinned against than sinning, had lost his life. Not even then was the struggle between kingly domination and the rights of the people to a voice in the government permanently decided. The "last and worser Charles," recalled to the throne of his ancestors, provoked another storm, which James II. was unwise enough to raise to fury, and this time the Stuart was expelled from England, finally and forever.

That awful tragedy in modern history, known as the French Revolution, in like manner was the direct consequence of long years of oppression and misery, coupled with ignorance and superstition. *That groundswell* was a fearful thing, wave following wave, until every city and hamlet in France had been baptized with the bloody spray. Every nation in Europe felt the successive shocks, and before their force was fully expended, more than one of them found themselves stranded on the shores of the nineteenth century, in the condition of battered wrecks after a storm.

The Revolution in our own country was another groundswell of gigantic proportions, having a corresponding origin in the resentment of a high-spirited people against manifest injustice. The monarchical principle was virtually swept

"Thou, too, Sail On!"

from the continent, and the founders of our glorious republic were left free to build, broad and strong, the framework of a popular government, the very best ever launched upon the sea of Time.

Let us hope also that it will prove the most enduring; for what American heart but thrills to the prayer in song of our best-loved poet—

"Thou, too, sail on, O Ship of State!
  Sail on, O Union, strong and great
Humanity with all its fears,
  With all the hopes of future years,
Is hanging breathless on thy fate!"

THE GROUNDSWELL OF TO-DAY.

If there be one danger of more threatening aspect than any other in the present juncture of affairs in the United States, it is the disturbing and corrupting influences flowing out of the existence of great moneyed corporations that, year by year, take on more and more of the characteristics of conscienceless and irresponsible monopolies. By various arts, extending even to the shameless purchase of legislative votes, these strive to shape the domestic policy of the State to their own ends, with less and less regard for the general welfare. The industrial classes are keenly sensitive to the effects of this policy of selfishness and greed, since upon them the burdens imposed by the "all-controlling few" fall the first and most heavily. What wonder, then, that we behold to-day another popular uprising, in earnest protest against attempted wrongs; or, that the farmers, emphatically the great producing class of the whole community, should seek a closer union in council, business plans and influence, and thus to roll onward the waves of their mighty *groundswell?*

A groundswell on approaching the shore is irresistible; the surging waters, as one mass upheaving and sweeping onward, bear all before them; no anchorage will hold. The only chance of safety is to give way by degrees, and thus allow the wave to spend its strength more gradually. Directly the force of one shock is past, the slack must be hauled in, and the vessel drawn back to its anchors, ready to be "slacked off" again at the approach of the next swell. Just so, the class at whose door lies the grievances of which the "Farmers' Movement" is the natural consequence, if they be wise, will yield with what grace they may to the pressure of public opinion. Persistence in a line of conduct constantly growing more and more intolerable will assuredly overwhelm them with disaster, if prolonged. Give way they must; and the people must see to it that whatsoever of wantonly usurped rights are now remanded to themselves, be maintained inviolate in the future.

"Watch 'em!"

TYPES AND ANTITYPES.

Our metaphor need not be enlarged upon. The people find a fitting type in the vast, majestic ocean; popular opinion in its waves, moving gently and quietly, when the elements around are at peace, but sweeping all before them, when lashed by the fury of a tornado.

There is another groundswell, not born of the winds, but of deep-hidden, volcanic fires. An earthquake occurs, and an island or a continent is upheaved. The on-moving waves thus resulting surge against the shores of an empire, engulfing not only the fishermen's craft, but the stately merchant-vessel and the man-of war; even the villages and cities that lie exposed are submerged. Here the antitype is the fire that lives deep in the heart, where lie the springs of human action.

What a mere tidal wave, as to force, is to the storm-begotten groundswell, this mighty rush of waters, originating in the throes of a submerged volcano, is to the angry passions of man as they burst forth after long repression. The tidal wave is easily avoided; the groundswell may be guarded against; but the moral groundswell generated of human passion, aggravated by long continued wrongs, *may* culminate in a wave so overwhelming as to carry a nation to its utter ruin.

CHAPTER II.

AGRICULTURE AND ITS SUBDIVISIONS.

WHAT AGRICULTURE EMBRACES.

Agriculture, in its broad sense, embraces husbandry, or the art of cultivating the soil and obtaining therefrom its increase in the shape of cereals and grasses; stock-breeding, and the feeding and fattening of the domestic animals; and all that pertains to the making and applying of manures, to draining, and, in general, to all other processes which go to increase the productive capacity of the soil.

Agriculture also includes the sub-industry of horticulture, which again is subdivided into vegetable gardening, floriculture, pomology, or the cultivation of fruits; arboriculture, or the cultivation of timber; forestry, or the conservation and culture of forests; and landscape gardening, or the beautifying of natural, or creation of artificial, scenery. These, in turn, are often infinitely subdivided; and especially has this been the case within the last thirty years, or since the multiplication of Agricultural Societies.

The breeder is not necessarily the fattener of cattle for market. The grain-farmer may not be either a breeder or feeder, except to a very limited extent. He may confine himself exclusively to the raising of grass for pasturage or hay; or the products from which he derives his revenue may be exclusively grain. The breeder, on the other hand, must raise both hay and grain, in order to enable him to prosecute his business successfully.

The fruit-grower is seldom engaged in other branches of horticulture, and the florist more rarely still; the vegetable gardener is least frequently of all engaged in other horticultural pursuits. The landscape gardener alone has to deal with all the branches of the noble profession of horticulture, which has been called "the Religion of Agriculture." If this metaphor be accepted, floriculture must certainly be termed the poetry of horticulture.

EFFECT OF SCIENCE ON AGRICULTURE.

Since the establishment of agricultural schools in Europe and the United States, the division of agriculture into its multiform sub-industries has been found exceedingly profitable. It is not too much to expect that, as science progresses in this direction, its subdivision will become more and more extensive. The day is certainly not far distant when pomology, forestry, floriculture, and many other branches of agriculture, will be more and more distinctively followed; just as threshing and draining are even now followed as distinct professions. The future is not remote in which steam-plowing, and hauling to the local market by steam, will be accomplished in connection with threshing and ditching, by persons who will make these their exclusive occupations.

From the Dark Ages until within the last fifty years there was no great and general advance of agriculture. There were improvements in various localities, it is true, but, at the close of the seventeenth century, England, then beginning to secure the mastery of the seas, had but one-half the area of the kingdom in arable and pasture land, the

English Farm Scene.—Shepherd and Flock.

remainder consisting of moor, forest, and fen. As late as the beginning of the nineteenth century much of the land in England either remained in forest or else was exhausted of its fertility. But all this is changed, and now, as Macaulay remarks, a hundred acres, which, under the old system, produced annually, as food for cattle and manures, not more than forty tons, under improved culture yields the vast increase of 577 tons.

THE FATHERS OF MODERN AGRICULTURE.

Until the commencement of the present century there was but little systematic cultivation in America. The forward movement was, undoubtedly, commenced by Washington (as good and conscientious a farmer as he was a statesman) and by Thomas Jefferson, whose scientific investigations into mechanics led him to make the first really valuable improvement in plows.

Great Britain is more indebted to Lord Bacon, undoubtedly, than to any of his contemporaries for the impetus which agriculture received in his day. This great philosopher taught men the inductive method—to inquire into and to discover by experiment, step by step, through the great alphabet of nature—soils, gases, elements, etc.—the true relation which each bears to each.

If all the votaries of agriculture had followed this great man's teachings we should have heard less of that *myth* the "Science of Agriculture." It might more truly be called the sum of all sciences, since, though it is made up of something of all sciences, nevertheless, it will never, in the nature of things, become in itself a true science.

Early in the eighteenth century Jethro Tull, one of the earliest and one of the best writers on agriculture that England ever had, did much, through the record of his experiments in new and improved modes of culture, to advance the customary system of tillage, and to reduce it to rule. Tull was the father of drill husbandry, and the inventor of the horse-hoe. He also invented, but failed to perfect, the threshing-machine, leaving the final triumph in this direction for American genius to achieve, more than a century later.

Arthur Young is also justly celebrated for his labors in behalf of agriculture. He traveled extensively over Europe, to observe the various methods of tillage which prevailed, and is said to have edited nearly one hundred volumes relating to the profession.

In Scotland, Lord Kames, and still more, Sir John Sinclair, were earnest and persevering patrons of agriculture. To the latter gentleman, Scotland is indebted for a complete agricultural survey of the country, with statistical accounts relating to it. The publication of the fruits of his labors had the important result, among others, of leading to the establishment of the Board of Agriculture, in 1793, by Mr. Pitt.

Sir Humphrey Davy was another benefactor of husbandry, deserving prominent mention. It was the result of his experiments which led to the establishment of Agricultural Chemistry as a recognized branch of modern science; and this is truly the "corner-stone of agriculture." Recognizing a plant as a living thing, he held that the laws of its existence must be studied in order to develop the most perfect growth. By experiments, and in his lectures, he demonstrated that plants derive their component parts either from the atmosphere by which they are surrounded, or from the soil in which they grow. These elements being principally carbon, nitrogen, oxygen, and hydrogen, he showed by analysis of soils and plants the relative nature of each, and the conditions necessary to best furnish the elements for growth, and proved that the process of vegetation depends upon their constant assimilation by the organs of plants, by means of moisture, light, and heat.

SCIENTIFIC EXPERIMENTS IN THE UNITED STATES.

In the United States but little scientific experimenting, having for its end the promotion of agriculture, was officially attempted until the endowment of Agricultural Colleges began; and but little has been done even at those institutions, except in a crude and confused way. In the practical application of science to agriculture, however, and in the invention and introduction of labor-saving machinery of the most diversified kinds, our people have become celebrated all over the civilized world.

In the construction of machinery for steam-plowing we do not yet compete with our English brethren, for the simple reason that our virgin soils, where steam-plowing is practicable, can not be advantageously worked by steam, except when an extraordinary depth of furrow is required, such, for instance, as in the cultivation of root crops; and these crops in our country, where corn is so cheap, can not be made profitable unless it be in special localities or seasons. Nevertheless, of late attention has been turned in this direction, and I confidently believe that in the Parvin motor will be found the principle which will eventually compete successfully with horse-power, not only in plowing our soils, but in all the operations of the farm where steam power is required, and also in hauling our grain to the railroad stations on our common country roads.

Our agricultural machinery, in general, has won the highest encomiums wherever exhibited, both in our own country and Europe, as models of strength combined with elegance and lightness.

The first cast-iron plow, made in New Jersey in 1797, has undergone various modifications, until now its mirror-like surface of polished steel, and the admirable adaptation of each part to the work required, would seem to leave but little more to be desired. Yet, not satisfied still, the mind of man is now seeking for some mechanism that shall entirely supersede the plow in the preparation of the soil for the perfect growth of the seed.

Science has enabled the farmer to plow his ground, sow his seed, cultivate his crops, harvest his grain, and make it ready for the stook, thresh, winnow, and send it to the market by the mere act of superintending machines, which do the work like so many creatures of intelligence. He mows his grass, makes it into hay, rakes it into windrows, cocks or loads it directly on the wagon, stacks or puts it in the barn, and even does the heavy work of feeding, entirely by machinery. Water is pumped for his stock and carried into his house by the agency of the wind or steam.

He digs, drains, makes roads, subsoils, and trench-plows his land; plants, hauls, and grinds his grain; prepares fodder for and feeds it to his stock; pumps, saws, and threshes; spades and hoes; loads and unloads; stacks his hay and straw, and does an infinity of other work besides, by the power of automatic sinews of iron and steel. How? By the power of mind applied to the direction of material forces; by true knowledge of cause and effect; in a word, by science. And yet, if asked the question to-day, it is highly probable that two-thirds of the farmers of this country would laugh at the idea of the existence of any intimate relation between science and agriculture.

STATUS OF AGRICULTURE IN ANCIENT TIMES.

It is well known that, at some periods of ancient times, and in some countries, agriculture was held to be an honorable calling, and kings, princes, and statesmen did not disdain to till the soil with their own hands. In ancient Egypt, where labored the men who reared the mighty pyramids, the priests and soldiers owned the lands, about six acres of the Delta of the Nile being allotted to each warrior. At war's alarm they sprang forth ready armed to fight for their estates and homes. In times of peace they grew and spun flax, and with the roots, herbs, wheat, and leguminous fruits which they raised, they supplied food for a large portion of the then known civilized earth.

The Carthaginians considered agriculture to be of all callings the most aristocratic, and the kings, princes, and nobles were among the most active cultivators of the soil. When the Romans finally subdued and laid waste the land, the only books which they deemed worthy of being carried away, it is said, were twenty-eight volumes of manuscripts relating to agriculture.

The Chinese, who have bridges constructed two thousand years ago, still consider agriculture so noble an art that a solemn ceremony is each year performed at which the emperor is required to turn the soil. This nation fed silkworms before Solomon reared his temple. They built the great wall around the empire while Europe was yet wrapped in the gloom of the Dark Ages. They cultivated cotton centuries before the discovery of America. In many respects, their knowledge and practice concerning the careful tilling of the soil is to-day superior to ours, with all our boasted enlightenment. A tract of fifty square miles about Shanghai is called the Garden of China; and, while we of the United States are lamenting our worn-out farms, and talking about emigrating to virgin lands, this people, for countless generations, have tilled the same soil, and, under their management, it is to-day as productive as ever.

Some of the States of ancient Greece esteemed agriculture as the mother of arts, and their agricultural products were exhibited at the Olympic games. With the Spartans, however, agriculture was contemned. It was left to the Helots, their slaves, whom they thought fit only to cultivate the soil. It is not strange, therefore, that they should have been obliged to sup black broth (whatever that may have been). Nor is it strange that they took a distaste to their wretched fare, and finally rivalled even the Athenians in luxury, the laws of Lycurgus to the contrary notwithstanding.

THE TRUE DEFINITION OF AGRICULTURE.

Agriculture is not simply getting the utmost present wealth from the soil with the least outlay of labor. It is not the mere rearing of flocks and herds, to convert into as much ready money as possible. It is not hewing down forests to such a degree that the next generation must replant. It is not a system of culture that will exhaust the soil before the farmer's hair turns gray. And most certainly it is not raising crops to sell at such price as the buyer may arbitrarily choose to offer.

High and progressive agriculture is such a system of tillage as shall give the greatest present returns, while the soil retains its full fertility, or, still better, increases its powers from year to year. It is such a system of breeding and feeding stock that, while the enhanced value of animals shall amply repay the labor and care bestowed, they shall improve in character and quality from generation to generation. It is such an intelligent appreciation of present conditions and future needs as, in clearing a timbered farm, shall lead to sparing trees enough for farm uses, and prevent the excessive denudation that will render a country arid and infertile from the want of rain and dew, or subject it to the unbroken force of sweeping and frightful storms. In improving a prairie farm, it is to set about planting the necessary timber that ultimately must be among the best paying crops on the farm. It is such a system of husbandry and rotation, by means of a diversified agriculture, that the farmer need not be dependent upon any one or two crops for his wealth. It is a business tact and thrift that always enables him to sell at the highest price, or at least on a strong and rising market. It is that counsel and assistance between neighbor and neighbor that draws close the bond of brotherhood, and by co-operation renders each one in the community helpful each to the other.

CO-OPERATION THE PANACEA.

It is by associated effort in Clubs, Granges, and other organizations of like social nature that much of this good can be accomplished. Communities in cities unite for the mutual protection of their interests; as witness the Trades' Unions and similar brotherhoods. Financiers have their Boards where they meet to lay plans, to deal in gold and paper money, and make stocks subserve their purposes of speculation. Railroad companies have their societies, and their yearly conventions, at which all assemble and organize new methods or combinations to secure the utmost returns for their investments.

Why should there not be organized effort among farmers? The greatest difficulty, heretofore, has been their apathy, and their segregation one from another. But now the persistent exertions of a few leaders have awakened them and broken up that apathy, and the wonderful increase of late years in Clubs and Granges has counteracted, in a great measure, the disability caused by their segregation. The whole continent is aroused to the depredations of capital upon labor, and the evil influences which monopolies are exercising upon the consciences of our public men.

There must now be no step backward. If the farmers of the country now fail in asserting and maintaining their just rights, they will cease to be free agents, and become fitting subjects for the virtual slavery into which they will then surely drift. Their only salvation is in their Societies, their Clubs, their Granges. In union there is strength, and in union there is growth.

CHAPTER III.

RELATION OF AGRICULTURE TO HORTICULTURE.

EDUCATION THE KEY-NOTE TO PROGRESS.

The history of agriculture will show that, until the discovery of the art of printing, and the dissemination of knowledge thereby, the farmer was either a slave outright, or, at best, a mere vassal, who had no rights of which his feudal lord might not dispossess him at will. The tiller of the soil was the pioneer who made his way into new countries, hewed down forests, reared flocks and herds, ditched and delved,

"Agriculture Speaking English."

reclaimed the wilds, fenced in fields, planted vineyards, and founded communities, too often only to find himself dispossessed by some armed tyrant, who ate of his providing, and reduced him to slavery. Thenceforth, he held nothing, except by the will of his master.

Such was agriculture until the era of the printing press, which not only marvelously lightened the burdens of scholastic training, but rendered comparatively easy the dissemination of knowledge among the masses. Then, to use the language of that old English farmer and writer, Evelyn, "Agriculture first began to speak English."

The savage is but little above the brute. His agriculture, if indeed he have any, consists simply in the planting, reaping, and storing away of the seeds of a few of the wild grasses, and digging a few of the wild roots that he may find growing beneath his tread. Emerging from barbarism, he gathers flocks and herds, and builds a permanent shelter for himself and family. Having a fixed habitation, he next learns to till the soil systematically as a means of subsistence. Art is now born, and manufactures begin to flourish. He plants a vineyard, becomes civilized, and horticulture and religion follow. Enlightenment ensues, and the cultivation of flowers comes in as a natural sequence, and with it poetry.

ADVANCED STATE OF HORTICULTURAL SCIENCE.

To show that husbandry is less progressive than its child, horticulture, we have only to observe the relative advance that has been made by agricultural and horticultural societies. The wide difference which this comparison will bring to light is due, chiefly, to the fact, that, while the prominent agricultural societies have, in most cases, confined their efforts to holding fairs, horticultural societies have been earnestly engaged in discussing the theory and practice of their art, comparing results, and educating themselves up to a high standard of excellence.

Such a proficiency is only attained among farmers by a certain class here and there, who have been educated to study the *principles* of their profession, precisely as the lawyer, the physician, and the divine study the principles of theirs. Associations of these learned professions have long been diligently employed in debating the various means of advancing their interests, and otherwise educating themselves to their respective callings, while agriculture has been, comparatively, standing still.

"The Wealth of Orchards," etc.

With horticulturists so situated that they have been able to avail themselves of the benefits of discussion, the attrition of mind against mind has made business men of them; has enlarged their ideas in various ways; and has led them to examine the principles and details of their art, and the studies relating thereto. They have made themselves especially conversant with botany and vegetable physiology, the effects of root and twig pruning, the circulation of the sap, fungous and other parasitic growths, the relation of the leaf and bark to the woody parts of the plant, cell growth, the effects of heat and cold on various portions of plants, acclimation, and the influence of the scion on the stock, with a great variety of similar practical details. The Transactions of the various Horticultural Societies existing in the United States constitute a compendium of knowledge relating to the arts in question that will compare favorably with those of any other societies extant.

Horticulture has been especially fortunate in securing the services of many scholarly minds, who have applied their scientific training to the elucidation of important questions that otherwise might have remained hidden for generations. It is a fact that among the leading horticulturists of to-day, a large proportion are men who have left the so-called learned professions to follow this fascinating branch of agriculture, where they have become actual life-workers. Thus it holds in its ranks teachers, physicians, clergymen, and painters, in about the order named. It is especially taken up by medical men, probably from the fact that their knowledge of anatomy and physiology in animals points them in the same direction as regards plants.

GARDENING OF OLD AND ITS PROGRESS.

Twelve years ago I wrote for the Transactions of the Illinois Horticultural Society an essay on gardening, in which I used the following language:

"It is more than probable that a higher state of systematic science has been attained within the last hundred years than had before been known since the foundation of the world. It is said that Egypt, 'the cradle of civilization,' so far perfected her tillage that the banks of the Nile were adorned with plantations, from the Cataract of Syrene to the shores of the

Delta; but this was not until Thebes, with her hundred gates, and the ancient cities of Memphis and Heliopolis were rising in grandeur, and the stupendous pyramids, obelisks, and temples of Egypt had become the wonders of the world.

"Solomon had not delighted to dwell in gardens, nor planted the 'vineyard of Baal-hamon' until after the Queen of Sheba had heard of his power and glory. The hanging gardens of Semiramis were works of art rather than of scientific culture, and the villas of Rome and Greece were more noted for their sculpture, statuary, and paintings, than for the extraordinary culture of their gardens.

"With the Dark Ages came the destruction of the arts and sciences, and the obliteration of almost every trace of agricultural and horticultural art as it had theretofore been taught. As returning civilization began to spread over Western Europe, gardens were again cultivated. And yet so gradual was the progress of horticulture, that, until the reign of Henry VIII, scarcely any kitchen vegetables had been cultivated in England. Since that time, with the increased facilities for knowledge, by means of cheap printing, it has made rapid strides toward that perfect science which it may ultimately reach.

"Kitchen gardening will not receive the attention it deserves from the farmer until scientific agriculture has become widely practiced. And yet a single half acre, well cultivated, will produce, from year to year, half the sustenance of a large family. Horticulturists, as a class, are intelligent, thinking people. Why? Because the products of the garden are better sustainers of the brain than hog and hominy. Show me a country without orchards and gardens, and you will there find a stolid, embruted race. But where the trees drop ripe fruits, and well-tilled gardens are swelling with vegetable wealth, and casting their sweet perfume of flowers over all, there we may be sure dwells an intelligent, thinking, onward-moving people, whose motto is Excelsior.

"Let one or two individuals in each neighborhood set the example, and it will not be long before others will follow, and soon gardens will be planted by all. Why, then, will not all decide to do something more for the next year than they have already done in the past, that our homes may be made more smiling and happy, from season to season? It is neither a small business nor unprofitable. Do you lack knowledge? Learn from books and other products of the teeming press—the depositories of all knowledge."

THE FUTURE INFLUENCE OF HORTICULTURE.

The words above, written twelve years ago for Illinois, would apply, in many situations, with as much force now. With wealth comes the desire for all that can make life comfortable and smooth. The road to wealth lies as much through the garden as the farm. That farmer who neglects this branch of his profession does justice neither to his God, his family, nor himself; for the garden gives health, and with health, thrift and economy; if wealth do not follow, certainly the man has but to blame himself.

Where once the painted savage lived by rapine and plunder, the cabins of the peaceful pioneer have been built.

These again have given place to comfortable dwellings, occupied with happy and intelligent faces. Begirt with well-tilled fields, prosperous farms have grown up all over our favored land. The lack yet remaining is orchards and gardens. Add but these, and it will not be long until flowers will blossom and stately trees grow up, shading smooth

"The Cabin of the Peaceful Pioneer."

lawns, and the next generation will bless the fathers who left them the inheritance. Each home will possess its garden, and this country, for which the All-Giver has done so much and man so little, will become the paradise and glory of the world—a country such as the ancients never knew.

It is a fact which can not be controverted that until horticulture is successfully practiced, high farming can not flourish, or rather high farming or improved agriculture follows, and is the result of, progress in horticultural art. The lessons learned through a study of the details of horticulture are found tc apply as well to husbandry, and the farmer soon learns that the careful saving and application of manure, thorough drainage, perfect disintegration and working of the soil, careful selection of seed, attention to meteorological influence, etc., are as much a part of good farming as of horticulture.

Hence, the farmer begins to read and reflect, study the effect of various manures on different crops, and the exact value of each crop in the rotation. He finds that the soil returns value just in proportion as it is fed. He sees again that feeding crops is not the only sustenance necessary to maintain the strength of the land he cultivates, but also that certain conditions of the soil enable it to store up plant food from the great storehouse of nature, the atmosphere. He is taught to study the anatomy and physiology of plants. From this the gradation is easy to that of animals; and hence the present superior condition of horses, cattle, sheep, swine, and other farm stock. At last he comes to know that agriculture is simply an unceasing transition from plant to animal, and from animal again to plant, in which nothing is lost, nothing gained. All was once dust, and to dust it again returns.

WHY ARE FARMERS BEHIND HORTICULTURISTS?

The principal reason, however, why farmers, as a class, are behind horticulturists is, that they have kept themselves isolated; have been too intent on the all-absorbing routine duties of the farm; have moved, plodding along in the grooves their forefathers hewed out; have not kept pace with the times; have neglected the higher education of the mind, to which members of other professions have devoted themselves so diligently; and have carried their not unjustifiable contempt of "book-farming" to an extent that has redounded to their own injury. They have stood still while others have been moving forward, until the wheel of time in its revolutions has shown them losers in the race of intelligent industry. They have cried "Help, Jupiter!" meanwhile withholding to put their own shoulders to the wheel of the car of progress.

These conditions must exist no longer. Henceforth, being now thoroughly awakened, they must not only labor steadily and with persistent aim, by and through their leaders, but they themselves must help, with brains and money, to work out their plans for emancipation from the shackles of a monopolizing power that seeks to reduce them to a mere serfdom. The ambition of the farmer should no longer be to send his son to a university, where he will be given an education totally unfitting him for rural life, unless he intends to become a lawyer, a doctor, or, as the good old Scotch housewife had it, qualify himself to "wag his pow in a pulpit."

A LITTLE KNOWLEDGE A DANGEROUS THING.

Our cities are too full already of ambitious young men who have received education sufficient only to make them consider themselves above honest toil. Failing to earn a livelihood by other means, they become mere penny-a-liners, or sink into degraded insignificance behind the bar of some saloon; or, perhaps, they mouth vile comedy, nonsense-songs, or worse, behind the footlights of disreputable haunts, where brutish humanity seeks its brutish amusements.

The picture is severe but not overdrawn. There are hundreds of once pure and intelligent young men, who, furnished an education superior to their former playmates, have felt themselves better than mere drudges on the farm, and have

5

sought the city, where, in their disdain of daily toil, they have gone down, step by step, until they have reached the lowest depths of degradation, and sometimes even of crime. Our penitentiaries are filled with just such backsliders from the ranks of honest industry, who once were good and true, and actuated by high moral principle.

Is there no remedy? Yes! *Make home attractive.* Cease the tomfoolery of shutting up from year's end to year's end the best room of the house, never to be opened save on state occasions, and then striking a chill to the innermost soul with its uncomfortable grandeur. Use the parlor as a gathering place where all may meet in social converse for mutual improvement. Furnish the room well and plainly, wasting no money on gorgeous furniture, easily ruined and a pleasure only to the eye. Educate the youth of the country to a taste for a literature that shall improve the mind. Fill the book-shelves with works pertaining to every-day life, interspersed with standard novels and poetry, written in the pure style of such writers as our own Irving and Bryant. Let us do this, and then assuredly shall be laid the broad and solid basis of an education that will make the generation next to come better and purer than that of to-day.

CHAPTER IV.

FARMERS' CLUBS IN GREAT BRITAIN.

IN SCOTLAND AND IRELAND.

Farmers' Clubs, publishing their Transactions are no "new invention," but have the venerable age of a full century and a half. In 1723, there was established, in Scotland, a society to which its founders gave the name of "Improvers in the Knowledge of Agriculture." It became extinct in 1755, but was succeeded by another, which was merged into the "Highland Agricultural Society." This association, in 1787 received a royal charter, and in 1834, it was re-chartered. Annual fairs were thenceforward held, at each of which premiums were given to the amount of £10,000.

In Ireland, an agricultural society was established in 1747. From the influence exerted by the members of this organization many others sprang up in various parts of the island, which were productive of great benefit, not only among the aristocratic landed gentry, for whom all these earlier organizations were instituted, but also among the small proprietors and tenant farmers, and, indirectly, among the laborers themselves.

The passage of the Irish Land Act is of too recent a date to enable an authoritative declaration to be made as to its efficacy. Viewed in the light of the steady decrease of emigration from that country since the law was enacted, it appears to be working well. Ireland seems to be entering on a career of unexampled prosperity, in which the farmers must participate. There has been a substantial increase in the wealth of the country during the unparalleled exodus which has taken place. The Land Act gives the tenant fixity of tenure; that is, they can not be ejected from their holdings until compensated for the money they have expended in improvements. These improvements sometimes amount to much more than the original value of the land. Thus, in some cases, the law amounts to a virtual handing over of the land from the landlord to the tenant, subject simply to a fixed annual rent.

THE FIRST FARMERS' CLUB IN ENGLAND.

In 1777, "The Bath Agricultural Society, of England," was organized, having for its aim the encouragement of agriculture, arts, manufactures, and commerce, in the counties of Somerset, Wilts, Gloucester, and Dorset. Through its volumes, published yearly, it disseminated a vast amount of practical information relative to the culture of the various crops then grown, and especially of those recently introduced. The breeding of cattle, horses, sheep, swine, and other stock, was fully treated of in their reports, which also contained much valuable data concerning manufactures, both general and as relating to agriculture, arts, and commerce.

Among the contributions to its literature we find such names as Dr. Falconer, Dr. Campbell, Sir Christopher Hawkins, Hobhouse, Arthur Young, M. DeSaussaure, Dr. J. Anderson, Dr. Fothergill, Rev. Alexander Campbell, Count DeBerchtold, Gen. Abercrombie, and other eminent men of the day. This shows the interest taken in agriculture, in

England, almost a century ago, by the best minds. This interest has borne abundant fruit, in making England to-day, for the number of acres cultivated, the most productive country in the world, both as to the variety of staples grown and the quantities obtained yearly from the soil.

We find, by the Transactions of the Bath Agricultural Society, for the year 1810, that there were then in Great Britain (besides the Board of Agriculture, of which Sir John Sinclair was President and no less a person than Arthur

Coat-of-Arms of Great Britain.

Young, Esq., Secretary) eighty-one Agricultural Societies in regular working order; and to show that they believed, also, in women's rights, we might point to the fact that one of them, the Badenach and Strathspey Society, had a woman for President, in the person of the celebrated Duchess of Gordon.

THE ROYAL AGRICULTURAL SOCIETY AND PRESENT ORGANIZATIONS OF ENGLAND.

The Royal Agricultural Society, which has exerted so wide-spread and beneficial an influence upon agriculture throughout the civilized world, was founded in 1838, and adopted for its motto, "PRACTICE WITH SCIENCE." Within seven years it had established, or had been the means of establishing, four hundred other societies; one hundred and fifty of these being *practical* Farmers' Clubs. Ten years later (in 1855), the societies and clubs amounted to over seven hundred. The most important of these clubs, the London Central Farmers' Club, became so firmly rooted, was so thoroughly supported, and its influence was so widely felt, that it received the appellation of the "Bridge Street Parliament," and gave rise to the aphorism by a celebrated English statesman, that "neither our fleets, however well manned, nor our armies, however valorous, nor our diplomacy, however successful, can do so much as the plow."

The Royal Agricultural Society owes much of its popularity to the deep interest manifested in it by the late Prince Consort—"the Farmer Prince"—who, indeed, always appreciated the fact that the welfare of the farmer meant the welfare of the nation at large. The Society yet continues to hold its annual exhibitions, which are peripatetic in their nature, and the distinction of being selected as the place for the yearly show is a much coveted one.

In most of the counties of England, there are County Agricultural Societies, which, also, hold annual exhibitions. These societies, as a rule, are in a healthy condition, and of great value to the farmers; but, now, the recognized representatives of the farming interests are the Chambers of Agriculture, composed of landlords, farmers, grain merchants, and others concerned in interests connected with the soil.

There is a Central Chamber, subordinate to which are County Chambers; and these, in turn, are the superiors of the local or district Chambers. These organizations are of quite recent growth, and the interest taken in them is immense.

CONDITION OF ENGLISH FARMERS.

It must be borne in mind that, in England, the relation of the farming class to the community at large is widely different from that which exists in our own country. There, the greater proportion of the farming land is in the hands of a few large proprietors, who rent their farms to a class of men, in nearly every case, possessing considerable capital. It is an actual fact that one hundred and sixty families own more than half of England, four-fifths of Scotland, and an immense proportion of Wales and Ireland.

The farmers of England, as a class, do not themselves work, but confine their personal share in the farm details to superintending the small army of laborers, (as an American farmer would consider them), who are the actual workers.

The parts of England which are suitable for modern, scientific farming, are few in number and not large in area. The smallness and irregular shapes of the inclosures, the diversified surface of the country, and the closeness with which each foot of ground has to be worked in order to realize a profit, in many cases preclude the employment of machinery. Hitherto, there has been little inducement to the English farmer to adopt the latter. Labor has been plentiful and cheap, and the prices of produce have generally been good.

Still, the present condition of most English farmers is very far from being satisfactory. Ground down by rent,

Shall we Emigrate?

rates, and taxes, oppressed by that vexatious and iniquitous remnant of feudalism, the game laws, and dictated to by their landlords at elections and elsewhere, their position is by no means enviable. Nor, as a class, do they now make a profit out of their business. There are many wealthy tradesmen and retired manufacturers who want a farm for purposes of pastime, and who care but little how much they lay out upon their hobby. The consequent competition for farms runs rents up to a figure that makes it impossible to obtain a living and fair interest for the capital invested. As a proof of the wide-spread discontent existing among English farmers, may be mentioned the immense and increasing numbers who annually expatriate themselves, and in the United States, Canada, Australia, New Zealand, and South America, seek that subsistence which unjust laws and extortionate landlords deny them at home.

With unlimited capital, a long lease of a good farm (which is not frequently obtainable), and a situation adapted for all modern appliances and improvements, a man of energy and education can still make farming pay in England; but so far as the mass of small farmers is concerned, the tendency of the age is to drive them to the wall and improve them out of existence. Small farms, as the tenancies expire, are lumped together and let to some pushing man of capital, to the exclusion of that class of tenant farmers who have heretofore been England's boast.

THE FARM LABORERS OF ENGLAND.

The condition of the farm laborers in England has for ages been a burning scandal. It is a natural consequence of the land laws of that country, that the village 'Squire and the parson (whose income is mainly derived from the rent of land) should be found rolling in wealth and luxury, while, hard by, the poor laborer, with his wife and almost invariably large family, is suffering from want of the actual necessaries of life.

Recently, under the leadership of Joseph Arch, a Warwickshire hedge-cutter and Primitive Methodist preacher, the laborers have roused themselves from the apathy of centuries, and have formed Unions, modeled after the Trades' Unions, the result of which has already shown itself in a marked amelioration of their lot. Arch has proven himself possessed of the sterling qualities of courage, modesty, and foresight, which go so far to form the character of a true leader of the people. In pursuance of his purpose to right the wrongs of his fellow-laborers, he left England and undertook a tour of observation through Canada and the United States. He expresses his determination, unless the grievances of his fellow-workers receive immediate attention, to organize a vast emigration scheme, which shall bring the landlords and farmers of England to a truer appreciation of the value of a man. He intends to devote five or six years to looking about, carefully avoiding haste, in order that he may not arrive at any conclusion likely to be disastrous to those whom he wishes to serve.

ENGLISH FARMERS AGITATING.

The farmers themselves, too, are arriving at the conclusion that they are an abused and really oppressed class. Now that voting by ballot has become the law of England, (though it has not yet been tried on a large scale), they hope to get at the true sentiments of their class, free from the intimidation and undue influence which their lords and masters have not scrupled to use hitherto. The "'Squirearchy," as the landlord class is called, are well aware that the scepter of power is passing from them. Therefore, being wise in their generation, they seek to conciliate the farmers by temporizing, and condescending patronage.

The meetings of the Chambers of Agriculture are at-

One of the Grievances of English Farmers.

tended by dukes, marquises, viscounts, earls, and so on, including the "knights of low degree" and esquires of still "less dignity." These blue-blood gentry are fully alive to the fact that, unless they can keep the farmers and the people in good humor, their power will depart from them, and, perhaps, their property as well. Therefore, they are eager to impart "what they know about farming" to their humble but restive dependents.

As it is, the grumblings are loud and deep. The justice of allowing thousands of fertile acres to lie waste, to no other end than that their noble owner may delight himself by the slaughter of partridges, pheasants, and hares, is questioned, and justly questioned, in view of the vast amount of farm produce that England is compelled to import to feed her teeming millions.

The people also begin to inquire whether it be a sufficient ground for their own and their children's suffering for bread that William the Norman passed bad laws and gave land, which did not belong to him, to his *sans culotte* followers eight hundred years ago. Pinched, as they are, by the scarcity and dearness of meat, they do not see the equity of allowing a land-owner to rob the country by raising a couple of rabbits, worth a shilling apiece, for the pleasure of shooting them, while on what those rabbits eat and spoil could be grown a sheep, furnishing a dozen times as much food. These, and similar questions, are being thoroughly agitated and debated. Parliament shows its knowledge that these grievances are real ones, and its desire that they should be shelved, by appointing commissioners to investigate them.

A GOOD TIME COMING.

It is evident, to all far-seeing minds, that the law of primogeniture in England is doomed, and that with it, or perhaps before it, will go down the connection of the Church with the State, which is intimately associated with those laws.

These relics of Norman barbarism, the primogeniture

laws, whereby "families" are built up at the expense of the nation, have already received a shattering blow by the late abolition of the purchase of commissions in the army. Commissions are now given only after the passage of examinations severe enough to eliminate from the candidates the hosts of younger sons and poor relations of whom army officers have hitherto been composed. Here is one avenue closed against the juniors. By and by will come the severance of Church and State, and the loss of the right to give away or sell the cure of souls. Then the landed gentry will have to provide for their entire families, instead of getting all their sons, save the eldest, supported at the public expense, as is the custom now. When this is forced upon them, they will no longer bar the correction of the ancient, unjust laws of entail and inheritance; and then, in natural sequence, will follow the breaking up of the large aggregations of land in single hands. Thus it is plain that the grievances of the English farmers, which consist in the actual existence of injurious laws, and not, as is the case with American farmers, in the evasion and open breaking of laws by high-handed aud too-powerful corporations, are in a fair way of being abolished. There, as here, it will have to be done by organization and concerted action. In both cases, the enemies of the farmers are well organized, wealthy, and unscrupulous; in both cases, it is a battle of the weak against the strong; and in both cases, the odds are greatly in the favor of the weak, if they will be true to themselves. They have the numerical majority, and it is only by fomenting divisions among them that their exactors can longer hope to continue their usurped power.

CHAPTER V.

AMERICAN FARMERS' CLUBS.

AT THE TIME OF THE REVOLUTION.

While eminent citizens of England were seeking, by every legitimate means, to foster the interests of agriculture, a corresponding class in the then infant States of America were not idle. Manufactures at that day were comparatively unknown, or only in their infancy. Then the foremost men of the nation were farmers, and derived their revenue directly from the soil. Of those engaged in the various professions of life, many still clung to the pursuit of their youth, and gave their farms their personal supervision. A large proportion of the heroes of the Revolution left the plow for the battle-field, and when the war was over returned again to their peaceful art.

Those, indeed, were days that may never again return. Then there was no swindling, no stock jobbing, no Credit Mobilier, no open buying and selling of votes, no fine art of lobbying, no overshadowing monopolies. The offer of a bribe was scorned, and the tempter held up to public indignation. If the first American bribe-taker, the traitor Arnold, could have been secured, he would have swung on a gibbet higher than Haman.

Alas! how changed. In this day of fraud and corruption, we see the bribe-taker and the swindling and drunken statesman honored and courted on every hand. They grow rich by gambling in gold and securities—the life-blood of the nation; they fatten and grow proud on panics, which shatter legitimate industries; when their bubbles burst they bring bankruptcy to the honest tradesman, and poverty

A Pennsylvania Barn-yard.

to innocent women and children, without any compunction. Why should they care? The law protects them, or at least connives at them. They have wealth. This species of crime is not odious, as it was in the days of our forefathers, when farmers were law-makers and the rulers in the land. It never will be made odious, until farmers again take the helm. This is a great work—how great has only lately begun to be appreciated. Happily the means of its accomplishment already exist, and this great social and political renovation may yet be brought about, through the agency of farmers' associations, under the various names of Clubs, Societies, Unions, or Granges.

CLUBS IN PENNSYLVANIA.

The first society formed in America was "The Philadelphia Society for Promoting Agriculture." This was established in March, 1785, by a number of citizens who, although but a small portion of them were actually engaged in farming, were actuated by a sense of the necessity of such an organization as an auxiliary to the development of the resources of the State and the agricultural interests of the country. It flourished for some years, and at its regular meetings much valuable information was elicited from practical men. This was published by the society, and thus disseminated through the country by means of the press. Among the awards made by this society was a gold medal to Mr. Mathewson, in 1790, for the best sample and greatest quantity of cheese.

Like many another benevolent association, it afterward lost much of its vitality; dark days came upon it, and it slumbered for years. In 1804, however, it was resuscitated through the patriotic exertions of Judge Peters, and thenceforward for a considerable period continued to do much good. It was finally incorporated by the Legislature of Pennsylvania in 1809, but has since died a natural death.

The example set by the earlier societies in Pennsylvania has not been lost. Local organizations and Boards of Agriculture, for holding fairs, etc., have sprung up in every part of the United States. These have exercised an immense power for good, not only in the locality where the original societies were organized, but throughout the land.

The seed sown has spread and borne abundant fruit in the newer States, as fast as the population has become sufficiently numerous to justify the formation of similar organizations; and, in fact, they have not been a whit behind the older sections of the country.

CLUBS IN THE SOUTH.

The first Agricultural Society ever incorporated in America was that established in South Carolina, in 1785, called

"When Cotton was King."

the "Society for the Promotion of Agriculture." Its objects included the institution of a farm for experiments in agriculture, and the importation and distribution of foreign productions suited to the climate of that State. Another prominent object was to direct the attention of farmers and planters to the economies connected with the agriculture of the State, and to enlist them generally in the improvement of their condition. The society accomplished an excellent work, among other things, that of introducing the cultivation of the olive and the vine into the State.

Societies for the promotion of agriculture were always regarded by the planters and statesmen of the South as being of the first importance; and naturally so, for the reason that agriculture always was the dominant—in fact, almost the exclusive—interest there; more than this, however, from the settlement of the country until about 1860, it was confined to special products, as, at first, tobacco, then cotton, and, later, sugar; these with blooded horses and cattle, comprising the chief sources of wealth of the southern planter. In the earlier history of the South, her clubs and societies were composed of men of wealth and position, and, like the earlier kindred societies of Great Britain, were exclusive in their nature.

More recently, Agricultural Societies in the South have taken on a more popular character, and the last five years has witnessed a wonderful increase in the number of clubs and similar organizations, which have had the effect to reawaken interest in this rich and diversified portion of our common country, and to induce emigration thither. It is to be hoped that this will be the means of developing the immense resources of this fertile region.

CLUBS IN NEW YORK.

A society for the "Advancement of Agriculture" was incorporated in New York in 1791, but it became defunct after a brief existence of ten years. In 1792, the Legislature of the same State incorporated another organization, under the title of the "Society for the Promotion of Agriculture, Manufactures, and Arts," and again, in 1804, a "Society for the Promotion of Useful Arts," in the recital of which arts, agriculture is first named. This society published seven volumes of Transactions previous to 1815.

The New York State Agricultural Society held its first regular fair in 1840, the small sum of twelve and a half cents being charged for admission. Since that time the society has grown in magnitude year by year, exercising a powerful influence upon the growth of agricultural art in the State. Clubs have multiplied, and the Legislature of the State, being finally roused to action, principally through the writings of Judge Buell and the efforts of his contemporaries, many of whom are still living, has done its duty toward agriculture.

The result has been the introduction of a systematic culture, under whose beneficent operations New York now stands the first State in the Union in the diversity and wealth of its products. Its agriculture has stimulated manufactures, built large cities, opened avenues of trade and commerce, and scattered all over it a population that has made it the Empire State of our great Republic. Its farmers have demonstrated that in a diversified agriculture consists the true wealth of a community, whether of a town, county, or State.

While this has been the case, however, its great maritime city, New York, has managed, through its vast aggregation of wealth, chiefly in the hands of a few unscrupulous individuals, to manipulate and get possession of the carrying trade to and from the West. It has bought legislatures and controlled the finances of the country. By a nod, a few of its money kings can signify how much or how little western farmers are to get for their produce. The unconscionable exactions of its railroad potentates have roused a bitter feeling of indignation, and just now it is waking up to the fact that, though powerful, it is not omnipotent. It begins to realize that, unless some change is made, the traffic which once poured money into its coffers will find other channels, and Montreal, Quebec, Boston, Baltimore, and New Orleans reign, perchance, in its stead.

"AMERICAN INSTITUTE FARMERS' CLUB."

This society, founded in 1843, had a more than usually active career for thirty years, or until the summer of 1873, when, from various causes, many of them of chronic standing, it ceased to hold its regular meetings. During the first twenty years of its existence, it effected a vast amount of good, and, through its published Transactions and the newspaper press, exercised an immense influence, reaching over the whole country. It has numbered many eminent men among its members, and its fairs, held annually in New York City, have always excited much interest.

Of late years, unfortunately, it has been managed by unpractical, theoretical men, and has lost its former hold on public attention, various rumors of "axe-grinding" and other irregularities becoming current. In the summer of 1873, its meetings ceased to be held, and, to all appearance, the Club was a thing of the past. A few months later, however, its meetings were resumed, and it is to be hoped that it will profit by its season of rest.

The Institute Farmers' Club has certainly borne a prominent and most honorable part in bringing the agriculture of the State to the advanced position which it now occupies; and, had its labors extended to no other field, it might well be proud of the manner in which its members strove for agricultural education during its days of vigor and practical endeavor. Let us hope that it will renew its youth, and more than emulate its former usefulness.

CLUBS IN MASSACHUSETTS.

But, away back beyond the date of the organization last named, we had Farmers' Clubs; for we find that, in 1803, in the old Bay State, the Trustees of the "Massachusetts Society for Promoting Agriculture," offered, among others, the following premiums:

"To the person who shall discover a cheap and effectual method of destroying the canker-worm, a premium of $100, or the society's Gold Medal."

1620—The Genius of History.

"For a heap of best compost manure from the common materials of the farm—for not less than 200 tons—with a description of the method, $50."

"For the most thrifty trees from seed, not less than 600, and not less than at the rate of 2,400 per acre, of oak, ash, elm, sugar, maple, beech, black and yellow birch, chestnut, walnut, or hickory, $25; or, if all of oak, $50; to be claimed on or before October 1, 1806."

"For accurate analyses of the constituent parts of several fertile soils, respectively so of poor soils, and how, by actual experiment, to remedy the evils, so that it can be practiced by *common farmers*, $50. And if it shall appear to the satisfaction of the Trustees, that the improvement is more than equal to the expense, then an additional $100."

The Old South.—Negro Quarters.

THE SPREAD OF AGRICULTURAL SOCIETIES.

From the beginnings thus imperfectly sketched, Agricultural Societies and Farmers' Clubs have multiplied and spread, until now there are none of the States, and but few of the Territories, which are destitute of more or less organizations of this character. These hold annual fairs, and distribute large amounts in premiums yearly, embracing the entire scope of agricultural and horticultural art, and domestic manufactures. Agricultural Societies are in active operation in nearly every county of the Northern States. In the South, the popular interest in these matters is spreading steadily, and deepening every-where. It will be but a few years, at most, before this section of the Union will be enabled to organize societies as generally as have the East and West.

THE PRESENT WANT AND FUTURE DUTY.

What is now wanted, and what is slowly being secured, is a unity of action by which the town and district clubs proper may become the integrals of the county societies, these again sustaining the same relation to the State Boards of Agriculture, which, in their turn, may form the constituent members of a National Society, whose duty it shall be to advance the true interests of the agricultural masses. The perfect organization thus outlined must be formed by the persistent action of the Clubs, Granges, Farmers' Unions, etc., that are now being organized in vast numbers throughout the land.

When the prime object for which these societies are now being instituted shall have been attained; that is, when the Transportation Companies have been brought back to a practical realization of their position as servants of the people, instead of being as now their masters; when the towering monopolies now overshadowing the land have been crippled;

and when a purer class of men have been elevated to public office, high and low, then these societies can settle down into the steady work pertaining to their position and the profession which they represent.

They can go on collecting data relating to the every-day economy of farm life, and make themselves useful to the country in a thousand various ways. Meanwhile, and always, it will behoove them to continue "standing guard" over the interests of the agricultural classes, and see to it that these do not again find themselves bound as with fetters of iron, and thrown helpless before the car of the Juggernaut, capital.

CHAPTER VI.

POWER OF THE FARMERS.

WHY FARMERS DO NOT WIELD POLITICAL POWER.

We have shown that heretofore our legislative bodies have been composed of professional men chiefly. There are a number of reasons why this has been the case; the principal one being that we are all too much inclined to be led away by what has been vulgarly called the gift of gab. A good talker, that is, one who is able, from a natural flow of words, to talk glibly, albeit without argument, naturally leads the masses the world over. Lawyers are, notably, sophists, and many of them sound reasoners and deep thinkers. Their education gives them such training that they naturally wield great influence. Hence their vast preponderance among those elected to do the legislation.

Another reason why farmers have not secured a proper representation is, that, as a class, they are not a reading people; and yet there is no calling in life, requiring continued manual labor, in which so much of that invaluable element, *brains,* can be exercised, or where so much is accomplished in this direction by natural thinkers, as that of the farmer. He may pursue any given train of thought while plowing, driving his team along the road, and during many other of his occupations, which the mechanic or artisan can not do.

The statistics of the book trade, however, show that the average farmer is not an average reader, either of books or newspapers—especially of those devoted to his profession. But farmers, although working slowly for the better in this respect, are nevertheless working surely. The rising generation is thirsting after knowledge, and when it has fairly entered the arena of public action must, if its predecessors do not, solve the problem of the social and political equality of the masses.

OUR DEFECTIVE EDUCATIONAL SYSTEM.

One great difficulty is that our "higher system" of education has tended to bring labor into contempt. Happily, this also is being changed. The elements of science are now taught in many of our common schools, though imperfectly, in most cases, and through the old groove-channels of the dead past. Our colleges are beginning to see the necessity of instruction in the practical application of science. Our agricultural colleges, especially, are manifesting a just appreciation of that higher education which teaches of things rather than of theories.

The "coming farmer" must be educated to a fairer and broader comprehension of the true status of the masses, and the advancement of the industries. He must study for his business, just as the merchant does for his, and as the professional man does for his. This attainment is growing easier every day; for, with the progressive settlement of a country, the agricultural masses become less and less segregated, and neighborhood Clubs, Granges, and social reunions are more and more possible.

If the farmer and the artisan longer refuse to do their share in the education to, and the legislation for, the great body politic, they will have none to blame save themselves. The initial point upon which all this must hinge, so far as concerns the farmer, is the neighborhood Club or Grange, in like manner as with Unions among artisans. The latter class, by the way, are still far in advance of the farmers in this respect. Their organizations can make themselves felt, and are growing daily in power and importance.

FARMERS MUST AROUSE THEMSELVES.

Farmers, you must arouse yourselves to the dignity and importance of your calling. You must educate yourselves to that intellectual status which will enable you to rule, as you are entitled to do by your numerical strength, instead of being ruled, as now, by classes in nowise your superiors, save as you permit them so to make themselves.

To do this, you must work, you must read, you must think! You must combine, and support the organizations for your elevation and advancement already founded. You must array yourselves in solid column, and insist, by your voting power, that the law-makers whom you elect do their duty, by subserving the interests of the whole people, and not those of merely a class.

A nation should be represented by its dominant industries. Agriculture is the dominant interest of the United States. You have the power, if you choose to use it. You represent a majority of the voting power, and your productions constitute one-half the gross annual value of all the products of all the varied industries of the country, or nearly four thousand millions of dollars.

The artisan should have his full share of representation, and the merchant, the manufacturer, and the other professions should have theirs. Nay, even the gambler in stocks ought, perhaps, to have what representation he is entitled to, although it would be somewhat difficult, under a just *pro rata,* to see just where his individual member of Congress would come in. Perhaps, New York and some other of the great cities might gain one by clubbing together.

There is one important point in this connection which farmers must constantly keep before their minds. It is that, having put their hands to the plow, there must be no looking back. "Revolutions never go backward," is a good saying and a true one. The agitation now going on must

Brought to the Bar at Last.

be continued, until the corruption now rife among our public men has received its death wound. The centralizing and monopolizing tendencies of capital must be unceasingly combatted until they be checked, or our country will soon be free only in name. The Transportation Companies must be made to feel that the power which created them can also regulate them; that, while their just rights will be respected, such vested interests as they claim, which are antagonistic to the public good, are, *de facto,* nullities.

The results of the Farmers' Movement have, already, unmistakably shown themselves. The infant Hercules has strangled the serpent in his cradle—witness the Illinois judicial elections, the Illinois "Railroad Law," and the panic precipitated among stock-jobbers by the prescience of their impending fate. And truly it is time that the many-headed hydra of corruption prepared for its approaching end.

NUMERICAL STRENGTH OF THE FARMERS.

Twenty years ago, the numerical strength of the Agricultural, compared with all other of the producing, classes in this country, was as three and a half to one. The relative difference in the number of farmers and that of the aggregate of mechanics and manufacturers was as five to one. The preponderance of the farmer over the so-called "learned professions" was in the proportion of fifty-six to one; and of all the producing classes over all the learned professions, as seventy-two to one.

Thus it will be seen that, over the whole country, it then took one individual out of seventy-three to bleed and blister, preach to, and plead for, the people of the United States. Nearly seven-eighths of the legislation of the country, however, has always been performed by one of these professions, namely, the law.

At the present time (using the latest tabulated statement which I have seen) the adult population of the United States is divided, as to occupations, as mentioned in the first table on the page following.

A glance at the second table reveals the fact that nearly one-half of the total earnings of the country are composed of the earnings of the agriculturist. But it will be observed that this sum, immense as it is, represents less than five hundred dollars *per caput, per annum*, for those actually engaged therein.

Agricultural pursuits	5,922,471
Domestic servants	975,734
Ordinary laborers	1,031,666
Trade and transportation	1,191,238
Manufactures	2,555,314
Miners	152,107
Total engaged in non-professional pursuits	11,828,530
Engaged in professional pursuits	677,393
Total	12,505,923

The value of the products of the several industries is estimated in approximate figures as follows:

Products of artisans, machinists, carpenters, blacksmiths, masons, and the like	$1,000,000,000
Leather manufactures	226,000,000
Iron and steel manufactures	120,000,000
Cotton manufactures	71,500,000
Woolen manufactures	66,000,000
Unskilled labor and distributors	1,600,000,000
Fisheries	100,000,000
Railway services	360,000,000
Agriculture	3,300,000,000
This makes the gross products of the country not quite	$7,000,000,000

REPRESENTATION OF THE FARMERS.

When we come to compare the actual amount of the representation of the farmers, both in our National and State legislatures, with the amount to which they are entitled, both in respect of their numbers and property, an astonishing disproportion is revealed. Of the two hundred and ninety-two Representatives in Congress, only six per cent. are farmers, while of the remainder sixty-five per cent. are lawyers; the residue is mostly composed of other professional men. In the State legislatures the proportions are not very different. As long as this is the case—as long as farmers suffer themselves to be represented by men who have no interests in common with themselves, whose advantage it is, indeed, that the laws should be as complicated and obscure as possible—farmers can not hope that their interests will receive proper attention.

If this state of things be suffered to continue, the farmers will have themselves to blame for their various grievances. They must no longer suffer the village caucus to be manipulated by the 'Squire, the doctor, the merchant, and the "bummer," to whom, hitherto, they have been too ready to leave the direction of their affairs. Farmers must attend the primary meetings and see that, for the town and county offices, as well as for the State and National legislatures, persons of their own class, or known to be in sympathy with them, be elected.

Our farmers are not by any means free from blame for the condition into which public affairs have drifted. They have allowed their business to monopolize their attention, blind to the fact that, while their assiduity may have netted them a dollar, designing rascals were laying their plans for robbing them of fifty cents. As a class, they neglected to inform themselves upon the current topics of the day. Therefore, they have fallen easy victims to swindlers of all shades—political swindlers chief of all. Now that they have awakened to their interests, we see the work of political regeneration making cheering progress, and still the tide is rising.

UNITED, EARNEST ACTION DEMANDED.

All other trades and professions, both in this country and in England, have their recognized organs. Most of them have an Association, Society, Club, Union, or something that answers the same purpose. They never indulge in bickerings and strife among themselves; but they are, at all times, willing to unite and sow dissension among the farmers. The latter, in this country, if united, as their enemies are, could carry any measure they please, by sheer weight of metal.

Some statisticians place the voting power of the farmers at less than two-fifths of the entire vote of the country. I am inclined to think that the actual power of the farmers far exceeds this proportion. But even if my estimate of their strength is somewhat in excess of the actual figures, it must be borne in mind that there are certain classes, in small towns and villages especially, whose interests are intimately connected with those of the farmers, and whose votes naturally belong with theirs, and in any distinctively drawn contest could be depended on by them.

I repeat that, in future, the farmer must, as a matter of self-preservation, take a more active interest in politics. The concerns of the nation, State, county, and township, must no longer be left to be manipulated by professional politicians, whose conception of the whole duty of man consists simply in looking sharp and making the most of every possible chance of advancing the interests of "Number One." The Clubs, Granges, and other organizations will eventually here find, perhaps, their most useful field. A scattering vote of the farmers would, of course, be ineffectual. What is to be done will have to be done in concert and *en masse.*

The Granges, by their regulations, can not discuss politics or religion at their meetings; but this does not prevent individual Patrons from using their judgment in selecting their candidates, nor does it preclude them from combining their votes, if they see proper to do so. When the Clubs and Granges have solidified their organizations (which they are now actively doing), then will be an excellent time for small politicians to stand from under.

UNION OF CLUBS AND GRANGES NECESSARY.

It is apparent to every one who has carefully followed up the Farmers' Movement that there has been a certain amount of jealousy and rivalry existing between the Granges and

The Motto for Farmers.

Clubs. These little differences have been fomented by certain interests, speaking through organs which have spared no means of sowing dissensions between them; on the one hand, decrying the Grange as being a secret society, and, on the other, stigmatizing the open workings of the Club as foolish, or, at least, ineffectual, from the facility with which politicians manipulate them.

It is absolutely essential that these petty differences should cease. The leading spirits both of the Clubs and Granges are well aware of this, and do their best to make common cause against the enemy. In those States where both Clubs and Granges exist, an organization, similar in character to that of the Illinois Farmers' Association, which consists of both orders, should be set on foot. From the first inception of the agitation against Transportation Companies and monopolies generally, one fact has been more and more clearly developing itself, namely, that the only remedy for the grievances of the farming community is a radical one—the substitution, in large degree, of farmers' representatives in our legislatures, State and National, for the present cliques of lawyers and politicians. Combined, the Granges and Clubs will shortly be able to effect this; separate and semi-antagonistical, they will fail utterly.

It is proper to say that I am not a member of the Order of Patrons of Husbandry. So far as I am informed, judging from the stand-point of an outside but much interested spectator, the secret feature of that order seems to be sufficient to disqualify it for receiving into its ranks our Roman Catholic farmers. At any rate, there are many most excellent citizens who are opposed, on principle, to secret societies of any kind. For these reasons it is necessary, if the organization of our farmers is to go to the length required to make it invincible, that there should be open Clubs, working conjointly with the Granges, and to the same end.

It is far from desirable, however, in my opinion, that our farmers should attempt to organize themselves into a political party; for even if they should succeed in the endeavor, they would but exchange King Log for King Stork. The easiest way out of their difficulties, it seems to me, clearly is for the farmers to vote for such men, and such men only, as they know to be identified with their interests and those of the *whole* people; in fact, that their policy should largely be "men, not measures."

Men of known worth and strength of character must be induced to take office—men whose sturdy integrity and intelligence shall make them proof against the sophistry and blandishments of the insinuating lobbyist, no matter in what disguise his "job" may be presented. When this is done, "politician" and "corruptionist" will cease to be synonyms, and the cloud of dishonor which now rests on our legislation will be lifted, and, let us hope, forever.

CHAPTER VII.

CO-OPERATION AMONG THE INDUSTRIES.

WHAT ORGANIZATION MAY ACCOMPLISH.

It can not be doubted that, if organizations of a social nature were established in every school district, auxiliary to County Societies having for their object the protection and advancement of the best interests of the agricultural classes; if these, again, were the units of a State Society or Club which, in similar manner, should guard and conserve all the varied elements concerned in making agriculture respectable and successful, and should secure for it a just share, through its own members, in the management of state affairs; and if, finally, these State organizations, through delegates elected each year, should meet at some designated point in the country to agree upon principles of action, and arrange and provide for the necessary means for carrying them out—it would be but a short time before the agricultural fraternity of the nation might—

First. Arrange for a co-operative system of trade.

Second. Purchase implements and machinery at wholesale rates.

Third. Dispose of grain and other agricultural products at the highest prices.

Fourth. Direct shipments on the most favorable terms, and at equitable rates to all.

Fifth. Store grain and negotiate advances, at the lowest rates of interest.

Sixth. Establish banks to be controlled by farmers.

Seventh. Replace the credit with a cash system in all the ordinary transactions of life.

Eighth. Through co-operation, sell or hold, as circumstances rendered necessary, the various products of the national industries, thus controlling, or entirely abolishing, the present system of gambling in the prime necessaries of life.

Ninth. Dispense with a large proportion of commission and middle men.

Tenth. Reduce railroad and water freights and fares to a minimum.

Eleventh. Break up monopolies, whether in trade, commerce, manufactures, or money.

Twelfth. Through co-operation of the farmers with mechanics and other laboring classes, establish manufactures at home, as near as possible to the production of the raw material, so that we might gradually produce at home nearly all that may be needed, in place of importing heavily from foreign countries.

Thirteenth. Encourage the breeding of superior stock.

Fourteenth. Establish a more thorough system of cultivation, and a greater diversity of products, thus preventing a glut of any one of them, such as there has been of corn during the last two seasons at the West.

Fifteenth. Promote education to the industries by insisting that every college or university which has received endowment from the State or General Government as such, shall use the funds for instruction in science, and the application of science to art.

Sixteenth. Through co-operation with the several industries of the country, present and future, insist upon a just representation of these industries in our State and National Governments, in proportion to the voting powers of each, and its legitimate importance and value in the nation.

SUPERIOR ORGANIZATION OF OTHER INDUSTRIES.

Many of the industrial classes, not only in the United States, but also throughout the civilized world, and especially in England, have been for years assiduously engaged in organizing for the elevation and advancement of their several trades and industries—socially, financially, and politically—by means of Unions and Societies of various kinds. For one reason or another, the most important of these industries, and the one upon which all others are based—Agriculture—has not yet been organized so as to present a united and solid front to the encroachments of capitalized power, as existing in corporations and monopolies, or the overweening political aspirations of the so-called learned professions. The result is, that, while the various Trades' Unions have measurably held their own as against these encroachments, the farmer, contenting himself with raising raw material with which to feed the great masses of progressive humanity, has suddenly found himself with but few rights which any one seemed bound to respect.

THE PENALTY PAID FOR PAST NEGLIGENCE.

Our farmers have helped to elect congressmen who legislated away the public lands in the most shameful manner to those who would divide the proceeds of this knavery with them to the largest extent. They have made legislatures which have granted to corporations vested rights dangerous in the highest degree to the well-being of the com-

Some of the Classes that should Co-operate.

munity at large. They have subsidized railroads with money obtained by the mortgage of their farms, which railroads, being completed, have been absorbed by the great trunk lines, controlled and manipulated by a handful of money-grabbing adventurers in the great cities of the East.

The American farmers' case, in a nut shell, is about as follows: He was a hard worker, and the lawyer legislated away his substance. Needing help and health and strength, the doctor purged and bled him; whereupon the undertaker, believing him nearly ready for the last rites, began preparing the shroud and coffin for his burial. By the lawyer we mean the politician; by the doctor, the railroad and other moneyed corporations; and by the undertaker, the consolidation of power, through monopoly, which, in its arrogance, has undertaken to say what the farmer shall receive as the price of his sweat and toil.

THE AGRICULTURAL PRESS A TRUSTY COUNSELOR.

Happily, during all this time, the farmer has had the stimulating counsel of the Agricultural press, which has maintained a stubborn front, and has been the means of setting on foot the organizations out of which deliverance is to come. The power of that press for good, however, has been limited, compared with the influence of the organs of other professions, first, from the fact that farmers are scattered over wide areas, while other professions are concentrated in villages and cities; and, second, because farmers, as a class, are not a reading people. In proportion to their numbers, they read less of general news and the current literature devoted to their profession than any other class, not even excepting the day laborers of the cities. They have had all along an overweening faith in the honesty of human nature, forgetting that faith without good works is of but little avail, and that among good works lies the faithful improvement of the privilege which Providence has given each class to use for its own good every legitimate means that is placed in its power.

The most available of these means are the journals devoted to the interests of agriculture, and good books. Next, are his organizations, at the meetings of which he may consult and debate. In short, he must first read, study, and reflect, and then he may intelligently resolve, wisely remedy, and thoroughly regenerate.

One of the great means for carrying forward the good work which is the immediate end and aim of the Farmers' Movement, is aggregation by co-operation—the bringing together of homogeneous bodies, and causing them to work unitedly to a particular end. The varied industries of which Agriculture consists are homogeneous. Husbandry, Stock-breeding and feeding, Dairying, Horticulture (including, as it does, Pomology, Arboriculture, Floriculture, Vegetable Gardening, and rural adornment)—these several professions make up over three-fourths in number of the population of civilized communities, and ought actually to represent a controlling power in the nation. Two reasons why they do not have been stated. Another might be mentioned, the result of their unavoidable segregation, namely, the lack of cohesion among the various parts which constitute the whole.

THE POWER OF THE MONEYED CLASSES CONSOLIDATED.

The commercial and manufacturing interests concentrate their power by aggregation, as at New York and Pittsburg, for instance; the agricultural, must always necessarily remain scattered broad-cast over the continent. The power of a corporation is represented by its money; that of the merchant by his goods and wares; that of the manufacturer by his fabrics; that of the farmer by his lands and their products. His monetary power lies in his crops. A single farmer's crop is of but little value to the commerce of the world, or of that of a nation. Aggregated, the agriculturists represent a power which all others may not equal.

Yet, in spite of this, as matters now are, the financier and gambler in stocks and bonds hold not only the farmer, but the entire industries of a nation as in the hollow of their hands. Should the farmers of a country withhold for a single season the produce of their labors, manufactures, trade, commerce, and every other industry would languish and lie prone in the dust. A wail would go up such as has not been heard since the seven lean seasons of Egypt.

The gold gamblers, the stock jobbers, the dealers in fictitious and watered stocks, however, have gone on from year to year "bulling" and "bearing" stocks, absorbing every dollar of successive inflations of the currency, buying and burying every coined eagle of the mint; tempting, subsidizing, purchasing, our legislatures, statesmen, and even the executive officers of the government, until the nation itself stands appalled at the enormity of the iniquity. The excitement dies away and is forgotten, for, when so many are corrupt, each is willing to cover his neighbor as with a mantle.

HOW PANICS ARE GENERATED.

The financier hurls masses of money against the stock of some particular corporation as an objective point; values are inflated; stock gamblers become wild; they buy and sell, until the wire-pullers, having gained their ends, unload at far higher prices than those at which they bought, leaving the struggling smaller fry to suffer their losses as best they may.

Again, a railroad is projected (a Pacific Railroad, for instance) through a region of swamps, mountains, and deserts. Congress is partly bribed and wholly duped to aid the scheme, and passes a law granting a territory equal in extent to Illinois and Indiana combined—a territory comprising land enough to found an empire. Financiers are posted off to Europe to negotiate the bonds. Banks are cajoled into lending the money, much of it deposited by customers, hoping to be reimbursed from the sale of lands before the bubble bursts. European capital has been bitten by this dog before, and is shy; it does not take the well-covered bait; there are rumors that all is not right; apprehension ensues. A great banking corporation, that has accumulated millions from the treasury of the nation, through the sale of its bonds, goes down. Consternation seizes the money kings, the brokers, and gamblers of Wall street, as bank after bank succumbs to the pressure. And now the banks can not pay, the merchant can not pay, the manufacturer can not pay, and—the laborer may starve. Business stagnates, the price of every commodity depreciates, and financial ruin engulfs thousands in quick succession.

Depreciated stocks and commodities are then quietly absorbed by those who set the ball in motion. By a series of such moves, these accumulate fortunes—ten, twenty, fifty, or even seventy millions of dollars, perhaps. They retire to their fastnesses, but only to issue forth, like Ghouls, at the chosen time, to again and again rob the graves of buried hopes and reputations, and revel once more in those fearful charnel houses—horror and despair.

This is no overdrawn picture. What care these money lords, who are seeking to carry the nation to a point where consolidated capital will hold a centralized government at its beck and to crush out the last vestige of that liberty which was gained by the labor and the life-blood of the heroes of the Revolution?

COMBINE, CONSOLIDATE, CONCENTRATE.

Co-operation was inaugurated by the original framers of Farmers' Clubs and kindred societies. Its growth has been slow, extending now over a century and a half. It is still continuing to take shape; witness the increased interest manifested in practical education, and in Clubs, Granges, Farmers' Unions, and Agricultural Conventions. It may be consolidated by a movement to unite the farmer and the artisan, which is even now engaging the talent of some of the best minds of the country.

Let the farmers of the country take hold unitedly in this matter of co-operation, using the calm judgment for which, as a class, they have always been noted, and they can hurl from power those who have pandered to the monopolizing tendency of capital. For it is this monopolizing power of centralized capital that is sapping the foundation of the people's liberties, and, through the open and unblushing purchase and sale of public men, rendering the government a byword of contempt. The farmers of the United States can accomplish this of themselves, if thoroughly combined. United with the other industrial classes, their power will be not merely irresistible, but overwhelming.

When crime and false intent—whether in the Judiciary, in the Legislature, in Congress, or in the departments of State—shall have been made odious; when the penitentiary shall receive the criminal of high degree, as the Bridewell does the thimble-rigger of the low dens of vice; when the statesman, bribed through Credit Mobiliers or with actual hard cash, to betray his constituents, shall be made to suffer the penalty of his crimes, as certainly and swiftly as does the sneak-thief, or the petty swindler at the street corners; when vice shall be thought hideous, because it *is* vice; when for proven corruption in office it shall be insisted that a

Fidelity.

man that be stripped of place and power, and buried politically, forever, without hope of resurrection; when all this is brought to pass, then shall we hope to see the beginning of the end. The raid on the railroads is but a trimming of the edges of the vast and horrid ulcer that is eating out the vitals of our free government—the ulcer whose real name is Corruption in Office!

CHAPTER VIII.

CONSTITUTION AND BUSINESS OF FARMERS' CLUBS.

PRELIMINARY STEPS IN ORGANIZATION.

Farmers in many communities are prevented from organizing Clubs for the reason that they are not conversant with the mode of organization. A few simple rules may suffice. Any number of individuals, male and female, (and in the organization of the social clubs it has been found necessary to perfect success that both sexes participate), may meet together and agree upon the time and place for meeting. It is also better, in summer, at least, that an afternoon be selected, and that the meeting be in the open air, when the weather is favorable.

It is also a pleasant adjunct to the social features to have a simple lunch provided, unless it be deemed preferable to make a pic-nic, each family furnishing its own basket of eatables. This latter plan certainly approves itself, as saving work to the hosts for the time being, and causing a subdivision of the labor and expense of the gathering, as well as adding to its enjoyability.

Until the machinery is well in motion, and the newness of the situation wears off, it is well to have the gatherings entirely informal and conversational; in fact, principally devoted to social chat upon the prospects of the crops, the probable yield, prices, and arrangements for mutual assistance in gathering and marketing, and the discussion of some general plan of co-operation. If there be musical talent among the members, let there be singing by all means, with instrumental accompaniments, if possible. There will always be found some among the members who will be able, even at the outset, to deliver short *extempore* addresses, or to prepare short practical essays on subjects connected with agriculture.

AFTERWORKINGS.

Gradually, debates may be introduced, taking care always that the exercises be not too long-continued at any one time.

"Going to the Club Meeting."

To vary this, the music and lunch will be in order. It will be found surprising how soon the genial influence will spread, and how eager all who are within walking or riding distance of the meeting will be to join in the work.

Thus Clubs may be instituted in every school district in the land, accomplishing great present good, and exercising a powerful influence upon the rising generation. And it will not be long until every man, woman and child will look forward to the day of meeting as a holiday, and a time of social enjoyment and improvement.

The first thing, of course, after organizing, will be to form a constitution under which to work.

The following is a simple, and yet comprehensive, constitution. It has been adopted, with slight modifications, by some of the most energetic and influential clubs in the West. The Club should meet on a fixed day in each month at the residence of one or another of its members.

MODEL FOR A CONSTITUTION.

I. This organization shall be known as the ——— County Farmers' Club, No. ——.

II. Its object shall be the improvement of its members in the theory and practice of Agriculture.

III. Its members, additional to its original number, shall consist of such persons as shall receive a two-thirds vote for admission, and pay the sum of one dollar, and such additional annual sum as may be annually fixed by a two-thirds vote of the members.

IV. Its officers shall consist of a President, Vice-President, Secretary, Treasurer, and Librarian (who shall constitute the Executive Committee, etc.), and the Chairmen of Standing Committees. The officers shall all be elected annually.

V. Its meetings shall be held monthly, and at such other times and places as the President may deem necessary to promote the aims of the Society.

VI. This Constitution may be amended at any regular meeting, said amendment having been proposed in writing at the next preceding meeting.

BY-LAWS.—1. The President shall preside at all meetings of the club and Executive Committee, and have power to call special meetings.

2. In the absence of the President, the Vice-President shall have the full powers of the President, and shall preside over the meeting during such absence or inability of the President.

3. The Secretary shall record the proceedings of the Club, and conduct its correspondence.

4. The Treasurer shall receive all moneys, and shall pay out the same on the written order of the President.

5. Regular meetings shall be held on the second Saturday of each month.

STANDING COMMITTEES, ORDER OF BUSINESS, ETC.

Standing committees take cognizance of all regular subjects, of which the most important (in the Northern States) may be named, as follows:

Soils and their improvement; Grasses, Pastures, and Meadows; Grains (Wheat, Oats, Corn, etc.) on Exhibition, and other farm crops; Fruits and Fruit Trees; Grass and Shrubbery; domestic animals; and library.

These may be grouped together, according to their importance, or each made the labor of a committee, three to five individuals constituting a committee.

The order of business may be as follows:

1. Reading minutes of last meeting.
2. Reports of Special Committees.
3. Unfinished Business.
4. New Business, Essays, Discussions, Report of Standing Committees.
5. Adjournment.

CO-OPERATION OF CLUBS.

One of the objects of designating the Clubs of a district or county by numbers is that it paves the way to co-operation. The several Clubs will thus be enabled to meet together each year for the discussion of matters of general interest, and to elect delegates to attend a yearly State Convention. These, again, can elect delegates for the National Convention, or Congress, which should also meet yearly. The Club may also have a local name, or a name indicating its special work, if any, such as Stock Breeding, Husbandry, Pomology, or General Horticulture, etc. At the yearly meetings, all these various branches of Agriculture should meet on common ground the interests of the whole being identical.

The meetings being held at the homes of the several members in succession, the Club will have a pleasant visit, and an opportunity to inspect the various systems of agriculture practiced. The comments elicited, and the general interchange of opinions, will be valuable and instructive to all. They will create and elevate taste, and tend to improve and simplify many of the processes of the farm, besides being the means of cultivating the social refinements, and the harmony of purpose so indispensable to the well-being of every community.

FORM OF ILLINOIS FARMERS' CLUBS' CONSTITUTION.

Subjoined is given the form of Constitution and By-Laws for Farmers' Clubs, as adopted by the Illinois (State) Farmer's Association. They are simple and practical in their construction.

CONSTITUTION.

I. This organization shall be known as the ——— Farmers' Club.

II. Its objects shall be improvement in the theory and practice of Agriculture and Horticulture; to promote the moral, intellectual, social, and pecuniary welfare of its members, and by active and cordial co-operation with other Clubs, and with its County Committee, to assist in carrying to a successful issue the object of the State Association.

III. Its members, other than the original ones, shall be elected by ballot, and all members shall be subject to pay an initiation fee of $——, and, thereafter, such sums as shall be necessary to defray the expenses of the Club.

State Seal of Illinois.

IV. Its officers shall consist of a President, Vice-President, Secretary, Corresponding Secretary, and Treasurer, who shall jointly constitute the Executive Committee, and shall be elected annually.

V. Its meetings shall be held monthly, and at such other times as the President may deem necessary for the good of the society.

VI. This Club shall become auxiliary to the County Association, whenever it shall be formed.

VII. This Constitution may be amended at any regular meeting, by a two-thirds vote of the members present, said amendment having been proposed in writing at a previous meeting.

BY-LAWS.—1. The President shall, when present, preside at all meetings of the Club and Executive Committee.

2. The Vice-President shall, during the absence or inability of the President, perform all the duties of the executive officer.

3. The Secretary shall record all the proceedings of the Club, and the Corresponding Secretary shall conduct its correspondence, and maintain an active correspondence with the County Committee, and other Clubs of the county and district.

4. The Treasurer shall receive all moneys paid into the Club, and disburse the same only on the order of the President and Secretary.

5. The regular meetings of this Club shall be held on the ——— day of each month, at —— o'clock.

The order of business shall be:

1. Reading minutes of last meeting.
2. Reports of Special Committees.
3. Unfinished Business.
4. New Business, Essays, Discussions, Reports of Standing Committees.

STATE ORGANIZATION—CONSTITUTION OF THE TENNESSEE FARMERS' ASSOCIATION.

As Societies increase in the towns and counties of a State, a general organization will be required. Below is appended the Constitution and By-Laws adopted by the Tennessee Farmers' Association, containing many excellent provisions, which may be modified to meet existing wants. This form may also be easily altered, so as to adapt it perfectly to county organizations. The Constitution is as follows:

CONSTITUTION.

I. We, the Farmers of Tennessee, in Convention assembled, in order to form a more perfect union, promote the general welfare, and secure the blessings of liberty to ourselves and our posterity, do establish this State organization, which shall be known as, and styled, the TENNESSEE FARMERS' ASSOCIATION.

II. Its object shall be the promotion of the moral, intellectual, social, and pecuniary welfare of the farmers of the State.

III. Its members shall consist of delegates from the

State Seal of Tennessee.

various Farmers' Clubs, Granges, and Agricultural and Horticultural Societies of the State, each of which shall be entitled to at least one delegate, and where the number of its members exceeds fifty, to one delegate additional for each one hundred members or fraction exceeding half that number. The members of the State Bureau of Agriculture, also the President and Professors of the Agricultural College of the State, shall be, *ex-officio*, members of this Association, and from counties, or from civil districts, in which no form of farmers' organization exists, farmers not delegates may be admitted by a vote of this Association. All members shall pay an annual fee of one dollar.

IV. Its officers shall consist of a President, and a Vice-President from each Congressional district of the State to be nominated by the delegates therefrom; of a Secretary and Treasurer, and these officers shall constitute the State Central Committee of this organization, with power to appoint an Executive Committee of three from its members; also, of a County Committee of one from each county in the State, to be nominated by the delegates from each county. Said officers shall be elected annually, and serve for one year, or until their successors are chosen. This organization shall meet annually, at such time and place as the Association, or, in case of its failure to designate, the State Central Committee may determine. Special meetings may be called by the Executive Committee.

V. This Constitution may be amended at any annual meeting by a two-thirds vote, provided said meeting be composed of delegates from one-half of the counties which are members of this Association.

BY-LAWS.—1. The President shall perform the duties of presiding officer, and have power to call meetings of the State Central Committee.

2. The Senior Vice-President shall, in the absence or disability of the President, perform the duties of that office. It shall be the duty of each Vice-President to secure the organization in each county of his district of a Farmers' Association, to be composed of delegates from the various Farmers' Clubs and Granges in the county, and of such other persons as the County Association may determine to admit.

3. The Secretary shall, under the direction of the Association and committees, open and maintain an active correspondence with the Vice-Presidents and County Committees, furnishing them with forms and Constitutions, and other documents and information to aid them in organization, and performing such other duties of correspondence as may be assigned him. He shall also keep a record of the proceedings of the Association, and of its Central and Executive Committees, and may be paid such compensation for his services as is found expedient and practicable.

4. The Treasurer shall hold the moneys of the Association, and disburse them upon the written order of the Presi-

dent and Secretary. He shall give such bond as the State Central Committee may require.

5. The State Central Committee shall have the general management of the affairs of the Association. It shall be their duty to promote and effect the thorough organization of the farmers of the State; to aid, by their advice and instruction, in such organization in all parts of the State; to ask and secure necessary legislation, State and National, upon matters affecting the farmers' interests; and, in general, to do all things in their power to further the objects and advance the interests of the Association.

6. The Executive Committee shall perform such duties as may be assigned to it by the State Central Committee, and may call special meetings.

7. These By-Laws may be amended at any annual meeting by a majority vote, provided said meeting is composed of delegates from one-half of the counties which are members of this Association.

CHAPTER IX.

INNER WORKINGS OF FARMERS' CLUBS.

FARMERS' CLUBS MUST BE SOCIAL.

If we could have Clubs throughout the length and breadth of the land, conducted on true social principles, so that the farmers of each neighborhood might meet together, both men and women, at stated times, especially during the winter months, and discuss matters of general interest (eschewing politics, of course), it would go a great way toward elevating the *status* of the fraternity. Heretofore, this has not been possible, but every day is making it easier and easier of accomplishment, as the country becomes more thickly settled, and facilities for locomotion increase. All that is wanted, is that individual leaders in each neighborhood inaugurate the movement, and hold out faithfully until it is accomplished. It would soon be found surprising how many facts could be gathered, even from the seemingly ignorant, which, stored up, would lay the foundation for future usefulness.

Thus each Farmers' Club would become the *nucleus*, from which agricultural societies, occupying a still higher plane, might be formed, to discuss and compile from the facts there gathered, some of the more important changes and transmutations that nature is working out so silently and with such seeming mystery.

Let these societies increase, until their ramifications extend upward through town, county, district, and State societies; and culminate in one grand, yearly convention for the whole nation, composed of delegates from each State or district. If this were accomplished, we could eventually so organize as to control—for good, I trust—the destinies of a country, the inhabitants of which are made up of the most energetic and intelligent of the working populations of the earth.

CLUBS MUST COLLECT FACTS.

It is the duty of every farmer in the land to endeavor to collect facts. Nay, there is not a farmer in the whole country but does so, and again loses or forgets them. Through Farmers' Clubs, these valuable data might be preserved, and eventually classified, by means of the county and State societies, into definite shape. This done, we should be surprised to see how long we had been groping in ignorance, simply for the want of organized study. Even the simplest operations of the farm, for the lack of accurate knowledge relating to the fixed and simple law that somewhere governs each and every thing in nature, is lost to the farmer, and, consequently, to the world.

The collection of experimental facts is the legitimate work of our Agricultural Colleges also. These facts should be supported by the results of isolated experiments that the working farmer is collecting every day in the year, and losing again for the want of some place and means suitable for putting them on record for the benefit of others. The aggregation of these isolated units from year to year, properly condensed into readable shape, would, in the end, furnish data valuable to science in the highest degree.

Let us illustrate. The farmer, being of an experimental turn of mind, throughout the course of a lifetime collects many facts—amasses a rich store of actual, practical, thoroughly-tested knowledge connected with his art. If a writer, he is likely to give the results through the public press; but if not, they are entirely lost at his death, unless, happily, the son succeeds the father, and happens to be imbued with the same love of experiment. Even in the former case, many of those who read his articles will not profit by them; for, having no personal acquaintance with him, they pass his writings by, as but the opinion of one unknown farmer—a man of like frailties of judgment with themselves. At all events, his contributions to agricultural science are not in their most valuable shape. But if the facts are gathered at our colleges, where the experiments carried out from year to year are chronicled and tabulated systematically, we shall, sooner or later, gather data that will be of immense value. If the professor die to-morrow, the observations and experiments are still carried forward by his successor.

In the case of the private individual, such records do not carry equal weight. To say nothing of the known fallibility of human judgment, there is, quite frequently, a disposition to suspect that the individual experimenter has some private end, or pet theory, to advance. Very much less of this feeling attaches to the work done, in the same direction, at a public institution. There the observer is supposed to be the servant of the people, and to be actuated by motives entirely above suspicion; and, hence, by virtue of his position, *he* can speak as one having authority.

SUBJECTS FOR DEBATE IN CLUBS, ETC.

While the local societies, founded solely on a social basis, must have a wide and beneficial effect upon our State Boards of Agriculture, this is not their only duty. The Granges

Not to be Trusted—The Patron versus the Politician.

are directly prohibited, by their fundamental regulations, from discussing politics, but this the Farmers' Clubs may do freely. Now, it would not be at all advisable to consider questions of politics from a partisan stand-point. But all matters pertaining to the welfare of the farmer, and the relation which each and every measure brought before the State and National Legislatures sustains to the interests of agriculture and the agricultural masses, should be freely discussed and debated. This would be one way to make and keep legislators honest.

If to this were added the firm resolve to send farmers in numbers proportionate to their ratio of voting power, to the Legislature, and also to Congress, a long stride would have been taken towards securing those rights for which the farmer is now struggling.

HORTICULTURISTS BETTER ORGANIZED THAN FARMERS.

I have already mentioned the undoubted fact that the average horticulturist is far in advance of the average farmer, as regards scientific familiarity with their respective callings. He has also made much further progress in the direction of organization.

In most of the older States, and many of the younger, there are active and thoroughly organized State societies in the interests of horticulture, the members of which meet regularly once a year. They discuss the experiences gained through the local societies, legislate upon such matters as are of general interest to the fraternity, and compile and publish the record of whatever is new or valuable to the profession. Their Transactions, often published at their own expense, will compare favorably with other literature pertaining to technical knowledge. So, also, the papers and essays contributed are, many of them, models of their class.

The educated farmer, in this country, is the exception; the educated horticulturist, the rule. The latter never allows any thing to escape his eye that may profitably be published, either in books, or in the journals devoted to the profession. He is constantly educating himself to a better and better acquaintance with the mysteries of nature. He reads, marks, learns, and inwardly digests, continually.

Brawn and Brains.

If one will only educate himself to it, it is perfectly easy to do as the horticulturist does—work with the brain while working with the hands. The operator at any labor, except such as is really laborious, as chopping, pitching, heavy lifting, etc., may employ the brain constantly. If the conversation usually carried on at ordinary labor were such as to expand the mind, rather than small talk, very small talk, sometimes, the civilized portion of the human family would soon be educated to a point where gossip would seem flat. Does the farmer thus educate himself to the minutia of his profession? The few do, the many do not.

ORGANIZED PLEASURE TAKING.

A prominent feature of the farmers' agitation, during 1873, was the organized observance of the Fourth of July by the Clubs and Granges. These bodies held meetings, throughout the West and North-west, at which it is estimated that fully two hundred thousand persons assisted. Immense gatherings took place all over Iowa, Illinois, Wisconsin, and Minnesota, chief in importance of which was the one in Livingston County, Ill., a county which, from the first, has taken a leading part in the movement. If any doubt had previously existed as to the hold which the movement had popularly secured, the gatherings on the "Farmers' Fourth," as it was known, must have been sufficient to satisfy the veriest Thomas.

Though Jupiter Pluvius was the reigning deity on the Farmer's Fourth of 1873, he was utterly unable to damp the enthusiasm of the meetings. Not that they were simply merry-makings. Far from it. The farmers were smarting under a sense of intolerable wrongs, and the seeking of redress for the past, and insurance against their repetition in the future, formed the principal topics of debate. However, I am hopeful that better days have dawned, and that, ere long, the fathers of the Farmers' Movement will be looked up to with the same veneration as that with which the Revolutionary forefathers were regarded after the liberation of our nation was achieved. Unless I am egregiously mistaken in the character of the Farmers' Movement, its success is certain, sooner or later. The utmost its enemies can do is to postpone their evil day by dividing the farmers' counsels; but postponement will only make the blow more severe when, at length, it does fall.

Hereafter, by all means, let the various societies combine and take an annual holiday on the Fourth, when they can join with their wives and children in merry-making, casting aside all business, except the addresses, without which a gathering of this sort would be incomplete.

CO-OPERATIVE BUYING AND SELLING.

If there existed the thorough neighborhood, county, State, and National organization of Clubs and Granges that I have advocated, co-operation in buying and selling would be an easy matter. Until this is accomplished, these Associations must work from their own individual bases, or through combination with such districts as may be enabled to join together.

The Treasurer of the Club may be the financial or purchasing agent, or some member of the Club may be appointed to that office separately. Suppose the Club, containing twenty to fifty members, intends to sell a certain amount of produce, for the purchase of necessary stores. The families represented in the Club require annually from fifty to one hundred dollars worth of dry goods and groceries each, according to size. The individual can not get as good a price on two to three hundred bushels of corn, a hundred bushels of wheat, a pair of steers, a half dozen fat hogs, or fifteen to twenty barrels of apples, as he who has from twenty to fifty times this quantity to dispose of at once.

The fiscal agent of the Club becomes the custodian of the property—say, a car load of hogs, another of cattle, ten cars of corn, half a dozen of wheat, and, perhaps, one or two of fruit. Accounts are opened with the grain merchant, the produce commission man, the cattle broker, etc., unless the respective dealers in the village or town consider it to their interest (which they soon come to do) to buy this property, and give cash in return, or such articles as may be wanted at fair prices. If not, the agent appointed makes the best terms he can for transportation, and sells in the best market he can find, buys the stores, and distributes to the several individuals of the Club. If the agent be a shrewd business man, consent to put aside his ordinary work, and does this business as a matter of accommodation to his Club, or at a lower rate than when done through the customary channels, money will be saved. If not, money is lost.

It is evident that, under the modern system, this plan can not be fully and permanently carried out, for the reason that the agent soon becomes the actual commission man or produce buyer, the actual merchant or middle man, with all the acquisitiveness of these classes. What may be done, legitimately, and with better results in most cases, is this: a community of farmers may combine to sell a certain quantity of produce, and buy for it certain other produce. A certain number of car loads of grain, for instance, may be delivered upon a fixed day, to be sold in the best market. With the proceeds certain goods are bought and distributed, according to the wants of the individuals. So with the purchase of farm machinery, etc. The principal of co-operation, however, can not be carried into practice with any economy, where competition is already sufficient to check a monopolizing tendency.

THE ADVANTAGE OF MUTUAL ASSISTANCE.

Farmers, from their isolation and peculiar position, have constantly felt the necessity of mutual assistance. In case of sickness, the neighbor must often go long distances for the doctor. In sparsely settled districts, when one farmer went to market, it has always been expected that he would do errands for his neighbors. In butchering, a reciprocity of service is extremely common, a return in kind in time of need being the only pay tendered or expected. Husking-bees, and other frolics of like nature, are always eagerly looked forward to by country-bred youth. These, and many other neighborly acts, have been common in every community of farmers from time immemorial. Through a close social organization among them, the principle may be applied in a variety of ways, keeping alive a kindly and generous feeling, one toward another, and proving of great material benefit, also, through co-operative assistance in carrying out the labors of the farm.

Neighborly Help.

The soil of one farm may become ready to plow, or sow, or harvest, days before another. In the Society, this might be arranged, and the labor mapped out in succession, so that much valuable time now lost might be saved. A.'s field may be plowed and seeded to-day, B.'s field to-morrow, and so on. If B. has double the land of A., he has, or should have, double the team. If he do one day's work for A. with two teams, he should receive in return two day's work with one team. The rich neighbor may, perhaps, have the better teams, and, therefore, the poor neighbor may receive more than he gave; but, again, the gain in having the work of both accomplished just when it should be, would more than balance this.

Plans may also be laid in the Council or Club, that will enable the farmer to successfully compete with his city neighbor, who is acutely educated to trade. The farmer owning a thousand acres or more is able to economize labor in a variety of small things, and thus saves, where the

10

workers of small farms must lose. Mutual assistance and co-operation will obviate this in a great degree.

A single instance will suffice to illustrate the point here presented. I once had occasion to purchase nineteen corn cultivators in one season, having increased the area of corn to require this additional number. Two of my neighbors wanted three each, making twenty-five in all. I wrote letters to several manufacturers, asking the lowest cash price for the quantity. The dealers at the nearest railroad town soon found out what I had done, and waited on me, offering to sell at prices lower than the factory price and freight would cost me, being content with the relative difference between the freight on my twenty-five, and the freight on car lots. They did not relish this interference with their prerogatives, but, of course, they could not help themselves. This was before the manufacturers combined to sell only through their agents. They are beginning to find that the project of forcing farmers to buy of whom they please, and as they please, is like having too many cooks in making broth—the dish is sure to be spoiled.

CHAPTER X.

THE ORDER OF PATRONS OF HUSBANDRY.

WHAT IS A GRANGE?

Webster says that the French word *grange* signifies a farm; *grangier*, a farmer; the Spanish word *grangear*, is to cultivate, and *grangero* a farmer. In Scotland, the buildings belonging to a grain-farm are called a grange; since, originally, the place where the rents and tithes due to the priesthood, and payable in grain, were deposited, was the grange, from the Latin word *granum*, grain. Shakespeare and Milton both use the word grange as meaning a farm-house, with the buildings and stables attached.

In England, "grange" is generally used to signify an old farm or manor house, surrounded by ancient trees, and sometimes by a moat or ditch. During the civil wars which devastated England up to two centuries ago, these manor houses and farm strongholds were made the scenes of bitter strife between tbe contending factions, and were often stubbornly defended. Hence, the term may be liberally construed as "stronghold"—happily expressive of the sense in which the Patrons of Husbandry use it.

The wealth of the farmer consists in his lands, buildings, stock, implements, and grain. Upon his cattle and grain are dependent, not only himself and his family, but also the entire community. In time of civil war, or other great national danger, the care of that which will support life is of vital importance. In time of strife, under the old baronial rule, neither party was especially careful to pay for what they wanted. If they found it, they took it, and the poor husbandman was left with nothing to maintain his family; hence, when able to do so, he made his house his stronghold.

The Patrons of Husbandry could scarcely have found a more appropriate designation for their places of meeting than the word Grange. It is, literally, their stronghold. The means of access may be aptly symbolized by the actual approaches of the Grange, as they existed in England during times of trouble, to-wit, a drawbridge and a ladder. Here the defenders meet—the Laborer and the Maid, the Cultivator and the Shepherdess, the Harvester and the Gleaner, the Husbandman and the Matron.

DEGREES OF THE ORDER SYMBOLIZED.

The above are the names of the degrees of the subordinate or local Granges, in which communities of farmers, their wives, and those of their children who are approaching maturity, meet to labor for the general good; to devise plans for social improvement; to discuss means for the mutual welfare of the fraternity; and to assist each other in the every day business of life. When the younger ones shall have arrived at the full age and stature of Husbandman and Matron, they will have climbed the first four steps of the ladder. To gain thus much, the candidate must have broken up the stubborn glebe of ignorance, and cultured it with the harrow and roller of good intent, that it may receive the seeds of education, which, in due time, shall return the husbandman an hundred-fold of knowledge. The succession of these four stages may be represented by the rise of man from the state of a savage. First, having neither flocks nor herds, primeval man gains a precarious subsistence by the chase and slaughter of such wild beasts as he may be able to overcome. While living this hand-to-mouth existence—to-day overburdened with meat and having no incentive to exertion, anon, driven by extreme want to resume his toil—but slight mental improvement is possible. Rising slowly in intelligence, he gathers flocks and herds, and emerges from his primeval barbarism, and the light of civilization begins to dawn upon him. Still his condition is that of a nomad, and improvable only to a limited extent; the pastoral life necessitates frequent changes of location as his flocks and herds exhaust the pasture.

In the course of time he seeks a more settled mode of life. He learns to till the soil in a rude way, and provide stores for the winter; gathers his fellows together into communities, makes laws for the general welfare, and becomes qualified to subdue and replenish the earth. The progress of struggling humanity, however, is still very slow. The discoveries and inventions of one generation are handed down to the next orally, and, necessarily, imperfectly; the craftsman hands down by word of mouth to his son the secrets of his trade. Thus, for ages, the improvement goes on, certain but slow, till the invention of the art of writing gives a vast impulse to the rate of progress. Thenceforward the advance is at an accelerating rate, and the achievements of man, once on record, relapse into oblivion no more. The higher, God-like nature becomes expanded, and man goes on, step by step, forming empires, surmounting difficulties apparently unconquerable but only met to be overcome; the rate of progress quickening, till, at length, he no longer advances step by step, but by leaps and bounds toward that perfection which he was created to attain.

HIGHER STAGES OF PROGRESS.

The Grange, whether it be allegorized as the fold for sheltering the flock, the storehouse of prosperous industry, or the place where all meet to enjoy the fruits of their mutual labors, is typical of the whole state of man. Here are gathered the golden grain, the ripe fruits, and the bright flowers of human progress; corresponding, respectively, to the Labors of Agriculture, the Religion of Agriculture, and the Poetry of Agriculture; the three—Husbandry, Pomology, and Gardening—comprising the whole art of Agriculture. This is the field where labor the Husbandman and the Matron, with their fellows. They have passed over the stile or ladder of the outer field of labor, and are now ready to enter the Orchard.

The Orchard is dedicated to Pomona. The Patrons reach this degree through a portal connecting the boundary of the field adjoining with the Orchard beyond. The ripe fruit of the trees planted therein is called Hope. The fruit will not be perfect unless, after the seeds are planted and the seedlings large enough to graft, the scions be properly placed, and guarded, nursed, watered, and pruned. They must be protected from the burning sun of summer by ample foliage, and by kindly mulching from the deadly frosts of winter; its blossoms must be shielded from the blasting east wind, and its overburdened boughs thinned of superfluous fruit, that all may be equal in size and beauty, and the perfect fruit brought, in due season, safely to the storehouse or Grange, to be shared with the fellow-laborers in the field and the fold.

The Orchard adjoins the Garden, represented by Flora, or Charity. It is divided from it by a beautiful hedge, from one side of which hang garlands of flowers; on the other side, fruits. The entrance to it is known only to those within. In it are winding paths, leading to bowers shaded by beautiful climbing plants. The most lovely flowers, gathered from every clime, grow, singly or in masses, everywhere, while foliage, plants and rare exotics are interspersed by the master minds who have labored to make it beautiful. A grassy slope, of the softest and smoothest turf, stretches away to a calm lake of pure water in the distance. In the lake is an island, reached by a rustic bridge. Upon the island are trees from every quarter of the globe, among whose branches song-birds nestle, while aquatic fowl are ever busy on the clear lake. A winding path from the bridge leads to a bower, formed by the interlacing branches of trees, over which climbing roses, honeysuckles, ivies, passion flowers, and trumpet vines are trailing in beautiful masses. The delicate perfume of flowers, the gentle breezes, cooled by ever-playing fountains, and birds of sweetest song or loveliest plumage, make this bower the fit court for the Goddess Flora, or Charity.

To the novice, upon entering, all seems enchantment. His perception has been rendered acute in the outer fields, and in the Orchard he has enjoyed the fruits of his labor. In the Garden the work is both for the true and the beautiful. The worker here must not only reflect upon the lines of beauty drawn throughout the garden, but must study the effect produced by ever-varying light and shade, the grouping of trees, the masses and lines of flowers, the emerald hue of the grassy turf, the gentle slope, the abrupt ascent, or the beetling cliff overhanging the torrent that dashes its waters over the rocky bed beneath, only, at last, to find rest in the glassy and peaceful lake beyond. As the Husbandman has studied the groundwork of his profession in the Field of Art, and in the Orchard of Hope has gathered the ripe fruits, the Religion of Agriculture—here, in the beautiful Garden, dedicated to Flora, the Poetry of Horticulture, he perfects himself in the science which underlies all art—the Science of Life.

He now sees before him the temple of Ceres, Faith, the goddess of the fruitful, productive earth; the inventress of Agriculture, without which man is a savage; the founder of civil society, which fixes the wandering savage to the soil, by making him a tender of flocks and herds. Softening his nature by degrees, she grants rights to property, and gives the protection of laws. He is no longer a barbarian, for now he has property, civil rights, and is a respecter of the property of others.

OBJECTS AND ADVANTAGES OF THE GRANGES.

We hear it constantly dinned in our ears, that "Agriculture is the most important and elevated occupation of any on earth." It is important as furnishing food for mankind, and elevated in proportion to the intelligence of the community which practices it. The farmer's vocation must depend for its relative status upon the intelligence of the individuals composing the fraternity. It is a mournful fact that the average farmer is not the equal of any of the other middle classes in education, and, consequently, not in business tact. One reason, as we have seen, is that he is isolated, in a great measure, from his kind, so that it is difficult for him to continue at school long enough to acquire more than the rudiments of an English education. The fault is too often with the parents, who, even when near schools, seem indifferent whether the child attend or not, or think they can't spare him or her from other work. Many of them fail to comprehend that this negligence on their part, is almost certain to have an evil influence on the future of the man.

This is, and should be, one of the legitimate fields of work for the Granges, because herein lies their power in the next generation. The child of to-day will be the man or woman then; the boy of to-day, the drudge and indifferent farmer, or the intelligent worker, and the successful tiller of the soil—the law maker or the ruler—according as his education has been neglected or fostered.

But a short time ago, the Order of Patrons of Husbandry was the vague idea of one individual; a year ago, a comparative handful of men and women; to-day, they are a vast army of earnest workers, strong in their will to resist the aggressions that have accumulated with each recurring year, to burden the farmer and carry the fraternity lower and lower in the social scale. Their watchwords are hailed and answered from the Atlantic to the Pacific—from the head waters of the Great Lakes, and the wild forests of Canada, to the everglades of Florida and the Texas plains whose shores are washed by the Gulf of Mexico. Their banners are unfurled, not alone to a nation, but over a continent. Political organizations arise, culminate, accomplish or fail of their ends, and die. They are weak from want of cohesion and unity of purpose. But the Grange was strong in its infancy, and while yet weak in numbers, because laboring with a unity of purpose for the right. It is still but a youth, with its best powers undeveloped; but the stripling David has already cast the stone that is to smite the Goliath of Monopoly in the forehead. Those who despised it a few months ago, in its supposed weakness, are now praying to it in its young strength. When it shall have arrived at its full stature, a giant in strength, irresistible if it remain pure in its intentions, it will wield a power such as no other social organization has known since the advent of man upon the earth.

WHAT A GRANGE IS NOT.

The Grange is not a political organization, and, notwithstanding the efforts of politicians to sway its destinies, so far they have signally failed. Therefore, any person, of whatsoever political creed, eligible to the rites of the Order, may become a member.

It is not a religious Order. Its record on that score is as broad as the Constitution of the United States. Hence, all persons may meet here—provided, simply, that they recognize a Supreme Being—on terms of perfect equality.

It is not an Order composed solely of the male sex. It includes both men and women, and herein is one great manifestation of sagacity in its founders. Herein, again, lies its pre-eminent strength; as the best bow-anchor it will hold the ship secure at its moorings, where, when not under sail fighting for the rights of the brotherhood, in its harbor of safety, no groundswells rising in the sea of discord can injure it.

It is not partisan in its nature, favoring one class at the expense of another; asking no more than simple justice at the hands of its enemies, nor desiring that which it is not willing to concede. The Grange teaches that "Human happiness is the acme of earthly ambition."

It is not sectional in its aims. For, while all are properly excluded from the Order, who have not a direct interest in Agriculture, it is not in antagonism with any industry, but rather seeks to foster and build up industries of every kind; holding that "Individual happiness depends upon the general prosperity."

What the "Granger" is Not—The Opinions of Some to the Contrary Notwithstanding. (123)

It is not even a secret society, except in the sense that every corporation, and every business firm, and even every family, are secret. The members simply do not tell the world all they know. Corporations have their secret transactions, known only to the officers. Every business firm has its secret marks or cipher, known only to its members and their assistants, by which they, and they only, know at what prices they buy, and at what prices they are willing to sell. Their books are not thrown open to the gaze, or curiosity, of any one who may choose to pry into their business.

And thus, dear reader, here you have, condensed in a nutshell, what a grange is, and what it is not. It is a social and business organization, for the promotion of the well-being of its individual members. It is not a conclave, seeking to do injury to any man or woman on earth.

CHAPTER XI.

THE ORIGIN OF THE ORDER.

HOW IT CAME ABOUT.

In January, 1866, Mr. O. H. Kelley, a native of Boston, but owning a farm in Minnesota, and at the time employed in the Department of Agriculture at Washington, was commissioned by President Johnson to make a tour of the South, to collect data as to its agricultural and mineral resources. He found the country struggling to recuperate from the effects of the war; the planters and farmers, few in number and widely scattered, with but little means for successfully carrying on their avocation.

Southern born planters have always been noted for their generous hospitality, and geniality, but it was not expected they would take kindly to a stranger and a government officer, whom they might naturally regard as an enemy. One reason, perhaps, for the generous spirit displayed by this people is that Freemasonry is largely established among them. The "mystic tie of brotherhood" saved many a poor soldier's life during the war, alleviated the sufferings of many wounded, and created countless friendships between individuals of the contending parties that will never be sundered while life lasts. Mr. Kelley, himself a Masonic brother, and of straightforward and pleasing address, made friends wherever he went, and traveled throughout the entire district south-east of the Mississippi, without an unpleasant incident; and, having satisfactorily executed the mission upon which he was sent, he returned North.

THE GERM-IDEA.

Feeling deeply the disabilities under which the southern planters labored, from the want of trained labor—themselves, from their antecedents, unfitted as yet to direct their affairs with practical efficiency—he gave much thought to the means to be employed to rouse the lower classes to an appreciation of the dignity of agriculture, and the necessity of steady work, through which they might make comfortable homes for themselves and their children.

While at Mobile, Ala., he thought deeply over the subject of practical co-operation by the union of the Agricultural Societies then existing. He knew that these societies were distinct and independent of each other, but he asked himself the question which had so often occurred to other minds, but without result, Why should not the Agricultural Societies co-operate for the general welfare of the farmers of the whole country? At least, why could not some plan be originated, by which these societies in the South could mutually assist each other in ameliorating the condition of the southern farmers?

Continuing to think and to talk upon this matter, he remembered, that, according to tradition, the tie that binds Mason to Mason had existed from time immemorial; he remembered that the hand of brotherhood had extended with civilization, until now in almost every land, and among nearly all people, the tie was found which bound man to man as brethren—religion, honor, and manhood being the only qualifications for the unity of brother with brother.

At last, he asked himself the question, Why should not the farmers, both North and South, unite in the same manner as the Masons, who have clung together for hundreds of years, for social and educational purposes, with a view to promote their common interests?

Why not? was the answer echoed back. And now the solution was reached. All that remained was to mould the germ-idea into practical, tangible shape. To do this, would require constant energy, untiring labor, and much self-sacrifice.

MATURING PLANS.

The future founder of the Order was not a man to shrink from the responsibility. During the remaining months of his stay in the South, he mentioned the project to prominent gentlemen whom he met. It was received with favor. The only difficulty was, with the means at his disposal, to unite individual to individual, and mind to mind, in the working out of plans that should harmonize conflicting views, and enable them to make the conception of his brain a beneficent reality, for the elevation of the masses, through the sweat of whose faces the nations eat their bread.

Mr. Kelley returned to Washington, and from thence to Minnesota, where he spent the succeeding summer, still revolving the project in his mind. In November, 1866, he returned to Washington, to take a clerkship in the Post-Office Department. He now began to move seriously toward developing the idea, that, within the last eighteen months, has spread over the entire West and South like a prairie fire, and is now making rapid progress, not only in the East, but even in Canada.

Among the gentlemen whose co-operation he sought, no one enlisted more heartily than Mr. William Saunders, then (as now) Superintendent of the gardens and grounds of the Department of Agriculture at Washington. Other gentlemen who cordially co-operated with Mr. Kelley, were Mr. William M. Ireland, chief clerk of the finance bureau of the Post-Office Department (which position he still holds), Rev. John Trimble, Jr., Rev. A. B. Grosh, so familiarly known from his connection with Odd Fellowship, and Mr. J. R. Thompson.

FORMING THE FIRST DEGREE OF THE ORDER.

The above were all members, with high rank, of secret social and benevolent orders, and therefore proficients in ritualism; and all are gentlemen of education and refinement. They met from time to time, canvassing the grand work and suggesting various means of promoting the organization. At length, acting upon the suggestions offered at the different meetings, Messrs. Kelley and Ireland, on the 5th of August, 1867, at their quarters at the United States Hotel, upon Pennsylvania Avenue at Washington, together compiled and worked out a draft of the First Degree of the Order.

Immediately after this date, Mr. Saunders was directed by the Commissioner of Agriculture to proceed to the West and South, upon business connected with the Department. Proceeding West, he wrote Mr. Kelley from Sandusky, O., on August 30th: "I have mentioned your Order to a good many, and all agree in considering the thing a grand idea." Among other prominent farmers and horticulturists whose attention Mr. Saunders called to the new Order, were, Mr. Anson Bartlett, of Ohio, who was subsequently elected Overseer of the National Grange, and Mr. Wm. Muir, of

Hon. WILLIAM SAUNDERS,
(First Master National Grange, and Member National Executive Committee.)

Missouri, the well-known horticulturist, (who was afterward elected Steward of the National Grange), then of the *Rural World*, and now one of the editors of the *Illustrated Journal of Agriculture.*

In St. Louis, Mr. Saunders conferred the First Degree. He reported progress, periodically, to the Agricultural Syndicate at Washington, and furnished the names of those who from time to time agreed to co-operate. The gentlemen previously mentioned, and others to whom the new movement was communicated, all took an earnest interest in the work, and thenceforward labored peristently for its success.

Besides those whose names have been given, correspondence was entered into with Mr. A. S. Moss and Mr. F. M. McDowell, of New York, and other prominent gentlemen in various States, connected with agriculture, from whom valuable suggestions were received in elaborating the ritual, and forming the ground-work of the Order.

THE FOUNDERS OF THE ORDER.

To Mr. Kelley, then, belongs the credit of originating the idea which was so energetically and promptly worked up and carried out by the worthy few heretofore mentioned. But it is due to Mr. Saunders more than to any other single individual that it became popularized among the farmers, and especially among horticulturists. His official position, his knowledge of the real wants of these classes, and his wide popularity as a working member in agriculture and agricultural art, gave him great personal influence. His persistent devotion to the interests of the Order, since his connection with it, has been singularly free from bias as to its objects and aims. While this is true, indeed of the great proportion of its officers, it is pre-eminently so of this earnest and honorable man.

It is a singular fact in connection with the Order, that, of the original members, not one of them, it is believed, except Mr. Kelley, ever organized a subordinate Grange. No less remarkable is the fact that, of those early correspondents who gave substantial aid and encouragement in earnest words of praise, not more than five or six have ever taken an active part in the practical work of the Order. Thomas B. Bryan, of Chicago, for instance, early in the organization, felt deeply its necessity, urged strongly its merits, and gave liberally of his means, while yet the Order was in its greatest straits. At various times, the funds freely given by this gentleman were urgently needed. These gifts, too, possessed the added merit of having been earned in legitimate and honorable business pursuits; and, unlike the large sums occasionally donated, with so much ostentation, by the railroad and other Wall Street jobbers to found religious and other institutions, his donations were neither given to divert public opinion, nor to cover up some nefarious scheme, by which the ill-gotten wealth was obtained, nor yet to smother by good deeds the cries of the struggling masses, by whose blood and sweat it was gathered.

SELECTING A NAME.

In September, 1867, a circular was prepared by the leaders in the movement, and sent out to individuals prominent in agriculture. This document stated what had been so far done toward organizing the system for association and cooperation. Suggestions were asked for, and, among other things, as to the proper name to be adopted, in case the project met their approval. Responses came, which, as a rule, were favorable to the work contemplated; suggestions were given, and the work on the ritual at last became so far advanced that it was imperative that a fitting and suggestive name should be decided on for the new Order, still, as it were, in embryo.

About forty titles in all were received for consideration. Among these were, "Agricultural Lodges," "Bee Hives," "Knights of Husbandry," "Knights of the Plow," "Temples of Industry," and "Tillers of the Soil." But the name that has since made the Order so famous, and which is so expressive of the true nature of the association, "Patrons of Husbandry," was happily adopted, as the title of the members, while another term, equally expressive, was decided on to indicate the hall or place of meeting, and thus the word "Grange" was wedded to enduring fame.

It would be well for all to remember this fact, and not mutilate the English language by calling the individuals Grangers, as is so often done, not only in contempt of the Order, but often, for want of knowing better, by those who do not feel inimical to the Order. The individual is a "Patron of Husbandry;" the place of meeting, a "Grange."

ORGANIZING THE "NATIONAL GRANGE."

On the fourth day of December, 1867, the National Grange was organized. Less than twenty persons assembled at the office of Mr. Wm. Saunders, in Washington, on 4½ Street, between Missouri Avenue and the old canal; but these were individuals from various States, who were actuated by a feeling unanimous in its resolve, to draw together the agricultural masses throughout the whole country, and endeavor, by precept and example, to show the necessity of such a thorough organization as should enable the fraternity to counteract the influences that had long been at work, in various directions, to divert the legitimate profits from the hands of the farmer.

After a free and most earnest discussion of the means best adapted to forward the project, it was resolved to organize the National Grange. A ballot for officers resulted in the election of the following: William Saunders, of the District of Columbia, Master; J. R. Thompson, of Vermont, Lecturer; Anson Bartlett, of Ohio, Overseer; Wm. Muir, of Missouri, Steward; A. S. Moss, of New York, Assistant Steward; Rev. A. B. Grosh, of Pennsylvania, Chaplain; Wm. M. Ireland, of Pennsylvania, Treasurer; O. H. Kelley, of Minnesota, Secretary; and Edward P. Faris, of Illinois, Gate-Keeper.

The persons thus elected were not all present, but they were all well known, and were selected because of their interest in the Order, and the constancy which they had shown in supporting the new movement. The majority of them had been earnest and untiring in the establishment of the Order; they had matured their plan of operation so far as possible; and it was necessary that sufficient time be given to carry out this plan, according to the pre-conceived idea. In the discussion of ways and means, it was decided, therefore, that this election should be for five years.

CHAPTER XII.

EARLY STRUGGLES AND THEIR FRUITION.

TESTING THE WORK ALREADY DONE.

Very soon after the establishment of the parent or National Grange, a subordinate Grange was organized at Washington, numbering about sixty members. This was intended, not only as a school of instruction, but also as a means of testing the efficiency of the ritual. The latter being found good, so far as it went, in January, 1868, a second circular was sent out to various portions of the States, in which the objects of the Order were announced.

Some of these objects were stated to be, " to advance education, to elevate and dignify the occupation of the farmer, and to protect its members against the numerous combinations by which their interests were injuriously affected."

Among the benefits to be derived, as stated by the circular, were: "Systematic arrangements for procuring and disseminating, in the most expeditious manner, information relative to crops, demand and supply, prices, markets, transportation throughout the country, and for the establishment of depots for the sale of special and general products in the cities; also, for the purchase and exchange of stock, seeds, and desired varieties of plants and trees, and for the purpose of procuring help at home or from abroad, and situations for persons seeking employment; also, for ascertaining and testing the merits of newly-invented farming implements, and those not in general use, and for detecting and exposing those that are unworthy, and for protecting, by all available means, the farming interests from fraud and deception of every kind."

CARRYING THE WORK FORWARD.

Four months had now elapsed since the organization of the National Grange. It wanted money, which had heretofore been taken freely from the pockets of the founders of the Order, to satisfy the necessary current expenses. These gentlemen were not wealthy, and the sums already advanced had been a heavy tax upon them. The organization now owed one hundred and fifty dollars, most of which was for printing. Progress had been made, it is true, through the circulars sent out and the personal efforts of the members; and it will also be seen that progress had been made in creating a debt, which, though small, was onerous, nevertheless, to men of moderate or limited means, who had already liberally furnished the "sinews of war."

To create new Granges, it was necessary that individuals familiar with the work should meet with the new candidates. The head officers, who were devoting their time to the organization, did not receive any compensation. How, then, could the money be raised to enable the proper officers to travel and disseminate the ritual of the Order?

Mr. Kelley, the Secretary, was found equal to the emergency, and even hopeful that he could make his necessary traveling expenses, from the ordinary fees derived from the granting of dispensations. It was, therefore, decided to send him out, on a salary of two thousand dollars a year, provided this amount could be realized out of the fees obtained from the establishment of the Granges in the various States. The National Grange, however, expressly stipulated that, if the fees did not meet the sum named, he should have no claim on that organization, and that it would assume the payment of no expenses whatever.

Hopeful and enthusiastic, Mr. Kelley immediately resigned his clerkship in the Post-office Department. Being furnished with a general letter of introduction, Harrisburg, Pa., was selected as the first point for trial. His ticket bought, he found himself with but two dollars and a half in currency of the United States, for expenses. How many men would have left a lucrative office, and thus launched out upon an unknown sea, on a voyage which might eventuate in the wreck of his fondest hopes? He carried nothing with him but the best wishes and earnest prayers of the brotherhood left behind.

THE FIRST FOUR DISPENSATIONS ISSUED.

Armed with the necessary power to grant dispensations for the organization of subordinate Granges, Mr. Kelley arrived at Harrisburg, where he enlisted the co-operation of a sufficient number of persons to form a Grange, and there the first dispensation was granted.

Proceeding from this point, he traveled on, talking, wherever opportunity offered, with the farmers whom he met; here and there meeting with hearty encouragement, but, in the majority of cases, finding the farmers afflicted with that species of conservatism which looks with doubt upon any thing that seems like breaking out of old ruts. They did not like to take stock in any chimerical venture, content to suffer the ills they had rather than fly to those they knew not of.

O. H. KELLEY, ESQ.,
Secretary of the National Grange.

At length, reaching Fredonia, N. Y., a second dispensation was granted. From here he went to Columbus, O., where another Grange was organized. From thence, in due course of travel, he went to Chicago, where the fourth dispensation was granted.

Of these four dispensations, the first two retained vital action, the third resulted in a total failure, and the fourth proved but little better. Before long, the Chicago Grange ceased to hold meetings, and became as virtually dead as the one in Ohio. In this condition it remained until November, 1873, when an effort was made to revive the interest of its members; and while this history is being written, strong hopes are entertained that the reorganization of this, the first Grange in Illinois, will be entirely successful. It has amply proved that large cities are not favorable to the growth of an Order for asserting the rights of the farmer.

The history of the Order will show that the principal obstacles to the successful prosecution of the enterprise lay with the farmers themselves. The reasons were, that they required to be roused by their enemies no less than by their friends—they had first to be educated to the proper point, through the well-organized and constantly increasing power of legalized monopolies, using their accumulated capital to bind still closer the shackles of the farmer and the other producing classes of the nation.

DISCOURAGEMENT, BUT NOT DESPAIR.

Discouraged, but not despairing, still urging the importance of the Order, and wanting only money to carry on the good work, Mr. Kelley, one month after leaving Washington, reached Minnesota, in which State, it will be recollected, his farm was situated. In this great grain-growing State he met with somewhat better success. Six Granges were organized before the close of the year, making ten in all. One of these, the North Star Grange, of St. Paul, deserves more than a passing notice. Its members took hold of the work with alacrity; they persisted, nowithstanding the difficulties under which the new organization labored; and, to its credit be it said, the Grange has never missed a meeting since.

Among those who most vigorously denounced the scheme, were the class who, while conducting their own affairs with secrecy, saw in the future of this organization a power that might combat and render nugatory their own schemes of aggrandizement. The journals devoted to this class were not slow in ringing the changes on the terrible abuse of power that would ensue, if the organization should prove successful and become powerful.

The journals of our large cities, acting in the interests of great organizations, were especially virulent. Even a portion of the religious press attempted to cast obloquy on the Order, having suddenly bethought itself that all secret orders were inimical to the interests of humanity; unaware, perhaps, that through secret societies and means some of the most self-sacrificing and disinterested actions that have ever cast a halo over the divine-human in man have been performed; and taking no note of the fact that the admission of wives and mothers into full communion with the Order was *the* element that must conserve the purity of the organization. Happily for the Order, and happily for its members, that this idea early suggested itself to the founders. Happy for humanity all over the earth, if this sacred element could pervade, not only each and every secret society, but all political organizations as well.

WORKING AGAINST DIFFICULTIES.

After reaching his farm in Minnesota, Mr. Kelley remained there until the early part of 1871. Meanwhile, he wrote and talked about the Order, made journeys, when necessary to grant dispensations, and, in connection with his brethren of the various Granges, encountered manifold discouragements with fortitude. But all working for a common purpose, the small nucleus of Granges slowly increased.

The first Grange established in Minnesota was at Itasca. In a short time, one was organized in Jasper County, Ind. Another was organized at Waukon, Iowa, at the home of Mr. Adams, the present Master of the National Grange. A few more Granges were organized in Iowa, Minnesota, Wisconsin, and Illinois; but, up to the beginning of 1873, the entire membership of the Order in the United States was not computed at over seventy-five thousand. Before the issue of this work, it will undoubtedly exceed seven hundred thousand. One reason for the slow growth of the Order until within the last eighteen months, was that the farmers still looked to their Clubs as the way out of their difficulties. But it was at last found that the only way to solve the problem of concentrated effort was by co-operation with and through the Granges.

Slowly, yet surely, the organization gained friends and strength. The annual meetings of the National Grange at Washington, which was working steadily forward, were regularly attended by the Masters of the State Granges; and, at length, the business of the Order had reached such magnitude that Mr. Kelley found that he must either relinquish his position as Secretary of the National Grange, or give up his farm. He proposed to continue his labors for the Order, and, in January, 1871, removed to Washington, whence, a year later, he removed his office to Georgetown, D. C., and here the headquarters of the National Grange have since remained. Since this date, the principal difficulties which originally embarrassed the movement have been overcome, and many conscientious men and women, who formerly opposed the Order from principle, have learned to view the matter in a different light, since they have found that the secret feature of the organization could not, by the rules of the Order itself, be used for evil. Thus it has come about that many heretofore bitterly opposed to the system are now its staunchest friends, and labor heartily in their new field of usefulness.

THE HEADQUARTERS OF THE ORDER.

As we have just mentioned, the Order has its headquarters at Georgetown, D. C. Here its vast business is carried on; the accounts are kept and compared, circulars, tracts, and pamphlets issued, correspondence conducted, dispensations granted, etc. Ten clerks are unremittingly engaged, finding it difficult to keep pace with the constantly increasing business of the office.

In 1872, more than five hundred thousand publications of various kinds were sent out. The number largely increased in 1873, corresponding with the growth of the Order. Franks have never been used, under any circumstances. In 1872, about two thousand five hundred dollars worth of postage stamps were used, while the express charges aggregated about one hundred dollars per month.

Notwithstanding the great drain on its treasury, the National Grange is in excellent financial condition. So much have its circumstances changed since the period of its early struggles, when "the forlorn hope" traveled westward, that it now has over thirty thousand dollars in bank, and does not owe a dollar. The motto, is "Pay as you go." This alone ought to commend it to every business man in the land. The Secretary writes: "I make no purchases, except C. O. D., and every clerk is paid promptly each Saturday night." The Constitution requires that moneys shall be deposited once a month, but it is proposed to alter this provision so as to require such deposits to be made weekly; indeed, this has been the practice of the National Secretary for a considerable time past. The depository has, we believe, always been the Farmers' Loan and Trust Company, of New York City.

It has been said that all new organizations must have the measles, whooping-cough, and other infantile complaints. This organization has fairly got through with these disorders; indeed they were taken very lightly, and no evils ensued. It is now fully grown, of mature vigor, clear in intellect, and with conscience unstained.

WONDERFUL GROWTH OF THE ORDER.

The Order of Patrons of Husbandry has been repeatedly decried as of mushroom growth, and it has as often been prophesied that its decay would be as speedy. Those who make this assertion are evidently conversant with its history for only the last two years, and even with that but imperfectly. It seems to have been forgotten that the organization is six years old, or else the assumption is made up from the old-fashioned stand-point that, in order to be respectable, an order must be covered with the dust of ages. Such is not the modern way of organizing reforms.

Let us look at the real growth of the Order. In the year 1868, ten subordinate Granges were organized; in 1869, thirty-nine; in 1870, thirty-nine; in 1871, one hundred and twenty-five; in 1872, one thousand one hundred and five. Since January 1, 1873, subordinate Granges have been organized as follows:

January	158
February	347
March	666
April	571
May	696
June	625
July	612
August	829
September	919
October	1050

What the Order is Not.

The number of Granges in the several States and Territories, according to the official list, on November 15, 1873, was:

Alabama	240
Arkansas	80
California	110
Georgia	327
Illinois	712
Indiana	587
Iowa	1830
Kansas	664
Kentucky	50
Louisiana	31
Massachusetts	14
Michigan	124
Minnesota	378
Missouri	1056
Mississippi	457
Maine	1
Nebraska	346
New Hampshire	8
New Jersey	19
New York	22

North Carolina	117	Wisconsin	245
Ohio	199	Colorado	2
Oregon	43	Dakota	29
Pennsylvania	37	Canada	8
South Carolina	188	Washington	5
Tennessee	219	Maryland	6
Texas	31	Florida	16
Vermont	30		
Virginia	8	Total	8260
West Virginia	21		

It will thus be seen that there are subordinate Granges established in thirty-six States and Territories, besides those in Canada, where, there is no reason to doubt, the Order will become as popular as it is in the United States. If it is of mushroom growth, its bitterest opponent can not deny that it has the sympathy and support of many of the leading minds of the United States and Canada. A reference to the statistics of the subordinate Granges established in 1873 will convince the most skeptical that the growth is entirely healthy; otherwise, its popularity could not so steadily increase.

STRENGTH OF THE ORDER.

The strength of the Order has been variously estimated. The membership of the subordinate Granges ranges from eleven to two hundred and fifty. Our figures show eight thousand two hundred and sixty Granges. Taking seventy as a fair average membership for each Grange, which is not too high an estimate, we have a total membership of nearly six hundred thousand. It will undoubtedly be increased, before the first of January, 1874, by a hundred thousand The female membership (included, of course, in the above estimate) is believed to be from seventy-five to one hundred thousand strong.

While, for the inception of this work, full credit should be accorded the originators, Messrs. Saunders and Kelley, and their worthy co-laborers, the rank and file—the working members—must not be forgotten. The Deputies especially have had an onerous task. They have had to battle with opposition, submit to reproach, disarm suspicion, and guard the Order at all points against the attacks of wily and insidious enemies. They have borne the emblems of the fraternity among foes difficult to overcome; they have had to steady the irresolute, and support the timid. With unbending purpose, and a firm reliance in the integrity of their cause, they have planted the banner of co-operative effort in every State of the Union. They have gathered a harvest of members—men whose strong arms have hewed out homes from the forest, or reared habitations on the prairie or the mountain slope, the plain or the hillside—all over the land. So far, this great army of the bone and sinew of the land have used their power in the most careful and considerate manner. The wonderful success of the organization might naturally have turned the heads of men who have long struggled hopelessly for their natural rights. That it has not thus far done so may certainly be accepted as evidence that the Order, in the future as in the past, will be actuated only by motives of honor, and a strict regard to justice and the inherent rights of man.

CHAPTER XIII.

AIMS AND OBJECTS OF THE ORDER.

SALIENT FEATURES OF THE ORDER.

Three salient and distinct features of the Order of Patrons of Husbandry are, respectively, its social, intellectual, and business elements.

The feature first named aims to bring together men and women, young and old, who, in social converse, may discuss whatever pertains to the well-being of the community. Purity of thought and expression are inculcated; and, while any question pertaining to innocent gossip may be broached, coarseness and backbiting are allowed no place.

In 1870, Mr. Saunders, at the annual meeting of the National Grange, of which he was then the Master, expressed himself as follows: "To make country homes and country society attractive, refined, and enjoyable, to balance exhaustive labors by instructive social amusements and accomplishments, is part of our mission and our aim."

Among the pleasant social features are the feasts provided, once a month, by the ladies in summer, not unfrequently taking the form of pic-nics in some grove. It is pleasant to record that this idea originated with a lady, Miss Carrie A. Hall, of Boston, Mass., who, with untiring zeal and self-abnegation, has devoted herself to the furtherance of the best interests of the Order almost from its inception. These banquets, whether held within the Grange or in the grove, help to bind together the various other features in one harmonious whole. The popularity of the pic-nics especially, leaves no doubt as to their utility, not only among the members themselves, but as exercising an influence upon many who would not otherwise become united with the fraternity. The lack of social enjoyment has long been felt among farmers, and this want the Grange supplies most thoroughly.

EDUCATING THE INTELLECTS.

Another want always felt most keenly by progressive farmers has been the difficulty experienced in meeting together for intellectual improvement. The Farmers' Clubs, except in a few isolated instances, have always failed in this. It seemed impossible to make the incongruous elements of masculine humanity cohere sufficiently for persistent effort in this direction; and only when the feminine element was permitted to unite therein has it ever become permanently successful.

In the ritual of the Grange, there is music to enliven, educate, and refine; many of the Granges already possess libraries, constantly added to, whose benefits all the members may share alike. While the Grange is a place where each sex and every condition in life, if respectable, may meet upon terms of perfect equality, the refining influences therein gained have already prevented many a young man from spending his time and means in the village saloons, or billiard halls, and many soul-destroying resorts of vice. The Grange has undoubtedly redeemed some who, but for its influence, would have gone from bad to worse, and have died drunkards, and perhaps have filled paupers' graves.

The Grange is intended to be the moral and intellectual

club-room, where husband and wife, father and mother, brother and sister, may meet, when the labors of the day permit, to improve themselves in that social and intellectual intercourse that has hitherto seemed unavailable to a class who compose at least two-fifths of the population of the country. If no other problem in human life were solved by the Patrons of Husbandry, this alone would stamp it indelibly as one of the most harmonizing institutions of either ancient or modern times.

THE BUSINESS FEATURE.

While the Patrons seek to inculcate precepts of morality, educate the intellectual, and provide innocent amusement, business is the chief aim of the Order. This includes plans for assisting each other in buying and selling; discussions on the best means for the improvement of tillage; on draining, landscape adornments, and the best methods of making home beautiful; and educating the members to a general knowledge of business, so that they will not become the prey of sharpers, who have heretofore found our agricultural classes only too easy dupes.

There is one class of swindlers to whom the farmers have especially fallen victims, the class called "scalpers" by railroad men. They sell tickets on their own account to any part of the world, cheating the purchaser when opportunity occurs. They are self-constituted agents, who buy up blocks of nursery trees and plants already culled until entirely worthless for practical use. These are sorted, tied into suitable bundles, to correspond to the orders taken from farmers by their agents, carefully labeled, and delivered as first-class stock of the varieties ordered. These tricks have filled the orchards of the unwary with fruits unsuited to the climate and locality, or even entirely spurious, wholly untrue to name.

Another species of sharpers are the various so-called agents, who are traveling over the country purporting to have bought goods at bankrupt sales, which goods they profess to sell at merely nominal prices. Still another stripe of these precious scamps are the swindlers in our cities who flood the country with circulars, proposing to sell tickets at from twenty-five cents to one dollar each, entitling the holder to select from a stock of goods to an amount many times their value.

These, then, are some of the objects for which the Order of Patrons of Husbandry was organized, namely, to abolish, through the social and intellectual elevation of the members, the nefarious practices of unscrupulous sharpers, who constantly prey upon those who, thrown seldom into contact with the world, have not the means of discerning the lurking swindle beneath.

A THIRST FOR KNOWLEDGE.

As the farmer gains information, he sees the necessity of supplementing his own empirical attainments with the knowledge richly stored in the books and journals devoted to his especial interests, of which heretofore by far too little use has been made, and which should be to the agriculturist what the technical books and journals are to the other several classes that compose a civilized nation. If the farmer ignores these means, he must continue not only to be the prey of sharpers and confidence men, but, in a great degree, to be worsted in the every-day transactions of legitimate business; for it is human nature to make money wherever one can, and in this the farmer is not different from other men.

He wins from his fellow, if he can. The higher his social and intellectual nature is developed, the less liable is he to depart from strict honesty and descend to meanness or

A Farm Scene.

downright dishonesty. Fair and honorable dealing marks the true business man; deceit and fraud belong only to the sharper and swindler.

THE SECRET NATURE OF THE ORDER.

It was considered necessary to the permanency of the organization, early in the inception of the Order, that its workings be secret. There are many reasons why this secrecy should be imperative. It was intended to bind the agricultural masses together firmly, but without severity. To use the expressive language of Mr. Saunders: "Unity of action can not be acquired without discipline, and discipline can not be enforced without significant organization; hence, we have a ceremony of initiation which binds us in mutual fraternity as with a band of iron; but, although its influence is so powerful, its application is as gentle as that of the silken thread that binds a wreath of flowers."

Why should it not be secret? No member of any business firm would long retain his position if he should allow the whole town to know the means used to forward the enterprises in which the firm was engaged; for, by this course, it would inevitably be bankrupted. If the lawyer was not bound by oaths to preserve inviolate the secrets entrusted to him by his clients, how could the ends of justice be subserved? If the physician should tell at the street corner, every thing that might come to his knowledge in the course of his practice, the social privacy of our homes and firesides would be gone, and all the decencies of life be outraged. If the divine should tell every idle gossip, each incident of sin or wrong done, that came to his ear, or if the priesthood should reveal the secrets of the confessional, what would be the result? Society would be convulsed to its center; for that which was innocent in itself would be magnified into absolute wrong, and that which was only venial would be contorted into the blackness of iniquity.

Persons in every vocation and degree of life have secrets that may not be told outside of the immediate circle in which they move. Even our political organizations have secrets that are not freely communicated. Our associations of every kind, and corporations, hold secrets essential to their success in business. Our legislative bodies, and even the Senate of the United States, hold executive sessions with closed doors.

While it might be freely confessed that a *political* organization, conducted with secrecy, would be likely to prove inimical to the liberties of the people, there can be no danger from the secrecy obligatory on the Patrons of Husbandry, one of whose fundamental principles is that politics shall not be discussed in meetings of the Order. Certainly, one thing has been proved, that women, from whom secrets were wrongfully supposed to leak as freely as water from a sieve, have proved themselves as trustworthy in this particular as men, thus disproving one more of the slanders against the sex.

THE SECRET FEATURE EXAGGERATED AND MISAPPREHENDED.

From first to last, there has been the wildest misapprehension of the extent and importance of the secrecy specialty of the Granges. This feature has been grossly misrepresented. Good people, in their anxiety to discountenance any thing savoring of Know-Nothingism or the like, have held up their hands in horror when asked to join. "What? Join a secret society? Never! *Never!!*" Straightway, they have gone home, and, with hair on end, outpoured to the partners of their bosom the unheard-of wickedness they have been tempted to perpetrate.

There exists, among persons who are not members and are therefore unacquainted with its workings, a fixed impression that the Order of Patrons of Husbandry is modeled after the German *Vehm Gericht*—a sort of agricultural "Holy League;" that it holds midnight sessions to which no one is admitted, except after giving certain cabalistic grips and passwords; that its councils are presided over by mysterious, closely-masked, scarlet-clad persons, in whose hands are the life and death, goods and chattels, of its members; that these head centres are entitled to require, and do require, neophytes to prove their fitness to join the Order by some deed of blood; that, at a sign of hesitancy, "Off with his head" is the command, and straightway the unfortunate trembler is minus his *caput*. In short, the general impression abroad is, that the Order of Patrons of Husbandry is a concatenation of masked meetings, grips, passwords, dark lanterns, stilettoes, poisoned chalices, skulls and crossbones, drowning in sacks, anonymous denunciations, and mysterious disappearances. And all this because it chooses to exclude outsiders from its business deliberation, and not to let their enemies know their every move.

The real state of the case (and, though not a member of the Order, I know it to be so—which is itself a proof that the secrecy required is not very rigorous) is, that this feature of the Grange is of the mildest character, and in very rare cases is it vigorously enforced. The wonderful spread of the Order is a guarantee that its principles are such as a good citizen may conscientiously subscribe to. In fact, the secrecy feature has been one of the greatest reasons for the marvelous success of the Order—perhaps *the* greatest, except the vigor which the leaders of the movement have shown in developing it.

THE REAL CHARACTER OF THE ORDER.

The real character and aims of the Order of Patrons of Husbandry were thus detailed to the writer by Col. A. B. Smedley, Master of the State Grange of Iowa:

It has no politics of a partisan character, yet it could hardly be expected that those consecrated to the work of reform and purification should consent to be longer in the leading-strings of political tricksters and demagogues, who have bartered their trusts for money. In fact, this Order proposes to invite office-seekers to back seats, while the people shall seek and designate their servants.

The Order is no respecter of persons, color, sects, or sexes, but has reference most positively to character, declining to admit drunkards, gamblers, professional politicians, or those whose pursuits or associations place them antagonistic to farm interests.

The Order means business, and will labor to bring the greatest good to the greatest number. Some of its general objects may be stated as follows, viz.:

1st. The ennoblement of labor, and the fraternity of the producing classes.

2d. Mutual instruction, and the lightening of labor by diffusing a better knowledge of its aims.

3d. Social culture, as also mental and moral development.

4th. Mutual relief in sickness and adversity.

5th. The prevention of litigation.

6th. Prevention of cruelty to animals.

7th. Bringing more nearly together the producer and consumer.

8th. The overthrow of the credit system.

9th. Building up and fostering our home industries.

10th. Mutual protection to husbandmen against sharpers and middle-men.

CHAPTER XIV.

OTHER PROMINENT FEATURES OF THE ORDER.

WOMAN'S MISSION IN THE GRANGE.

This subject has already been touched upon, but will bear amplifying. During the early days of the Order, every means was used by its enemies to throw disrepute upon this feature of the plan of association. All sorts of charges—moral, philosophical, humorous, satirical, and vindictive—were hurled against it. Time, however, has proved the excellence and strength of this element. One firm friend it has had, from first to last, in that brotherhood who acknowledge the mystic tie wherever on earth it is habitable for man; who are bound with a cord of union that can not be broken; who recognize that all men are the children of one God, and who follow the divine precept, "Love ye one another."

Mr. Saunders, in an address heretofore quoted from, said of the work of women in the Grange: "Their assistance in the workings of the Order is proving of incalculable value; it is, indeed, doubtful whether the objects of the institution, especially in regard to the refinements of education, and all that tends to brighten hearths and enliven homes, could have been accomplished without their presence and aid."

Woman's work in the Grange is to elevate and refine. If her influence were felt and acknowledged in every secret organization having for its object the rounding off the rough edges of every-day life, its power for good would be greater than it was ever before able to exercise in any one single direction; for, as is truly said in one of the circulars sent out by the Patrons: "Every husband and brother knows that where he can be accompanied by his wife or sister, no lessons will be learned but those of purity and truth."

WOMEN AS KEEPERS OF SECRETS.

Another fear, early expressed, was that women could not keep a secret. It is unnecessary to say that this idea is now thoroughly exploded. In all the workings of the Order nothing is yet believed to have escaped the lips of one of the female members where it should not be told. The reason is obvious. The wives and daughters of farmers are not surrounded by the false glitter and deceptions of fashionable life. They share the labors and the sorrows of their families; they are treated as the equals of, and co-workers with, the men. Their tastes are simple, their aspirations pure.

Many a city belle envies the robust health, the blending of the rose with the lily, characterizing the country girl. The one is engaged in frivolities and fashionable dissipation, such as drive the carmine from the cheek; the other takes a healthy, practical interest in the affairs of daily life around her. The mere votary of fashion may be able to keep her own secrets, but she does not always keep those of her friend. The rural wife or maiden keeps not only her own, but also those of her friends which may not be told.

Maidens as true and faithful abound also in our cities, but they are not found in the circles of those butterflies who worship at the altar of fashion, but rather around the fireside of the God-fearing man of business, the artisan and

The Matron at Home.

the mechanic. If the lately-established Order of Patrons of Industry should do for the working classes of our cities what the Patrons of Husbandry have done and will do for our rural population, the united strength of these organizations will become a power for good absolutely irresistible; and they can sweep from the land the last vestige of corruption and fraud, even to the cleansing of the Augean stables of party politics and "ring" jobbery.

HOW THE PATRONS PREVENT LAW SUITS.

Lawyers make our laws, and in framing them it is not strange that they should so arrange them as to make the most capital for themselves. As now constituted, the majority of our legislative enactments are such a mass of verbiage that none but an adept, educated to the art, can unravel the tangled skein. Indeed, so intricate are they that even the lawyers themselves, nay, even our best judges, are not able to pronounce upon their meaning with precision.

Many of the Granges have incorporated into their constitutions a clause binding the members, when differences arise between them, to submit their cases to arbitration. Here is a beneficent expedient that, if rigidly adhered to, will save to the members not only enough to pay the working expenses of the Grange, but also, in the course of a few years, to stock each organization so electing with a library amply sufficient to meet all their ordinary wants.

In some instances this method of settling disputes has entirely done away with the petty suits that are constantly stirring up neighborhood strife, and filling the pockets of pettifogging lawyers, growing rich, in many cases, from the results of their own machinations. If this class, who are held in contempt by the honorable portion of their profession, persist in stirring up strife, let the quarrels by all means be settled by the Granges without their further intervention. A Patron who refuses to abide by the pledge he takes in this respect when he signs the constitution, should justly be considered to have a greater love for the law than justice, and properly ought to be subject to Grange discipline, even to expulsion.

The time and money often wantonly squandered in litigation (to say nothing of the ill-feeling engendered), if properly expended, would, in many cases, save the farmer's family much needless suffering, and not unfrequently lift the mortgage from the farm, and leave its possessor in the undisturbed enjoyment of the results of his previous hard labors. This clause in the constitution of Granges we believe to have been first started in that enterprising banner State, Iowa. May her people long enjoy the results of their struggle against extortion.

THE COLORED BROTHER AS A PATRON.

It has been said that, sooner or later, the colored element in our population, and especially at the South, would clamor for admittance into the Order; and that this question would prove annoying and difficult of adjustment. This is one of the myths gotten up originally in Washington, and dispatched to a daily paper of New York city, apparently for the purpose of not only exciting prejudice among those outside the Order, but also of creating discord within. But the bomb fell harmless; the still-born myth failed to stir up the feeling among Southern Patrons that was intended.

On the other hand, it is a gratifying fact that in no portion of the country, except the Western States, has the Order made so rapid progress as at the South. There, at least, the colored element gives no trouble. Why should it in this Order, any more than in Masonry, for instance? No individual, unless he or she be a farmer, or at least connected with agricultural pursuits, and respectable, is admitted into the Order.

Cotton Plant.

The constitution of the Order does not allow either politics or religion to interfere with the work. Every individual member is as free and untrammeled in these matters as though not a Patron. Nor does the constitution contain any reference to color. If the requisite number of persons of color should apply for a dispensation, it would be issued; or, if not, it would be a proceeding, on the part of the officer refusing, of an entirely arbitrary character, for which he could not readily account to the National Grange. It is to be hoped, indeed, that Granges, composed of persons of color, will be established all over the South and elsewhere, provided the agricultural element is strong enough to support one. In the North there will rarely be any necessity for Granges of colored brethren, for, there, comparatively few persons of color take to farming regularly. Their tropical nature leads them to engage in such labor in cities as save them from exposure to the weather in winter. There is nothing in the ritual of the Order that precludes the admission of any person on account of nationality or color, no matter what it be. There is an especial field of usefulness for the Grange at the South. It would be just the school, combining the esthetic with the practical, in which to educate the freedmen, who, having just emerged from slavery, requires every possible agency for informing, refining, and elevating his untutored nature, and fitting him for his duties as a man and citizen.

NO GRANGES SPEAKING FOREIGN LANGUAGES.

It has also been flung in the teeth of the Patrons that no German Granges have been established. With the same truth, and to the same point, it might be observed that there have been no Irish, nor French, nor Swedish, nor Dutch Granges established. The fact is, there should not be, except in certain special localities, or in settlements sufficiently large for organization, where the inhabitants have not yet learned to speak our language. In such exceptional cases the ritual should be translated into the language required, that the perfect affiliation of all farmers might be secured.

Where the community of any nationality is sufficiently strong to allow the formation of a Grange, although they might speak English in the most imperfect manner, there could be no objection to dispensations therefor. Indeed, being subordinate to the National and State Granges, it would help to cement and bind together the whole with a still stronger bond of unity, and in a closer brotherhood. It is to be hoped that the Order will work strongly in this direction, granting dispensations in every language, if need be, that is spoken in the United States.

It is unquestionably true that all the foreign nationalities in our midst, and especially the German, who are naturally imbued with a strong fraternal feeling, prefer to join beneficiary societies having their own branches. The feature in question could work no harm among the Patrons, any more than among other order, in the country. On the contrary, it might be the means of still further consolidating the agricultural masses.

THE ILLINOIS "STAATS-ZEITUNG" ON THE GRANGES.

The following extract from this leading German newspaper well expresses the feeling which should govern this matter:

"A German recently publicly protested against the 'Granges.' He thought the control of the reform movement ought not to be left in the hands of secret societies with mystic signs and ceremonies of inauguration. Like the country, he regarded its welfare, and the furthering of the same, as the common privilege and duty of all; and here, where every laudable object may be openly prosecuted, so patriotic an undertaking must not become the exclusive property of a few, nor yet must it be enveloped in a mantle of secrecy, and surrounded with a mysterious hocus-pocus. Such secrecy and hocus-pocus is hypocrisy and deception on the one hand, and superstition and folly on the other.

"The man who wrote this views the thing in too gloomy a light. Deception and folly can not be discovered in the farmer associations. The thing, of course, would be wrong if they sought to accomplish a specific political object in a secret manner. But, as is to be seen from the declarations of the chiefs of the Order, politics is not really the object. Not in their capacity as members of granges do the farmers take part in politics, but in their capacity of members of public farmers' associations, who publicly discuss, and in their resolutions publicly declare, what they want. We will only point to the county conventions of the farmers in Illinois, and to their platforms and nominations.

"Not a few German farmers belong to the English-American granges. But their participation in the Order would be far greater if there were German granges, which, of course, would be just as subordinate to the principal body as are German Odd Fellow lodges to the Grand Lodges of their Order."

SOME OF THE UNJUST CHARGES AGAINST THE GRANGES.

It has been asserted that the Granges were simply organized for political effort, which in time would become apparent; that the ritual is simply a cheap glitter that, in a short time, would lose its power, and end in dissolution, leaving the farmer worse off than before; that, if successful, they would crush manufactures, and involve the country in financial ruin; that the Order is fatally defective in coherence, from the want of education and intelligence among the rank and file of the Order; with many more harsh things of the same general tenor.

The first proposition has already been sufficiently disproved by the action of the Granges themselves. The second is well known in the Order to be incorrect, unless by cheap glitter is meant the simplicity of the ritual and the few ceremonies of initiation. The saving in purchases of every kind needed by the members is a feature that must inevitably bind together this most remarkable social organization of any age. The want of intelligence and education has more foundation in truth, if by this is meant that the average farmer lacks the training that would enable him to cope with those shrewd fellows whose only aim in life is the gathering together of the almighty dollar, from every available source, and by whatsoever means possible.

It is conceded that agriculture is the ground-work of national wealth; and that the prosperity of the country depends upon the prosperity of the agricultural interests. Yet the farmer of the West has seen himself grow poorer and poorer each year, although his granaries were overflowing with the cereals, while millions far away wanted cheap food. While in one nation thousands were starving, the Western farmer, in many localities, was burning his corn for fuel, because freights were so high that he could not transport it.

The fault, it must be said, was not *all* with the railways, exorbitant as were their charges, and grasping as were their combinations to extend their power. The farmers of the West had been raising too much of the raw material for export. They had failed to keep up with the progress of the age, and did not diversify their agriculture to meet the requirements of the times. Therefore, education to a proper business managment is one of the tenets of the Order.

SOME GAINS OF THE GRANGES.

They have gained much socially, in having been enabled to bring together neighborhoods between which social intercourse had previously seemed impossible. Instances are recorded where families have ridden fifteen miles, regularly, to attend the meetings of the Order. The reason was, the gathering was not only made the occasion when friends could meet together in social converse, but the ritual, both written and unwritten, tends to expand the mind; the aim and scope of the work in general being to make the members better and more intelligent men and women. For as the action of flint upon steel elicits sparks, so the attrition of mind with mind elicits ideas and stimulates the intellect.

The educational features are, by lectures and discussions, to show the true value of business qualifications, not only in buying and selling, but also as applied to the everyday routine of farm life. The Patron will be a better business man and a better farmer as well. The work of the

Order not only shows the business relation of individual to individual, but also the business relation of the individual to the Government, and to the community in which he or she lives.

Buying cheaper and selling dearer, are simply incidents that come in correlatively in the work. A certain class of business men have endeavored to inculcate the idea that the Order was to make a raid upon the various industries of the country, in order to concentrate all business in the hands of the Patrons themselves. But the truth is, the Patrons do not propose interference with any legitimate business; and they seek, by every lawful means, to build up manufactures everywhere. When a business or manufacture becomes an onerous monopoly, that seeks to obtain excessive profits by crushing out the weak who seek the same line of business, the counteracting of this iniquity must undoubtedly be regarded as legitimate and proper work for the Granges. They are seeking to build up business, not kill it.

A CASE IN POINT.

The cost of shipping agricultural machinery and manufactured implements is exceedingly great. It occurred to the Patrons of Iowa that much of this expense might be reduced by making at least some of these at home. Plow factories were started under the auspices of the Order, and now a large percentage of the plows used by the members of the Order, are manufactured in this State, and at prices materially below what they cost under the old *regime*, when they had to go through the hands of the various agents, employed by manufacturers for the purpose of enabling them to keep up the retail price to the farmer.

Some of the more sagacious of the manufacturers have

retracted their overbearing diction to deal with the Granges only through the manufacturers' agents, and they acknowledge that their profits remain unimpaired. In the end, all manufacturers must come under the same system, or go to the wall. One of their great savings, and one not previously estimated, is, that they are not obliged to keep immense stocks scattered all over the land, constantly depreciating in value, and in various ways entailing a considerable percentage of losses. The new system of direct purchases will eventually do away with a class of middle men or agents, many of whom have been but little better than "grain scalpers," living as they did, and growing rich from their inordinate commissions, and having a monopoly of the articles sold. One of the very proper aims of the Patrons is to do away with such exactions.

CO-OPERATION OF INDEPENDENT ORGANIZATIONS NECESSARY TO ULTIMATE SUCCESS.

Every Grange, Farmers' Club, Farmers' Union, Farmers' Co-operative Association, and every similar organization of whatsoever name that has sprung up throughout the land, since the banner of resistance to monopoly has been raised, must not only co-operate with other Granges, Clubs, Unions, etc., but these several organizations must learn to work unitedly, as one coherent whole, toward all legitimate ends that it may seem necessary to secure.

The assumption is reiterated and insisted on, that all these bodies must assist and co-operate with each other upon all vital questions, whether social, financial, or even political.

Some of the leading partisan journals of the day begin to see the beginning of the end, and are endeavoring to prejudice public opinion against all combinations of farmers. At first, many of the politicians and political editors were especially anxious to assist in working out the problems that agitated the agricultural masses. The more sensible of them are now inclined to allow these organizations to manage their own affairs. This is especially true of the Granges, and for a cogent reason, namely, they can not, to use a slang phrase, get the inside track.

One of the leading journals of Chicago, which, when not indecent or vulgar, is bitterness itself, in calling attention to the meeting of the Illinois Farmers' Association which held its annual session at Decatur, on the 16th of December last, headed a double-leaded leader on the subject, "Agricultural Jackasses," and rounded it off with "Dam phool;" by such terms referring to men like Professor Turner, W. C. Flagg, and others of justly high standing for intelligence and philosophical breadth of mind.

If these men are not capable of discussing questions relating to agriculture, and agricultural interests, as connected with national or political economy, it is not probable that the penny-a-liner of the Chicago Times will ever shine in that direction. That journal might well be proud if its entire staff possessed a moiety of the scholarly attainments that belong to either of the two working farmers above named.

CHAPTER XV.

LAWS AND BY-LAWS OF THE ORDER.

OFFICERS AND CONSTITUTION OF THE NATIONAL GRANGE.

The officers of the National Grange, at present, are as follows: Master—*Dudley W. Adams*, Waukon, Iowa; Overseer—*Thomas Taylor*, Columbia, S. C.; Lecturer—*T. A. Thompson*, Plainview, Wabasha Co., Minnesota; Steward—*A. J. Vaughan*, Early Grove, Marshall Co., Mississippi; Assistant Steward—*G. W. Thompson*, New Brunswick, New Jersey; Chaplain—*Rev. A. B. Grosh*, Washington, D. C.; Treasurer—*F. M. McDowell*, Corning, New York; Secretary—*O. H. Kelley*, Washington, D. C.; Gate-Keeper —*O. Dinwiddie*, Orchard Grove, Lake Co., Indiana; Ceres —*Mrs. D. W. Adams*, Waukon, Iowa; Pomona—*Mrs. O. H. Kelley*, Washington, D. C.; Flora—*Mrs. J. C. Abbott*, Clarkesville, Butler Co., Iowa; Lady Assistant Steward—*Miss C. A. Hall*, Washington, D. C.; Executive Committee — *William Saunders*, Washington, D. C.; *D. Wyatt Aiken*, Cokesbury, Abbeville Co., S. C.; *E. R. Shankland*, Dubuque, Iowa.

PREAMBLE TO THE CONSTITUTION.

Human happiness is the acme of earthly ambition. Individual happiness depends on general prosperity.

The prosperity of a nation is in proportion to the value of its productions.

The soil is the source from whence we derive all that constitutes wealth; without it, we would have no agriculture, no manufactures, no commerce. Of all the material gifts of the Creator, the various productions of the vegetable world are of the first importance. The art of agriculture is the parent and precursor of all arts, and its products the foundation of all wealth.

The productions of the earth are subject to the influence of natural laws, invariable and indisputable; the amount produced will, consequently, be in proportion to the intelligence of the producer, and success will depend upon his knowledge of the action of these laws, and the proper application of their principles.

Hence, knowledge is the foundation of happiness.

The ultimate object of this organization is mutual instruction and protection, to lighten labor by diffusing a knowledge of its aims and purposes, to expand the mind by tracing the beautiful laws the Great Creator has established in the universe, and to enlarge our views of Creative wisdom and power.

To those who read aright, history proves that in all ages society is fragmentary, and successful results of general welfare can be secured only by general effort. Unity of action can not be acquired without discipline, and discipline can not be enforced without significant organization; hence, we have a ceremony of initiation, which binds us in mutual fraternity as with a band of iron; but although its influence is so powerful, its application is as gentle as that of the silken thread that binds a wreath of flowers.

The Patrons of Husbandry consist of the following:

CONSTITUTION.

ARTICLE I.—*Officers.*—Section 1. The officers of a Grange, either National, State, or Subordinate, consist of and rank as follows: Master, Overseer, Lecturer, Steward, Assistant Steward, Chaplain, Treasurer, Secretary, Gate-Keeper, Ceres, Pomona, Flora, and Lady Assistant Steward. It is their duty to see that the laws of the Order are carried out.

Sec. 2. *How Chosen.*—In the Subordinate Granges they shall be chosen annually; in the State Granges once in two years, and in the National Grange once in three years. All elections to be by ballot.

Vacancies by death or resignation to be filled at a special election at the next regular meeting thereof—officers so chosen to serve until the annual meeting.

Sec. 3. The Master of the National Grange may appoint members of the Order as Deputies to organize Granges where no State Grange exists.

Sec. 4. There shall be an Executive Committee of the National Grange, consisting of three members, whose term of office shall be three years, and one of whom shall be elected each year.

Sec. 5. The officers of the respective Granges shall be addressed as "Worthy."

ARTICLE II.—*Meetings.*—Section 1. Subordinate Granges shall meet once each month, and may hold intermediate meetings as may be deemed necessary for the good of the Order. All business meetings are confined to the fourth degree.

Sec. 2. State Granges shall meet annually, at such time and place as the Grange shall from year to year determine.

Sec. 3. The National Grange shall meet annually, on the first Wednesday in February, at such place as the Grange may from year to year determine. Should the National Grange adjourn without selecting the place of meeting, the Executive Committee shall appoint the place, and notify the Secretary of the National Grange and the Masters of State Granges, at least thirty days before the day appointed.

ARTICLE III.—*Laws.*—The National Grange, at its annual session, shall frame, amend, or repeal such laws as the good of the Order may require. All laws of State and Subordinate Granges must conform to this Constitution and the laws adopted by the National Grange.

ARTICLE IV.—*Ritual.*—The Ritual adopted by the National Grange shall be used in all Subordinate Granges, and any desired alteration in the same must be submitted to, and receive the sanction of, the National Grange.

ARTICLE V.—*Membership.*—Any person interested in agricultural pursuits, of the age of sixteen years (female), and eighteen years (male), duly proposed, elected, and complying with the rules and regulations of the Order, is entitled to membership and the benefit of the degrees taken. Every application must be accompanied by the fee of membership. If rejected, the money will be refunded. Applications must be certified by members, and balloted for at a subsequent meeting. It shall require three negative votes to reject an applicant.

ARTICLE VI.—*Fees for Membership.*—The minimum fee for membership in a Subordinate Grange shall be, for men five dollars, and for women two dollars, for the four degrees, except charter members, who shall pay—men three dollars and women fifty cents.

ARTICLE VII.—*Dues.*—Section 1. The minimum of regular monthly dues shall be ten cents from each member, and each Grange may otherwise regulate its own dues.

Sec. 2. The Secretary of each Subordinate Grange shall report quarterly to the Secretary of the State Grange the names of all persons initiated or passed to higher degrees.

Sec. 3. The Treasurer of each Subordinate Grange shall report quarterly, and pay to the Treasurer of his State Grange, the sum of one dollar for each man, and fifty cents for each woman, initiated during that quarter; also, a quarterly due of six cents for each member.

Sec. 4. The Secretary of each State Grange shall report quarterly to the Secretary of the National Grange the membership in his State, and the degrees conferred during the quarter.

Sec. 5. The Treasurer of each State Grange shall deposit, to the credit of the National Grange of Patrons of Husbandry, with some banking or trust company in New York (to be selected by the Executive Committee), in quarterly installments, the annual due of ten cents for each member of his State, and forward the receipts for the same to the Treasurer of the National Grange.

Sec. 6. All moneys deposited with said company shall be paid out only upon the drafts of the Treasurer, signed by the Master and countersigned by the Secretary.

Sec. 7. No State Grange shall be entitled to representation in the National Grange whose dues are unpaid for more than one quarter.

Article VIII.—*Requirements.*—Section 1. Reports from Subordinate Granges relative to crops, implements, stock, or any other matters called for by the National Grange, must be certified to by the Master and Secretary, and under seal of the Grange giving the same.

Sec. 2. All printed matter, on whatever subject, and all information issued by the National or State to Subordinate Granges, shall be made known to the members without unnecessary delay.

Sec. 3. If any brothers or sisters of the Order are sick, it shall be the duty of the Patrons to visit them, and see that they are well provided with all things needful.

Sec. 4. Any member found guilty of wanton cruelty to animals shall be expelled from the Order.

Sec. 5. The officers of Subordinate Granges shall be on the alert in devising means by which the interests of the whole Order may be advanced; but no plan of work shall be adopted by State or Subordinate Granges without first submitting it to, and receiving the sanction of, the National Grange.

Article IX.—*Charters and Dispensations.*—Section 1. All charters and dispensations issue directly from the National Grange.

Sec. 2. Nine men and four women, having received the four subordinate degrees, may receive a dispensation to organize a Subordinate Grange.

Sec. 3. Applications for dispensations shall be made to the Secretary of the National Grange, and be signed by the persons applying for the same, and be accompanied by a fee of fifteen dollars.

Sec. 4. Charter members are those persons only whose names are upon the application, and whose fees were paid at the time of organization. Their number shall not be less than nine men and four women, nor more then twenty men and ten women.

Sec. 5. Fifteen Subordinate Granges, working in a State, can apply for authority to organize a State Grange.

Sec. 6. When State Granges are organized, dispensations will be replaced by charters, issued without further fee.

Sec. 7. All charters must pass through the State Granges for record, and receive the seal and official signatures of the same.

Sec. 8. No Grange shall confer more than one degree (either First, Second, Third, or Fourth) at the same meeting.

Sec. 9. After a State Grange is organized, all applications for charters must pass through the same, and be approved by the Master and Secretary.

Article X.—*Duties of Offiers.*—The duties of the officers of the National, State, and Subordinate Granges shall be prescribed by laws of the same.

Article XI.—*Treasurers.*—Section 1. The Treasurers of the National, State, and Subordinate Granges shall give bonds, to be approved by the respective Granges.

Sec. 2. In all Granges, bills must be approved by the Master and countersigned by the Secretary, before the Treasurer can pay the same.

Article XII.—*Restrictions.*—Religious or political questions will not be tolerated as subjects of discussion in the work of the Order, and no political or religious tests for membership shall be applied.

Article XIII.—*Amendments.*—This Constitution can be altered or amended by a two-thirds vote of the National Grange at any annual meeting, and when such alteration or amendment shall have been ratified by three-fourths of the State Granges, and the same reported to the Secretary of the National Grange, it shall be of full force.

BY-LAWS.

Article 1. The fourth day of December, the birthday of the Patrons of Husbandry, shall be celebrated as the anniversary of the Order.

Art. 2. Not less than the representation of ten States, present at any meeting of the National Grange, shall constitute a quorum for the transaction of business.

Art. 3. At the annual meeting of each State Grange, it may elect a proxy to represent the State Grange in the National Grange, in case of the inability of the Master to attend, but such proxy shall not thereby be entitled to the Sixth degree.

Art. 4. Questions of administration and jurisprudence, arising in and between State Granges, and appeals from the action and decision thereof, shall be referred to the Master and Executive Committee of the National Grange, whose decision shall be respected and obeyed until overruled by action of the National Grange.

ART. 5. It shall be the duty of the Master to preside at meetings of the National Grange; to see that all officers and members of committees properly perform their respective duties; to see that the Constitution, By-Laws, and resolutions of the National Grange, and the usages of the Order, are observed and obeyed; to sign all drafts drawn upon the treasury, and, generally, to perform all duties pertaining to such office.

ART. 6. It shall be the duty of the Secretary to keep a record of all proceedings of the National Grange; to keep a just and true account of all moneys received and paid out by him; to countersign all drafts upon the treasury; to conduct the correspondence of the National Grange, and, generally, to act as the administrative officer of the National Grange, under the direction of the Master and the Executive Committee.

It shall be his duty, at least once each month, to deposit with the Fiscal Agency holding the funds of the National Grange, all moneys that may have come into his hands, and forward a duplicate receipt therefor to the Treasurer, and to make a full report of all transactions to the National Grange at each annual session.

It shall be his further duty to procure a monthly report from the Fiscal Agency with whom the funds of the National Grange are deposited, of all moneys received and paid out by them during each month, and send a copy of such report to the Executive Committee and the Master of the National Grange.

ART. 7. It shall be the duty of the Treasurer to issue all drafts upon the Fiscal Agency of the Order, said drafts having been previously signed by the Master and countersigned by the Secretary of the National Grange.

He shall report monthly to the Master of the National Grange, through the office of the Secretary, a statement of all receipts of deposits made by him, and of all drafts or checks signed by him during the previous month.

He shall report to the National Grange, at each annual session, a statement of all receipts of deposits made by him, and of all drafts or checks signed by him since his last annual report.

ART. 8. It shall be the duty of the Lecturer to visit, for the good of the Order, such portions of the United States as the Executive Committee may direct, for which services he shall receive compensation.

ART. 9. It shall be the duty of the Executive Committee to exercise a general supervision of the affairs of the Order during the recess of the National Grange; to instruct the Secretary in regard to printing and disbursements, and to place in his hands a contingent fund; to decide all questions and appeals referred to them by the officers and members of State Granges; and to lay before the National Grange, at each session, a report of all such questions and appeals, and their decisions thereon.

ART. 10. Such compensation for time and service shall be given the Master, Lecturer, Secretary, Treasurer, and Executive Committee, as the National Grange may, from time to time, determine.

Whenever General Deputies are appointed by the Master of the National Grange, said Deputies shall receive such compensation for time and services as may be determined by the Executive Committee: *Provided*, In no case shall pay from the National Grange be given General Deputies in any State after the formation of its State Grange.

ART. 11. The financial existence of Subordinate Granges shall date from the first day of January, first day of April, first day of July, and the first day of October subsequent to the day of their organization, from which date their first quarter shall commence.

State Granges shall date their financial existence three months after the first day of January, first of April, first of July, and first of October, immediately following their organization.

ART. 12. Each State Grange shall be entitled to send one representative, who shall be the Master thereof, or his proxy, to all meetings of the National Grange. He shall receive mileage, at the rate of five cents per mile, both ways, computed by the nearest practicable route, to be paid as follows: The Master and Secretary of the National Grange shall give such Representative an order for the amount on the Treasurer of the State Grange which he represents, and this order shall be receivable by the National Grange in payment of State dues.

ART. 13. Special meetings of the National Grange shall be called by the Master upon the application of the Masters of ten State Granges, one month's notice of such meeting being given to all members of the National Grange. No alterations or amendments to the By-Laws or Ritual shall be made at any special meeting.

ART. 14. These By-Laws may be altered or amended at any annual meeting of the National Grange, by a two-thirds vote of the members present.

The Manual containing the Constitution of the National Grange has the following pertinent remarks, relating to the work of subordinate Granges, and their legitimate sphere of action:

First, we organize the Granges, and study to become familiar with the work of the Lodge room. We study to take in the essence and

"What Shall we do with Him?" The "Granger's" Advent among the Politicians. (175)

spirit of our beautiful and elevating Ritual. We also get acquainted with each other. As a people, we pay too little regard to the social and fraternal element in society. There are, perhaps, reasons why this is so, growing out of our earnest practical life in developing a new country, but it is none the less true that our happiness and well-being would be better promoted by cultivating more fully our social natures.

After the organizing period has passed, we come to the business or material phase of our work. Here we need to be governed by a large and enlightened wisdom. We are suffering from the oppression of corporations. Manufacturers combine against us, and, owing to circumstances by which we are surrounded, we, perhaps, do not understand, at present, just the best and most business-like method of remedying the evil. We need, then, to carefully study and mature our plans before we begin to act. We talk over among ourselves what we desire to do, and compare opinions as to the best methods of arriving at results. Having perfected our plans, we should be more than careful that we carry out in good faith, and in a business-like way, all agreements and contracts.

State Seal of Missouri.

CONSTITUTION OF STATE GRANGES.

The following is stated, by authority, to be among the most perfect of the Constitutions of the State Granges, especially those articles (III and XXIII) entitled "Legislative" and "Councils:"

CONSTITUTION OF THE STATE GRANGE OF MISSOURI.

ARTICLE I.—This Grange shall be known as the Missouri State Grange of the Patrons of Husbandry.

ARTICLE II.—*Members.*—The members of the State Grange shall be composed of Masters of Subordinate Granges and their wives, who are Matrons. Past Masters and their wives, who are Matrons, are honorary members, and shall be eligible to hold office, but not entitled to vote.

ARTICLE III.—*Legislative.*—The legislative and all other powers of this Grange shall be vested in certain of its members, to be selected as follows: All members of the State Grange, resident in each county, shall meet on the first Tuesday in February, at such place as they may from time to time designate, and elect one of their members for the county at large, and one additional member for each eight Granges, or fraction equal to five. *Providing*, nothing in this act shall be construed to prevent Masters and Past Masters and their wives, who are Matrons, from attending the meetings of the State Grange, and receiving the Fifth degree.

ARTICLE IV.—*Meetings.*—This Grange shall hold regular annual meetings on the third Wednesday in February, at such place as the Grange may, from time to time, determine. Special meetings may be called by the Master and Secretary, upon the written request of the Executive Committee; written notices of such meeting being given to each Subordinate Grange thirty days preceding, or by a vote of the Grange at a regular meeting.

ARTICLE V.—*Duties of Officers.*—Fifty members shall constitute a quorum for the transaction of business, but a less number may adjourn from day to day.

ARTICLE VI.—It shall be the duty of the Master to open and preside at all meetings of the Grange, and, in conjunction with the Secretary, call special meetings of the Grange.

ARTICLE VII.—The duties of the Lecturer shall be such as usually devolve upon that officer in a Subordinate Grange.

ARTICLE VIII.—It shall be the duty of the Overseer to assist the Master in preserving order, and he shall preside over the Grange in the absence of the Master. In case of a vacancy in the office of Master, he shall fill the same until the next annual meeting.

ARTICLE IX.—It shall be the duty of the Steward to have charge of the Inner Gate.

ARTICLE X.—The Assistant Steward shall assist the Steward in the performance of his duties.

ARTICLE XI.—Section 1. The Secretary shall keep an accurate record of all proceedings of the Grange, make out all necessary returns to the National Grange, keep the accounts of the Subordinate Granges with the State Grange, and pay over quarterly to the Treasurer all moneys coming into his hands, and take a receipt for the same. He shall also keep a complete register of the number and names of all Subordinate Granges, and the name and address of the Master and Secretary.

Sec. 2. The Secretary shall receive as compensation for his services, a sum of money, not exceeding One Thousand Dollars per annum, to be paid quarterly.

Sec. 3. It shall be the duty of Secretaries of Subordinate Granges to report quarterly to the Secretary of the State Grange statistical information in regard to the condition of crops, stock, prices, and other information that may be for the good of the Order—under Seal of his Grange.

The Secretaries of Subordinate Granges shall report to the Secretary of this Grange, all rejections or expulsions from their respective Granges, and the Secretary of this Grange shall report the same to all Subordinate Granges in the State.

Article XII.—It shall be the duty of the Treasurer of the State Grange to receive all moneys, giving his receipt for the same; to keep an accurate account thereof, and pay them out on the order of the Master of the State Grange, countersigned by the Secretary; he shall render a full account of his office at each annual meeting, and deliver to his successor in office all moneys, books, and papers pertaining to his office, and he shall give bonds in a sufficient amount to secure the money that may be placed in his hands; said bond to be approved by the Executive Committee. The Treasurer of each Subordinate Grange shall report quarterly, and pay to the Treasurer of the State Grange the sum of one dollar for each man, and fifty cents for each woman initiated during that quarter; also a quarterly due of six cents for each member.

The Treasurer of the State Grange shall send a receipt for the same to the Treasurer, and a duplicate to the Secretary of the Subordinate Grange, who shall forward his duplicate copy to the Secretary of the State Grange in his quarterly report.

Article XIII.—It shall be the duty of the Gate-keeper to see that the gates are properly guarded.

Article XIV.—The duties of the Chaplain and the Lady Officers shall be such as are defined by the Constitution of the National Grange, and in the Manual adopted for our use.

Article XV.—*Elections.* All elections shall be by ballot, and a majority vote elects.

Article XVI.—*Committees.* All committees, unless otherwise ordered, shall consist of five members, and shall be appointed as follows: three members by the Master, and two by the Overseer.

Article XVII.—At the regular annual meeting a Committee of Finance shall be appointed, whose duty it shall be to audit all accounts previous to their being paid. To them shall be referred the reports of the Secretary and Treasurer for examination.

Article XVIII.—The Executive Committee shall consist of six members, to be elected by ballot, three for one year and three for two years, and at each annual meeting hereafter three members shall be elected, to hold their office for two years. The members of this committee shall select one of their number for Chairman, who shall not have a vote, except in case of a tie. They shall have authority to act in all matters of interest to the Order when the State Grange is not in session; shall provide for the welfare of the Order in business matters, and shall fill all vacancies in office occurring in the State Grange, unless otherwise provided for. They shall be allowed pay for all their necessary expenses incurred in the transaction of business for the Order, and shall report their acts in detail to the State Grange on the first day of the annual meeting.

ARTICLE XIX.—*Official and Fiscal Year.* The official year of Subordinate Granges shall commence on the first Saturday in July, and the fiscal year shall commence on the first days of January, April, July, and October succeeding their organization. The fiscal year of this Grange shall commence on the first day of October.

ARTICLE XX.—*Quarterly Dues.* The Secretary shall see that the quarterly dues of Subordinate Granges are promptly paid, and in case the dues remain delinquent two quarters, the delinquent Grange shall be reported to the Master of the State Grange. On receiving such notice, it shall be the duty of the Master to warn the delinquent Grange, and if the dues are not forwarded in thirty days it shall be the duty of the Master to advise the Master of the National Grange of such delinquency, and recommend the revocal of the charter of the delinquent Grange; and any Grange whose charter has been thus revoked, may petition the State Grange for reinstatement.

ARTICLE XXI.—*Applications.*—Section 1. Persons making application for membership in our Order shall apply to the Subordinate Grange nearest to them, unless good, sufficient reasons exists for doing otherwise, which reasons must be submitted in writing. In such case the Grange shall judge the reasons, and, if thought best, it shall consult the Grange nearest the applicant.

Sec. 2. Any person, whose application for membership shall have been rejected, may renew such application at the expiration of six months thereafter.

Sec. 3. No application for membership in this Order shall be entertained, unless it shall be known that the agricultural interests of the applicant predominates over all other interests, financially.

ARTICLE XXII.—*Deputies.*—Section 1. There shall be appointed by the Master of the State Grange at least one Deputy in each county, where a proper person can be found, who shall be nominated by a majority of the Masters present from said county. In case of vacancy or non-representation in any county, then the Master may appoint a Deputy for such county or counties.

Sec. 2. It shall be the duty of the Deputies so appointed to organize new Granges, on application having been made to them by those desiring such an organization; to install officers of Granges when the same have been elected; and they shall be vigilant that no disorder shall obtain in the Granges under their jurisdiction, and shall promptly report any such disorder to the Master. Deputies shall receive, for organizing new Granges, their necessary traveling expenses. The Deputies shall be appointed for one year, but shall be subject to removal, for cause, by the Master. No other Granges shall hereafter be recognized except those organized by Deputies appointed as herein specified, excepting only those organized by the Master of the State Grange.

Sec. 3. In counties where there is no organization, the Deputies appointed by the Master shall receive as compensation for their services ten dollars for each Grange organized, said compensation and expenses to be taken from the fees paid by the charter members organized by said Deputies.

ARTICLE XXIII.—*Councils.*—It shall be lawful for Subordinate Granges to form themselves into associations to be called Councils, for the purpose of facilitating the transaction of business, of buying, selling, and shipping, and for such other purposes as may seem for the good of the Order.

They shall be governed, and the membership decided, by such laws, as the Council may from time to time make, not in conflict with the constitution of the National and State Granges.

They may elect a business agent to act in concert with the Executive Committee, and it shall be their duty to inform the Master of the State Grange of any irregularities practiced by Deputies within their jurisdiction.

ARTICLE XXIV.—*Amendments.*—This Constitution may be amended or revised at any regular meeting of the Grange, by a vote of two-thirds of the members present.

BY-LAWS OF THE STATE GRANGE OF MISSOURI.

ARTICLE I.—*Order of Business.*—Section 1. Opening the Grange.
Sec. 2. Calling of Roll by counties and presentation of credentials.
Sec. 3. Conferring the fifth degree.
Sec. 4. Reports of Standing Committees.
Sec. 5. Reports of Special Committees.
Sec. 6. Unfinished Business.
Sec. 7. Election of Officers.
Sec. 8. Appointment of Committees.
Sec. 9. New Business.
Sec. 10. Suggestions for the good of the Order.

ARTICLE II.—*Rules of Order.*—Section 1. When the presiding officer takes the chair, the officers and members shall take their respective stations, and at the sound of the gavel there shall be a general silence. The Grange shall then proceed to open in regular form.

Sec. 2. No question shall be stated unless moved by two members, or be open for consideration unless stated by the Master. And when a question is before the Grange, no motion shall be received, unless to close; to lay on table; the previous question; to postpone; to refer; or to amend. They shall have precedence in the order in which they are arranged, the first three of which shall be decided without debate.

Sec. 3. Any member may call for a division of a question when the sense of it will permit.

Sec. 4. The yeas and nays may be ordered by the Master, on the call of any member, duly seconded.

Sec. 5. After any question (except one of indefinite postponement) has been decided, any member who voted in the majority may, at the same or next meeting, move for a reconsideration therof; but no discussion of the main question shall be allowed unless reconsidered.

Sec. 6. No member shall speak more than once on the same subject, nor occupy more than five minutes, except by the consent of a majority of the members. And no member, while speaking, shall name another by his or her proper name, but shall use the appropriate designation belonging to his or her standing in the Grange.

Sec. 7. The Master or any member may call a brother or sister to order while speaking; when the debate is suspended, and the brother or sister shall not speak until the point of order be determined, unless to appeal from the chair, when he or she may use the words following, and no others: "Master, I respectfully appeal from the decision of the chair to the Grange." Whereupon the Grange shall proceed to vote on the question: "Will the Grange sustain the decision of the chair?"

Sec. 8. When a brother or sister intends to speak on a question, he or she shall rise in his or her place and respectfully address his or her remarks to the Worthy Master, confining him or herself to the question, and avoid personality. Should more than one member rise to speak at the same time, the Worthy Master shall determine who is entitled to the floor.

Sec. 9. When a brother or sister has been called to order by the Worthy Master for the manifestation of temper or improper feelings, he or she shall not be allowed to speak again on the subject under discussion in the Grange, at that meeting, except to apologize.

Sec. 10. On the call of five members, a majority of the Grange may demand that the previous question shall be put, which shall always be in this form: "Shall the main question now be put?" And until it is decided, shall preclude all amendments to the main question and all further debate.

Sec. 11. All motions or resolutions offered in the Grange shall be reduced to writing, if required.

Sec. 12. When standing or special committees are appointed, the individual first named is considered as the chairman, although each has a right to elect its own chairman. Committees are required to meet and attend to the matters assigned them with system and regularity, and not by separate consultation, or in a loose or indefinite manner.

Sec. 13. The Worthy Master, by virtue of his office, may attend all meetings of committees, take part in their deliberations (without voting, however), and urge them to action. In the appointment of committees, the Worthy Master, who should ever preserve a courteous and conciliatory deportment to all, not overlooking the humblest member, has many opportunities of bringing humble merit into notice, and of testing and making available the capabilities of those around him. He should carefully avoid both petulancy and favoritism, and act with strict impartiality.

Article III.—*Deputies.*—Deputies appointed to organize Granges by the Master of the State Grange, shall be examined by the Master or Lecturer of the State Grange (applying to the one nearest to his residence) as to his qualifications, and, if found competent, a commission shall be given him, certified by the Secretary of the State Grange, under seal of the Grange.

Article IV.—*Lecturer.*—It shall be the duty of the Lecturer to visit Granges by order of the Executive Committee, to see that the work is properly done, and to instruct the members, for which he shall receive such compensation as said committee may determine. He may also be appointed a Deputy by the Master of the State Grange, to organize Granges in counties where there are none, for which he shall receive such compensation as is provided for in Art. XXII of the Constitution.

Article V.—In organizing new Granges, Deputies must not allow them to be located so near together as to prevent their having from fifty to one hundred members.

Article VI.—*County Meetings.*—It shall be the duty of the Secretaries of the County Meetings, called in accordance with Art. III of the Constitution, to immediately inform the Secretary of the State Grange of such meeting, and the officers of the same; also, to furnish the Secretary of the State Grange the names of the representatives chosen, and to furnish to each representative a written certificate of such election, under Seal of some Grange in the county.

Article VII.—*Minutes.*—The minutes of the State Grange shall be approved each morning while in session, and before final adjournment shall be read by the Secretary and approved as a whole.

Article VIII.—*Mileage.*—Sec. 1. That each member in attendance upon this meeting of the State Grange be required to report, under the seal of his Grange, to the Secretary of the State Grange, the number of miles traveled by him to reach the place of meeting of State Grange.

Sec. 2. That the Secretary of this Grange be required to exchange for this an order upon the Treasury of the respective Subordinate Granges equal in amount to a mileage of five cents going and returning from place of meeting of State Grange, and $2.00 per day during time of attendance, and going to and returning from the same.

Sec. 3. That these orders shall be cashed by the Treasurers of Subordinate Granges, and received from them by the Treasurer of the State Grange in lieu of cash in their quarterly reports.

ARTICLE IX.—*Miscellaneous.*—Smoking within the hall is forbidden while the Grange is in session.

COUNTY COUNCILS—CONSTITUTION, ETC.

In some of the States where the Order of Patrons of Husbandry has become strong, it has been found advisable to organize County Councils. In Iowa and Missouri, as well as in some other States, the By-laws of the organization provide for such. One of the principal objects of the Granges is the more perfect transaction of business, especially buying and selling.

It is lawful for these Subordinate Granges to form themselves into associations, to be called Councils, for the purpose of facilitating the transaction of business—of buying, selling, and shipping, and for such purposes as may seem for the good of the Order. They are governed, and the membership decided, by such laws as the Council may from time to time make, not in conflict with the Constitution of the National and State Granges. They elect business agents to act in concert with the Executive Committee, a part of whose duty it is to inform the Master of the State Grange of any irregularities practiced by Deputies within their jurisdiction. Subjoined are the Constitution and By-laws of the Scotland County, Missouri, Council of Patrons of Husbandry, which are the most comprehensive that have come under my notice.

PREAMBLE.

Whereas, Other classes and professions of men have formed combinations to protect their own interests; and,

Whereas, Many of these combinations are working indirectly against the best interests of the farmer; therefore, in order to form a more perfect union, secure our rights, and protect our interests against the encroachments of such combinations, we the representatives of Subordinate Granges of Patrons of Husbandry, in —— County, acting under the State Grange of ——, do hereby form ourselves into a mutual operative association, and adopt the following articles of confederation:

CONSTITUTION.

ARTICLE I.—*Name.*—This association shall be called the —— County Central Association of Patrons of Husbandry.

ARTICLE II.—*Objects.*—The objects of this association shall be the promotion and attainment of the united and uniform action of the Granges of which it is composed, in all matters affecting their interest and welfare; in bringing the producers and consumers of agricultural implements and products closer together by buying and selling through this association, or through such parties as may make arrangements with it to buy or sell such articles or implements as we may need, and to transact such other business as may be necessary to secure these ends.

ARTICLE III.—*Membership.*—Section 1. This association shall be composed of Subordinate Granges in regular working order, who have complied with the rules and regulations of this association.

Sec. 2. All Granges in regular working order may become members of this association by the payment of five dollars to the Secretary, and may retain such membership by the payment of annual dues in a sum equal to five cents for each of its members.

ARTICLE IV.—*Representation.*—Section 1. Each Grange belonging to the association shall be entitled to representation as follows: One delegate at large, and one delegate to every fifty members or moiety thereof. And all members of Subordinate Granges belonging to this association, in good and regular standing in their respective Granges, shall be members of this association, and entitled to all its rights and privileges except voting.

Sec. 2. Individual members of Granges not belonging to this association, may become members of the same by the payment of fifty cents each, and any number of such members on the payment of five dollars shall be entitled to all the rights and privileges of a Grange, but no Grange shall be entitled to more than one representative at large.

Article V.—*Officers.*—Section 1. The officers of this association shall be a President, Vice-President, Secretary, Treasurer, Doorkeeper, and three Trustees, whose powers and duties shall be fully defined in the By-laws of this association.

Sec. 2. There shall be an Executive Committee of five, consisting of President, Secretary, and three Trustees.

Sec. 3. These officers shall be elected annually by ballot at the first regular meeting in each year, to be held on the first Tuesday in September. A majority of all the votes cast shall be necessary to a choice.

Article VI.—*Laws.*—Section 1. This association shall have power to make all laws necessary for its government; also, to alter, repeal, or modify such laws as may be found objectionable or inoperative, and to alter and amend this Constitution, whenever it shall be deemed necessary, by a two-thirds majority of its delegates; proposed amendments, alterations or modification to be presented in writing and lay over three months.

Article VII.—*Meetings.*—Section 1. The regular meetings of this association shall be as follows: An annual meeting and three quarterly meetings, to be held at such places as may be designated by the association and its trustees—the annual meeting on the first Tuesday in September, at 10 o'clock A. M., and the quarterly meetings to be held on the first Tuesday of December, March, and June in each year, at 10 o'clock A. M.

Sec. 2. Special meetings may be called by the President and Secretary whenever it is deemed necessary for the good of the association, and the Secretary shall give each Grange at least ten days notice of such special meeting.

BY-LAWS.

Article I.—*Duties of officers.*—Section 1. It shall be the duty of the President to preside at all meetings of the association, sign all orders drawn on the Treasurer, and perform other duties ordinarily required of such presiding officer.

Sec. 2. It shall be the duty of the Vice-President to perform the duties of the President in his absence, or whenever required to do so.

Sec. 3. It shall be the duty of the Secretary to keep an accurate record of the proceedings of this association, conduct its correspondence, receive and pay over all moneys to the Treasurer, taking his receipt for the same, draw and countersign all orders on the Treasurer, make a full report of the condition of the association and doings of the Executive Committee at the annual and each quarterly meeting, and have his books ready for inspection by the Trustees at any time.

Sec. 4. It shall be the duty of the Treasurer to receive from the Secretary all moneys belonging to the association, giving his receipt for the same; to keep accurate account of all such moneys received; to pay all orders drawn on him by the President and countersigned by the Secretary; to make a report of all moneys received and paid out by him at the annual and each quarterly meeting, and to deliver to his successor all moneys and other property belonging to the association.

Sec. 5. It shall be the duty of the Door-keeper to examine the members before opening meeting, and perform such other duties as may be required by the President or association.

Sec. 6. It shall be the duty of Trustees to examine all bills and accounts of the officers and members of this association; also, the books and papers of the Secretary and Treasurer when required to do so by the association, and report on all matters they may have on hand at the annual and each quarterly meeting, or whenever required to do so.

Sec. 7. It shall be the duty of the Executive Committee to see that all the laws and resolutions of the association are enforced in all its business transactions, when it is not in session.

Article II.—*Vacancies.*—Vacancies in any of the offices of this association may be filled by the Executive Committee until the next regular meeting, when an election shall be had to fill the rest of said vacancies.

Article III.—*Compensation.*—Section 1. The Executive Committee shall be allowed two dollars per day for time actually spent in the services of the association, except at meetings of the association.

Sec. 2. All bills and accounts against the association shall be presented in writing, and shall specify the articles or services charged for.

Article IV.—The Secretary and Treasurer shall each be required to give such bond for faithful performance of duty and safe keeping of funds as shall be required and approved by the Trustees.

Article V.—*Order of business.*—1. President calls to order.

2. Door-keeper examines members.
3. Secretary calls the roll of Granges.
4. President appoints Committee on Credentials.
5. Reading minutes of last meeting.
6. Reports of Committees, Special and Standing.
7. Bills and accounts.
8. Unfinished business.
9. New business.
10. Reports of delegates as to progress, work, and news.
11. Suggestions for the good of the association.

CONSTITUTION OF SUBORDINATE GRANGES.

The Constitutions of Subordinate Granges are founded upon those of the State Granges, *mutatis mutandis.*

The following form was prepared by Secretary W. H. Baxter, of the State Grange of California, and Master of Napa Grange, No. 2; and we give it, to make our series complete.

CONSTITUTION.

Article I.—Section 1. This Grange shall be known and distinguished as —— Grange, No. —, Patrons of Husbandry of the State of California.

Officers.—Sec. 2. The officers shall consist of and rank as follows: Master, Overseer, Lecturer, Steward, Assistant Steward, Chaplain, Treasurer, Secretary, Gate-Keeper, Ceres, Pomona, Flora, and Lady Assistant Steward. It is their duty to see that the laws of the Order are carried out.

Sec. 3. The officers of this Grange shall be chosen annually, and elected by ballot. Vacancies by death, resignation, or otherwise, to be filled at a special election at the next regular meeting thereof. Officers so chosen to serve until the annual meeting.

Sec. 4. There shall be an Executive Committee of this Grange, consisting of three members, whose term of office shall be three years, one of whom shall be elected each year.

Sec. 5. The officers of the respective Granges shall be addressed as "Worthy."

Sec. 6. Nominations for officers shall be made only at the two meetings immediately preceding that of the regular election, except when the nominees for an office all decline. Election of officers shall take place at the last regular meeting of the term, who shall be installed at the first regular meeting in the new term, provided the installing officer be present; if absent, it must be postponed until the proper officer can attend.

Sec. 7. Any officer absenting himself from the meetings of the Grange three successive times, except in case of sickness, or absence from home on business, or for misconduct as an officer, may be removed by a vote of two-thirds of the members voting, at the next meeting after a resolution therefor has been offered in the Grange.

Sec. 8. No person shall be eligible to, or hold, office in this Grange who is not clear of all pecuniary charges on the books, or charges of any and every kind whatsoever, and shall not have attained the Fourth Degree of the Order.

Article II.—*Meetings.*—Section 1. This Grange shall meet once in each month, and may hold such intermediate meetings as may be deemed necessary for the good of the Order.

Sec. 2. All business meetings are confined to the Fourth Degree.

ARTICLE III.—*Laws.*—This Constitution, and the By-Laws formed under it for the guidance of this Grange, must conform with the Constitution and the Laws adopted by the National Grange.

ARTICLE IV.—*Ritual.*—The Ritual adopted by the National Grange shall be used in this Grange, and any desired alteration in the same must be submitted to, and receive the sanction of, the National Grange.

ARTICLE V.—*Membership.*—Any person interested in agricultural pursuits, of the age of sixteen years (female), and eighteen years (male), duly proposed, elected, and complying with the rules and regulations of the Order, is entitled to membership and the benefit of degrees taken. Every application must be accompanied by the fee of membership. If rejected, the money will be refunded. Applications must be certified by members, and balloted for at a subsequent meeting. It shall require three negative votes to reject an applicant.

Sec. 2. All candidates for membership must be of good moral character and industrious habits, and whose interest in agriculture is paramount to all other interests, and believe in the existence of a Supreme Being, the Creator and Preserver of the universe, and be proposed in the Grange nearest his residence, unless good and sufficient reasons appear for his being proposed in this Grange.

ARTICLE VI.—*Application for Membership.*—Section 1. The name of a person offered for membership, with his age, residence, and occupation, and, in conformity with the form prescribed by the National Grange, shall forthwith be referred to a committee of three members for investigation, who shall report at the next regular meeting (unless circumstances prevent), when the candidate may be balloted for with ball ballots; and if any, or less than three, cubes shall appear, further balloting or announcement shall be deferred until the next regular meeting. During this interval the member casting the cube may (and it is his duty to) inform the Worthy Master of the cause thereof, and the Master shall, at the next regular meeting, state the reason, if any is given, to the Grange, without exposing the name of the person; and if the person who shall have cast the cube fail to inform the Master of the reason thereof, the Master shall, at the next regular meeting, if no other objection be made, declare the applicant duly elected; but if reasons are given, or other objections be made, then the ballot shall again be held, and if no more than two cubes appear, the candidate shall be declared elected.

Sec. 2. No reconsideration of an unfavorable ballot can be had unless all the persons who shall have cast cubes against an applicant voluntarily make a motion for a reconsideration of the ballot, when a vote on the reconsideration shall be taken by ballot, and if all the ballots cast be in favor, the reconsideration shall be had; the application shall then lie over till the succeeding meeting, when another ballot shall be had, and if the same be unanimously in favor of the applicant, he shall be elected; but if one or more cubes appear, the applicant shall be rejected. A favorable balloting can be reconsidered at any meeting prior to the admission of a candidate, provided a majority of the members present agree thereto.

Sec. 3. When a candidate has been rejected, notice thereof shall be sent by the Secretary of this Grange to all the Granges in this county and district.

Sec. 4. A proposition may be withdrawn at any time before the candidate shall have been balloted for, with consent of a majority of members present voting in favor the same.

Sec. 5. If any person shall gain admittance to this Grange upon a petition containing any false representation, such person shall be expelled.

ARTICLE VII.—*Fees and Dues.*—Section 1. The minimum fee for membership in a Subordinate Grange shall be, for men five dollars, and for women two dollars; for the four degrees, except charter members, who shall pay, men three dollars, and women fifty cents.

Sec. 2. The dues in this Grange shall be in conformity with "Article VII" of the Constitution of the National Grange regulating the same, and the By-Laws of this Grange.

ARTICLE VIII.—*Requirements.*—All requirements applicable to Subordinate Granges by the Constitution of the National Grange in Articles VIII and IX are hereby made part of the Constitution of this Grange.

ARTICTE IX.—*Duties of Officers.*—The duties of the officers of this Grange shall be prescribed by the By-Laws of the same.

ARTICLE X.—Section 1. The Treasurer shall give bonds to be approved by the Executive Committee of this Grange.

Sec. 2. All bills must be audited by the Finance Committee and approved by the Master and countersigned by the Secretary before the Treasurer can pay the same.

ARTICLE XI.—*Restriction.*—Religious or political questions shall not be tolerated as subjects of discussion in the work of the Order, and no political or religious tests for membership shall be applied.

ARTICLE XII.—*Penalties and Suspension.*—Section 1. *Clause* 1. Any member neglecting to pay the dues required by the By-Laws of this Grange for the space of twelve months, shall be notified by the Secretary of the Grange in writing, and if, after receiving such notification, such member still neglect to pay said dues for the space of one month, shall, upon vote of the majority of members present voting, be suspended from membership. Provided, that no person shall be suspended until after the fact of said dues being in arrears and unpaid for six months shall have been announced in open Grange at two regular meetings prior to such suspension.

Clause 2. Any member suspended as above may be reinstated on payment of the dues which caused suspension, and all accruing dues intervening, on a two-thirds vote of the members of the Grange present voting in favor of said reinstatement. Provided, that no member so suspended shall be entitled to any of the benefits or privileges of the Order during said suspension; nor shall a dismissal card be granted until all delinquencies are liquidated, and all charges withdrawn, should there be any; and then, upon a vote of the Grange and payment for withdrawal card, such dismissal may be granted.

Sec. 2. Any member who shall violate any of the principles of the Order, or offend against the Constitution, By-Laws, or Rules of Order of this Grange, shall be fined, reprimanded, suspended, or expelled, as the By-Laws may direct, or the Grange determine.

Sec. 3. Every member shall be entitled to a fair trial, and no member shall be put on trial, unless charges, duly specifying the offense, shall be submitted to the Grange in writing, and signed by a member of the Grange, and a copy, under seal of the Grange, be served upon the member accused.

Sec. 4. Such charges shall be referred to a committee of five members, peers of the accused, who shall summon the parties and try the case. They shall keep full minutes of the proceedings and report the same to the Grange with their verdict; the witnesses shall give their testimony on oath or affirmation, and no testimony shall be taken without an opportunity for cross-examination by the accused. Upon judgment being rendered, an appeal may be taken, at any time within one month, to the State Grange, in the persons of its Executive Committee, whose decree shall be final. If no appeal be taken, the verdict, being ratified by the Grange, shall be final. If exceptions to the report of the Committee be filed, the Grange may determine upon their merits, and either sustain the report or refer the same back, or to another Committee, or grant a new trial. If the Grange deem the exceptions ill-founded, it shall proceed to pronounce its judgment and affix the penalty.

Sec. 5. If the accused refuse or neglect to stand trial when duly summoned, the committee shall report such refusal or neglect as contempt of the Grange, which report shall be conclusive, and the punishment shall be expulsion.

Article XIII.—The funds and property of this Grange shall be held exclusively as a trust fund, to be devoted to the uses of the Grange, as may be required, from time to time, under and by the direction of such action as may be taken in the Grange, by its members, at any regular meeting.

Article XIV.—The officers for the term about expiring shall prepare and deliver to their successors in office all books, papers, funds, and other Grange property on their retiring from office, taking a receipt for the same, being careful to have all the business of the Grange recorded and finished so far as it may have progressed.

ARTICLE XV.—Withdrawal and dismissal cards may be granted to members who are clear of the books, by a majority vote, in conformity with Article XII.

ARTICLE XVI.—The masculine pronoun shall be constructed to include both sexes, and any question in regard to the meaning of any part of these Articles shall be determined by the Master of the State Grange.

ARTICLE XVII.—Section 1. This Grange may make, alter, or rescind such By-Laws, Rules, and Resolutions, from time to time, as may be deemed expedient, provided they do not in any wise contravene the Constitution and By-Laws of the National Grange or the State Grange of California.

Sec. 2. The By-Laws of this Grange are in force from the time of their adoption.

Sec. 3. This Constitution may be amended or revised at any regular meeting of the Grange, by a vote of two-thirds of the members present, upon notification having been given in open Grange at four regular meetings preceding such proposed change.

FORM OF BY-LAWS FOR SUBORDINATE GRANGES.

The following are the By-Laws proposed for the Subordinate Grange in the State of Iowa. They are not obligatory, however, but may be adopted or modified, as the Grange may see fit:

ARTICLE I.—Section 1. This Grange shall be known and distinguished as ——— Grange, No. —, of the State of Iowa.

Sec. 2. The regular meetings of this Grange shall be held ——.

Sec. 3. The time of meeting from the first of October to the first of April shall be ———, and from the first of April to the first of October shall be ———. Special meetings may be called by the Grange or the Master of the Grange, or, in his absence, by the Overseer, when deemed necessary for the good of the Grange.

Sec. 4. —— members shall constitute a quorum for the transaction of business.

Sec. 5. The Grange shall be opened at the above appointed time, in the Fourth Degree, if a sufficient number of members be present.

ARTICLE II.—*Membership.*—The members of this Grange are all who have been or may be initiated in, or affiliated therewith, who have subscribed to the roll-books, and who have not withdrawn, or been excluded for unworthy conduct or non-payment of dues.

ARTICLE III.—*Officers.*—The officers of this Grange shall be ranked and titled as follows: Master, Overseer, Lecturer, Steward, Assistant Steward, Chaplain, Treasurer, Secretary, Gate-Keeper, Ceres, Flora, Pomona, and Lady Assistant Steward. It is their duty to see that the laws of the Order are carried out.

How Chosen.—The officers of this Grange shall be chosen annually at the last regular meeting in December, and installed at the first meeting in January.

All elections shall be by ballot.

ARTICLE IV.—*Duties of Officers.*—Section 1.—*Master.*—It shall be the duty of the Master to preside at all meetings of the Grange; to see that all officers and members of committees perform their respective duties, as enjoined by the several charges and these By-laws; to inspect and announce the result of all balloting and other votes of the Grange; see that all the laws and usages of the Order are duly understood and obeyed; to sign all orders drawn on the Treasurer, with the consent and approbation of the Grange; and perform such other duties as may be required by the Ritual or Grange, properly devolving upon that office.

Sec. 2.—*Overseer.*—It shall be the duty of the Overseer to assist the Master in preserving order and decorum in the Grange, preside in the absence of the Master, and perform all other duties devolving upon that office.

Sec. 3.—*Lecturer.*—It shall be the duty of the Lecturer to always be prepared with some useful information to read, or cause to be read, when no regular business is before the meeting, and see particularly that all addresses, lectures, and other information provided for the good of the Order and members of this Grange are distributed to them.

Sec. 4—*Steward.*—It shall be the duty of the Steward to preside in the absence of the Master, Overseer, or Past Master; to have charge of the Inner Gate; to see that the field is properly arranged for labor; the working tools in their places; to conduct the ballot; and to provide for the introduction and accommodation of candidates.

Sec. 5.—*Assistant Steward.*—It shall be the duty of the Assistant Steward to have charge of the candidates during initiation, and to see that the regalias are properly distributed and cared for; also, to give all due assistance to the Steward.

Sec. 6.—*Treasurer.*—It shall be the duty of the Treasurer to receive all moneys, giving his receipt for the same; to keep an accurate account of said moneys, and pay them out on the order of the Master, with the consent of the Grange; to transmit all moneys due the State Grange to the Treasurer thereof, at the request of the Secretary; to render his books and a statement of his accounts with the Grange to the Finance Committee, when called upon to do so; and to deliver to his successor all moneys, books, vouchers, etc., having reference to the finance of the Grange.

Sec. 7.—*Secretary.*—It shall be the duty of the Secretary to record accurately all the proceedings of the Grange; to make out all necessary returns for the State and National Granges; to report to the Treasurer at the end of each quarter the amount due the State Grange; to keep accounts of members with the Grange; to receive and pay over to the Treasurer all moneys, taking his receipt therefor; to draw and countersign all orders voted by the Grange, and to perform such other duties as may devolve upon that office.

Sec. 8.—*Gate Keeper.*—It shall be the duty of the Gate-Keeper to see that the Gates are properly guarded, and to perform such other duties as may be required.

ARTICLE V.—*Applications for Membership.*—Applications for membership must be made in the form prescribed by the National Grange, and when made shall be announced in open Grange, and referred to a Committee of Investigation, consisting of three brothers or sisters, two appointed by the Master and one by the Overseer, which shall take the application in charge, and report at the next regular meeting.

ARTICLE VI.—*Fees and Dues.*—Section 1. The fees for conferring four degrees, for males, in this Grange shall be two dollars for the First degree, and one dollar for each subsequent degree, which shall accompany the petition.

The fees for conferring the four degrees on women shall be fifty cents for each degree, the money to accompany the petition in all cases.

Sec. 2. The regular dues of this Grange shall be ten (10) cents per month for each member.

ARTICLE VII.—*Committees.*—Section 1. All special committees, unless otherwise ordered, shall consist of three members each.

Sec. 2. The Master, on the night of his installation, shall appoint a standing Committee on Finance, to consist of three members.

Sec. 3. It shall be the duty of the Committee on Finance to audit all bills and accounts previous to their being passed upon by the Grange, and they shall be authorized to examine the books and accounts of any officer, or member of any committee of the Grange, whenever they think proper, and shall report, as speedily as possible, on all matters they may have on hand.

Sec. 4. At the first regular meeting in each year there shall be elected by ballot three Trustees, who shall have charge of all property of the Grange, as well as all business in which the Grange shall have an interest.

ARTICLE VIII.—*Charges.*—Section I. If at any time it shall appear that a member, by his or her general conduct, either morally or otherwise, shall be working against the best interests of the Order, charges may be preferred against the offending member, in accordance with the provisions of the following article, and they may be expelled, or subjected to such penalties as a majority of the Grange may direct.

Sec. 2. In no case shall members of a Grange enter into litigation with each other, until they shall have presented a plain statement of their differences to the Trustees of their Grange, and shall have allowed them an opportunity to adjust them, if possible.

Article IX.—*Suspensions, Withdrawals, etc.*—Section 1. No brother or sister of this Grange shall be suspended or expelled from membership unless charges be preferred in writing, duly specifying the offense, presented by a brother or sister in good standing, and the accused being allowed full opportunity to make his or her defense.

Sec. 2. Any member desirous of withdrawing from this Grange must pay all indebtedness thereto, and obtain the consent of the Grange.

Article X.—*Amendments.*—All propositions for amending or repealing these By-Laws, or any part of them, shall be presented in writing at a regular meeting, and shall lie over until the next regular meeting, when it may be acted upon, if agreed to by two-thirds of all the members present.

RULES OF ORDER.

1. When the presiding officer takes the chair, the officers and members shall take their respective stations, and at the sound of the gavel there shall be a general silence. The Grange shall then proceed to open in regular form.

2. No question shall be stated unless moved by two members, or be open for consideration unless stated by the Master. And when a question is before the Grange, no motion shall be received, unless to close, to lay on the table, the previous question, to postpone, to refer, or to amend. They shall have precedence in the order in which they are arranged, the first three of which shall be decided without debate.

3. Any member may call for a division of a question when the sense of it will permit.

4. The yeas and nays may be ordered by the Master, on the call of any member, duly seconded.

5. After any question (except one of indefinite postponement) has been decided, any member who voted in the majority, may, at the same or next meeting, move for a reconsideration thereof; but no discussion of the main question shall be allowed unless reconsidered.

6. No member shall speak more than once on the same subject, until all the members wishing to speak have had an opportunity to do so, nor more than twice without permission from the chair. And no member, while speaking, shall name another member by his or her proper name, but shall use the appropriate designation belonging to his or her standing in the Grange.

7. The Master or any member may call a brother or sister to order while speaking; when the debate shall be suspended, and the brother or sister shall not speak until the point of order be determined, unless to appeal from the Chair, when he or she may use the words following, and no others: "Master, I respectfully appeal from the decision of the Chair to the Grange." Whereupon the Grange shall proceed to vote on the question: "Will the Grange sustain the decision of the Chair?"

8. When a brother or sister intends to speak on a question, he or she shall rise in his or her place and respectfully address his or her remarks to the Worthy Master, confining him or herself to the question, and avoid personality. Should more than one member rise to speak at the same time, the Worthy Master shall determine who is entitled to the floor.

9. When a brother or sister has been called to order by the Worthy Master for the manifestation of temper or improper feelings, he or she shall not be allowed to speak again on the subject under discussion in the Grange, at that meeting, except to apologize.

10. On the call of five members, a majority of the Grange may demand that the previous question shall be put, which shall always be in this form: "Shall the main question now be put?" And until it is decided, shall preclude all amendments to the main question and all further debate.

11. All motions or resolutions offered in the Grange shall be reduced to writing, if required.

12. When standing or special committees are appointed, the individual first named is considered as the chairman, although each has a right to elect its own chairman. Committees are required to meet and attend to the matters assigned them with system and regularity, and not by separate consultation, or in a loose and indefinite manner.

13. The Worthy Master, by virtue of his office, may attend all meetings of committees, take part in their deliberations (without voting, however), and urge them to action. In the appointment of committees, the Worthy Master, who should ever preserve a courteous and conciliatory deportment to all, not overlooking the humblest member, has many opportunities for bringing humble merit into notice, and of testing and making available the capabilities of those around him. He should carefully avoid both petulancy and favoritism, and act with strict impartiality.

CHAPTER XVI.

THE MOVEMENT TOWARD CO-OPERATION.

WHAT ARE THE FARMERS' GRIEVANCES?

The question has often been asked, What are the farmers' grievances? These have never, at the conventions, been fully defined; but they may be summed up in a few words: The agricultural classes suffer, and always have suffered, from the rapacity of capital, aggregated and centralized.

There are two principal ways in which capital is employed to overreach them. The first is through the combination of those who buy their produce, thereby creating a protected monopoly, limited, it is true, but, nevertheless, uniformly successful. In this class I do not mean to include the ordinary country merchant, who buys produce, or trades and barters for it, but those rings, great and small, which are formed to gamble in the necessaries of life in our cities. Their ramifications sometimes extend to the regular dealers in the principal railroad towns, and sometimes even to the leading railroad officials themselves, but oftener are confined to a few of the great distributing centers, as New York, Buffalo, Cincinnati, Chicago, St. Louis, etc. The minor combinations in the ordinary railroad towns are merely local and of short duration, so that the intelligent man may hold his produce, and thus assist in breaking them. If farmers were even partially organized, these lesser combinations would be impossible.

FARMERS' TROUBLES OF MODERN GROWTH.

Up to the breaking out of the war, these grievances were principally confined to the exactions of local dealers, and the commission men at the distributing point, or, as they were called, middle men. During the war, and, more especially since then, a variety of schemes to centralize capital for the purpose of fictitiously lowering or increasing values, has led to gigantic combinations, which have always tended to enrich the wealthy and impoverish the poor. While these combinations have operated against all classes, the farmers have been the greatest sufferers, and especially those of the West, since, from the nature of the situation, and the limited amount of manufactures, they have been compelled to sell their produce in foreign markets.

Lands were granted by the government, in the most wholesale manner, toward the building of railroads in every direction. Combinations and consolidations were formed, stocks were watered, the Credit Mobilier was put in operation. At last, the fact was painfully unearthed that even some of our most eminent statesmen (without respect to party, and men who had been heretofore regarded as of the strictest integrity) had become implicated. As to the rank and file of mere politicians, that class was always rotten to the core; they always lived on corruption, and they expected always to do so.

OPERATIONS OF RAILROAD RINGS.

Railroad combinations and consolidations were formed, operated by a few individuals in Wall Street, who virtually controlled the railroad system of the United States. Vanderbilt, Tom Scott, Daniel Drew, and Jay Gould, were the potentates to whom all must bow the knee. A handful of such men have sought to control the inland navigation of the country, that of the great lakes being the first objective base, from which they hoped, apparently, to extend their supremacy to the rivers.

For years, their scheme seemed to prosper, and "all went merry as a marriage bell." The farmer saw his profits growing less and less, with each successive season. Still he managed to live and pay his taxes, and if he complained at all, it was but in a whisper. At last, the three great corn seasons in the West filled the great granary of the world to overflowing. The price of their grand staple went down, down, down, and did not rally; eight cents per bushel was all that the farmer received in some localities. The farmer began to ask himself the reason, why, when it cost only a certain moderate sum to transport a car-load from Chicago to New York, nearly a thousand miles, it should cost nearly one-half the amount to transport the same car from his market town to Chicago, or St. Louis, distant perhaps less than one hundred miles.

In expostulating against this wrong, he naturally blamed the management of these local roads, forgetting that many of the leading lines in the West were really operated by individuals in the great seaboard cities, who either owned or controlled the greater part of the stock, and who were, by the unjust discriminations on local traffic, eking out dividends on watered stock, or assisting to swell the lesser profits of the great through transportation lines between Chicago, St. Louis, and Cincinnati, at the West, and Boston, New York, and Philadelphia, at the East. This was but another means of assisting the merchants and forwarders (the middle men) of our great cities, and for what? Simply to keep them still. The great "operators" could not fleece both classes, and so the farmer must pay for all.

The great mistake made by the railroad magnates, East and West, was in not heeding the smaller tidal waves that were as mere ripples to the great September groundswell that convulsed the country. The question may well be seriously asked, Will it require a still greater explosion of long-suppressed fires, a more terrible disorganization of business than that through which we have just passed, to show this class of men that henceforward their power for evil is circumscribed, and that they must conform to the requirements of justice? We believe it most certainly will, unless the Government itself can be purified of the class of politicians, who pander to the great money lords of the East. The signs of the times persistently misread or unheeded, there may come a wide-spread financial ruin, such as no civilized people ever suffered. What a humiliation to a nation of boasted freemen, who have allowed their law-makers to become utterly corrupt, and their laws vicious and one-sided, through the buying and selling of human consciences!

WHERE THE BLAME ORIGINALLY LIES.

Much of the evil we have mentioned arises from the want of a business education among the masses of the farmers themselves. For this, however, they are not entirely to blame; their isolation one from another has, in a measure, prevented it. Congress, while yet it was pure, endowed schools for the instruction of the masses to the industries. Let them allow mere scholiasts to fritter this endowment away, and they will be utterly lost.

Looking at the grievances entailed since the settlement of

the country, by the common methods of barter and sale, it will become obvious to the most casual observer that their lack of education has made the masses, constantly, the prey of sharpers. It is not the reading and thinking portion of the agricultural world who are readily victimized. And I would that these words, uttered in all singleness of purpose, might be taken home by each individual reader. Let him ask if he really has done himself and his children justice, in using all the means for education that were available. If so, the words do not apply to him.

I repeat, that American farmers, as a class, have been content to exist from year to year, and decade to decade, in this dull, unprogressive manner. They have been seeking to disenthrall themselves for generations, but have failed from the fact that, until within the last twenty years they have not been a reading, thinking class. They have received education sufficient to enable them to read intelligently their Bible, hymn-book, and, at long intervals, perhaps, a newspaper—the last, in too many cases, borrowed from some more enterprising neighbor; but the fact itself is patent and incontrovertible that they have been much behind other classes in their practical information concerning the ordinary, every-day affairs of the business world. Hence, not knowing the true values of what they had to sell, they were continually overreached by the buyer, who had made it his especial business to inform himself on this point.

THE VILLAGE MERCHANT AS AN EXTORTIONER.

The farmer saw the merchant, whom for want of a better name he began to call a middle man, accumulating wealth from year to year, and living in apparent comfort from the profits of bargain and sale, while he himself had a hard pull to get along, and pay the interest on the mortgage, large or small, as the case might be, on his farm. If he had any thing to sell, say a load of wheat, it was taken to market. The merchant was asked, "What are you paying for wheat?" He might think the price offered too small, but the next dealer was asked, and the next, and the next, and the price was always the same. Here was a combination—a monopoly, if you choose to call it so—by which, two, three or a dozen country merchants ruled the price of produce in the town. The farmer might sell or not, he was not obliged, there was no coercion; for could he not haul it back to his granary? But if he did, what then? Haul it back once more, and take the price offered, at last.

Here and there, scattered far or near, were individual farmers, who had educated themselves to business habits, had regularly read the journals devoted to their interests, and had kept a close account of the profit and loss of the farm. This exceptional class, when prices were low, held their grain, and, when the market was right, sold in bulk, buying, perhaps, of their neighbors to make good the quantity contracted for. Here, again, was another monopoly, and a legitimate one, which simply illustrates the advantages of educating one's self to his business in life. The enterprising farmer was coerced into this course, from the fact that no means seemed available to enable him to co-operate with his fellows for a more general good.

THE GROWTH OF GRIEVANCES.

By and by, a few individuals in a neighborhood would form a Club or Society, to discuss their real or supposed grievances, and systems of cultivation; gradually, newspapers would find their way into the homes of the members; and, as knowledge begets a thirst for more, the number of these would increase; and so, in the course of a few years, not only a more intelligent system of agriculture, but also a more correct idea of doing business would be introduced.

In the development of all new countries, the first settlers act in the capacity of merchants in selling their crops to those who come later. These, again, join them in selling to others, until, at last, the country becoming overstocked with the raw material, a village springs up, and the farmers sell to the merchants, who make an exclusive business of buying produce, or bartering needed wares therefor. Up to this point, there has been no trouble. The new comers needed all that was produced for purposes of sale. The population was a community to themselves; their tastes and lives were simple, and they cared but little how the great outside world was going on. It is only with the advent of high civilization that oppressive monopolies can exist.

The exact time when transportation charges begin to pinch the farmer, it is evident, is when a country begins to produce more than it can consume. When all that he can raise, or even more, is wanted, the farmer fixes his price; when a surplus is produced, it must be exported to be turned into cash. The merchant, or middle man, steps in and buys in hopes of reaping a profit. Another merchant comes in, and a healthy competition is created; they combine together and form a monopoly. To counteract this evil, the farmers, too, must combine, and face it boldly.

THE BUILDING OF RAILROADS AND ITS EFFECTS.

Dating from about the year 1848, there was a general feeling among the farmers throughout Illinois, that they were not receiving the just reward of their labor. The country was settling up, and the cost of transporting produce to St. Louis and Chicago, the principal distributing points, over the common roads was so great that it left the farmer little or nothing to carry back to his family. The country villages were few and far between. Railroads had not been built, and it was with the greatest difficulty that the farmer could gather enough money to pay his taxes. The construction of railroads began, but before these were in operation a feeling of awakening had so grown upon the popular mind that Farmers' Clubs began organizing, though, at first, more to discuss matters of cultivation than any thing else.

In 1852, the exactions of the country merchants, or middle men, as they were even then called, came in for a great share of the blame, and justly, beyond a doubt. They were the protected monopolists, who, by the force of their cohesion, controlled prices, and, while they grew rich themselves, oppressed the farmers. I do not stop here to ask, Would not, and does not, the farmer seek to do the same, if opportunity or circumstances favor? I am now simply writing history.

In the year just named, the Michigan Southern Railroad was completed to Chicago. The Galena Union, now Northwestern, was stretching westward, and the Illinois Central was nearly completed. The opening of these lines gave partial relief, and caused towns and villages to spring up as if by magic along their routes. Heretofore, the only commodity that brought the farmer any returns in cash was the live stock which he fattened and sold to the drover, to be driven on foot to the nearest point where it could be packed and distributed.

Agriculture, which before had been languishing, suddenly became remunerative. With the advent of the towns along the road came increased immigration. The farmer again had a home maket; he could again, in great measure, deal without the intervention of a middle man. Other towns sprang up, and other immigration followed. Soon a large more formed, and the farmer again found himself on relatively-losing ground, although not so badly off as before.

THE CENTRALIA, ILLS., CONVENTION.

The feeling that relief must be had finally gained such strength that a general convention or congress was called, and held at Centralia, on the fifteenth of September, 1858. The discussions of this body were earnest in tone and comprehensive in scope. They resulted in the following platform, declaration of principles, and plan of operations:

FARMER'S PLATFORM OF 1858.

"We believe that the time has come when the producing classes should assert, not only their independence, but their supremacy; that non-producers can not be relied upon as guarantees of fairness; and that laws enacted and administered by lawyers are not a true standard of popular sentiment.

"We believe that a general application to commerce of the principle that the majority should rule, would increase the income and diminish the outlay of producers, and, at the same time, elevate the standard of mercantile morality.

"We believe that the producer of a commodity and the purchaser of it should, together, have more voice in fixing its price than he who simply carries it from one to the other.

"We believe that the true method of guarding against commercial revulsions is to bring the producer and consumer as near together as possible, thus diminishing the alarming number and the more alarming power of non-producers.

"We believe that in union there is strength, and that in union alone can the necessarily isolated condition of farmers be so strengthened as to enable them to cope, on equal terms, with men whose callings are, in their very nature, a permanent and self-created combination of interests.

"We believe that system of commerce to be the best which transacts the most business, with the least tax on production, and which, instead of being a master, is merely a servant.

In Union there is Strength.

"We believe that good prices are as necessary to the prosperity of farmers as good crops, and, in order to create such a power as to insure as much uniformity in prices as in products, farmers must keep out of debt; and that, in order to keep out of debt, they must pay for what they buy and exact the same from others."

DECLARATION OF PRINCIPLES.

"These truths we hold to be self-evident, that, as production both precedes barter and employs more labor and capital, it is more worthy the care and attention of governments and of individuals; that in the honorable transaction of a legitimate business there is no necessity for secret cost-marks; that, in all well-regulated communities, there should be the smallest possible number of non-producers that is necessary to the welfare of the human race; that labor and capital employed in agriculture should receive as much reward as labor and capital employed in any other pursuit; that, as the exchanger is merely an agent between the producer and consumer, he should not have a chief voice in the establishment of prices; that the interests of agriculture and of commerce can only be considered as identical when each has an equal share in regulating barter; and that the principal road to honor and distinction, in this country, should lead through productive industry."

PLAN OF OPERATIONS.

"*First.* The formation of Farmers' Clubs wherever practical, the object of which shall be to produce concert of action on all matters connected with their interests.

"*Second.* The establishment, as far as possible, of the ready pay system in all pecuniary transactions.

"*Third.* The formation of wholesale purchasing and selling agencies in the great centers of commerce, so that producers may, in a great measure, have it in their power to save the profits of retailers.

"*Fourth.* The organization of such a power as to insure the creation of a national agricultural bureau, the main object of which shall be an annual or semi-annual census of all our national products, and the collection and dissemination of valuable seeds, plants, and facts.

"*Fifth.* The election of producers to all places of public trust and honor the general rule, and the election of non-producers the exception."

CHAPTER XVII.

THE NATIONAL AGRICULTURAL CONGRESS OF 1872.

REVIVAL OF CLUBS AT THE SOUTH.

Soon after the close of the late war, the more far-seeing citizens of the South began to consider seriously the importance of organizing for the promotion of agriculture in that fertile section. They recognized the fact that the produce of the land is the basis of all national wealth, and they felt this to be especially true of their portion of the country, for the reason that it had always been essentially an agricultural region; and they noted with sadness that, during the war, its agriculture had languished, and its manufactures had been entirely broken up.

Societies for the advancement of agriculture and its kindred interests consequently sprang up and flourished, and eventually a general association was formed, which assumed the name of the "Agricultural Congress." At the second session of this body, held at Selma, Alabama, in December, 1871, the importance of the undertaking was generally recognized. It was essentially a Southern institution, and composed of Southern men. Its officers were as follows: President, Dr. R. J. Spurr, of Kentucky: Vice-Presidents—Hon. Reuben Gentry, of the same State; General William J. Hardee, of Alabama; Major R. R. Hurt, of Tennessee;

Hon. W. H. Foote, of Mississippi; W. M. Lawton, Esq., of South Carolina; Hon. B. Compton, of Maryland; Hon. Mark A. Cooper, of Georgia; Hon. D. F. Kenney, of Louisiana; Hon. Asa Hodges, of Arkansas; Hon. Lee R. Shryock, of Missouri; Hon. F. Watts, of the District of Columbia; and General C. H. Dupont, of Florida: Secretary and Treasurer, Charles W. Greene, of Tennessee.

A Virginia Tobacco Barn.

President Spurr, in his circular address, stated the object of the association to be to hold consultations upon Agriculture and kindred interests, ignoring all partisan politics; to represent, in a general head, the local organizations; and to co-operate with these in promoting the general welfare. The Association recognized the fundamental principle that agriculture being the foundation-stone of our prosperity as a people, the farmers of the country should have proper representation in the councils of the State and Nation; and it was held to be within the province of the Congress to assist in securing such representation. The intention of this organization was to unite every Agricultural Society throughout the land, but especially those of the Southern and Western States, into one body, in which there should be a delegation from each of these societies, the basis of representation being one delegate to each fifty members or fraction thereof, and to include representatives from any society, whether State, County, District, or Township Association.

THE TENNESSEE ASSOCIATION.

Another organization, the Tennessee Agricultural and Mechanics' Association, was also in existence at this time, embracing among its members gentlemen from all sections of the country, but principally from the Southern States. Its President was F. J. LeMoyne, of Pennsylvania; Secretary, J. B. Killebrew, of Tennessee; Treasurer, F. H. French, of the same State.

In October, 1871, at the instance of this association, there was held at Nashville, Tennessee, an Agricultural Congress, consisting of delegates from eleven States, and representing more than forty different Agricultural Societies and associations. The same body, by agreement with this Congress, appointed a session to be held at St. Louis for the purpose of consolidating, and making the organization truly national.

At the Nashville meeting, a committee was appointed to prepare and publish an address to the people, setting forth the aims of the Congress, and calling for a general participation therein by agriculturists of all the States and Territories, who were invited to send in delegates from their various associations.

THE FIRST NATIONAL AGRICULTURAL CONGRESS.

Accordingly, on the 27th day of May, 1872, the two societies, numbering about three hundred delegates, met at Masonic Hall, St. Louis, in convention. Colonel Arthur B. Barrett, President of the St. Louis Agricultural and Mechanical Association, called the assembly to order, whereupon the Rev. Dr. Means, of Georgia, in a prayer strongly marked for its fervid eloquence, invoked the blessing of the Almighty upon the deliberations of the assembly, praying that the work accomplished might inaugurate a unity of action that should redound to the welfare of the struggling industries of the nation, of which agriculture was the true corner-stone.

Colonel Barrett, in his address of welcome, alluding to the unity of interests which had called the convention together, said he felt that the common cause demanded a united action on the part of every farmer; every one who would advance the pursuits of agriculture through our broad land, should unite in that common purpose of advancing such interest. It was one ramifying the whole country, representing three-fourths of the brain and muscle of the land, and when associated for good can accomplish every thing. No Congress could stand before its will. It could dictate the policy of the country; it could open national highways to the sea; and all that was necessary would be to unite in one common, earnest desire to promote that end.

General William H. Jackson, of Tennessee, proposed a general vote of thanks of the two bodies to the St. Louis Agricultural and Mechanical Association, for the cordial welcome that has been extended to them. This was heartily and unanimously concurred in.

Each organization retired to a separate apartment where, after deliberation, it elected a committee to act with that of the other as a joint committee. On the part of the Congress the following gentlemen were appointed: Major R. B. Hurt, Jackson, Tennessee; D. E. Beatty, Illinois; T. W. Woodward, South Carolina; Suel Foster, Iowa; Governor H. W. Foote, Mississippi; O. P. Whitcomb, Minnesota; Professor W. H. Jamison, Alabama; James B. Clark, Kentucky; E. B. Whitman, Georgia; Lee R. Shryock, Missouri; John W. Foote, North Carolina.

For the Agricultural Association the names of the committee were as follows: H. M. McAllister, Pennsylvania; E. W. West, Illinois; R. M. Patton, Alabama; O. H. Jones, Georgia; John Scott, Iowa; Gen. W. H. Jackson, Tennessee; A. B. Barrett, Missouri; H. Rawlings, Indiana; John Saul, District of Columbia; Commodore M. F. Maury, Virginia and North Carolina; F. McArdle, Montana, and M. W. Wood, Kentucky.

Secretary Greene, of the Congress, being engaged in the main hall, Jonathan Periam, of Chicago, was requested to act with Secretary Killebrew, of Tennessee, for the joint committee. The association then adjourned until the next day for the purpose of allowing the committee to deliberate. Upon reassembling, the committee reported that they had agreed upon a consolidation of the two organizations, under the name of the National Agricultural Congress, and had also agreed upon the basis of a constitution, which announcement was received with hearty and reiterated applause.

On motion of Major Lee R. Shryock, it was resolved that a committee of one from each State be appointed to report permanent officers to the National Congress. The delegates from each State then conferred with each other, and appointed the following committee to name their permanent officers:

Virginia, Commodore M. F. Maury; South Carolina, Major Thomas W. Woodward; Georgia, E. B. Whitman; Alabama, Governor R. M. Patton; Mississippi, J. L. Power; Tennessee, Colonel R. J. Chester; Kentucky, Colonel J. B. Clarke; Pennsylvania, H. N. McAllister; Ohio, Dr. John A. Warder; Indiana, Hon. John Sutherland; Illinois, Professor J. B. Turner; Missouri, Colonel John H. Harris; Iowa, J. H. Bacon; Kansas, Major J. R. Hudson; District of Columbia, John Saul.

On motion, there were added Dr. R. J. Spurr and Dr. F. J. LeMoyne, the ex-presidents of the original societies.

The committee retired, and upon returning to the hall, Commodore Maury said that he was instructed by the nominating committee to report the following names, which they unanimously recommend for adoption: For President, Hon. John P. Reynolds, of Illinois. [Cheers.] For Secretary, Charles W. Greene, of Tennessee. [Cheers.] For Treasurer, Major L. R. Shryock, of St. Louis, Mo. [Cheers.]

Mr. Starr moved that the report be received, and that the present chairman cast the vote of the association for the officers reported.

General Jackson moved that they be declared chosen by acclamation.

The motion was carried, and the President said that, in obedience to the power conferred upon him, he voted for the names presented by the committee as presiding officer, Secretary and Treasurer of this Congress.

A committee, consisting of General Jackson and Governor Patton, were appointed to escort the President-elect to the chair.

General Jackson, in introducing Mr. Reynolds, made one

of his characteristic and pleasant speeches, and, in conclusion, said: "It is with feelings of peculiar pleasure I present the Hon. J. P. Reynolds, of Illinois, a gentleman so well and favorably known to the agriculturists throughout the length and breadth of the land, who has devoted so much of his time and resources to this great work; who is now, to use a farmer's phrase, in harness, and who is one of the most active workers in the cause. I say it affords me peculiar pleasure. The committees have shown themselves wise in selecting such a one to conduct this enterprise, as it will be conducted under his leadership to a successful issue. I am gratified to present to you the eminent gentleman from Illinois."

President Reynolds, in returning thanks, tersely reviewed the objects and aims of the Congress, and referred briefly to its future scope and power. He thought the association, in its aims and in its character, and in all other respects, was certainly one to which the American people might look with some sort of hope, and aid in the grand interests for which all were working. He said it would be a waste of words to now make any suggestion to the assembly; indeed, at this late stage it would be a waste of time. He, therefore, asked to be excused from making any extended remarks, and tendered his thanks for the honor conferred on him.

The President appointed the following committee on revision of the Constitution: Dr. LeMoyne, of Pennsylvania; Dr. Spurr, of Kentucky; General Jackson, of Tennessee; Mr. McArdle, of Montana Territory; John Scott, of Iowa; John A. Warder, of Ohio, and General Marmaduke, of Missouri.

Mr. French moved that the delegates make nominations for Vice-Presidents in the various States. Carried; whereupon the following Vice-Presidents were chosen: Alabama,

C. C. Langdon, Mobile; District of Columbia, John Saul, Washington; Georgia, O. H. Jones, Atlanta; Illinois, Hon. A. M. Garland, Springfield; Indiana,. F. C. Johnson, New Albany; Iowa, Dr. J. M. Shaffer, Fairfield; Kansas, George F. Anthony, Leavenworth; Kentucky, Dr. James H. Moore, Harrisburg; Minnesota, J. H. Stevens, Minneapolis; Mississippi, Dr. J. O. Wharton, Terry; Missouri, Arthur B. Barrett, St. Louis; North Carolina, William F. Kornigny, Goldsboro; Ohio, Norton S. Townsend, Avon; Pennsylvania, A. Boyd Hamilton, Harrisburg; Tennessee, General W. H. Jackson, Nashville; Virginia, Commodore M. F. Maury, Lexington; South Carolina, William M. Lawton, Charleston; Maryland, Henry A. Parr, Baltimore.

Mr. J. B. Killebrew offered the following in relation to Farmers' Clubs:

Resolved, That this Congress do earnestly recommend to farmers in various districts and townships through the United States to organize themselves into Clubs, and have monthly meetings, and with this organization disseminate through the newspapers the facts they may gather in the interest of practical agriculture. Adopted.

On motion of Dr. Spurr, amended by Dr. Spalding, it was resolved that a committee be appointed to whom any resolutions might be referred. The chair appointed Dr. Spurr, Mr. G. B. Whitman, Dr. J. A. Warder, and Gen. Jackson.

As showing the wide scope taken in the deliberations of this Congress, on motion and after considerable discussion, the President, assisted by the members, selected the following committees: On Meteorology—Com. Maury, Professor Turner, Rev. A. Means. On Forest Culture—R. S. Elliot, Dr. Warder, W. C. Flagg. On Experimental Agriculture—Dr. Spalding, Gen. W. H. Jackson, Chas. V. Riley. On Agricultural Education—Col. R. E. Withers, H. M. McAllister,

T. K. Hudson. On Grasses—L. D. Morse, M. Williams, O. H. P. Lear. On Transportation and Commerce—Gen. Marmaduke, W. D. Williams, R. M. Patton. On Fertilizers—Prof. Jamison, M. F. Fontain, J. C. Burroughs. On Labor and Emigration—W. M. Lawton, Geo. Edmunds, E. B. Whitman, Wm. M. Wielandy. On Live Stock—Dr. Spurr, D. B. Gilham, D. H. Jones. On Horticulture—Dr. E. S. Hull, F. H. French, J. L. Ratliff.

The reading of an essay on immigration, by Mr. Lawton, of South Carolina, which was politically violent and inflammatory in its nature, gave rise to the following resolution, by Mr. Flagg, of Illinois:

Resolved, That, inasmuch as topics supposed to have a remote political bearing have been regarded as not proper subjects for discussion by this convention, therefore, all speakers and essayists be requested to avoid such allusions to the "late unpleasantness" as may be denunciatory of persons differing in political opinions, and calculated to disturb the harmony of the meeting.

Mr. Anthony, of Kansas, begged leave to inquire if the resolution was retroactive. He could wish that it were, for Mr. Lawton's essay on immigration was one purely political in character, and one eminently qualified to revive the old feeling of difference between the North and South. He would not be willing to give even a tacit support to such a paper. He did not wish to discuss the question, but moved an amendment that the essay mentioned be not spread upon the records.

Mr. Withers said the question was out of order, and could not come up unless a motion to print was before the house. Mr. Anthony said he understood that all essays read became a part of official proceedings, and, if so, he wished the essay on immigration eliminated.

The chair explained that but one essay read had thus far been ordered printed. A special order would be necessary. The resolution of Mr. Flagg was then read, and passed unanimously.

It is worthy of remark that this discussion was conducted in the most friendly spirit, both North and South, all parties holding alike that it was in bad taste, and that hereafter all subjects having a political bearing ought, properly, to be ruled out of order.

Mr. Scott, of Illinois, offered the following resolution, relating to the preservation of timber:

WHEREAS, The destruction of our forests will ultimately bring about drouths injurious to the agricultural interests of the country; therefore, be it

Resolved, That the preservation of our forests, and the artificial planting of forest trees on our vast prairies, are subjects of most vital importance to the agriculturist, as well as the people of the United States.

This was referred to the committee on forest trees.

Mr. F. C. Johnson, of Indiana, offered a resolution instructing all agricultural and horticultural societies to offer premiums for the best agricultural and horticultural papers, and to do all in their power to contribute to the extension of their circulation. Adopted.

Mr. H. J. Schulte offered the following:

Resolved, That a memorial be forwarded from this body to the next United States Congress, urging it to reserve at least six sections of timber in each of the congressional townships of the present government land covered with forest, in order to avoid the extremes of drouth resulting from the want of timber or trees. Referred to committee on forests.

Mr. J. B. Killebrew offered the following important resolution, which was adopted:

Resolved, That the farmers in every district and township in the United States organize themselves into Clubs for monthly meetings, to collect and disseminate the facts that they may gather in the interest and practice of Agriculture.

On motion of Mr. Whitman, a committee of five was appointed, to whom all resolutions might, at the pleasure of the Congress, be referred without debate.

The convention then proceeded to discuss the different sections of the Constitution. Several minor amendments were adopted. The title of the association was changed to that of the National Agricultural Society, but a reconsideration was voted, and the old title of the National Agricultural Congress was finally retained.

Com. Maury's paper on Meteorology was the most important paper read before the Congress. It related to the influence of rain storms, winds, dews, etc., their volume and distribution, and the influence exercised by the planting of timber. It comprehended, in its scope, the continuous meteorological observations throughout the world, by the combined governments of every land. "By this means," said the eminent lecturer, "we may eventually foretell the seasons with a great degree of certainty." The address also comprehended the regular publishing of reliable crop reports, through which the farmer might keep himself informed in relation to the future of prices, from the appearance of the crops throughout the world.

Gov. Patton, of Alabama, from the Committee on Transportation, submitted the following resolutions:

Resolved, That this Congress appoint a special committee of three to consider the subject in all its bearings, and to report at the next meeting of this body such information acquired as may seem to be necessary.

Resolved, That this Congress invite such correspondence from all parts of the country, to be addressed to the chairman of said committee, furnishing full and complete data upon which to base a report.

The report of the committee was received and the resolutions adopted.

Mr. Fontaine, of Georgia, submitted a preamble and resolution on the subject of fertilizing. The preamble recited that the annual outlay for fertilizing is $25,000,000. It was, therefore, recommended that each county society represented in this Congress, or hereafter to be admitted, should, through its secretary, forward to the Secretary of the Congress approximate statements giving the amount of fertilizers used, their money value, kinds used, and cost of transportation, with the distance transported.

The following resolution was offered and adopted:

Resolved, That the Congress of the United States, which has heretofore so liberally protected the manufacturing interests of the country, be memorialized to aid the Agriculture of the United States by admitting, free of duty, the following chemicals which we think contain all the great essentials of plant food, to the end that the manufacture of fertilizers be cheapened and agricultural interest proportionably benefited: nitrate of potash, nitrate of soda, salt, gypsum, sulphate of ammonia, German salts of potash, or potash in any form, and sulphuric acid.

Gen. Jackson read a series of resolutions, reported from the committee to whom Com. Maury's address was referred. The resolutions appealed to every agricultural or mechanical society, club, and association, in behalf of the movement, soliciting their co-operation by memorials to Congress, and otherwise. Further, they looked to the raising of a committee of one from each State of the Union to exert itself in favor of Com. Maury's plan. They requested all journals to note the proceedings and give them their sanction. The resolutions were adopted.

Mr. R. S. Elliott, of Kansas, read the report of the Committee on Forest Culture.

To carry out the views embodied in the report the committee submitted the following resolutions:

1. That we recommend farmers throughout the United States to plant their hilly or otherwise waste lands, and at least ten per cent. of their farms, with trees, in such manner as to provide shelter belts or clumps of rapid growing and useful timber.

2. That we solicit the Legislatures of the several States to pass laws providing bounties for planting trees, encouraging the planting of the highways, and for the provision of State nurseries of young timber trees, and also the appointment of an "arbor day" for the annual planting of trees, as has already been done in the State of Nebraska.

3. That we ask the Congress of the United States to require, so far as practicable, that railroad companies and settlers hereafter receiving the benefit of the homestead and other acts donating lands, shall plant with timber trees one-tenth of the land so donated.

The importance of this subject was thoroughly discussed, and the resolutions were adopted.

Professer Turner, of Jacksonville, Ill., read an able and characteristic essay on the education of farmers. The subject was treated eloquently, and the essay was marked by the originality and profound thought for which the professor is noted. The lecturer showed that common school education throughout the United States, as it was now administered, was exerting its whole force to drive men away from the farm and from industrial pursuits; that farmers and industrial men were the only class of men in the United States that could rectify the matter. Teachers can not do it. In the elucidation of his subject, he pointed out what he conceived to be radical errors in our common school system, and showed how the common school discipline was calculated to unfit boys for the active duties of life. On motion of General Jackson, a vote of thanks was tendered Professor Turner. Some discussion occurred on a proposition to adopt the speaker's positions and print the address, but no action was taken.

After assembling in the afternoon, the preliminary business being finished, an address on practical entomology was delivered by Professor C. V. Riley, State Entomologist of Missouri. A vote of thanks was tendered the eminent speaker.

The committee to whom was referred a resolution memorializing Congress to make additional land grants for Agricultural College purposes, reported that in their judgment the proposition for further national aid for Agricultural Colleges was one of pre-eminent merit, provided such guards and guarantees could be thrown around it as to secure the end sought. The lands already donated had generally been frittered away. The committee conclude by an expression of their belief that it was the duty of Congress to pass a declaratory act so clear as to settle all controversy, and to withhold all further aid until such time that it was found that the true ends of the original appropriation were being reached by these institutions.

Several essays which were prepared, but not read for want of time, were referred to appropriate committees.

After the usual votes of thanks, the Congress adjourned to meet at Indianapolis, at ten o'clock A. M., on the fourth Wednesday of May, 1873.

Thus ended one of the most important conventions ever held by the farmers of America; important as showing their earnestness of purpose, and the uniform good feeling prevailing between different sections of the country. It was not expected that the way would prove free of all difficulties.

It was especially felt that to be successful the Congress must be sustained by the agricultural masses throughout the nation, and especially by the Industrial Societies, Farmers' Clubs, and other organizations relating to agriculture, over the length and breadth of the land. The door was opened, however, and the way made clear.

CHAPTER XVIII.

THE FIRST BLOOMINGTON, ILLS., CONVENTION.

EFFECT OF THE WAR ON AGRICULTURE.

From 1858 to the breaking out of the war, the subject of the various taxes which all products paid before they reached the consumer, were earnestly and frequently discussed. But soon there were mutterings of another kind, and when the dogs of war were at length let loose, convulsing the country from the Atlantic to the Pacific, and from the great lakes to the Gulf, all questions were dropped other than which related to the salvation of our national unity. Production was stimulated, trade flourished, prices were more and more inflated, money was plenty, and farmers prospered, and readily sold their surplus at remunerative prices.

All forgotten, save the Nation's Unity.

The war, however, brought into existence a horde of speculators, who exercised their enterprise and craft, not only in the processes of moving, maintaining, and operating large armies, but in other matters as well. Speculation became rife in our cities in every possible direction, but especially in money and in stocks, the latter either real or fictitious, made to represent money. Thus was built up that system of hollow unreality in monetary affairs, coupled almost constantly with fraud and corruption, that has lately culminated in the failure of Jay Cooke & Co., and a general collapse of stocks of every kind, showing at once the entire rottenness of the whole system of building apparently colossal but really fictitious fortunes upon the bulling and bearing of stocks.

THE END OF ENDURANCE.

The encroachments and vexatious discriminations of the transportation companies, and the exactions of agents and middle men, had all been increasing, the farmers meanwhile steadily growing poorer and poorer. On all sides were heard the mutterings of discontent, like the scattering, desultory fire of skirmishers, preliminary to a general engagement.

The enemy laughed at the writhings of their captives, bound, as they had them, with iron bands. "Pay us three, or four, or *five* bushels of corn, and we will take one to New York for you! You object? Then keep your corn! Burn it, or let it rot! Ingrates! After all that we have done for you!"

Again, it was the middle men who spoke: "You want a plow, a reaper, a thresher? Pay us, then, three or four times its cost, or you must do without. You will buy it direct? No, you will not buy it direct from the maker! We have stopped that little game! You have it from us, or not at all."

The wealthy farmer found that farming did not pay; the

well-to-do saw his capital disappearing; while the one with small means sold out and went West to seek that market which a new, rapidly-developing country always affords. Railroad companies consolidated; they grew rich, and had to water their stocks, to keep down the dividends to a figure which would not call up blushes of shame to the manipula-

The Monopolists' Mistake—NOT the type of the Farmer.

tors. Meantime, the farmers' needs become more and more pressing. Money they must have, and their crops were sold at a loss. Even the less thoughtful began to wonder where the robbery was going to cease. "Let us organize," became the cry.

Early in 1869, the agitation began to assume definite shape. Local meetings were held in many districts, and plans were mooted (though all but despairingly, in some cases) for a general organization similar to the Trades' Unions, which, in England, and to a smaller degree in the United States, were obtaining great power, in some instances having successfully combatted and dictated terms to over-reaching capital.

THE BUGLE-CALL.

In March, 1869, the Hon. Henry C. Wheeler, a farmer of Du Page County, Illinois, who had distinguished himself by his efforts to stir up his fellow-workers to a due sense of their power, issued a call for a convention of farmers of the North-west, to be held at Bloomington, Illinois, on the following 20th of April. This document possesses great interest, as a forcible statement of the case of the producers against their enemies, and, still more, as leading to the first clearly-defined protest of an organization of farmers against the extortions of the monopolists, who were eating out their substance. Mr. Wheeler's manifesto was published in the principal papers of the North-west, and was as follows:

THE TRANSPORTATION QUESTION.

THE RELATION OF THE CARRYING TO THE PRODUCING INTEREST OF THE COUNTRY—CALL FOR A CONVENTION.

To the Farmers of the North-west: Will you permit a working farmer, whose entire interest is identified with yours, to address to you a word of warning?

A crisis in our affairs is approaching, and dangers threaten.

You are aware that the price of many of our leading staples is so low that they can not be transported to the markets of Europe, or even to our own seaboard, and leave a margin for profits, by reason of the excessive rates of transportation.

During the war but little attention was given to the great increase in the price of freights, as the price of produce was proportionately high; but we look in vain for any abatement, now that we are obliged to accept less than half the former prices for much that we raise.

We look in vain for any diminution in the carrying rates, to correspond with the rapidly-declining prices of the means of living, and of materials for constructing boats, cars, engines, and track; but, on the other hand, we see a total ignoring of that rule of reciprocity between the carrying and producing interests which prevails in every other department of trade and commerce.

Does it not behoove us, then, to inquire earnestly how long we can stand this descending scale on the one hand, and the ascending on the other, and which party must inevitably and speedily go to the wall?

I by no means counsel *hostility* to the carrying interest—it is one of the producer's best friends; but, like the fire that cooks our food and warms our dwelling, it may also become the hardest of masters. The fire fiend laughs as he escapes from our control, and in an hour licks up and sweeps away the accumulations of years of toil.

As we cherish the fire fiend, so we welcome the clangor of the carrier fiend as he approaches our dwellings, opening up communication with the busy marts of trade. But it needs no great stretch of imagination to hear also the cach! cach! cachinations of the carrier fiend as he speeds beyond our reach, and leaving no alternative but compliance with his exorbitant demands.

Many of us are not aware of the gigantic proportions the carrying interest is assuming. Less than forty years since the first railroad fire was kindled on this continent, but which now, like a mighty conflagration, is crackling and roaring over every prairie and through every mountain gorge. The first year produced fifteen miles; the last, 5,000.

On the same mammoth scale goes on the work or organization and direction. By the use of almost unlimited means, it enlists in its service the finest talents of the land as officers, attorneys, agents, and lobbyists; gives free passes and splendid entertainments to the representatives of the people; and even transports whole legislatures into exceeding high mountains, showing them the kingdoms of the world, with lavish promises of reward for fealty and support: witness its land grants and franchise secured from the powers that be, such as no similar interest ever acquired even in the Old World.

In Europe every corporation returns its franchises to the Crown within a specified time, while here their titles are more secure than the farmers' warranty deeds.

Do you say that you are out of debt, and can stop producing when it does not pay?

I tell you, my friends, that the carrying interest, with its present momentum unchecked, will soon acquire the power to tax your unincumbered possessions into leaseholds, and you and me into tenants at will.

I fancy I hear the response: "These things are so, but what can we do?"

Rather, my friends, what can we *not* do? What power can withstand the combined and concentrated force of the producing interest of this Republic? But what avails our strength if, like Polyphemus in the fable, we are unable to use it for want of eyesight; or, like a mighty army without discipline, every man fighting on his own hook; or, worse, reposing in fancied security while Delilahs of the enemy have well nigh shorn away the last lock of strength? In this respect we constitute a solitary exception, every other interest having long since protected itself by union and organization.

As a measure calculated to bring all interested, as it were, within speaking distance, and as a stepping stone to an efficient organization, I propose that the farmers of the great North-west concentrate their efforts, power, and means, as the great transportation companies have done theirs, and accomplish something, instead of frittering away their efforts in doing nothing.

And, to this end, I suggest a convention of those opposed to the present tendency to monopoly and extortionate charges by our transportation companies, to meet at Bloomington, Illinois, on the 20th day of April next, for the purpose of discussion, and the appointment of a committee to raise funds to be expended in the employment of the highest order of legal talent, to put in form of report and argument an exposition of the rights, wrongs, interests, and injuries (with their remedies) of the producing masses of the North-west, and lay it before the authorities of each State and of the general government. Congress is now in session, and the Constitutional Convention of this State will then again be convened. Farmers, now is the time for action!

The call was responded to, and, accordingly, on the day designated a large number of the leading farmers from various counties of Illinois, met at Bloomington, in mass convention. An organization was effected by the election of officers, as follows: President, Hon. J. H. Bryant, of Bureau County. Vice-Presidents, Messrs. William Smith, of McLean; S. H. McCrea, of Cook; E. S. Topping, of Whiteside; Lewis Ellsworth, of Du Page; John Davis, of Macon; W. W. Miller, of St. Clair; E. S. Hull, of Madison; A. M. Brown, of Pulaski; G. W. Hered, of Marion; W. Seldengale, of Knox; M. L. Dunlap, of Champaign; and K. K. Jones, of Adams.

GOVERNOR PALMER'S LETTER.

The Governer of Illinois, Gen. John M. Palmer, in a letter to the Convention, expressed the hope that the first work attempted would be to convince the people of the State that they had the power to rid themselves of the burdens of which they so justly complained. Upon the practice of corrupting legislators with money, he said: "Whether public men now in office are corrupt or not, it will be the fault of the people themselves if those hereafter selected are so. The people, rejecting all the sophistry by which the real questions that concern them are concealed or mystified, must hereafter investigate for themselves, and take care of their own interests." He hoped the Convention would assert, and prepare to maintain, that there is no interest in this country that is or can be beyond the control of the law.

The state of the question between the producing interest of the State and the transporting interest, he held to be, "that the whole subject of freights, and all subjects that are dependent on, or collateral thereto, are absolutely under the control of the owners and managers of railway lines, and that practically they may and do grasp, and appropriate to their own use, such proportion of the value of the products of the farmers and workshops of the country as they, in the exercise of their uncontrolled discretion, may determine. The object of the people of the State must be to overthrow this pretension, and to establish the doctrine that freights, and all that relates to the transportation, storage, and sale of the products of the industry of the country, shall be relieved from the arbitrary rule of monopolies, and be subjected to such regulations as may harmonize with reason and justice." He hoped the work of the convention would be to call the attention of the people to these opposing propositions, and to urge them to support that which is most reasonable and just, and also to suggest the means by which success might be secured for the right.

GENERAL BUSINESS OF THE CONVENTION.

The various phases of the transportation and warehouse questions were earnestly discussed by the delegates, and, as a rule, in an impartial spirit, only a small proportion of the speakers indulging in appeals to the passions of the audience. Strong resolutions were passed, denouncing the wrongs under which the producers labored, and the necessity of prompt and consecutive action to obviate these wrongs. A motion to send an official copy of the resolution to the President of the Constitutional Convention, then in session, was carried, and the following declaration was adopted:

"This Convention declares, First: That the present rates of taxation and transportation are unreasonable and oppressive, and ought to be reduced.

"Second: That our legal rights to transportation and market ought to be clearly set forth and defined.

"Third: That if there be any legal remedy under existing laws for the wrongs we suffer, such remedy ought to be ascertained and enforced.

"Fourth: That, if there be no such remedy, measures should be taken to secure one by appropriate legislation.

"Fifth: That statistics should be collected and published to show the relation of North-western products to those of the rest of the country.

"Sixth: That nothing can be accomplished for the enforcement of our rights, and the redress of our wrongs, without an efficient organization on the well-known principles that give the great corporations such tremendous power.

"Seventh: That, with honest pay for honest labor, and compensation commensurate with great service, we can secure the assistance and support of the highest order of learning, ability, and skill.

"Eighth: That this Convention should appoint a commissioner of agricultural and carrying statistics, to prepare and publish, with the aid of eminent counsel, a report of the products of the North-west, the rights to market and transportation, and the remedies available for existing wrongs, the expenses thereof to be defrayed by subscription price for such report."

Hon. H. C. Wheeler was promptly elected Statistician, and after the appointment of an Executive Committee, the Convention adjourned.

ONLY A PARTIAL SUCCESS, AND WHY.

Great results were expected from the meeting of this body. Nothing practical, however, came of it, except that it was the entering wedge, that opened the way to further work in the same direction.

It was obvious to all thinking men that the Statistician could not work without money, and that no working farmer could stand the necessary drain upon his pocket in collecting statistics, and in employing legal talent to sift existing laws. Thus, so far as remedying abuses, the first Bloomington Convention was a failure. Not so, however, as to its moral bearings. It was the plow that broke into the stubborn soil of monopoly. But plowing alone, the farmer well knows, avails but little, without the further aid of the harrow and the roller. The harrow was subsequently applied at the Kewanee and other Conventions. It now looks as though the iron roller of the farmer must be set in motion to crush all smooth, and render the stubborn glebe fit for good seed. But all will come in good time. How shall it be brought about? Must it be by taking pattern of the railroad engineer? He, seeing an obstruction before him which he can not avoid, drives his engine at its highest speed full upon it.

The good farmer, in laying out lands, does not put his hand to the plow and look back. In the case we are considering, as in many others, there were crooked furrows made, for, in looking about to see where the money was to come from, the team pulled awry.

CHAPTER XIX.

THE KEWANEE (ILLINOIS) CONVENTION.

ORIGIN OF THE CONVENTION.

In the spring of 1872, the Farmers' Club of Avon suggested to a number of corresponding Clubs the advisability of holding a convention, in order to compare notes, discuss subjects of interest to the fraternity, inquire into the causes of the depressed condition of Agriculture in the West, and propose remedies therefor. A correspondence ensued among men prominent in the Clubs, in which S. M. Smith, of Kewanee; Edward Maynard, of St. David; John McAdams, of Avon; J. Howard, of Smithfield; A. M. Garland, of Springfield, Secretary of the State Board of Agriculture; W. T. R. Finnessy, of Kewanee; John Prickett, of Lewistown, and others, participated. Mr. Finnessy thought that the movement would place farmers in a "higher position." Mr. Garland expressed the opinion that the "idea concerning a unity of effort among Farmers' Clubs," etc., was "in the right direction." Mr. Howard deemed something of the kind "very necessary." Mr. McAdams desired greatly the "more thorough organization of our farmers." It was the hope of Mr. Maynard that those having the matter in charge would "act promptly." The Club of which Mr. Prickett was a member was "decidedly in favor of the measure." Many others added pertinent and encouraging words.

A few disapproved of the proposition, but the notes of dissent were drowned in the general unanimity, and it was eventually decided to issue a formal call for a convention of delegates, to meet at Kewanee, on the 16th and 17th of October, 1872.

This call was made by Mr. S. M. Smith, both a cultured and working farmer, "for the purpose of comparing views, and consulting together on the best means of organizing a general union of farmers, for their mutual benefit and protection against the monopolizing tendencies of the age." Delegates were invoked to attend in the following words: "Come, then, farmers, and help us to make the meeting a success in numbers, intelligence, and results."

THE DELEGATES AND THEIR DIFFICULTIES.

About fifty delegates answered the call, composed of members of the various organizations then existing in Illinois. Nearly all were strangers to each other; they had met with undefined ideas of their wrongs; opinions as to the future had not been matured; and no plans or remedies for future action had been devised. They had come together, hoping almost against hope, that they might find a way out of their difficulties. But order soon came out of chaos. The delegates were eminent as farmers, and also as thinkers; many of them were men of wealth, and some of them were well known for their political prominence.

The Convention was an entire success, and became historic as the first convention of farmers who had really succeeded in making their power felt.

Among those present were the Hon. L. D. Whiting, of

Bureau County, State Senator; Henry C. Lawrence, brother of Judge Lawrence; C. C. Buell, formerly a prominent educator, but now a farmer of Whiteside County; Colonel A. Woodford, one of the originators of the Grange in Illinois; James Smith, Jr., a farmer of Madison County; C. A. Barney, of Bureau County, well known by his contributions to the press; D. H. Goran, a large stock-raiser of Fulton County, and H. D. Carson, an extensive stock-grower of Weathersfield, Henry County. The county last named was also represented by C. C. Blish, who is said to "feed more cattle" than any man in that part of the State; M. B. Potter, a large farmer; C. H. Loomis, who "farms three hundred acres," and G. N. Paliner, a noted hedge-raiser.

Character was also given to the meeting by the presence of such men as Messrs. King, of Madison; McElroy, of Champaign; Saddoris, of Rock Island, and Prickett and Campbell, of Fulton. Many other gentlemen of equal local prominence were in attendance. All the delegates were farmers. The bone, sinew, and brain of the agricultural population of the State were fairly represented.

Letters were read from General Ross, of Avon, A. M. Garland, of Springfield, Hon. M. L. Dunlap, of Champaign, and others, who were unable to be present, but who fully sympathized with the ends in view.

BUSINESS OF THE MEETING.

The convention organized by the election of Hon. L. D. Whiting, President; Colonel A. Woodford, Vice-President; and S. M. Smith and L. W. Beer, Secretaries.

A committee, appointed for the purpose, recommended as subjects for consideration: "How can farmers, through their Clubs and other organizations, accomplish a saving to their members in purchasing, selling, and in transportation?"

"Benefits and results attainable through Farmers' Clubs and kindred organizations."

The discussion on these subjects was animated and interesting. Several delegates from different Clubs spoke of the benefits that had accrued to the members from their organization, enabling them to make a large saving in the cost of nearly all the supplies they needed. So far as the experience of those associations represented was concerned, they

Steamboat and Railway Cars.

had all worked harmoniously, and much to the advantage of the members pecuniarily, aside from their refining and instructive social features.

The subject of transportation by railroad was considered, and thoroughly shown up. It was stated by one member that eighteen years previously a car load of cattle could be sent from Abingdon to Chicago for twenty dollars, and that for the same service fifty dollars was then the tariff. The relative prices from other points was given, showing a large advance within a few years on that class of shipments.

A State Central Committee was appointed, and also an Executive Committee of three to fill vacancies, if any should occur, in the Central Committee. The appointment of these committees and the passage of a series of stirring resolutions constituted the important business of the Convention. The resolutions were as follows:

Resolved, That the agricultural interests of this country are the primary source of its growth, wealth, and prosperity; and that the protection and development of these are essential to the prosperity of every related industry, and also of every other vocation or business.

Resolved, That the immediate objects and purposes of the Convention should be to devise some means, or system of means, to cheapen the process of production, and lessen the expense of transportation.

Resolved, That the success of co-operative effort, as illustrated in the accumulation of capital for the carrying forward of immense business enterprises; in the combination of workingmen for the increase of wages, or the restriction of the hours of labor; in the formation of rings for controlling the price of agricultural or manufactured products, and for "bulling" or "bearing" the markets of every kind; and in the thorough and efficient organization of political parties for partisan ends, should teach the farmer the lesson, both of its efficiency and its adaptation to the particular needs, if applied with intelligence and wisdom.

Resolved, That it is the duty of Farmers' Clubs, and similar organizations, to put forth their best efforts for extending and multiplying these organizations, until they shall compass the industrial interest of the entire West.

Resolved, That this Convention regards with favor the growth and prosperity of the organization called Patrons of Husbandry, and accept the evidences of its benefits and efficiency with hopeful expectations of its future usefulness.

Resolved, That the destruction of Canada thistles and noxious weeds is a matter of vital importance to the agricultural interests of the West; and this Convention would commend the action of the Legislature of Illinois in its efforts to accomplish this object.

Resolved, That the strength or weakness of the Railroad Law, so-called, should be determined by its thorough trial and enforcement; and this Convention would demand additional legislation on the subject, if required.

Resolved, That this Convention appoint a State Central Committee of one, and a committee of one from each county, whose duties shall be to act as a medium of communication between the various farmers' organizations.

Resolved, That the Convention return a vote of thanks to the citizens of Kewanee and the Wethersfield Farmers' Club, for the very generous hospitality extended to the members of this Convention; and that especial thanks are due the aforesaid Club for inaugurating and carrying to so successful an issue this Convention.

These resolutions have sometimes been referred to as the first formal protest by the farmers against the oppressions under which they labored. This, however, is an error. The first protest was made at Bloomington, in 1869, as noticed in the last chapter. That was the entering wedge, this the maul that struck it home. We shall soon see that it required still harder pounding, and the use of still other wedges, to widen the rent in the gnarled log of monopoly, each individual splinter of which will hold its own until severed with the keen edge of the axe.

A motion was adopted that "all Farmers' Clubs, Protective Associations, and Granges, now existing in this State, and not represented in this Convention, or which may hereafter be organized, be requested to report their name, officers, and location to the State Central Committee."

The Executive Committee above referred to consisted of L. F. Ross, John Prickett, and William Beem.

The State and County Committees were elected as follows: For State Central Committee, Hon. W. C. Flagg, Moro, Illinois. For County Committee, H. H. Gibson, Madison County; W. F. P. Hennesy, Fulton County; O. H. Loomis, Henry County; L. D. Whiting, Bureau County; Cyrus Humphrey, Knox County; G. W. McElroy, Champaign County; Joseph Wright, Whiteside County; Henry Saddoris, Rock Island County; H. C. Lawrence, Warren County.

The Executive Committee was empowered to appoint for other counties as Clubs might report.

SPEECHES AND POETRY.

Various stirring addresses, interspersed with songs by the Kewanee Glee Club, were delivered toward the close of the Convention, one, upon the subject of education, by Mr. C. C. Buell, being exceedingly well delivered. Mr. S. M. Smith, since widely known as one of the great champions of the cause, made a strong speech, in which he called attention to the growing taste among the rural population for home adornment, and recited the following extract from the beautiful poem of John G. Whittier, "Among the Hills:"

I look across the lapse of half a century,
And call to mind old homesteads, where no flower
Told that the spring had come, but evil weeds,
Nightshade and rough-leaved burdock in the place
Of the sweet doorway greeting of the rose
And honeysuckle; where the house walls seemed
Blistering in sun, without a tree or vine
To cast the tremulous shadow of its leaves
Across the curtainless windows, from whose panes
Fluttered the signal rag of shiftlessness;
Within, the cluttered kitchen-floor, unwashed
(Broom-clean, I think they called it); the best room
Stifling with cellar damp, shut from the air
In hot midsummer, bookless, pictureless,
Save the inevitable sampler hung
Over the fire-place, or a mourning-piece,
A green-haired woman, peony-cheeked, beneath
Impossible windows; the wide-throated hearth
Bristling with faded pine-boughs, half concealing
The piled-up rubbish at the chimney's back;

And, in sad keeping with all things about them,
Shrill, querulous women, sour and sullen men,
Untidy, loveless, old before their time,
With scarce a human interest, save their own
Monotonous round of small economies,
Or the poor scandal of the neighborhood;
Blind to the beauty every-where revealed,
Treading the May-flowers with regardless feet;

"For them the Bobolink sang not."

For them the song-sparrow and the bobolink
Sang not, nor winds made music in the leaves;
For them in vain October's holocaust
Burned gold and crimson over all the hills,
The sacramental mystery of the woods.
Church-goers, fearful of the unseen Powers,
But grumbling over pulpit tax and pew rent,
Saving, as shrewd economists, their souls
And winter pork with the least possible outlay
Of salt and sanctity; in daily life
Showing as little actual comprehension
Of Christian charity, and love, and duty,
As if the Sermon on the Mount had been
Outdated, like a last year's almanac;
Rich in broad woodlands and in half-tilled fields,

And yet so pinched, and bare, and comfortless,
The veriest straggler limping on his rounds,
The sun and air his sole inheritance,
Laughed at a poverty that paid its taxes,
And hugged his rags in self-complacency!
Not such should be the homesteads of a land
Where whoso wisely wills and acts may dwell
As king and lawgiver, in broad-acred state,
With beauty, art, taste, culture, books, to make
His hour of leisure richer than a life
Of fourscore to the barons of old time.
Our yeoman should be equal to his home
Set in the fair, green valleys, purple walled—
A man to match his mountains, not to creep
Dwarfed and abased below them.

RESULTS OF THE DISCUSSION.

One of the most important features of the Kewanee Convention was, that, though it was called a Convention of Farmers' Clubs, it was attended by many influential members of the Order of Patrons of Husbandry. Up to this time there had been, or was supposed to have been, a degree of jealousy existing between the two forms of association. These differences had been fomented and magnified by designing persons who wished to see the associations antagonistic, in the hope that the agitation would prove a failure. The unanimity which marked this meeting showed that no ill-feeling existed between the two organizations.

This Convention, upon the whole, may be characterized as the most important meeting held up to that time, as far as Western farmers are concerned. An immense stride was there taken toward effecting the organizations that have since developed into a power before which their foes, at first derisive, now tremble. Not the least good effected was that each delegate carried home to his constituents a keener perception of the importance of the questions at issue, of the necessity of concerted action, and of the possibility, which was before doubted, of the producing classes eventually defeating their powerful antagonists. These opinions speedily spread throughout the West, and public opinion became ripe for carrying forward the grand movement for securing cooperation of effort.

Meantime, meetings were being held throughout the West, and Farmers' Associations were forming rapidly. As the agitation developed, and grievances were ventilated, it became apparent that a ball was set in motion which would not stop until greater questions than the robberies by the transportation companies and middle men had received their quietus. Attention began to be directed to the iniquitous working of the tariff laws, which protect monopolies at the expense of the people, and absolutely impede the establishment of those home manufactures which they ostentatiously pretend to protect.

CHAPTER XX.

THE SECOND BLOOMINGTON (ILL.) CONVENTION.

THE STORM GATHERING.

The Executive Committee elected at the Kewanee Convention, set immediately to work. Meetings were held, speeches made, and, from a variety of causes, the existing feeling became still further intensified. Undoubtedly, one of the principal causes was the extraordinarily low price of corn.

The corn crop of the West, in 1872, was the largest which had ever been gathered, aggregating, for the United States, 1,092,000,000 bushels. This, succeeding the large crops of 1871, had filled every crib and available storehouse to overflowing. There was not sufficient stock in the country to which even the half of this crop might be fed, and in consequence the markets were glutted. In many portions of Illinois, Iowa, and Kansas, it was freely burned as fuel, being actually cheaper, at existing prices, than either wood or coal. Ten cents per bushel was the ruling price, at points remote from transportation, and in many places it could not be sold at all.

Here was the last feather that broke the camel's back. In many instances, it required six or seven bushels of corn to get one other bushel to the eastern markets. First, were heard mutterings in Iowa from the Patrons of Husbandry; and with these mingled the voices of fellow-sufferers in Kansas. Then other sources of still greater discontent aroused indignation, and soon it became evident that a storm was gathering, compared with which all previous demonstrations had been but the patterings of an April shower.

THE CALL FOR THE CONVENTION.

In compliance with the duty assigned them, the Executive Committee appointed at Kewanee issued a call for a State Convention, to be held at Bloomington, on the 15th and 16th days of January 1873, of which call the following is the more essential portion:

FARMERS' CONVENTION.

"Equal and exact justice to all; special privileges to none."

The undersigned, the Executive Committee appointed by the Convention of delegates from Farmers' Clubs, held at Kewanee, Oct.

The Demand of the Industries.

16th and 17th, 1872, in pursuance of the duties assigned them, do hereby invite each Farmers' Club, Grange, or other agricultural, horticultural, or industrial association of the State of Illinois, to send delegates for every thirty-three members, and fraction in excess of that number, (*Provided*, That every organization shall be entitled to at least one delegate), to an Illinois Farmers' State Convention, to be held in the City of Bloomigton, Wednesday and Thursday, Jan. 15 and 16, 1873, commencing at 9 A. M. on Wednesday, with three sessions each day—at 9 A. M., 2 P. M., and 7 P. M.

The purpose of said Convention is to perfect the organization made at Kewanee, by the formation of a State Farmers' Association from said delegates, adoption of a constitution, and for securing the organization and representation of associations in every county, and, if possible, in every township, of the State; to discuss and insist upon reform in railway transportation, the sale of agricultural implements, the sale of farm products by commission merchants, and such other abuses as have grown up in our midst, and are now taxing and impoverishing producers and consumers; and to transact such other business as may be brought before the Convention.

OPENING OF BUSINESS.

This call was earnestly responded to, and the assemblage of delegates was a large one. A temporary organization was effected by the election of Hon. L. D. Whiting, of Bureau Co., as chairman, and Mr. S. M. Smith, of Henry Co., and S. P. Tufts, of Marion Co., as secretaries. Mr. Whiting stated the grievances of the people, and some of the propositions for a remedy. Coming from the source whence they did, his remarks are worthy of recapitulation. He alluded to the fact that, in response to the Executive Committee, he had left his public duties to meet the association, again to testify his sympathy with the purposes of the convention, and catch inspiration from its spirit. He said:

"This is an age and an era of organization. We behold it, and feel its effects in various ways. Nearly every profession, calling, and pursuit, except our own, associate, organize, and combine, to promote their interests. The agriculturists, isolated and scattered, away from

Life on a Prairie Farm—Receiving Reports at Evening.

the post-office, and telegraph, and lecture-room, is the last to move. If he felt himself pressed and overburdened by high prices for all he bought, and low prices for all he sold, he has sought to cure the evil by more rigid economy and longer and harder hours of labor. While most other pursuits push up the prices of their commodities, if need be by shortening their hours of labor, and sometimes by wholly stopping the wheels, we have met this by more desperate struggles to multiply our productions, and to hurry them upon the market. Poverty, if not actual bankruptcy, stares the farmer in the face.

"There are remedies for all evils, so there must be somewhere a cure for the ills that threaten the fraternity. For some months past the producers in various and widely-separated places have been almost spontaneously coming together in local organization. This convention of the farmers of Illinois is to consider the matter of binding together these local societies by a State organization.

"As it was somewhat new for our people to attempt any general organization, the question was very naturally asked, What is the purpose?

"No one is authorized, or able, especially in advance, to pronounce fully for any movement. He would answer as he saw it from his own stand-point. Farmers' Associations are intended for mutual improvement in our calling,—to call forth new thoughts, and diffuse useful information among ourselves, so as to produce better results with less labor—for social enjoyment, and for intellectual and moral improvement. Such associations will afford the opportunity for neighborhood co-operation in rural improvement, stock-breeding, dairying, farmers' insurance—perhaps in buying and selling, to some extent, and so, generally, to effect for our class what organization has done for others.

"But we desire, also, to understand more fully the relation between agriculture and the government, and, especially, to see that justice is done on matters of taxation. As *cheap transportation* is vital to our prosperity, we mean, in some manner, to solve this problem, and it is to this matter especially I shall call attention.

"The West must long remain an exporting and an importing country, to an enormous and increasing extent. The prices of our products go up or down, as transportation varies its scale. As all interests of a country prosper when its chief staples bring a good price, so the West generally—all classes, professions, and trades are nearly equally interested in cheap transportation."

THE RAILROAD ABUSES.

In discussing the question of railroad transportation, Mr. Whiting said he believed railroads to be in perfect harmony with the genius of the age; remembered their feeble beginnings in America; had watched with pride and hope their marvelous growth, until now more than sixty thousand miles stretched their network from the Great Lakes to the Gulf of Mexico, and from the Atlantic to the Pacific. They are nearly as vital to the present civilization as the air we breathe, and he wanted to see every neighborhood penetrated with them; and no wise man would desire to cripple them by injustice.

It had been confidently believed that their multiplication would lead to competition, "which is the most natural and best regulator of business. But of this the country now despairs. Railroad kings have learned to flank competition by combination."

"The whole railroad system is being consolidated in a few organizations, each of which represents hundreds of millions of dollars. Already, the country is parceled out in lots and vast regions to the different systems. Like hostile invading armies, they levy contributions limited only by the ability of their victims to pay. These exactions are again aggravated by unjustly discriminating against persons and places. If competition shows itself at a few points, they remorsely double up on others within their grasp. They levy an Internal Revenue tax by their own fiat, and to fill their own coffers. If this blood-money was well applied, it might be some compensation, but it is now certain that in many cases, instead of going to the stockholders, it is gobbled by some favorites and head-centers, and spent in gambling and riotous living. So enormous is the robbery that ex-president Gould, a few weeks ago, to compromise a little dispute in a settlement, without much ceremony handed over seven or eight millions. . . . . If the tidal-wave now rising does not win, it must be followed by such a succession of others, each higher and stronger, till the railroad Pharaohs are brought to judgment. By their power over freights they may 'bull' or 'bear' the market at will. They may make *real* fortunes for their favorites, as easily as the Frenchman fancied he made a thousand dollars before breakfast by marking up his goods. . . . . I look to 'competition' as the most natural, legitimate, and effectual cure. As this competition will not come of itself, and as individually we can not apply it, Government must be invoked in the matter. The water lines already have done much. The lakes and the Erie Canal save us millions annually. The ocean around by Cape Horn is a regulator to some extent to the Pacific Railroad. I would therefore open new lines of water. . . . Although it would cost money, did not, does not, railroad extortion cost money? Who can tell how much? Which is better, to pay something for permanent relief or be perpetually robbed? . . . , I have suggested these as means for bringing competition. I do not surrender the claim that Government can and ought to regulate railroads by fixing maximum rates, and forbidding unjust discrimination. The government power of eminent domain was invoked by them in their construction on the ground that they were to be public institutions. The people never clothed their legislators with power to contract away, for all time, the inherent rights of the people. In our advancing civilization, public interest and public necessity will not be thwarted by old and musty cob-web precedents. 'Dartmouth College' may have been well enough for that day, and for an institution of learning; but it can not much longer be made a standard rule and hobby-horse for railroads. These vast corporations, which stretch from sea to sea, and cover the whole country like an enveloping atmosphere, can not much longer shield their extortions by quoting a law decision concerning a school. The judge or lawyer who shall narrow his visions to this infinitesimal point when dealing with the great question, will be laughed to scorn."

He believed the "Dartmouth decision," which Webster had wrung from the judges, would prove that a little learning was a dangerous thing; held that the railroads of Illinois were in open rebellion against the constitution and laws of the State, which commands the legislature to act, but which law they were only seeking "mildly to enforce."

"Let us institute the necessary machinery and apply the proper force to execute the law. If we can not name the specific measures of relief on some great matters, there are yet objects enough of a lesser kind, and clearly within our reach, to induce organization. In the meantime the great question will be studied, and when the true solution shall appear we shall have a power to execute. The truth is, there are, no doubt, many ways of relief. Just now none of these ways are practical for the want of a compact organization. Difficulties will disappear as we gather in strength. As the stars reduced themselves to order, when the great Newton proclaimed true nature's law, so will wrong and monopolies yield up their grasp when confronted by a united people."

THE FARMERS IN COUNCIL.

While the Committee on Credentials was deliberating, there was an informal discussion entered into upon the grievances of the farmers, and the scope of work to be performed.

Mr. Creed, of Marion County, stated that there were thirty farmers' organizations in his county; that they were originally organized as a protection against horse thieves. He urged the thorough organization of the farmers in the State, by which means they could become united in demanding a voice in the control of affairs affecting their interests. Mr. Ewing, of Macon, thought the Convention should confine its action to one or two main points or questions. They should limit action mainly to the great question of transportation. Mr. Wiley believed every county should organize, with Clubs in every school district. Through such organizations, the evils complained of could be remedied. Law-makers, who were careful observers, would not resist the demands of such organizations. Mr. Perry, of Marshall County, thought we should be striking at the root of the evil, if we turned our attention to the aggregation of capital in the hands of monopolies. Mr. Phoenix, of McLean County, said that now all organizations tended to monopolies. It was soulless brains against muscle that ailed us. We were sold soul and body, in bonds, in Europe and at home. He thought the enfranchisement of women would cure our troubles.

Mr. Ellice, of Bureau County, said that, through the organization of Farmers' Clubs, they would be enabled to procure the greatest recompense from their labor. They had succeeded in producing, while corporations had succeeded in getting the profits; while the farmers poll a three-fifth vote, they have had little or nothing to do with legislation. They should make their political power felt by sending representatives of the farmers to the Legislature and National Congress. To control monopolies, we must do it through legislation, and that requires political action.

Mr. S. M. Smith, of Kewanee, said that, before we talked about using our strength politically, we had first better learn what our strength was. We must first have organizations, complete, compact, and thorough, extending into every school district. The gist of the mass of letters he had received since the Kewanee meeting was: "Men and brethren, what shall we do to secure relief from these monopolies?" The movement then organized would, if wise and discreet, sweep like a prairie fire, not only through this State, but throughout the great North-west. We all know and feel the existing evils. The question to decide is, how to remedy them.

The Committee on Credentials having reported two hundred and seventy-five regularly-appointed delegates in attendance, and the Convention being thus ready for work, permanent officers were elected, as follows:

President—Hon. Willard C. Flagg, of Madison County; Vice-Presidents—S. P. Tufts, O. E. Fanning, H. C. Lawrence, John H. Bryant, and M. M. Hooton; Secretaries—S. M. Smith and S. P. Tufts; Treasurer—Duncan McKay.

Several hours were given up to the discussion of Farmers' Associations as business organizations. The fact was clearly brought out that these organizations had, for two years past, made large savings to the members, both in selling their products and in purchasing supplies, so that there had been already a large advantage gained through co-operation. The experience varied somewhat, as it necessarily would, in different parts of the State, but the advantages every-where were decided.

RAILWAY LEGISLATION AND RAILWAY REFORM.

The President addressed the Convention on the subject of railway legislation and railway reform, giving a history of the railway systems in various countries, their growth, costs, tariffs, etc. He said:

"These systems have grown up under various governmental provisions, and may be classed as follows:

"1. Roads built, owned, and managed by governments, as in the case of Russia and other despotic countries.

"2. Roads partly built and controlled by government, so that private and government enterprise compete on parallel lines, as in the case of Belgium.

"3. Roads built on guarantees and subsidies offered by government to private companies, as in France, Austria, India, and in the case of our own Pacific and Illinois Central roads.

"4. Roads built under charters granted by government.

"Looking at all these facts, and at others, not in the line of argument, I can not pronounce the railway systems of England and

America a success. I see the necessity of a recognition of the truth long ago enunciated by John Stuart Mill, that roads, canals, and railways, as well as gas and water companies, 'are always in a great degree, practical monopolies, and a government which concedes such monopoly to a private company, does much the same thing as if it allowed an individual or an association to levy any tax they choose for their own benefit on all the malt produced in the country, or on all the cotton imported.'

* * * * * * * *

"What is the most feasible manner of controlling the power we have evoked, is the proper subject for the deliberation of this Convention. It may be direct regulation by act of our General Assembly; it may be by the condemnation of the franchises that have been abused, and perhaps forfeited; it may be by enforcing the principle of our State Constitution, and making the railroads in the State in fact what they are in theory—public highways; it may be national legislation, under the constitutional power to regulate commerce among the several States, or other power, if amendment be necessary, so that the vast combinations of lines that already more than half span the continent shall be made subject to one general and equitable law of freight and passenger rates. It may be by building or condemning national railways that shall traverse the continent, north and south, east and west, and, running with fixed rates, compel the private companies to reasonable rates. It may be one or many. But that relief must be had is certain.

"If neither legislatures, nor courts, nor executives can furnish it, the people themselves can. But I believe and maintain that there is an adequate remedy in all, and that we only need to insist and require that our officers do their duty. The unjust judge that decides that the people have no rights that the railroad corporations are bound to respect, should be retired to private life. The legislative railway attorney should be excused from further service. It is certain that all who falter or fear must make way for better men, and our courts, our legislatures, and our executive officers should be required to be a unit in making the railway corporations what they were intended to be—the servants of the public, doing fair work for fair pay."

CHARTERS AND CONTRACTS.

An earnest discussion ensued on charters and contracts. Mr. H. C. Lawrence, of McDonough County, held that the charters granted the railroads under the old constitution of Illinois were in the nature of contracts, and, therefore, the evils complained of could not feasibly be corrected by litigation. He did not favor the project of a grand competing trunk line to the seaboard. He thought the State had the power of condemnation of the roads. He would rather resort to this power, and pay for them what they were worth, but not the fictitious values placed on them by the excessive watering of stock.

Mr. J. H. Rowell, one of the volunteer counsel in the famous McLean County (Illinois) Suit, gave, at some length, a history of the case. The points of his address were substantially as follows:

The power of eminent domain, and the power of taxation, have been lawfully used in the construction of railways. They are, therefore, public highways. The corporators are the trustees of the public engaged in administering a public trust. They are a part of the machinery of the State—are political officers as truly as are the sheriff and circuit clerk. Like them, they receive compensation for their time and capital by being permitted to charge fees, and, like them, their fees may be established by the legislature, the power that created them.

If it is a good law (and it is), what need has the State or nation to build more lines of railroad? We own all the roads now; freight cars, locomotives, depots, the road-bed, ties, and iron, all belong to the State, the corporation having a qualified property in them, and the right to perpetually execute the trust, if they obey the law; for this is the condition under which they invested their capital. Let us regulate what roads we now have, and see how that works before we build more.

A permanent railroad bureau is needed, as one of the executive departments of the State, which should be charged with the duty of overlooking the railroad property, examining into the cost of management, the amount of traffic, the appliances for speed and safety, the exclusion of blood-sucking fast freight lines, and the enforcement of the law. It is idle to talk about enforcing obedience from these masterful monopolies by private effort. It will be found altogether too costly and unequal. The State must take it in hand, as it does the punishment of crime, and the penalty for willful disobedience must be forfeiture.

The courts move slowly, but whenever public opinion becomes crystalized conviction, they never fail to give it the voice of authority. A good old maxim of the law tells us that when the reason for a law ceases, the law itself ceases. By its aid, many a musty precedent has been swept away, and given place to a juster and better rule.

With the producers of Illinois organized and united; with an enlightened understanding of the issues involved, not forgetting that the lawyers may be found necessary evils in the fight; with faith in the purity and eminent ability of our Supreme Court, the speaker hoped, within the six months following the Convention, to hear the voice which should emancipate the people from the tyranny of railway monopoly.

RIGHTS OF THE PEOPLE versus *RAILROADS.*

Mr. R. J. Benjamin, a well-known lawyer of Bloomington, in a long and logical argument, which he sustained by many quoted authorities, presented the rights of the people and corporations, and believed that if the matters at issue were pressed to a final termination in the courts, justice would be done the people, without depriving the corporations of any just or equitable compensation for the legitimate capital represented by them.

A letter was read from Colonel Morgan, one of the Railway Commissioners, in which he suggested that the questions for discussion were, in a large degree, the same as had officially come before the commission. First, it ought to be conceded that the railroads have a right to present to the courts their construction of certain laws. If the laws are valid, the courts will sustain them, and if invalid, the roads have a right to oppose them. He called attention to the case recently tested in McLean County, wherein the validity of the present law was sustained. The case had been appealed, and if the Supreme Court of the State should affirm, the railroad would undoubtedly carry it to the Supreme Court of the United States. In this case, it could hardly be expected that a final decision would be reached before 1876. The combined capital invested in railroads in the State was not less than $200,000,000. It is this immense power of capital that had to be opposed.

Subsequent to the reading of the letter, Colonel Morgan

arrived in Bloomington, and, upon his arrival at the Convention, was loudly called for. Coming forward, he said that he had not designed to take part in the deliberations of the Convention, but would say that he had accepted the appointment on the commission with the firm conviction that in that position he was bound to do his duty. In this State, the contest is against railroad companies that claimed the right to fix the rate of transportation in their own way, and this by reason of an irrevocable contract. Thanks to Judge Tipton, that so-called right had received its first knock-down. Who will set it on its feet again? He believed that retrospective relief could and must be obtained; and that the fictitious railroad capital of the United States must be forever blotted out, and no more, under any form, be permitted to rest as a wrongful burden on the people. He believed this could be done. Every railroad had been taking secretly and fraudulently from the people, and putting into the pockets of dishonest managers. Reasonable rates, he hoped, would some time be a reality.

FORMATION OF THE ILLINOIS STATE FARMERS' ASSOCIATION.

The Committee on State Organization presented its report by the Secretary, S. T K. Prime, embodying a constitution, as follows:

ARTICLE I. This organization shall be known as the Illinois State Farmers' Association.

ARTICLE II. Its object shall be the promotion of the moral, intellectual, social, and pecuniary welfare of the farmers of Illinois.

ARTICLE III. Its members shall consist of delegates from the various Farmers' Clubs, Granges, and Agricultural and Horticultural Societies of the State, each of which shall be entitled to at least one delegate, and where the number of its members exceed fifty, to one delegate for every one hundred members or fraction exceeding half that number. The members of the State Board of Agriculture shall be, *ex-officio*, members of this association, and from counties or parts of counties in which Clubs, Granges, or other Agricultural or Horticultural Societies are not organized, persons, not delegates, may be admitted by vote of this association. All members shall pay an annual fee of $1.

ARTICLE IV. Its officers shall consist of a President, a Vice-President from each Congressional District of the State, (to be nominated by the delegates therefrom,) of a Secretary and Treasurer; and these officers shall constitute the State Central Committee of this organization, with power to appoint an Executive Committee of three from the members, also a County Committee of one from each county in the State, to be nominated by the delegates. Said officers shall be elected annually and serve for one year, until their successors are elected. This organization shall meet annually at such time and place as the Association, or, in case of its failure to designate, the State Central Committee, may determine. Special meetings may be called by the Executive Committee.

In the discussion upon the report of the Committee, the Constitution and By-laws were considered *seriatim*. Mr. Somers, of McLean County, moved to amend the title by calling it "The Farmers' and Mechanics' Association," but the amendment was lost, and each clause of the constitution was adopted in the form reported by the Committee.

The officers elected were: President, W. C. Flagg; Vice-Presidents—first Congressional District, A. H. Dolton; second, Daniel Worthington; third, N. S. Church; fourth, P. B. Richards; fifth, D. W. Dame; sixth, Rufus Hoard; seventh, H. R. Conklin; eighth, William Colon; ninth, L. F. Ross; tenth, H. C. Lawrence; eleventh, T. Butterworth; twelfth, Benj. Dornblaser: thirteenth, Joshua Brown; fourteenth, J. B. Porterfield; fifteenth, David Morrison; sixteenth, Dr. M. M. Hooton; seventeenth, T. Smith, Jr.; eighteenth, John M. Ferris; nineteenth, Richard Richardson; Secretary, S. M. Smith; Treasurer, Duncan McKay.

THE RESOLUTIONS.

The Committee on Resolutions reported as follows:

WHEREAS, The Constitution of Illinois requires the Legislature to pass laws to correct abuses and prevent unjust discrimination and extortion by railroads; and,

WHEREAS, The Legislature has complied with this provision of the Constitution; and,

WHEREAS, The Railroads in the State of Illinois stand in open defiance of the laws, by charging rates greatly in excess of what the laws allow, and by unjust discriminations and extortions; and,

WHEREAS, These exactions and extortions bear most heavily upon the producing classes; therefore, be it

Resolved, That this convention of farmers and producers insist upon the enforcement of these laws.

Resolved, That in obedience to the universal law that the creature is not above the creator, we declare our unalterable conviction that all corporations are subject to regulation by law.

Resolved, That we call upon every department of the State government—the executive, legislative, and judicial—in their joint and several capacities, to execute the Constitution and laws now in force; and if amendments or new laws are needed to enforce obedience, we call for their speedy enactment.

Resolved, That cheap transportation is of vital interest to the West, and that every combination to increase the price above what is just and legitimate is a conspiracy against the rights of the people, and a robbery which we loudly protest against.

Resolved, That in the efforts of our officers to execute the laws in question, no narrow policy should be pursued by the Legislature, but that the magnitude of the matter at stake demands that ample appropriations be made, to enable those in charge of the object to act with vigor and effect.

Resolved, That the power of this, and all local organizations, should be wielded at the ballot-box by the election to all offices, from highest to lowest—legislative, executive, and judicial—of such, and only such, persons as sympathize with us in this movement, and believe, as we do, that there is a rightful remedy for this wrong, and that it can and must be enforced; and to this end we pledge our votes at all elections where they will have a bearing against the wrong in question.

Resolved, That the late decision in the McLean County Circuit Court, sustaining the constitutionality of our railroad law, is sound, and we hail it with satisfaction.

Resolved, That persons traveling upon the railroads of the State, having tendered to the conductor the legal fare, are in line of their duty, and as they have complied with all their legal obligations, are entitled to the protection of the civil power of the State; and any conductor or other officer or employee of the road attempting to disturb any such person, or eject him from the cars, are violators of the peace and dignity of the State, and should be punished by exemplary penalties.

The railroad question was again brought up, by Mr. Stephen R. Moore, of Kankakee, who reviewed the subject, and offered the following resolutions, which were referred to the appropriate committee. They are as follows:

Resolved, That all transportation companies, lines, and persons shall have the right to run their cars, said roads paying as toll therefor such compensation as the Board of Directors shall determine upon.

Resolved, That the Board of Directors for the management of the said roads shall be elected by the lower House of Representatives of the State named as corporators.

Resolved, That one Senator and Representative be requested to appoint three persons who shall be empowered to proceed to the Legislatures of States through which the road will pass, and ask co-operation by the States, and request that each State will appoint three persons, who shall constitute a joint committee.

Resolved, That the charter for the constitution of such national railway should be granted by the national government, and said railway shall forever remain a public highway.

Resolved, That the States through which this national freight road shall be built shall become corporators under said charter.

Resolved, That in the States through which, and along which, the road should be built, the people thereof shall construct the same through the territory of said States respectively.

Resolved, That said railway shall ever remain under the control of said States, which States shall exercise the power of regulating the tariff rates.

Resolved, That it is the sense of this convention that a double track, steel rail, freight railway should be built from Lincoln, Neb., in the West, crossing the States of Iowa and Missouri as near upon a line as may be, running thence East on air line to Youngstown, near the eastern boundary of Ohio; thence following the Gardner survey to some point in Pennsylvania, to be determined upon hereafter; from thence with three diverging lines running to New York, Philadelphia, and Baltimore; and that said railway should be used exclusively for a freight line. The committee to prepare a charter for the construction of the road, to submit it to the respective State Legislatures for approval, and, when approved, to present the same to Congress, and ask for its passage.

Resolved, That the chairman appoint a committee of five to present these resolutions to the Legislature, and ask that body to carry out their spirit.

Mr. Carter, from the Committee on Resolutions, submitted a report, as follows:

Resolved, That we recommend to our Legislature the enactment of a law making it a misdemeanor for any county or State officer to accept a free pass from any railroad, while holding office.

Resolved, That we view with favor the opening of feasible water communications, and all propositions to so improve and enlarge the great water line of the lakes and the St. Lawrence as to practically bring tide water to Chicago; and, for this purpose, completing the Illinois river improvement, and the extension of the canal to Rock Island, so as to connect the vast interior river system with the ocean commerce at our great commercial city, meet our approbation.

Resolved, That it is the sense of this convention that, in the appointment of Railroad and Warehouse Commissioners, at least one of the members of that commission should be a man whose business interests, sympathies, and knowledge of the experiences and wants of the farmer class, should fairly constitute him a representative man of that class, and who shall be so recommended by them.

Resolved. That in order to accomplish the ends arrived at by this Convention, we earnestly recommend the organization of the farmers throughout the State into Clubs, and Granges of Patrons of Husbandry.

The following resolution was offered and adopted:

Resolved, That this Convention appoint Capt. J. H. Rowell and R. W. Benjamin to proceed to our Legislature, and procure an act condemning all railroads that are running in violation of the law, and we further recommend that a commission be appointed to take charge of such road or roads, and run them in compliance with the law.

Resolved, That this Convention hails with joy and pleasure the late action taken in Congress by representatives Shellabarger, of Ohio, and Hawley, of Illinois, as the harbinger of better things to come.

The following miscellaneous resolutions were offered and referred to the Committee on Resolutions:

Resolved, That the Secretary of this Convention be instructed to forward to Hons. Shellabarger, of Ohio, and Hawley, of Illinois, and to the President of the Senate and the Speaker of the House of Representatives, copies of the resolutions of this Convention, with request that they be laid before the respective Houses.

Resolved, That the names of the persons composing the meeting at Kewanee, on the 15th and 16th of October, 1872, be inscribed on a suitable tablet, for permanent preservation by this society.

Resolved, That in view of the power of the press, this Convention urge upon the Farmers' Clubs over this State, the great importance of reporting their proceedings to their local papers, and, so far as practicable, to the papers having a State circulation.

Resolved, That the Legislature of this State be requested to instruct our Senators, and request our Representatives in Congress, in view of the depressed condition of the agricultural interests of this State and all others dependent thereon, except that of railway transactions, to insist upon the utmost economy in appropriations and frugality in expenditure of national moneys consonant with the necessities of the country.

Resolved, That we are in favor of removing the duties on iron, lumber, and salt.

Resolved, That farmers buy no implements of those manufacturers or their agents who have entered into any conspiracy agreeing not to sell their implements to Farmers' Associations.

Resolved, That this Convention respectfully call the attention of the General Assembly to the bill introduced by Senator Vaughn, of Knox County, in 1871, affixing reasonable maximum rates of freights on railroads, and that we urge the immediate passage of that or some similar bill.

Resolutions of thanks to the city of Bloomington, the Board of Trade, and citizens generally, for their hospitality, closed this Convention, which must ever rank with the most important of its class, not only from the business actually transacted, but from the life which it infused into the Farmers' Movement. The Association formed at this meeting has since grown and flourished. It comprises members of both Clubs and Granges, and, on that account alone, its value to the farming interest throughout the West is incalculable; for it is by the union of these organizations that the farmers' wrongs are to be righted.

CHAPTER XXI.

THE PATRONS OF IOWA AND THEIR WORK.

TWO MEETINGS OF THE STATE GRANGE.

The Order of Patrons of Husbandry early obtained a strong foothold in Iowa, and this, for a considerable time past, has been the banner State in the number of its Granges, etc. Nearly two thousand Granges are now in working operation there, and their influence is powerfully felt in almost every county.

The last annual meeting of the State Grange was held at Des Moines, on the ninth and tenth of December, 1873. Grand Master Smedley, in his opening address, reviewed the growth of the Order in the State, showing that the number of Subordinate Granges increased, during the preceding year, from seven hundred and eighty-eight to one thousand eight hundred and thirty-eight, with an aggregate membership of one hundred thousand. He warned the members that the success of the Order depended upon the observance of their rules, prohibiting the introduction of politics into the Order. During the afternoon, a prominent member made a speech favoring the formation of a new political party.

After a sharp contest, concluded late on the tenth, the following officers were elected: Col. A. B. Smedley (re-elected), Master; J. M. Dixon, Overseer; J. G. H. Little,

Secretary; J. W. Wilkinson, Lecturer; William Duane Wilson, Chaplain; D. W. Prindle, Steward; Jonathan Thacher, Assistant Steward; M. L. Devon, Treasurer; Executive Committee—J. W. Whitman, E. R. Shankland, and —— Clark.

From a more perfect report of the annual meeting of the Iowa State Grange, held on the twenty-eighth of January, 1873, I quote the following points, not only as embodying important information concerning the workings of the Order in its greatest stronghold, but also as showing the tendencies of the Farmers' Movement. This meeting was attended by

State Seal of Iowa.

over one thousand delegates from the various Granges of the State, representing forty thousand of the farmers of Iowa. But for the railroad blockade, caused by the unprecedented snow-storms that had visited the West, it is estimated that over two thousand delegates would have assembled, As it was, however, the large hall used for the occasion barely accommodated the number present.

RAILROADS, LAND GRANTS, SALARIES, AND GRANGE AGENTS.

One of the memorials presented, asked Congress to build a double track freight railroad to the seaboard, and another asked the Legislature of Iowa to build a system of narrow guage railroads in the State. The following resolution was adopted with respect to the land-grant bill then before Congress:

"*Resolved*, By the State Grange of the Patrons of Husbandry, that the Worthy Master be requested to telegraph to President Grant their earnest desire that he interpose his veto on the bill recently passed by the House of Representatives of the United States, making or confirming additional grants of lands to railroads in this State."

A memorial was adopted asking the legislature to regulate railroad tariffs. Resolutions were passed appointing a Grange agent for each railroad in the State; and organizing the entire Grange of Iowa into a company for the reduction of express rates.

The report of the Finance Committee, which was adopted, recommended that the Master should receive a salary of seven hundred dollars per annum, each member of the Executive Committee one hundred and fifty dollars, and the Treasurer two hundred dollars.

A motion was adopted that the memorial of the Grange in regard to railroad legislation be presented to the President of the Senate and the Speaker of the House.

At the meeting of the Executive Committee, there were appointed a State Agent, and an agent for each of the main lines of the East and West railroads in the State, whose duty it should be to attend to all railroad interests of the Granges, such as making freight rates, and seeing to prompt and safe shipment of all Grange freights.

A. B. Smedley, of Howard County, the newly-elected Master of the State Grange and Chairman of the Executive Committee, was appointed Grange Agent for the McGregor Western Railroad; E. R. Shankland, of Dubuque, agent for the Dubuque & Sioux City Railroad; Spencer Day, of Marshalltown, for the Chicago & North-western Railroad; O. H. P. Buchanan, of Mt. Pleasant, for the Burlington & Missouri River Railroad; J. D. Whitman, of Des Moines, as agent for the State at large, and also for the Chicago, Rock Island & Pacific Railroad.

SPEECH OF GRAND MASTER A. B. SMEDLEY.

At the festivities at Epworth, Iowa, on the seventeenth of September, 1873, Col. A. B. Smedley, one of the master spirits in this great Order, in an eloquent address, enunciated sentiments which can not fail to find an echo in the heart of every delver of the soil. The following extracts will show the tenor of his address:

* * * * * * *

The darkness, bigotry, and intolerance of feudal Europe drove to the bleak shores of New England a few souls, in whose hearts responded the divine element of freedom. What seemed to them darkness, privation, and trial was the birth of a new nation, which should be the home of the oppressed of all lands. Human slavery, relic of the dark ages, cursed our nation. The time came when slavery and freedom could not exist together; through trial, through

"Through Trial, Toil, and Blood."

toil and blood and anguish, slavery went down into the realms of the past, and freedom was triumphant. 'T is true that in a thousand homes are empty seats; 't is true that in a multitude of hearts there are vacant chambers; but God's purposes are accomplished, and the stain that for so long had darkened our fair nation's fame was effaced, and we began to say we were a nation of freemen.

But we had scarcely begun to congratulate ourselves on our success when a new enemy appeared. Circumstances growing partly out of a long and terrible war, and partly from other causes, had led to the creation of immense and powerful corporations, which threatened the safety, prosperity, and happiness of the people. Thoughtful men began to be troubled, and to look with painful anxiety as to the probable result of a condition which threatened to usurp the government, which destroyed confidence in our judiciary, and which held in their hands the prosperity of all industrial and producing classes. The national banks, although created to meet the exigency of the darkest days of the war—the system designed by good men, and serving, for a time, a wise purpose—had become an enormous power, and one which, in the hands of designing men, might be used as an instrument of oppression. Our system of railroads, designed by the beneficent genius of good men, to bring vast and incalculable blessings to all—the capitalist and the laborer alike—had become a power beyond the control of the government, and an engine of unheard-of oppression. Here were new enemies. Here was an unhappy condition, and honest men began to look about for means of relief. It was seen that the whole agricultural interests of the country, more especially of the West, was made productive or unproductive, just as the whim or caprice of those who controlled these corporations led. The industry of a whole commonwealth might, and oftentimes was, made of just such a nature as they desired, and people were simply tools in their hands, with just such remuneration as they pleased to give them. Men came to see that it was only a question of time when these monopoly interests should be as absolute in their ownership of the agricultural and producing classes of the country as the nobles of Russia are of the serfs. We saw, too, that this evil was gaining in strength every day, and unless some means was found

Danger!

to check this dangerous and growing evil, absolute serfdom would be the result.

In casting about for some means of relief, various plans were devised. We, from time to time, heard of the Laborers' Unions of Europe, of the Internationals of France, and of late years we have been studying the old system of the freehold cities of Germany, with their perfect system of guilds and associations of labor, which all finally went down under the iron heel of despotism. While looking for light, while casting about for relief, there were rumors of a new organization, peculiarly American in its character, and one which was designed to unite together, in one common bond of brotherhood, the laboring and producing classes. This new organization was called the Patrons of Husbandry. Born of a great and almost terrible need, in obedience to the divine law of supply and demand, in our day and hour of need, this organization came to strengthen our hands, and to form a united interest from the Atlantic to the Pacific slope. I remember very distinctly the first time I read the preamble to the National Constitution of the National Grange. Volumes might be written and not more clearly express man's relation to his brother man, and to the Father.

* * * * * * * * *

I have sometimes been pained at the tenacity with which some members of our Order cling, with an absorbing purpose, to simply the pecuniary aspect of our work. Brothers, this is commendable, but it is not all. Our sons and daughters must be educated. Educated, not only in books, but in that broader education which takes in all of the human character. Nowhere can this be so well done as in the Grange room. Here the highest and broadest moral sentiments are taught, line upon line, and precept upon precept. The highest attributes of human character are here brought forward. Meanness and bitterness are rebuked, and the mind is expanded. Not alone, however, are our children educated in the Grange room. We ourselves are benefited. How many men and women are learning how business men do business, and the relations all sustain to the government and to commerce. When our Order has passed the elementary stages, and has become, so to speak, solidified, no class of people in our land will be as learned, as broad in their views, as farmers. I look for the time to come when from the farms and shops of Iowa will go forth men who will fill our executive and legislative halls; when intelligence will become so broad and general that it will be impossible for our judiciary to be corrupt; and when we shall cease to hear of venal legislators and corrupt public servants.

No experiment of modern times has been so important as the one under consideration. The farmers of this nation are on trial before the world. The question is now to be settled as to whether they are capable of self-government; as to whether they are competent to do business, and whether they are susceptible of a high condition of educational advancement. The experiment is now to be tried, practically, as to whether woman is competent to assume equal and like responsibilities with man; as to whether our wives, mothers, daughters, and friends shall work with us, joining hands in all life's duties.

Sisters and brothers, do we feel the importance of this trial? Are we fully aware of the importance of this experiment? Do we realize just what it means? That it means, upon the one hand, a servile, slavish, and secondary condition; on the other, manhood and womanhood in their highest and broadest sense? It means, on the one hand, comparative poverty; on the other, affluence. It means, on the one hand, ignorance; on the other, enlightenment. It means serfdom on the one hand, and freedom on the other. It means that our children shall be the future hewers of wood and drawers of water in the nation, or American citizens, brave, strong, self-reliant, and competent for all places of trust and responsibility. It means that labor shall be a degradation, or that work shall be ennobled, elevated, and a badge of conferring honor. Again I say, do we fully realize the importance of this experiment? Do we take in all its power and significance?

* * * * * * * * *

Let us, then, with clean hands and pure hearts, consecrate all that is best and noblest in us, to the success of a work more patient and sublime in its character than any ever before undertaken. Let each lay upon the altar of this new Order whatever he or she may have of selfish ambition or of mercenary motive, and, joining hands, let us covenant that our best and highest thought and action shall be dedicated to the cause of justice and humanity. Let us pledge, each to the other, that we will labor faithfully, patiently, earnestly, and persistently to purify and lift up ourselves, State and Nation being ever in mind. Let us remember that if we would triumph in the unequal conflict upon which we now enter, we must fear God, obey our laws, maintain our honors, not forgetting that a good matron, as well as a good husbandman, has taken solemn obligations and assumed grave responsibilities. And now may the Great Master of the universe bless us in our labor, and sustain and abide with us, both here and when our work here is finished.

CHAPTER XXII.

THE KANSAS FARMERS' CO-OPERATIVE ASSOCIATION.

THE STATE CONVENTION AT TOPEKA.

On the 26th of March, 1873, a mass convention of the farmers of Kansas was held at Topeka, at which was formed the now powerful organization known as the "Farmers' Co-operative Association of the State of Kansas." The meeting originated with the Manhattan Farmers' Club, which passed resolutions requesting the Secretary of the State Board of Agriculture, Mr. Alfred Gray, to call a State Convention, to be composed of delegates from Farmers' Clubs. This was done, and, subsequently, the call was enlarged so as to include Farmers' Unions, Granges, and other similar organizations.

While the formal initiatory business of the Convention was being transacted, Mr. Henry Bronson, Dr. Lawrence, and Mr. Van Winkle delivered addresses on the incidents of taxation, and farmers' grievances generally. The speaker first mentioned declared that it was because of a false financial system, and a false political system no longer bearable, saddled on the people, that the farmers have come here to see if they can not be righted. It is useless to say they can do nothing; for they have the votes and the power, though want of organization has kept them from accomplishing these reforms. Just so soon as organization is effected they will be as strong as they are now weak. It matters not whether this be done by Farmers' Unions or by the Patrons of Husbandry, and he would never quarrel with the means that accomplished these ends, and desired all to work with the means and tools that suited best; but there should be no antagonism. They had strong powers to combat, and when they met them in fight should be confident that they were strong enough to cope with the enemy. He counseled them to avoid divisions, and believed that there was a working force in the land that would culminate in a strength sufficient to make their efforts a success.

State Seal of Kansas.

The verification of credentials having been concluded, the Committee on Organization recommended the following named gentlemen:

Hon. John Davis for President; Jonathan Weaver and Alfred Taylor for Vice-Presidents; J. K. Hudson for Secretary; and J. T. Stevens, Assistant Secretary. The President-elect briefly thanked the Convention, and business was proceeded with.

After adopting a resolution limiting speeches to ten minutes, a committee was appointed to draft a constitution for a permanent organization. In the course of the discussion which preceded this action, Governor Robinson said that the only benefit which the farmer could hope for was by well-considered organization. The old question of demand and supply was obsolete and played out; none of the great interests were using it. It was, instead, the new word of combination which determines the price at which iron and other commodities are sold from New York to San Francisco. All classes, whether they be mechanics, engineers, shoemakers, or boot-blacks, combine and fix the price for their different products or labor. We have parallel lines of railroad, but they combine and do not compete. If the poor farmers were to combine and withhold their hands, the people would perish. There was but one course for the farmer to pursue, and he would not give one fig for any thing they would accomplish unless they adopted it. He advocated county and State organizations, auxiliary to a National one, all to be in correspondence with headquarters; and that the National Directory should set the price for farm products in our cities; who should find out all the statistics of interest to the farmer, average of grain and cost, and have an intelligent information of the prices determined in all our great cities. The State organizations should, within their limits, gather up such statistics and fix prices, and county societies should do the same. The farmer would then handle the same weapons, and be on the same footing with dealers in iron, wool, and cotton. He urged organization, and when organized, to correspond with headquarters, and agree to abide in good faith with the Board of Directory as to the movement of grain and prices. We can then obtain laws, regulate railroads and the price of every commodity to be bought by the farmer. They will give it up when this state of affairs occurs. While he did not advise any political action, his advice was to vote for the known friends of the farmer, wherever they might be found, and they would soon find out that they had plenty of friends. He hoped that some steps would be taken by the Convention in the right direction.

RESOLUTIONS AND DEBATE THEREON.

Various resolutions were submitted and referred to a committee, which, subsequently, reported the following:

Resolved, That organization is the great want of the producing classes at the present time, and we recommend every farmer in the State to become a member of some Farmers' Club, Grange of the Patrons of Husbandry, or other local organization.

Resolved, That the taxes assessed and charged upon the people, both by national, State, and local governments, are oppressive and unjust, and vast sums of money are collected far beyond the needs of an economical administration of government.

Resolved, That we respectfully request our Senators and Representatives in Congress to vote for, and secure, an amendment to the tariff laws of the United States, so that salt and lumber shall be placed on the free list, and that there shall be made a material reduction of the duty on iron, and that such articles as do not pay the cost of collection be also placed on the free list.

Resolved, That we demand that the Legislature of our State shall pass a law limiting railroad freights and fares to a just and fair sum, and that unjust discriminations against local freights be prohibited.

Resolved, That the act passed by the last Legislature, exempting bonds, notes, mortgages, and judgments from taxation, is unjust, oppressive, and a palpable violation of our State constitution, and we call upon all assessors and the county boards to see that said securities are taxed at their fair value.

A debate ensued on the first resolution. Mr. Lines objected to the Granges on the ground of their secrecy feature, and moved that the words "Granges of Patrons of Husbandry" be stricken out. After a discussion, in which it appeared that Mr. Lines was almost alone in his views, the amendment was withdrawn, and the orginal resolution was afterward carried. The second resolution was passed unanimously.

On the tariff resolution a lively discussion took place, in which statistics were given by Major Miller, of the State Agricultural College, showing that the tariff on iron did not account for the difference in the price of that article in the United States and England. Mr. Christopher gave some details about the Syracuse salt ring, and their manner of crowding out competition. Mr. Van Winkle moved to amend the resolution by leaving out salt and iron. The amendment was lost, and the resolution carried.

When the resolution on railroad freights came on for consideration, Mr. Lines moved, as a substitute:

That we earnestly request the Legislature of our State, at its next session, to enact a law regulating freights and fares upon our railroads upon a basis of justice; and that we further request our members in Congress to urge the favorable action of that body, where the same power exists beyond all doubt, to the same end, and, if need be, to construct national highways at the expense of the government.

After a discussion, this was adopted instead of the original resolution.

The other resolutions, after discussion, were adopted.

CONSTITUTION, BY-LAWS, AND OFFICERS.

The report of the Committee on Permanent Organization was then taken up. It embodied a Preamble and Constitution, as follows:

PREAMBLE.

As a means of obtaining a more perfect uniformity of action among the farmers of the State, in order that we may secure a more equal division of the profits arising from the different vocations of life, of diminishing the unreasonable transportation tariff now charged by railroad companies, and of breaking down monopolies of every character, we, whose names are hereto subscribed, do pledge ourselves to sustain the following Constitution and By-Laws:

CONSTITUTION OF THE FARMERS' CO-OPERATIVE ASSOCIATION OF THE STATE OF KANSAS.

ARTICLE I. This Association shall be called the Farmers' Co-operative Association of the State of Kansas.

ART. II. The objects of this Association shall be the collection of statistics relative to the products of the State, their amount, cost, and value; to assist the farmers in securing just compensation for their labor; to co-operate with similar organizations in other States in procuring cheap transportation and remunerative prices for surplus products, and act generally in the interest of the producing class.

ART. III. The officers of this Association shall be elected annually by ballot, and shall consist of a President, Vice-President, Secretary, Treasurer, and an Executive Committee of five, who, with the President, Vice-President, Secretary, and Treasurer, shall constitute a Board of Directors. It shall be the duty of the several officers to discharge the duties usually devolving upon such officers respectively.

ART. IV. The Secretary, in addition to recording the proceedings of the Association and Board of Directors, shall conduct a correspondence with auxiliary associations of whatever name, transmit to them all information of interest to farmers, and perform such other duties as the Association or Directors may require.

ART. V. The Board of Directors shall have the general supervision of the interests of the Association, and provide for carrying into effect the provisions of Article II of this Constitution.

ART. VI. The terms of office after the first shall be one year, or until their successors are elected, and the annual meeting and election shall be held on the second Tuesday in January of each year.

ART. VII. Any county, township, or district organization in this State, whether called Union, Grange, Club, or other name, who shall forward to the Treasurer the sum of five dollars for each county society, and one dollar for all other local societies, and such assessments as shall be made, from time to time, by the Executive Committee for the benefit of the Association, whose Secretary shall correspond with the Secretary of this Association, and whose members shall co-operate in its general objects, may become auxiliary to this Association and be entitled to all its benefits.

ART. VIII. Each representative district shall be entitled to send two delegates to all meetings of the Association. Such delegates to be elected by all the auxiliary farmers' organizations in such district.

ART. IX. The Directors shall have power to call delegate conventions whenever they shall deem it expedient.

ART. X. All claims and accounts shall be audited by the Board of Directors, and no money shall be paid out of the treasury except upon its order.

ART. XI. This constitution may be altered or amended at any regular meeting of this Association by a vote of two-thirds of the members present.

The same Committee reported the following resolutions, which were adopted:

Resolved, That the act relating to the collection of statistics and industries, approved March 6, 1873, and an act relating to District and County Agricultural Societies and Farmers' Clubs, approved March 6, 1873, meet with the approval of this Convention, so far as they go in the accomplishment of the objects sought by this Convention.

Resolved, That the Farmers' Co-operative Association of the State of Kansas co-operate with the State Board of Agriculture, and the State organization of the Patrons of Husbandry.

After discussion, the report and Constitution were adopted.

The Convention proceeded to the election of officers, with the following result:

John Davis, of Riley Co., President; J. K. Hudson, of Wyandotte, Vice-President; H. Bronson, of Douglas, Treasurer; Alfred Gray, Secretary and Corresponding Secretary. Directors—T. B. Smith, of Douglas; John Mings, of Osage; O. W. Bill, of Riley; A. H. Grass, of Montgomery; and J. S. Van Winkle, of Leavenworth.

LOCAL ORGANIZATIONS, ETC.

Mr. Alfred Gray was elected Corresponding Agent to communicate with the principal manufacturers of agricultural implements, and dealers in the same, with a view to obtaining low rates of purchase, and also to make application for reduced rates of transportation on all the different railroads, and forward a statement of advantages obtained monthly to each of the different organizations of farmers within the State.

Mr. Coleman, of Douglas, offered the following resolution, which was adopted:

Resolved, That it is the sense of this Convention that the farmers of Kansas, while they are ready to denounce in unmeasured terms every monopoly that strikes at their interests in the shape of robbery and oppression, are equally ready to admit any and all wrongs and errors of their own that have brought them into the dilemma which all complain of to-day.

Various other resolutions were adopted, among others one recommending a form of constitution for use by the local organizations of Kansas, as follows, after passing which the Convention adjourned *sine die:*

PREAMBLE.

We, the undersigned, farmers of ——— Township, ——— County, Kansas, and vicinity, for the better protection and further advancement of our interests, hereby form ourselves into an organization; and for the government of the Association we adopt the following Constitution:

CONSTITUTION.

ARTICLE I. This organization shall be known as ———

ART. II. Section 1. The officers of the organization shall consist of a President, Vice-President, Secretary, and Treasurer.

Sec. 2. The President shall preside at all meetings of the Association, preserve order, give the casting vote in case of a tie, call special meetings when deemed necessary, and perform all other duties belonging to his office.

Sec. 3. The Vice-President shall preside in the absence of the President, and shall perform all the duties of that officer.

Sec. 4. The Secretary shall keep correct minutes of the proceedings of the organization, and record the same in a book provided for that purpose. He shall attest all orders signed by the President, sign membership cards, and perform all other duties pertaining to the office of Secretary.

Sec. 5. The Treasurer shall receive all moneys paid into the organization, and pay out the same upon the order of the President, attested by the Secretary, and may be required to give such security as the organization may deem necessary.

Art. III. Sec. 1. No person shall become a member of this organization unless he is a farmer, or is practically interested in farming.

Sec. 2. Every member of this organization shall subscribe to the Constitution, and abide by the decisions of the Association.

Art. IV. This Constitution may be amended on one week's notice in writing, by a two-thirds vote of the members present.

CHAPTER XXIII.

THE SPRINGFIELD (ILLINOIS) CONVENTION.

GROWTH OF THE MOVEMENT AND CALL OF THE CONVENTION.

Immediately after its organization, as narrated in Chapter XX, the Illinois State Farmers' Association set itself vigorously to work reorganizing the existing local Societies and inaugurating new ones; and within three months over a thousand organizations had been perfected in the State, in response to the appeal made from Bloomington. Early in the following Spring, the Legislature of Illinois being then in session, it was considered desirable that another combined effort should be made, for the purpose of impressing upon the legislature the earnestness of the movement, and the fact that the people were determined that railroad matters should be legislated upon both speedily and effectually. A call was therefore made for a State Convention, to be held at Springfield, Illinois.

Pursuant to this call, a gathering of delegates met April 2, 1873, more than three hundred in number, and representing Farmers' Associations in seventy-two counties. They were called to order by the President of the State Association, Mr. Flagg, who briefly stated the object for which they had met. After an informal debate touching various minor subjects, a permanent organization was affected as follows: President, D. W. Dame, of Carroll Co.; Vice-Presidents—State at large, W. C. Flagg, of Madison, and E. Smith, of Bureau, with an additional Vice-President from each congressional district, as follows: James Creed, Marion; S. S. Morgan, Livingston; W. E. Magill, Mason; T. McD. Richards, McHenry; C. W. Marsh, DeKalb; John D. Armstrong, LaSalle; A. N. Harris, Stark; J. H. Pickrell, Macon; A. M. Hulling, Ford; Gen. W. B. Anderson, Jefferson; H. W. Rincker, Shelby; Charles Snoad, Will; Thomas Hendrickson, Vermillion; W. E. Alcorn, Richland; D. Gore, Macoupin, R. N. Coffeen, Champaign; T. Butterworth, Adams; Joseph B. Barger, Gallatin; Gen. J. McConnell, Sangamon. Secretaries, S. P. Tufts, Marion; L. R. Morris, Macon.

GOV. BEVERIDGE ON THE MOVEMENT.

Gov. Beveridge, of Illinois, addressed the meeting at considerable length. In the course of his speech he said:

"I recognize the fact that the producing interest is the grandest and noblest interest asking for our protection, our fostering, and our care. A large proportion of the people of this State are engaged in production; in cultivating the soil, in bringing out from our fertile prairie soil the richness placed there by the Creator; and it will always be the case in this State that the farming interest will be the largest interest in the State, made so by nature. But we can't get along without other interests. We can not well get along without the professional interests, and yet I know we sometimes think that lawyers do not amount to much; but if lawyers do not amount to much, when we get sick we like to have the doctor; and if we do not care much about Sunday, when we are about to die we like to have a preacher. Now these professional interests must be preserved; the manufacturing interests must not be crippled; the commercial interest must not be crippled; and the transportation, or railroad interest must not be abolished. Now, as a producing class, we can not get along without the railroads. They are two great interests that must subserve each other. Take away from the State the railroads of the State, and where will the producing interests go to? On the other hand, the railroad interests can not get along without the producing interests. Let every farmer in this State cease producing—let him go to other States and other countries; let them cease cultivating the soil, and what interests would the railroads have in occupying their lines of track over the prairies? These two interests must go together, hand in hand, working for each other's good and each other's benefit.

Now, having said so much, I recognize this fact, that the railroad interests of this State, or the railroads of this State, are exacting from the producing class, and from the commercial, the professional, and the manufacturing classes, extortionate rates for passenger and

"Other Interests Also."

freight tariffs. I recognize the fact that this great interest, wielding a capital of nearly two hundred and fifty million dollars, if not more, as a unit readily combining all its powers and all its forces, is exacting of the people of this State too much money—making too many discriminations. Then, what I wish to say to this convention, gentlemen, is, that when you make this war upon railroads, do not make it upon them to abolish them, but make your war to bring them within subjection of the legislature, of the law of the land. (Cheers, and cries of "That's the talk.")

"There is thrust in our faces, from time to time, the Dartmouth College decision; there is thrust in our faces the argument that the granting of charters to these corporations is a contract between the people of the State and the corporations, in pursuance of the Constitution of the United States, and can not be impaired. Well, now, it may be so; I can not tell—neither can you tell—what our courts will hold to; but I predict that the time is coming, and I want you to be patient—it won't come this afternoon, it won't come next week, it won't come this year, it won't, perhaps, in five years, it may not come, perhaps, until after a struggle of a quarter of a century, but the time is coming, if you are as determined and persistent in your efforts as you are enthusiastic to-day, and have been, when public opinion will mould the character of our courts, and compel them to reverse that decision in the Dartmouth College case. I say that the time is coming when our courts will not hold that these charters are a contract between the people of the State and the corporations, but, they will hold that they are, as in my opinion, but mere grants of power which enable them to contract in getting the road-bed, enable them to contract in furnishing means of transportation, enable them to contract with you in carrying your freight and your person; and that the amount of power can and must be controlled by the legislature giving that power. I say the time is coming when our courts will hold that the creature is not greater than the Creator; that the corporations created by law are not greater than the legislature that created them; that these corporations, called in one sense persons, are not more sacred in their vested rights than are the vested rights of you or me, of the rights given me by the great God himself."

Gov. Beveridge then explained the difficulties with which legislation on the subject of regulating railroads was beset, stating that many persons who imagine they could settle the whole question in half a day would find, on consideration, that it was a most difficult question.

GOV. PALMER ON RAILWAY MONOPOLIES.

Ex-Governor Palmer followed in a strong speech. He said:

* * * * * * * * *

"The germ of this whole subject of vested rights is the Dartmouth College case. The State never made a being more lofty than the being that God makes, and no corporation can have rights superior to the rights of the citizens. The roads have a right to take your lands, for you gave it to them; but they have no right to go beyond the limits of reason and justice in making their charges for carrying freights and passengers. The principles of free government prohibit the right to do injustice to the people. No government can be superior to the people themselves, and when the people of Illinois determine that they will not submit to exactions, they will begin to cease. When it is understood that men will not submit to them their liberties are safe, and then only. Laws must be submitted to and obeyed, so long as they are in force. But when laws do not accomplish that for which they were framed they should be changed. You must look at this railway question from a radical stand-point, and must take the position that whatever it is necessary to do you will do. You have declared railways to be highways; that they are under the control of the legislature, and that their officers are public agents. The managers of these railways are in Wall Street, New York, and your troubles begin there among the jobbers in these stocks. There, and in other large cities, railway stocks are personal property, and pass from hand to hand, and you never know who owns them. They are the subjects upon which men gamble. Now, you should repeal the laws that make them personal property, and have them so managed that you would know of their transfers and who owned the stocks. You can not, as it now is, get at the real managers of these western railways. I would sweep out of existence the laws by which these stocks are made personal property. I would fix it so the stock could not be watered. Who knows what the roads in this State cost? No one except railway men, for the stocks are watered, and watered to death. I would declare these railways to be highways, and allow farmers and others to put cars upon these tracks, and compete with the railway companies in their own business, and when this can be done, much will have been accomplished. We are but in the infancy of this business, and men are now living who will see railways multiplied indefinitely, and you must study this thing with a view to getting at what is to be. You remember, in Jackson's time, how men shook at the idea of having a corporation control thirty-six millions! Why, there are men here who can remember how that idea made men shake. What do you see now? Men who control untold millions to corrupt the people. A man in Pennsylvania who can raise the price of every

A Model Monopolist.

thing that you raise, for his own benefit and prosperity, keeps whispering, 'Do n't interfere with vested rights.'"

THE RESOLUTIONS.

A resolution was offered and passed, condemning the back-pay steal, and censuring the President for signing the bill. The committee appointed to draft resolutions submitted the following:

Resolved, By the Farmers of Illinois in Mass Meeting Assembled, That all chartered monopolies, not regulated and controlled by law, have proved in that respect detrimental to the public prosperity, corrupting in their management, and dangerous to republican institutions.

Resolved, That the railways of the world, except in those countries where they have been held under the strict regulation and supervision of the government, have proved themselves arbitrary, extortionate, and as opposed to free institutions and free commerce between States as were the feudal barons of the middle ages.

Resolved, That we hold, declare, and resolve that this despotism, which defies our laws, plunders our shippers, impoverishes our people, and corrupts our government, shall be subdued and made to subserve the public interest at whatever cost.

Resolved, That we believe the State did not and could not confer any of its sovereign power upon any corporation, and that now is the most favorable time to settle the question, so that it may never be hereafter misunderstood that a State can not create a corporation it can not thereafter control.

Resolved, That in view of the present extortions, we look with alarm upon the future of an interest which can combine in the hands of a few men a capital of nearly $250,000,000, and we believe it essential to the prosperity of all classes that this contest continue until these corporations acknowledge the supremacy of law.

Resolved, That we regard it as the undoubted power, and the imperative duty of the legislature, to pass laws fixing reasonable maximum rates for freight and passengers, without classification of roads, and that we urge upon our General Assembly the passage of such laws.

Resolved, That the existing statute, providing for a classification of railroads with a view to adjusting a tariff of charges according to the gross amount of earnings, is a delusion and a snare, and is so framed that the railroads are able to classify themselves, and that it ought to be carefully modified or repealed.

Resolved, That inasmuch as the Supreme Court has clearly pointed out the way to reach unjust discriminations made by the railroads of this State, we can see no reason for delay on the part of the Legislature in enacting the necessary laws on the subject, and we urge immediate action thereon.

Resolved, That we urge the passage of a bill enforcing the principle that railroads are public highways, and requiring railroads to make connections with all roads whose tracks meet or cross their own, and to receive and transmit cars and trains offered over their roads at reasonable maximum rates, whether offered at such crossings, or at stations along their roads, and empowering the making of connections by municipal corporations for that purpose, and for the public use.

Resolved, That we heartily indorse the action of the General Assembly looking to the enforcement of the performance of their duties by monopolies as common carriers; and that, in addition thereto, we believe that railroads should be required to carry all freight and passengers offered from the country through which they pass, and not permitted to limit the amount of their business and destroy its natural increase.

Resolved, That the constitution and laws of Illinois are as binding upon railroad corporations as upon the citizens, and that the State must require obedience to the law from all alike, whether the same be deemed constitutional or not by the parties affected, until repealed or declared unconstitutional.

Resolved, That we indorse most fully the action of those who tender legal rates of fare upon the railroads, and refuse to pay more; and that it is the duty of the Legislature to provide by law for the defense by the State of Illinois of suits commenced, or that hereafter may be commenced, by railroad companies against individuals who have in good faith insisted, or hereafter may insist, upon the right to ride on railroads at legal rates.

Resolved, That the presentation of railroad passes to our legislators, whatever may be the spirit and intent with which they are accepted, are demoralizing in their influence; and we look to our

Legislature, now in session, to rise above personal considerations of pecuniary interest or convenience, and to pass a law making it a misdemeanor for any Senator, or other State or county officers, to accept any railroad pass, knowing, as we do, that the people look upon the acceptance of these passes with decided and almost universal disapprobation.

* * * * * * * *

WHEREAS, The Constitution of 1848, Article X, prohibits the Legislature from granting special railroad charters in the following words: "And corporations not possessing banking powers or privileges, may be formed under general law, but shall not be created by special acts, except for municipal purposes; and in cases where, in the judgment of the General Assembly, the objects of the corporation can not be attained under general laws," therefore,

Resolved, That it is extremely doubtful whether any railroad charter granted since April 1, 1848, by the Legislature of Illinois is of any validity, and that the vested rights of railroad monopolies in this State exist only by assumption of the monopolies and the sufferance of the people.

* * * * * * * *

WHEREAS, The Constitution of 1870, Article XI, Section 13, prohibits any railroad company from issuing watered stock, in these words: "No railroad corporation shall issue any stock or bonds except for money, labor, or property actually received and applied to the purposes for which such corporation was created; and all stock, dividends, and other fictitious increase of the capital, stock, or indebtedness of any such corporation shall be void. The capital stock of no railroad corporation shall be increased for any purpose, except upon giving sixty days' public notice in such manner as may be provided by law;" and,

WHEREAS, This article of the Constitution has probably been violated by nearly all the railroad companies in the State; therefore,

Resolved, That it is the duty of the Railroad Commissioners to look carefully into this matter, and to commence proceedings in all clear cases by *quo warranto*, or otherwise, against all railroad companies which have disregarded this important provision of the organic law of the State.

Resolved, That we regard the improvement of the Illinois River as not sectional, but of great importance; and we request the members of the House of Representatives to vote for the bill now pending for the improvement of that river, as it will give our State absolutely into the hands of the people.

Resolved, That we demand of Congress a repeal of all laws preventing the competition of small vessels, which may choose to engage in the carrying trade on our inland lakes between ports in the United States, without regard to nationality.

Resolved, That we are in favor of the immediate repeal of the protective duties on iron, steel, lumber, and all materials which enter into the construction of railroad cars, steamships, sailing vessels, agricultural implements, etc., and that we urge upon Congress immediate action for this purpose, that cheap railroads and cheap ships are necessary to cheap freights; and that we invite the railroad companies to co-operate with us to that end.

DIVIDED COUNSELS.

In the debate which arose upon the resolutions, it became apparent that the friends of free trade and of protection were about equally represented. A long discussion of a disorderly character took place, and various expedients were resorted to for the purpose of impeding action. One delegate said that party wire-pullers were at work to use the Convention to forward local improvements, and for political purposes. Finally, the resolutions were taken separately, and passed unanimously, until the question of passes to legislators and other government officers came up. This brought on an excited debate. It was passed, however, with an addition that the Legislature was requested to enact a law restricting members' pay to the time when actually in service. The resolution relating to the Illinois River was laid on the table amid much excitement. The tariff resolution was objected to, as being a side issue and not connected with the objects of the Convention. The meeting seemed about equally divided, but the chairman declared the resolution carried.

Additional resolutions were adopted, as follows: Requesting the Legislature to pass a railroad law before it adjourned; that the practice of legislators voting on questions on which they are directly interested, is contrary to public morality; that it is one of the necessary measures of railroad reform that the laws that make the stocks of railroad corporations personal property, be repealed, and the law so amended as to withdraw such stock from speculation, and give to them the permanency and certainty of ownership of the railroads themselves; demanding that railroads be no longer assessed taxes at less than one-tenth of their value; and recommending that farmers keep a "farm expenses" account, so that the actual cost of production may be ascertained and made public. Some minor work closed the first day's proceedings.

CONCERNING RECONSIDERATION.

On reassembling, it appeared that there were but seventy-five delegates present, the remainder of those present on the first day having gone home, considering the main business of the Convention over. The advocates of the Illinois River improvement made an effort to revive the resolution relating thereto, but failed.

Senator Castle delivered a talented address, in which he enlarged upon the power of the railroads, and said that the question to be settled first was, "Do the railroads control the State, or does the State control the railroads?" Let the aims be single until these corporations acknowledge the supremacy of the law, and yield obedience thereto.

Mr. S. M. Smith said the tariff resolution was a bone of

contention, and ought not to have been introduced. The Convention should have confined itself to the railroad question, and left out all disturbing issues. He ended by moving that the vote by which the tariff resolution was adopted be reconsidered. It was also moved to reconsider the resolution censuring the President. It was decided that the consideration of the two resolutions be postponed, and the Convention adjourned.

CHAPTER XXIV.

THE TEST CASE ON THE UNCONSTITUTIONAL ILLINOIS RAILROAD LAW.

THE McLEAN COUNTY TEST CASE.

In obedience to the demand for action regulating railroads and preventing unjust discriminations, the Legislature of Illinois, in April, 1871, passed a bill entitled "An Act to prevent unjust discriminations and extortions in the rates to be charged by the different railroads in this State for the transportation of freight on said roads." This act declared that no railroad corporation should charge for the transportation of property on its road, for any distance, the same, nor any larger or greater amount, as toll or compensation, than was at the same time charged or collected for the transportation of similar quantities of the same class of property over a greater distance upon the same road, nor should any railroad corporation charge or collect for the transportation of property over any portion of its road, a greater amount as toll or compensation than should be charged or collected by it for the transportation of similar quantities of property of the same class over any other portion of its road of equal distance; and that different charges for receiving, handling, and delivering freight at different points should not be made. The act further provided that any willful violation of its provisions should be deemed a forfeiture of the franchises of the corporation offending, and that, for such cause, it might be proceeded against by information in the nature of a *quo warranto*, to judgment of ouster and final execution.

Doubts having been expressed of the validity of this law, it was determined to institute a test case. This was accordingly done, information being laid by the railroad and warehouse commissioners in the Circuit Court of McLean County, in the name of the people of Illinois against the Chicago and Alton Railroad Company. The information charged that said company had repeatedly charged for transporting lumber from Chicago to Lexington, a distance of one hundred and ten miles, the sum of five dollars and sixty-five cents per one thousand feet, while, at the same time, it had only charged for the transportation of like lumber from Chicago to Bloomington, a distance of one hundred and twenty-six miles, the sum of five dollars per thousand feet. These acts, the information alleged, had forfeited the charter of the Company.

The Company admitted the facts, and stated that the rates to Bloomington were unreasonably low, but no one except the Company was injured thereby; and that said charges were adopted in order to compete with the Illinois Central Railroad Company, and to protect the customers of appellant from injury, by a reduction of rates from Chicago to Bloomington on the Illinois Central Railroad. In short, the company insisted that, although the acts charged against them were in contravention of the act of April, 1871, still such charges were lawful, for the reason that the said act was in violation of the Constitution of the State, and also of that of the United States.

JUDGE TIPTON'S DECISION.

The case was heard before Judge Tipton, who gave judgment against the company. Judge Tipton delivered an elaborate opinion, in which he considered fully the character of the laws under which the suit was brought, and cited numerous authorities to prove that corporations have no rights that can be maintained against the welfare of the people, and that railroad companies can not be so hedged about by special charters that they can override and oppose the public by unjust discriminations and extortionate charges. He said:

"The very object of granting charters to railroad companies by the State, was that the people should have the right of transportation of the products of the country to and from the great centers of trade, without unjust discrimination. The particular method by which this object should be attained rests only in the discretion of the legislature. If it has the power to legislate on the subject at all, its legislation must control, whether the courts deem the provisions wise or unwise. The legislature has determined that discrimination between communities—that is, a greater charge for a less distance over the same road—is unjust and hurtful to the interests of the people at large.

"The effect of such discrimination is to transfer, by artificial means, the natural advantages possessed by one community to another less favorably situated. To allow this is to subordinate the general interests of the public to the real or supposed advantage of the particular railroad corporation by whose action the unnatural effect is produced, and would be to abandon the right and duty of the legislature to afford by law equal protection to all citizens of the State. By former reasoning it will be seen that railroad corporations do not hold their property and franchises by a higher tenure than the citizen holds his farm or other property. * * * * *

"Railways are improved public highways, and therefore can be constructed by the aid of the right of eminent domain; and the corporations so created are public agents, created for the practical administration of the public property (right of way) put into their hands as such agents, to be administered to subserve public interests.

"The lines of railways in this State are public highways. Their use is for the people at large, for travelers and shippers. They are compelled, as before stated, to receive and transport passengers and freight according to the usage of the corporations. The public have an easement over the roads, the right to which, in its proper exercise, is as sacred as the right of individual property, or the right

The Highway of Civilization.

of the corporation to collect tolls or compensation. The right to the use resides in the public, and is above the control of the corporation. In the very act of fixing tolls or rates, the corporations are only exercising the power delegated to them as public agents, in the administration of the public property, which is put into their hands by the exercise of the highest power of sovereignty. The legislature evidently has power to protect the public right in the use of easement, and to protect it in the enjoyment of it, at reasonable rates and without discrimination; as much right to enforce such protection as the corporation has to assert its claim to the right of way, and to exact tolls for the use of it. The road, *sub-modo*, with all its rolling stock, buildings, fixtures, machine shops, and other property pertaining to it, is private property, owned and operated by the corporation for the mutual benefit of the public and the corporation. The principles of the common law, and their charters accepted by them, and which clothe them with such ample powers, impose duties on them to the public, which they must discharge; and the manner of enforcing a faithful performance of these duties is within the legislative power of the State. The provision in defendant's charter, authorizing the President and Directors to fix the rates of compensation for the transportation of persons and property does not change the legal effect from what it would have been had no such provision been contained in the charter."

THE THREE-CENT-A-MILE WAR.

Thus the first game in the great contest with monopolies must be scored to the people. The railroad company immediately appealed to the Supreme Court of Illinois. The more hot-headed of the farmers imagined that victory was permanently secured, and, incited by demagogues who wished to gain notoriety, boarded trains *en masse*, and insisted on riding for three cents a mile, the maximum fixed by the law. In some cases they gained their ends, but in others ludicrous incidents occurred. A party of farmers, *en route* for the second Bloomington Convention, boarded a train and tendered their three cents, whereupon the train was shunted to a side-track, while an overwhelming force of the company's employees were sent for. Meantime, the farmers employed their enforced leisure in singing, and having a good time generally. A large force of brakemen and laborers coming up, the farmers capitulated at discretion, and paid the extra fare. On arriving at the scene of the

Convention, where news of the occurrence had preceded them, they were met by a band of music, and were the lions of the day.

Other cases were less creditable to the persons concerned. Some hotspurs, having tendered the fare fixed by law, refused either to be ejected from the train, or to pay the extra money, producing revolvers and knives in support of the legality of their proceedings. It is due to the farmers to say that this high-handed way of settling the difficulty was almost unanimously condemned. It was universally conceded among all intelligent men that riding for three cents a mile, behind a knife or revolver, proved nothing. One case of this sort went to trial. An Illinois Central Railroad conductor was arrested and fined for putting a farmer off his train who would not "come down" with more than three cents. The decision was against the company, which again immediately appealed. Of course, it went by the board, when the law under which it was made was, shortly afterward, declared unconstitutional.

THE ARGUMENT ON THE APPEAL.

The appeal of the Chicago & Alton Railroad Company from Judge Tipton's decision came before the Supreme Court of Illinois in the January term of 1873. The case for the appellant (the company) was prepared with great ability, and set forth the reasons why the Illinois law was unconstitutional, basing them upon the following facts:

1st. The company was especially authorized by law to charge such rates of toll as its President and Directors should from time to time establish.

2d. The said authority to charge toll was a contract between the State and the appellant; in support of which the famous Dartmouth College decision was principally relied on.

3d. Charging a greater compensation for transporting persons and property a shorter distance than for a longer one is not necessarily unreasonable or an unjust discrimination. In support of this, it was alleged that in the case in dispute the toll to Lexington was reasonable, and that the toll to Bloomington was too low, but that no one was injured thereby save the company. Examples were given of many cases before the English courts where companies had been upheld in similar cases.

4th. The judicial department of the government has the sole authority to determine between the public and the appellant what rates are reasonable and what are unreasonable, and what discriminations are just and what are unjust.

5th. The power of the General Assembly to pass all such laws as are necessary to promote the health, safety, morals, good order, and general welfare of the inhabitants of the State, did not authorize the passage of the Act of April 7, 1871.

DECISION OF THE SUPREME COURT—THE LAW UNCONSTITUTIONAL.

In rendering its decision, the Supreme Court first quoted from the constitution of the State of Illinois, as follows:

> "The General Assembly shall pass laws to correct abuses and prevent unjust discrimination and extortion in the rate of freight and passenger tariffs on the different roads in this State, and enforce such laws by adequate penalties, to the extent, if necessary for that purpose, of forfeiture of their property and franchises." Art. XI., Sec. 15.

The court argued that the discrimination forbidden by the common law, and by the constitutional enactment in accordance therewith, was against *unjust* discrimination, while the law under consideration was directed against all discriminations, whether they could be shown to be unjust or not. The decision continues:

This provision, expressly directing the Legislature to pass laws to prevent *unjust* discrimination, is a recognition of the palpable fact that there may be discriminations which are not unjust, and by implication it restrains the power of the Legislature to a prohibition of those which are unjust. That was undoubtedly the object of the Legislature in passing the existing law. This is clearly shown by its title. But the act itself goes further. It forbids any discrimination whatever, under any circumstances whatever, and whether just or unjust, in the charges for transporting the same classes of freight over equal distances, even though moving in opposite directions, and does not permit the companies to show that the discrimination is not unjust. The mere proof of the discrimination makes out a case against the railway companies, which they are not allowed to meet by evidence showing the reason or propriety of the discrimination, and then, upon this sort of *ex-parte* trial, imposes as a penalty for the offense a forfeiture of the franchise, which would often be equivalent to a fine of millions of dollars. The object of the law is commendable, but such a proceeding, to be followed by such a penalty for the first offense, can not be sustained. It could only have been authorized through the inadvertence of the Legislature. The law as it now stands makes an offense out of an act which might be shown not to be an offense, but an exercise of a wise discretion really beneficial to the people of the State; and, while debarring the companies from all right of explanation, confiscates their franchises upon the first conviction. The Legislature can not raise a conclusive presumption of guilt against a natural person from any act that may be innocent in itself, taking from him the privilege of showing the actual innocence or propriety of the act, and confiscating his property as a penalty for the supposed offense. Those provisions of our constitution which forbid the deprivation of life, liberty, or property, except by due process of law, and which guarantee the right of trial by jury "as heretofore enjoyed," and the right in all criminal prosecutions to appear and defend in person and by counsel, would all be violated by such a law. These provisions, it is true, are designed to apply only to natural persons; but artificial persons must be permitted to invoke the spirit of justice which prompted them, so far as may be necessary to protect their property and franchises against the operation of a law that substantially condemns without a trial.

* * * * * * *

The opinion of the court is, that while the Legislature has an unquestionable power to prohibit unjust discrimination in railway freights, no prosecution can be maintained under the existing act until amended; because it does not prohibit unjust discriminations merely, but discrimination of any character, and because it does not allow the companies to explain the reason of the discrimination, but forfeits their franchise upon an arbitrary and conclusive presumption of guilt, to be drawn from the proof of an act that might be shown to be perfectly innocent. In these particulars, the existing act violates the spirit of the constitution.

The judgment of the Circuit Court, ousting the appellant of its franchises, must therefore be reversed.

The court advised further, that before this act could be enforced it must be so amended as to correspond with the requirements of the constitution, by directing its prohibition against unjust discriminations. The court did not question the power of the State to regulate railway rates; and, furthermore, it expressed an opinion as to what is or is not a discrimination, which is of much importance:

If a farmer, living three miles from the Springfield station, upon this company's road, is charged fifteen cents per bushel for shipping his corn to Chicago, is it just that a farmer living twenty miles nearer Chicago should be charged a higher sum? Certainly not, unless the railroad company can show a peculiar state of affairs to justify the discrimination, and this must be something more than the mere fact that there are competing lines at one point, and not at the other. The discrimination, in such a case, is as much a discrimination between individuals as it would be in reference to two persons living in the same locality, and shipping at the same station, unless, as before stated, a satisfactory reason can be given for discrimination between the points of shipment; and such a reason, in the case supposed, it is not very easy to conceive. * * * * * * *

The only issue to be made under a law properly framed would be whether there was an unjust discrimination or not. If on the trial of such an issue the prosecution proves a permanently established discrimination, like that disclosed by the present record, and the company can show no other reason for it than the existence of a competing line at the favored points, the defense must be held unsatisfactory, notwithstanding witnesses may testify that they believe, as a matter of theoretical opinion, that the rates to Lexington are reasonable. They can not be reasonable, and the discrimination must be unjust, if the lesser rates for the greater distance have been established merely because the company has ceased to exercise at that point a practical monopoly.

CHAPTER XXV.

THE NEW ILLINOIS RAILROAD LAW AND ITS WORKINGS.

THE RAILROAD COMMISSION SQUABBLE.

The existing railroad law of Illinois having been pronounced unconstitutional, and the Legislature being at the time in session, the amendment of the act was immediately and diligently set about; in fact, so diligently as to excite the apprehension among the farmers that their legislators were going to "talk the subject to death." This feeling began to strengthen as measure after measure was mooted, yet always put aside. The Springfield Convention, of which a condensed report has already been given, was called with a view of enlightening the Legislature as to the earnestness of the popular desire for an efficient law.

About this time (March, 1873) the term of office of the Railroad and Warehouse Commissioners expired. The farmers began agitating for the appointment to the office of persons identified with agricultural interests. Governor Beveridge, however, nominated Messrs. McCrea, Robinson, and Stilwell—one of whom is a banker, another a lawyer. This raised a storm about the Governor's ears which he will not readily forget. Protest after protest, memorials and resolutions without end, were sent in, and the Governor, wisely yielding to the pressure, finally conferred the vacant offices on gentlemen intimately connected with farming pursuits, and of approved honor—Messrs. J. M. Pearson, H. D. Cooke, and David A. Brown.

THE NEW RAILROAD LAW.

Meanwhile, the Legislature was debating the various measures submitted, and eventually passed a law which is here given:

An Act to prevent extortion and unjust discrimination in the rates charged for the transportation of passengers and freights on railroads in this State, and to repeal an act entitled, "An Act to prevent unjust discriminations and extortions in the rates to be charged by the different railroads in this State for the transportation of freights on said roads," approved April 7th, A. D. 1871.

Section 1. Be it enacted, by the people of the State of Illinois, represented in the General Assembly. If any railroad corporation, organized or doing business in this State, under any act of incorporation, or general law of this State, now in force, or which may hereafter be enacted, or any railroad corporation organized, or which may hereafter be organized under the laws of any other State, and doing business in this State, shall charge, collect, demand, or receive more than a fair and reasonable rate of toll or compensation, for the transportation of passengers or freight, of any description, or for the use and transportation of any railroad car upon its track, or any of the branches thereof, or upon any railroad within this State, which it has the right, license, or permission to use, operate, or control, the the same shall be deemed guilty of extortion, and upon conviction thereof shall be dealt with as hereinafter provided.

Sec. 2. If any railroad corporation aforesaid shall make any unjust discrimination in its rates or charges of toll or compensation for the transportation of passengers or freight of any description, or for the use and transportation of any railroad car upon its said road, or upon any branches thereof, or upon any railroads connected therewith, which it has the right, license, or permission to operate, control, or use, within this State, the same shall be deemed guilty of having violated the provisions of this act, and upon conviction thereof shall be dealt with as hereinafter provided.

Sec. 3. If any such railroad corporation shall charge, collect, or receive, for the transportation of any passengers, or freight of any description, upon its railroad, for any distance within this State, the same, or a greater amount of toll or compensation than is at the same time charged, collected, or received for the transportation, in the same direction, for any passenger, or like quantity of freight of the same class, over a greater distance of the same railroad; or if it shall charge, collect, or receive, at any point upon its railroad, a higher rate of toll or compensation for receiving, handling, or delivering freight of the same class or like quantity, than it shall, at the same time, charge, collect, or receive at any other point upon the same road; or if it shall charge, collect, or receive, for the transportation of any passenger, or freight of any description, over its railroad, a greater amount as toll or compensation than shall, at the same time, be charged, collected, or received by it for the transportation of any passenger, or like quantity of freight of the same class, being transported in the same direction, over any portion of the same railroad, of equal distance; or if it shall charge, collect, or receive from any person or persons a higher or greater amount of toll or compensation than it shall, at the same time, charge, collect, or receive from any other person or persons, for receiving, handling, or delivering freight of the same class and like quantity, at the same point upon its railroad; or if it shall charge, collect, or receive from any person or persons, for the transportation of any freight upon its railroad, a higher or greater rate of toll or compensation than it shall, at the same time, charge, collect, or receive from any other person or persons, for the transportation of the like quantity of freight of the same class, being transported from the same point, in the same direction, over equal distances of the same railroad; or if it shall charge, collect, or receive from any person or persons, for the use and transportation of any railroad car or cars upon its railroad, for any distance, the same or a greater amount of toll or compensation than is, at the same time, charged, collected, or received from any other person or persons, for the use and transportation of any railroad car of the same class or number, for a like purpose, being transported in the same direction, over a greater distance of the same railroad; or if it shall charge, collect, or receive from any person or persons, for the use and transportation of any railroad car or cars upon its railroad, a higher or greater rate of toll or compensation than it shall, at the same time, charge, collect, or receive from any other person or persons for the use and transportation on any railroad car or cars of the same class or number, for a like purpose, being transported from the same point, in the same direction, over an equal distance of the same railroad; all such discriminating rates, charges, collections, or receipts, whether made directly, or by means of any rebate, drawback,

Obsolete Method of Transportation in the Tobacco Country.

or other shift or evasion, shall be deemed and taken, against such railroad corporation, as *prima facie* evidence of the unjust discriminations prohibited by the provisions of this act; and it shall not be deemed a sufficient excuse or justification of such discriminations on the part of such railroad corporation, that the railway station or point at which it shall charge, collect, or receive the same or less rates of toll or compensation, for the transportation of such passenger or freight, or for the use and transportation of such railroad car the greater distance than for the shorter distance, is a railway station or point at which there exists competition with any other railroad or means of transportation. This section shall not be construed so as to exclude other evidence tending to show any unjust discrimination in freight and passenger rates. The provisions of this section shall extend and apply to any railroad, the branches thereof, and any road or roads which any railroad corporation has the right, license, or permission to use, operate, or control, wholly or in part within this State; *Provided*, however, that nothing herein contained shall be so construed as to prevent railroad corporations from issuing commutation, excursion, or thousand-mile tickets, as the same are now issued by such corporations.

Sec. 4. Any such railroad corporation guilty of extortion, or of making any unjust discrimination as to passenger or freight rates, or the rates for the use and transportation of railroad cars, or in receiving, handling, or delivering freights, shall, upon conviction thereof, be fined in any sum not less than one thousand dollars ($1,000), nor more than five thousand dollars ($5,000), for the first offense; and for the second offense not less than five thousand dollars ($5,000), nor more than ten thousand dollars ($10,000), and for the third offense not less than ten thousand dollars ($10,000), nor more than twenty thousand dollars ($20,000); and for every subsequent offense, and conviction thereof, shall be liable to a fine of twenty-five thousand dollars ($25,000); *Provided*, That in all cases under this act either party shall have the right of trial by jury.

Sec. 5. The fines hereinbefore provided for, may be recovered in an action of debt, in the name of the people of the State of Illinois, and there may be several counts joined in the same declaration, as to extortion and unjust discrimination, and as to passenger and freight rates, and rates for the use and transportation of railroad cars, and for receiving, handling, or delivering freights. If, upon the trial of any causes instituted under this act, the jury shall find for the people, they shall assess and return with their verdict the amount of the fine to be imposed upon the defendant, at any sum not less than one thousand dollars ($1,000), nor more than five thousand dollars ($5,000), and the court shall render judgment accordingly; and if the jury shall find for the people, and that the defendant has been once before convicted of a violation of the provisions of this act, they shall return such finding with their verdict, and shall assess and retnrn with their verdicf the amount of the fine to be imposed upon the defendant, at any sum not less than five thousand dollars ($5,000), nor more than ten thousand dollars ($10,000); and the court shall render judgment accordingly; and if the jury shall find for the people, and that the defendant has been twice before convicted of a violation of the provisions of this act, with respect to extortion or unjust discrimination, they shall return such finding with their verdict, and shall assess and return with their verdict, the amount of fine to be imposed upon the defendant, at any sum not less than ten thousand dollars ($10,000), nor more than twenty thousand dollars ($20,000); and in like manner for every subsequent offense, and conviction, such defendant shall be liable to a fine of twenty-five thousand dollars ($25,000); *Provided*, that in all cases under the provisions of this act, a preponderance of evidence in favor of the people shall be sufficient to authorize a verdict and judgment for the people.

Sec. 6. If any such railroad corporation shall, in violation of any of the provisions of this act, ask, demand, charge, or receive of any person or corporation any extortionate charge or charges, for the transportation of any passengers, goods, merchandise, or property, or for receiving, handling, or delivering freights, or shall make any unjust discriminations against any person or corporation in its charges therefor, the person or corporation so offended against may, for each offense, recover of such railroad corporations, in any form of action, three times the amount of the damages sustained by the party aggrieved, together with costs of suit, and a reasonable attorney's fee, to be fixed by the court where the same is heard, on appeal or otherwise, and taxed as a part of the costs of the case.

Sec. 7. It shall be the duty of the Railroad and Warehouse Commissioners to personally investigate and ascertain whether the provisions of this act are violated by any railroad corporation in this State, and to visit the various stations upon the line of each railroad for that purpose as often as practicable; and whenever the facts, in any manner ascertained by said commissioners, shall in their judgment warrant such prosecution, it shall be the duty of said commissioners to immediately cause suits to be commenced and prosecuted against any railroad corporations which may violate the provisions of this act. Such suits and prosecutions may be instituted in any county in this

State, through or into which the line of the railroad corporation sued for violating this act may extend. And such railroad and warehouse commissioners are hereby authorized, when the facts of the case presented to them shall, in their judgment, warrant the commencement of such action, to employ counsel to assist the attorney-general in conducting such suits on behalf of the State. No suits commenced by said commissioners shall be dismissed, except said railroad and warehouse commissioners and the attorney-general shall consent thereto.

Sec. 8. The railroad and warehouse commissioners are hereby directed to make, for each of the railroad corporations doing business in this State, as soon as practicable, a schedule of reasonable maximum rates of charges for the transportation of passengers and freight and cars on each of said railroads; and said schedule shall, in all suits brought against any such railroad corporations, wherein is in any way involved the charges of any such railroad corporation, for the transportation of any passenger or freight or cars, or unjust discrimination in relation thereto, be deemed and taken, in all courts of this State, as *prima facie* evidence that the rates therein fixed are reasonable maximum rates of charges for the transportation of passengers and freight and cars upon the railroads for which said schedules may have been respectively prepared. Said commissioners shall, from time to time, and so often as circumstances may require, change and revise said schedules. When such schedules shall have been made or revised, as aforesaid, it shall be the duty of said commissioners to cause publication thereof to be made for three successive weeks, in some public newspaper in the city of Springfield, in this State; *Provided*, that the schedules thus prepared shall not be taken as *prima facie* evidence, as herein provided, until schedules shall have been prepared and published as aforesaid, for all the railroad companies now organized under the laws of this State, and until the 15th day of January, A. D. 1874, or until ten days after the meeting of the next session of the general assembly, provided a session of the general assembly shall be held previous to the 15th of day of January aforesaid. All such schedules, purporting to be printed and established as aforesaid, shall be received and held, in all such suits, as *prima facie* the schedules of said commissioners, without further proof than the production of the paper in which they were published, together with the certificate of the publisher of said paper that the schedule therein contained, is a true copy of the schedule furnished for publication by said commissioners, and that it has been published the above specified time; and any such paper, purporting to have been published at said city, and to be a public newspaper, shall be presumed to have been so published at the date thereof, and to be a public newspaper.

Sec. 9. In all cases under the provisions of this act, the rules of evidence shall be the same as in other civil actions, except as hereinbefore otherwise provided. All fines recovered under the provisions of this act shall be paid into the county treasurer of the county in which the suit is tried, by the person collecting the same, in the manner now provided by law, to be used for county purposes. The remedies hereby given shall be regarded as cumulative to the remedies now given by law against railroad corporations; and this act shall not be construed as repealing any statute giving such remedies. Suits commenced under the provisions of this act shall have precedence over all other business, except criminal business.

Sec. 10. The term "railroad corporation," contained in this act, shall be deemed and taken to mean all corporations, companies, or individuals now owning or operating, or which may hereafter own or operate, any railroad, in whole or in part, in this State; and the provisions of this act shall apply to all persons, firms, and companies, and to all associations of persons, whether incorporated or otherwise, that shall do business as common carriers upon any of the lines of railways in this State (street railways excepted), the same as to railroad corporations hereinbefore mentioned.

Sec. 11. An act entitled "An act to prevent unjust discriminations and extortions in the rates to be charged by the different railroads in this State for the transportation of freight on said roads," approved April 7, A. D. 1871, is hereby repealed; but such repeal shall not affect nor repeal any penalty incurred, or right accrued, under said act prior to the time this act takes effect, nor any proceedings or prosecutions to enforce such rights or penalties.

WORKING OF THE NEW LAW.

The new Railroad Law has been thoroughly and conscientiously carried out by the Commissioners, as far as settling schedules of freight and passenger charges is concerned. It soon became apparent, however, that State legislation could not give other than very partial relief to the producing class;

the through lines re-adjusted their rates, so as to oblige other States to make up what was withheld from them in Illinois. The 44th Congress will have to face this question, beset as it is, with difficulties. And if that Congress dare to trifle with this subject—to truckle to the monopolists—to waste its time in whitewashing thieves and land-sharks, instead of looking after the interests of the people, its master, a ball will be set in motion which will stop — where?

The Illinois State Fair of 1873, at Peoria, was taken advantage of, to hold a conference between the Central Committee of the State Farmer's Association and the Railroad Commissioners. The schedule of tariffs, etc., was explained by the Commissioners, and questions propounded by the Committee, to whom the answers given were satisfactory. The Commissioners had everv confidence in the law, as far as it went, though they considered it susceptible of improvement.

In the course of their investigations, it appeared that the Commissioners had carefully examined the tariffs for the leading roads for a series of years. Finding that as business increased, the rates of transportation had steadily advanced, they had fairly and candidly considered the interests of the roads, and endeavored to establish such rates as would do them no injustice, and which would stand. Railway officials had been courteously treated, though they had generally ignored the Board, frequently submitting intricate questions through inferior officers and agents. The rates adopted were by comparison with the old company rates, and were simply intended as a maximum, leaving the railway companies to fix lower rates if they wished. The law permitted no unjust discriminations, either of special lines or individuals. It was important that it should be understood that the Commissioners' tariffs were in force now, and that railway companies were liable to fine for non-compliance. In every case of violation of the act, the offending company would be rigorously prosecuted.

The Commissioners had a fund of $35,000 for paying expenses of test cases. They and their counsel expressed themselves satisfied with the law, and did not consider that it could be materially improved by amendments, and thought the enforcement of the law would accomplish the ends for which it was devised. They believed the railway companies throughout the country were combined to secure the repeal of the law, and that, to do so, they would use every agency at their command. It behooved the people of the State, especially clubs and societies, to act promptly and decisively, instructing their representatives to sustain the law as it stands, and the Commissioners in its enforcement.

CHAPTER XXVI.

THE ILLINOIS JUDICIAL ELECTIONS.

THE FIRST CHARGE ALONG THE LINE.

The judicial elections in Illinois, in the summer of 1873, have the distinction of being the occasion on which the Farmers' Movement first showed its strength. There had been plenty of speeches made, resolutions passed, and memorials drafted, and the several bodies were in a tolerably well organized shape. Farmers had become aware that the only remedy for their grievances was a radical one—the use of the ballot-box. The first opportunity for a display of their power came in June, 1873, when the time came around for the election of Judges for the local courts, and two Justices for the Supreme Bench.

One of the retiring Justices was Chief Justice Lawrence, a gentleman of unblemished name, and a jurist of very high attainments. It was before Judge Lawrence that the appeal from the ruling of Judge Tipton, in the McLean County test case, was heard, and it was by him that the decision that the Illinois railroad law was unconstitutional was rendered. The attorneys of the Fifth Judicial District, where the election was to take place, memoralized Judge Lawrence to allow himself to be put in nomination for re-election, to which he consented. The farmers felt themselves slighted in not being consulted in the matter, and resolved to hold a meeting on the subject, not with any intention of supplanting Judge Lawrence (whom the originators of the Convention intended to nominate), but with the object of showing that the people were determined to be consulted on questions affecting their interests. Unfortunately, between the calling and the meeting of the Convention, Judge Lawrence, in accepting the nomination, expressed himself in contemptuous terms about the power of the people. This put the farmers on their mettle. They considered themselves as much entitled to be represented as any other class, and determined to run a candidate of their own. Such was the origin of the Princeton Convention.

THE PRINCETON CONVENTION.

This meeting ventilated farmers' grievances fully, and unanimously passed the following resolutions:

Resolved, That the provisions of the Constitution of 1870, of the State of Illinois, in regard to railroads, are, equally with the other provisions of the Constitution, the supreme law of the State, and our Legislature should provide the necessary legislation to execute such provisions, and our courts should sustain and adopt the same.

Resolved, That the charters of the railroads in this State are not contracts in the sense that they are paramount to the Constitution and laws of this State, and that the provisions of the Constitution of the State in regard to railroads, and necessary legislation to enforce the same, are not repugnant to the Constitution of the United States.

Resolved, That the railroads in this State are public highways, and their operators common carriers, and the General Assembly, as required by the Constitution of this State, should pass laws establishing reasonable maximum rates of charge for the transportation of passengers and freight on the different railroads in this State, and should also pass laws to correct abuses and to define and prevent extortion in the rate of freight and passenger tariffs on such roads;

and such legislation should be sustained and enforced by the judiciary of the State.

Resolved, That we will support no man for office who is not in accordance with the sentiments of these resolutions; and that we recommend to the anti-monopolists of this State to nominate such candidates for Supreme and Circuit Judges as are pledged to sustain the Constitution and laws of this State in accordance therewith.

A Princeton Convention Man.

The Convention, with great unanimity, then nominated Hon. Alfred M. Craig, of Knox County, as candidate for the Supreme Judgeship. No pledge was required from Judge Craig, and no questions were asked in respect to his opinions on any subject. His record as a member of the Convention which framed the present Constitution of Illinois was such as to satisfy his supporters that his sentiments were in harmony with their own. He was known to be an able and accomplished lawyer, though not possessing the profound legal knowledge of his opponent.

In nearly all the judicial districts, farmers' candidates were put in nomination for the vacant offices, and in those cases in which there was any opposition there was a degree of bitterness shown which would have been better in place in a partisan political contest.

THE RESULT AT THE POLLS.

In nearly every circuit, where the farmers nominated a candidate, they were successful, and the exceptional cases were uniformly in sections where their organization had not been fully perfected.

The grand, central point, attracting universal attention, was, of course, the Fifth District, where the Lawrence-Craig contest was going on. There the opposition to the farmers' candidate was powerful, united, and determined. Judge Lawrence had the support of all the legal talent of the State. Some of the leading journals espoused his cause, and in his own county every local interest that could possibly be brought to bear was arrayed against his opponent. On the other hand, however, he had to contend with the active, relentless animosity of the Chicago *Journal*, the editor of which, a short time previously, he had fined for contempt of court. The State Farmers' Association did not take an active part in the contest, some of its officers not sympathizing with the opposition to Judge Lawrence. Yet the farmers voted together manfully, and Craig was elected by a majority of about 3,000.

THE RESULT OF THE ELECTION MISCONSTRUED.

This judicial contest attracted much attention, particularly in the East, where, up to this time, the Farmers' Movement had been reckoned of small account. The Eastern journals, misinformed of the true state of the case, stigmatized it as an attempt to pack the judiciary in favor of a class; declared that the judges were pledged beforehand to decide cases regardless of the law; that it was to punish Judge Lawrence for conscientiously deciding a case in favor of a railroad that Judge Craig was elected; that it was an outrage which ought to be denounced every-where, etc.

The utmost that can be alleged against Judge Craig is, that he accepted a nomination from a convention which had made a certain declaration of principles, but which will all bear examination, and to which no one can reasonably object. Judge Craig gave no pledge whatever, and the wording of the resolutions of the Princeton Convention merely expressed the resolution of the farmers to support only candidates who would decide cases in strict accordance with the law and the Constitution of the State.

Still, it was an understood thing with the farmers of Illinois that, in the judicial contest, the battle between

8,000 Majority for Craig.

monopolies and the people had begun in earnest. They were anxious to know, at the mouth of a judiciary unbiased and above suspicion, whether the railway acts of the State were unconstitutional or not. If there were barriers by reason of which an honest judge could not confirm existing laws, they wanted to know it in order that the State Constitution might be amended. If necessary, they even looked forward to initiating a movement for amending the Constitution of the United States.

CHAPTER XXVII.

THE AMERICAN CHEAP TRANSPORTATION ASSOCIATION.

THE GRAIN GROWERS' TRANSPORTATION AND LOAN ASSOCIATION.

Subsequent to the first convention at Bloomington, Illinois, there was a meeting held in New York City, at which was formed the "Grain Growers' Transportation and Loan Association," a grand co-operative scheme, whose capital was placed at $10,000,000, in 200,000 shares of $50 each. It was organized under the laws of the State of New York, with a numerous Board of Trustees, as follows: E. R. Shankland, President Iowa Agricultural Society; John Scott, Ex-Lieutenant-Governor, S. B. Dumont, and John Grinnell, all of Iowa; O. P. Whitcomb, Wm. L. Ames, and Charles A. Wheaton, respectively, President, member of Executive Committee, and Treasurer of the State Agricultural Society of Minnesota; B. R. Hinckley, President, and Wm. R. Taylor, member of the Executive Committee, Wisconsin Agricultural Society; Edward Pier, of Wisconsin; Henry C. Wheeler, Commissioner of Statistics Illinois Farmers' Convention; Aaron T. Bates, and Carlos Glazier, of Illinois; Samuel Edwards, President Illinois Horticultural Society, and Samuel P. Adams, Michigan.

It was thought that farmers would subscribe liberally,

from the fact that the trustees were, principally, well-known agriculturists, and all of them business men of high standing. The scheme looked well on paper; but it was unwieldy, and, I believe, the trustees never elected their officers. Certainly, the capital stock was never subscribed. The sub-

Constituents of the S. P. C. A., for whose Transportation Congress has already Legislated.

ject of transportation, however, continued to interest New York, whose merchants began to foresee that, if some remedy were not instituted, a large portion of the grain trade would be diverted from that city.

THE FARMERS' AND PRODUCERS' CONVENTION.

Finally, another Convention was decided on, to meet on the 6th of May, 1873. This was known as "the Farmers' and Producers' Convention." Pursuant to call, it assembled at the Astor House, in New York city, and organized by the election of the venerable Hon. Josiah Quincy, of Boston, Massachusetts, as President, and R. H. Ferguson, of Troy,

New York, Secretary, with Vice-Presidents from various States.

President Quincy, in his address to the Convention, said that he had spent a large part of his life in building railroads, and he felt very keenly the danger growing out of immense railroad monopolies. He appreciated their great benefits, but was aware of their danger to the people. The great granaries of the West held enough to supply the East with food, but it depends on one or two men to say what shall be paid for that food when delivered in Eastern cities. He thought something must be done to take this matter out of the hands of the few men. It was a matter that interested deeply the whole country, and should not be controlled by a very few. The object of this Association was to counteract the great evil. Railroads have power to bribe Legislatures, and will continue to dictate laws until the people shall have come together and asserted their rights. The rights of railroad shareholders are not to be infringed upon, but the paramount right of the whole people to cheap transportation must be asserted and secured.

The Constitution and By-Laws reported provided that the organization shall be known as "The National American Cheap Transportation Association," whose object shall be the cheapening and equalization of railroad transportation rates throughout the United States, and to make provision also for a subordinate association in each State, and regulate minor matters for the guidance and government of national and State associations.

After the discussion of the subject that had brought the gentlemen together from the various States of the Union, a committee was appointed which drafted resolutions and submitted them to the Convention.

THE RESOLUTIONS.

WHEREAS, The productive industries of the United States—plantation and farm, mine and factory, commercial and mercantile—are not only the sources of all our national and individual wealth, but also elements on which our very national and individual existence depend; and,

WHEREAS, All national products are fruits of labor and capital, and as neither labor nor capital will continue actively employed without an equivalent measurably just; and,

WHEREAS, The great national industries are only sustained and prospered by the interchange of products of one section of the country for those of another; and,

WHEREAS, The existing rates of transportation for the varied products of the Union from one part of the country to another, and to foreign countries, as well as the transit cost of commodities required in exchange, are in many instances injurious, and to certain interests absolutely destructive, arising in part at least from an insufficiency of avenues; and,

WHEREAS, The great national want of the nation to-day is relief from the present rates of transit upon American products; therefore, be it

Resolved, 1. That it is the duty of the hour, and the mission of this association, to obtain from Congress, and the different State Legislatures such legislation as may be necessary to control and limit by law, within proper constitutional and legitimate limits, rates and charges of existing lines of transportation; to increase, where practicable, the capacity of our water-ways, and to aid such new avenues, both water and rail, as our immensely increasing internal commerce demands, so that the producer may be justly rewarded for his honest toil, the consumers have cheap products, and our almost limitless surplus find foreign markets at rates to compete with the world.

2. That cheap transportation, both of persons and property, is most conducive to free movement of the people; that the widest interchange and consumption of the produce of the different parts of the Union is essential to the welfare and prosperity of the country.

3. That constant and frequent association of the inhabitants of remote parts of the United States is not only desirable, but necessary, for the maintenance of a homogenous and harmonious population within the vast area of our territory.

4. That the different parts of the country also demand the freest possible interchange of industrial products of the varied climates and industries of the United States, so that breadstuffs, textile fabrics, lumber, iron, sugar, and various other products, local in their production but general in their consumption, may all reach the consumer at the least practicable cost for transportation; and that an arbitrary and unnecessary tax levied by the transporter over and above a fair remuneration for his investment is a burden upon the producer and consumer that it is the part of wise statesmanship to remove.

5. That certain leading railway corporations of the country, although chartered to subserve the public welfare, and endowed with the right of eminent domain solely for that purpose, have proved themselves practically monopolists, and become the tools of avaricious and unscrupulous capitalists, to be used to plunder the public, enrich themselves, and impoverish the country through which they run.

6. That many of the railway corporations have not only disregarded public convenience and prosperity, but have oppressed citizens, bribed our Legislatures, and defied our executives and judges, and stand today the most menacing danger to American liberty and to republican government.

7. That the present system of railway management having failed to meet the just expectations and demands of a long-suffering people, it must be radically reformed and controlled by the strong hand of the law, both State and national, and railway corporations compelled to perform their proper functions as servants and not masters of the people.

8. That, to this end, we invoke the aid of all fair-minded men in all the States of the Union in excluding from the halls of legislation, from our executive offices, and from the bench, all railway officials, railway attorneys, or other hirelings who prostitute public office to the base uses of private gain.

9. That, leaving different sections and interests that desire cheap transportation to work out the problem in such manner as they may deem best, we earnestly invoke their careful consideration, their energetic and their resolute will in regulating and controlling rates of transportation, and in giving remunerative wages to the producer and cheap products to the consumer, untaxed by unearned charges for their carriage.

10. That we invite the people of the various States to organize sub-

sidiary associations, State, county, and town, to co-operate with the national associations. The power to accomplish the purposes desired rests absolutely with the suffering millions; and relief is within their reach and control. United action and the near future will give, as certain as its need for all time and the good of all, the true solution of the problem of cheap transportation.

The resolutions were taken up and discussed at length, and, finally, were adopted unanimously.

On motion the following committee was appointed to draft an address to the people: Hon. Josiah Quincy, Boston, Mass.;

Loading a Steamboat on the Mississippi.

M. D. Wilbur, Michigan; Horace H. Day, New York City; R. H. Ferguson, Troy, New York; Henry Bronson, Kansas; J. A. Noonan, Milwaukee; and W. H. C. Price, New York.

The Convention then adjourned to meet in Washington, January, 1874, at the call of the Executive Committee.

PRESIDENT QUINCY'S CALL FOR THE WASHINGTON CONVENTION.

The call for this Convention, to be held in Washington in January, 1874, was looked forward to with the greatest interest. In November, 1873, it was promulgated, and was as follows:

In the month of May, 1873, delegates from several States met in New York for the purpose of forming an American Cheap Transportation Association. The organization was effected by the election of a president, secretary, and treasurer, together with vice-presidents from the several States represented. It was voted that a meeting of the officers or delegates of the several State Associations then existing, together with those of any other State Association that might be formed, should be held in Washington in the month of January, 1874. It was also voted that an address should be prepared and published, setting forth the complaints against the management of some of the railroads, together with suggestions of measures that might tend to relieve the people from undue exactions, and facilitate transportation between the different Staies. As the residences of the gentlemen appointed to prepare the address were too distant to permit their personal conference, it was thought best that they should submit their views to the President of the Association, who was authorized to present their general drift to the people, when issuing the call for the January meeting. As the address has not been submitted to the other members of the committee, the chairman is alone responsible for the form it has taken.

The subject should not be approached without a grateful acknowledgment of the blessings which the railroad has conferred upon our country. Of all the mighty powers that are so rapidly changing the face of the world this takes precedence as an educator and civilizer. This mighty interest has absorbed the largest capitalists, the most active minds, and the most gifted projectors of our time. Much money has been made by it, and a great part of that money has been honestly and honorably earned. Enterprising capitalists who took great risks, far-sighted men of business who gave vigorous thought to the internal development of their country, have made large fortunes and have richly deserved them. They have provided the people with a most valuable servant. But the time has come when it is evident that this excellent servant is capable of becoming a most tyrannical master. We are threatened with the curse of special rights, special privileges, special favors, special powers, and the monopolies of cliques and rings. An *imperium in imperio*, controlled by the ablest executives that money can purchase, acts with peculiar advantages under a popular government. If that eternal vigilance, which has been called the price of liberty, is not exercised; if an aggressive power is not boldly met and restrained by wise and reasonable legislation,—we are inviting those bad and lawless remedies which are too often worse than the injustice they assail.

Among the many charges that have been preferred against the managers of American railroads the mention of a few will be sufficient for the purposes of this address. Mr. Rufus Hatch, in his circular upon "Frauds in Railroad Management," offers statements to show that at the time of his publication the watering of the stock of the Hudson River and the New York Central Railroads amounted to $57,576,700, which exceeded the capital actually paid in by $7,368,400. He likewise asserts that the watering in the Cleveland, Painesville and Ashtabula, the Buffalo and Erie, and the Cleveland and Toledo, together with the excess of new capital over old, amounted to $20,065,870; and this watering of the Lake Shore, added to that of the Hudson River and New York Central, amounted to $77,644,770, equaling $79,000 a mile for the whole distance from Chicago to New York, and paying on every mile an annual dividend of $6,325.

Mr. Geo. O. Jones, at a recent hearing before the Congressional Committee on Transportation, corroborated these statements, and estimates that New York pays $10,000,000 a year on watered stock. It is also charged against some of the managers of the great line of railroad that, while Congress has granted immense tracts of land in order to reduce the cost of roads and the fares for transportation, means have been employed to separate the railroads from these grants for the purpose of dishonestly appropriating these benefits. Railroads thus favored by the government have been constructed at great cost, through the issue of bonds, and then leased to lines of which their managers had the control. Rings have thus obtained possession of land and shares at nominal prices, and have imposed upon the people such taxes as their directors might choose to levy.

It is charged that while our several States have granted charters authorizing railroad corporations to take the land of any citizens, and to issue shares for the construction of their roads, and permitting them to collect a liberal interest for all moneys invested, shares have been issued gratuitously to stockholders, with the view of exacting interest upon fictitious values; and also that officers or influential shareholders who have been interested in express companies, mineral land companies, and other associations, have caused peculiar privileges to be given to such bodies, enabling them to gain unjust advantages over all others who depend upon railroad transportation for the transaction of their business. It is also asserted that accommodation has been refused to those who have made themselves obnoxious by exposing the unjust proceedings above specified, and that shippers of merchandise not in favor with inner rings have been denied fair opportunities for competition.

Finally, it is alleged that no action of individuals is capable of resisting corporations wielding the vast power and backed by the immense wealth at the disposal of railroad managers. It is alleged that some of these members have already packed conventions, bribed legislators, and subsidized judges, and have obtained, through corrupt means, an influence subversive of the rights of the people and most perilous to republican institutions.

The Cheap Transportation Association asks that these charges, brought by responsible citizens against the managers of railroads, be thoroughly investigated. We assert that it is the right and duty of Congress to inquire how its liberal grants of land have been appropriated. They were granted to give temporary credit to certain railroad corporations, and to constitute a sinking fund which would ultimately pay off debts contracted in the construction of roads. They were granted, in the interest of the country, to reduce rates of transportation to the cost of maintaining the roads. Should it be found that these grants, covering an area greater than many of our States, have been obtained under false pretenses, and used for private aggrandizement, we ask that they be reclaimed from those who unjustly hold them in possession.

Our several States have surrendered the privilege of righting their own wrongs, upon the understanding that Congress will do it for them. The railroad power of the State of New York, for instance, may levy for the benefit of watered stock the estimated tax of ten cents per bushel upon corn and wheat, and the farmers of the West and citizens of New England have no remedy except through the action of the General Government. For this reason we are forced to ask Congress for a thorough investigation of the measures that have been adopted to effect the interchange of products among our States—measures that are alleged to have destroyed the value of the productions of one section, and to have increased the cost of the necessaries of life in another. We ask for a thorough investigation into special contracts made for the transportation of freight and passengers that have given the contractors advantages over their fellow-citizens.

We ask Congress to consider whether it be not expedient to make certain laws for the regulation of railroads, in order to meet such wrongs and avert such dangers as an investigation may bring to light; and whether it be not expedient to create a permanent Railroad Commission, with power, upon substantial complaints, to send for persons and papers, to lay injunctions, and to abate violations of the laws. Railroad managers, as common carriers, should be required by law to give no privileges to one customer above another under similar circumstances. All deviations in price from the published schedule made to companies or to individuals should be duly recorded in books, at all times open to the inspection of the Railroad Commission, as well as to citizens who make proper application to examine them.

It is proposed to ask Congress to consider the expediency of establishing national railroads or canals for the purpose of carrying freight between distant States and the seaboard, or to require existing roads to draw cars for individuals or companies at fixed rates.

But it is unnecessary further to anticipate the action of the meeting of the Association, which is hereby called to meet at Washington on Wednesday, the 14th day of January, 1874. At this meeting delegates from all kindred State organizations are invited to appear.

JOSIAH QUINCY,

President of the American Cheap Transportation Association.

CHAPTER XXVIII

THE NATIONAL AGRICULTURAL CONGRESS OF 1873.

OPENING FORMALITIES, ETC.

Pursuant to adjournment, as mentioned in Chapter XVII, the National Agricultural Congress held its second session at Indianapolis, May 28, 1873, with a large attendance of highly intelligent delegates from twenty-five States. In the absence of the President, Hon. John P. Reynolds, A. M. Garland, Esq., of Illinois, was called to the chair.

Governor Hendricks, of Indiana, delivered an address of welcome, and was followed by Mayor Mitchell, of Indianapolis, and Hon. John Sutherland, of the Indiana State Board of Agriculture, in some pleasant remarks of similar tenor. General W. H. Jackson, of Tennessee, in responding, on behalf of the Congress, gave a short history of the gathering and its objects, concluding his remarks as follows:

"I regard it as a matter of great importance to all the interests of the country. The reason that actuated us in the formation of this organization was to have greater unity and concert of action among the agricultural classes, whom, we thought, ought to have a voice in the affairs of the State and nation. There was lack of concert of action, and of that cohesiveness which exists in all other classes. We have combinations of capitalists in mining and in manufacturing, in seafaring, in commerce, and the thousand channels through which capital seeks accumulation. We desire that this association may dignify and ennoble this most ancient and venerable calling, so that it will have the effect of bringing about a wide diffusion of knowledge, and increase the general and individual prosperity of our citizens; and in proportion as we can have a wider diffusion of knowledge and elevate that class to which they belong, we believe that it will increase the general prosperity of the whole country. These associations will have the effect, if there be lingering prejudices and asperities engendered in the times past, to smooth them over and cause them to be forgotten.

"This is one of the grand ideas in my mind—it is one of the most pleasant ideas to my mind—that it will unite the people of all the sections of this broad land, to consult together as to the material interests of the whole country.

"And here let me disclaim, as I am familiar with the origin and inception of this movement, that by our unity and concert of action we desire to crush and oppress any interests in this broad land. I recognize them as all important in their places, but we simply wish, by unity of action, to promote the paramount interests of this great class which we are here representing. That is the idea that is intended, as I say, by the wide diffusion of knowledge growing out of the reported practical experiments. All these minor societies, all State societies, will be tributary to this grand National Agricultural Congress, and it will have the effect of spreading through the country, more readily, improved implements and methods of recuperation, fertilization and culture.

"These are some of the ideas we have in coming together.

"Members of this body, let prudence and caution and wisdom guard all your deliberations. We are not here, as some suppose, to fight railroads. We regard the railroad interests of the country as one of the grand interests of the country. We regard the railroad interests and agricultural, as hinging on each other, and so intimately connected that one can not be withdrawn without great detriment to the other. Therefore, we want to see the railroad interest cherished in every way; but we feel that they, as well as middle men who handle our produce, are getting a greater share of the profits than by right they are entitled to. We simply ask and shall endeavor to seek the line of equity as between the true producer and the carrier, and having found that line, we dare maintain our rights.

A Farm in Indiana.

That is the idea. We want nothing but a fair line, and we should proceed in such a cautious way as not to do any thing imprudent. I thank you, gentlemen, for the call that has been made upon me of responding; and I thank you, gentlemen, for this Convention, for the very kind welcome extended."

FINANCIAL, HORTICULTURAL, AND ENTOMOLOGICAL.

Secretary Greene, in his annual report, alluded to the difficulty under which he labored in consequence of the neglect of the societies whom the Congress represented, (three thousand in number,) to send their quota of the expenses, and spoke highly of the manner in which the agricultural press had seconded his exertions. He estimated that there were then in existence at least ten thousand societies under different names. Of these, two-thirds had been organized during the six months last preceding. Commodore Maury's system of weather signals, as explained to the last Congress, had been established, and it was important that it should be extended, but the appropriations from Congress were small compared with the value of the undertaking. The financial report showed an excess of expenditures over income of $350.

Professor Riley, of Missouri, read a paper on the "cotton worm and its destruction," which he appropriately prefaced with the remark that he offered it as "a proposition whereby millions of dollars may be saved to the people of the South." He proposed an inexpensive remedy for the destruction of this pestiferous insect, whose appearance in the cotton-field strikes dismay to the heart of the planter.

The Committee on Horticulture and Entomology made a report wherein they recommended that Congress be asked to provide that railroad companies and homesteaders, receiving the benefit of acts donating land, shall plant with timber trees one-half of the land so donated; that our Agricultural Colleges should give more attention to forestry, as in similar institutions in Europe; asking railroad companies to co-operate in restoring the timber growth; and directing attention to the practical importance of the science of entomology, and declaring that each State should appoint an entomologist.

The "eight-hour law" was discussed at length, but no decision was arrived at thereon.

EXHAUSTIVE REPORT ON THE TRANSPORTATION QUESTION.

A committee appointed on the transportation question delivered the following exhaustive report:

1. The cheap transportation of persons and property is a national necessity. Our country is immense, and its climate, productions, and wants very varied and diverse in its different parts. The eminent thinker, Dr. Draper, in his "Civil Policy of America," has stated that he regards cheap transportation, even looking at it simply as a means of commingling, fraternizing, and unifying our population, as a natural necessity. Even more true, if possible, is the statement that the greatest good of the masses of the people is to be observed by furnishing all articles, whose production is local, but whose consumption is general and necessary, at the lowest possible cost of transportation. Eight States in the Northwest produced 800,000,000 of cereals in 1862—eighty bushels for every man, woman, or child of its population, and enough, properly distributed, to feed the whole forty millions of the nation, whilst the East had not grain enough to last her more than three months of the year, and the four Southeastern States of South Carolina, Georgia, Alabama, and Florida, required fifty millions of bushels more grain than they grew. Pennsylvania has exhaustless mines of coal. Massachusetts, with her immense factories, has none. The Southern States have a soil eminently adapted to the production of cotton and sugar—arti-

cles sought and needed by all portions of the more Northern States. Missouri has her immense mines of iron, whose manufacture and use goes every-where. The Pacific coast has her wines, her wheat, and her minerals, valuable to all. To fetch and carry these raw products and the secondary products of their manufacture from producer to consumer, at the lowest possible cost, is the worthy and most desirable object of the day. It will remove an oppressive burden that now rests like an incubus upon the producing interests of the country, and give cheap food, cheap clothing, and cheap fuel to the people every-where.

2. In examining into this subject, we find that, in the first place, the present avenues for freight transportation are insufficient, or, at least, as now organized and operated, do not do their proper work. Our water routes are obstructed by falls and rapids that are not overcome; by shoals and sand bars that are not removed; and for months of the year are blockaded by ice or by low water. The railways, being used both for passenger and freight transportation, can carry only relatively small amounts of freight, and both water and railway routes are blockaded by an insufficiency of warehouses, elevators, and other means of transferring freight at our principal inland and seaboard cities.

3. We find, moreover, that rates charged by these transportation companies are exorbitant, as compared with the necessary cost, and are really prohibitory in their character at points remote from the great markets. The rates by water, while considerably lower, are still much above the necessary cost, and in the northern part of the country are inoperative during the winter season. The charges of elevators and other warehouses have, at many points, been also exorbitant and oppressive. Thus, in seasons of plenty, the producer finds the price of his products reduced below the cost of production, and in seasons of scarcity the consumer must pay unwarrantable and unbearable prices for the necessaries of life. Not only this, but inasmuch as the seaboard prices, except in cases of local scarcity, fix the producers' prices at his own locality, the result is that the high prices of freight are a cause of loss to the producer even upon what he sells at home. With an immense region of wheat and other grain-growing country opening up in the north-west, these evils to our special farming interests threaten to be greatly aggravated and increased in the future.

4. We may add that the unjust discriminations of railway corporations have greatly aggravated and intensified this evil. Discriminations are unduly exciting and building up the prosperity of competing points, and depressing and destroying that of other points; real estate is depreciated, manufactures and agriculture languish, and the country even becomes depopulated by reason of unjust discriminations.

5. In view of these facts, your Committee believe that due encouragement should be given to the opening of new routes, and the improvement of the old ones, so as to furnish transportation at cheap rates between all parts of the Republic. Among these we would call attention to the following, which, from a cursory examination, seem to have more or less merit: The Niagara Ship Canal, the Caughnawaga and Champlain Canal route, from the St. Lawrence to New York; the Fox River Canal, of Wisconsin; the James River and Kanawha Through Water Line; the Illinois and Michigan Canal and Illinois River Improvement; the Atlantic and Great Western Canal; and the Mississippi and Appalachicola Canal along the Gulf Coast.

6. The Southern Pacific and Northern Pacific Railroads are aided by grants of land, and their construction, it is believed, secured, and we believe will be an important means of relieving the pressure of trans-continental transportation. The scheme of the Eastern and Western Transportation Company also promises a valuable new through route from the Northwest to the Atlantic.

7. We call attention to, and ask an investigation of, the merits of the narrow gauge railways, as much cheaper in their construction and operation than the existing railways; of freight tracks or railways adapted especially to cheap transportation; and of tram-railways laid upon the common highways of the country, which we believe can be done at a cost not exceeding that of Macadamized roads.

8. We recommend that efforts be made and persevered in, until all railway corporations shall be subject to legislative regulation. so as to insure the absolute and perpetual prohibition and prevention of extortionate charges and unjust discriminations.

9. We recommend that all men who believe that the rights of the people should be protected from the extortions and discriminations of transportation monopolies. should unite in reforming the execu-

tive, judicial, and legislative departments of our National and State governments by excluding therefrom the proprietors and servants of such monopolies.

10. We deprecate, finally, the practice of executive, judicial, and legislative officers in accepting favors from transportation corporations, whose interests are more or less in conflict with those of the people, whom such officers are elected to serve.

We further recommend the adoption of the following supplemental report:

We, the farmers of the United States, in Congress assembled, respectfully represent to the Senate and House of Representatives of the 43d Congress, that the great want of the whole country, and especially the West and North-west, is increased facilities for transportation between the valleys of the Ohio and Mississippi and the Atlantic seaboard; that, in consequence of the rapidly increasing products of the West, and the corresponding increase of its demand for the manufacturing, mechanical and other products of the East, the necessity to meet this want is daily becoming more imperative.

That to respond to this want the best interests of the country demand continuous water line communication between the East and West as public highways, made for the use of all on equal terms, and subject to such tolls only as may be necessary to keep the same in repair.

That the central water line through Virginia, by way of the James River and Kanawha Canal, in connection with the proper improvements of the Ohio and Kanawha Rivers, is eminently of that character, from its directness across the very center of our country from north to south, with easy connections with the entire system of navigation of the great center basin, free from the climatic objections of frost in winter and heat in summer, and from interruption in time of war, with great capacity for freight; and it will furnish the cheapest, shortest, and most direct outlet from the Mississippi to the Atlantic.

That the character and feasibility of this improvement has been thoroughly investigated and indorsed by eminent engineers in the service of the State of Virginia through a long series of years; that the survey more recently made by the General Government entirely confirms the feasibility and eminent value of this work to the whole country; and a bid is now pending before Congress, by which it is asked that this work may be completed by the General Government, the States of Virginia and West Virginia surrendering all ownership, jurisdiction, and control over the same.

That in the completion of this work, by cheapening the cost of transportation of heavy products between East and West, and by investing with value the products of the region through which it passes, there will be a saving and profit annually to be shared in by the whole country, greater than the entire cost of the work.

This National Congress of Farmers of the entire country respectfully request that the next Congress of the United States take into favorable consideration the bill now pending for the completion of this great central water line.

Resolved, That a copy of these resolutions be furnished to the President of the United States, and President of the Senate, and Speaker of the House of Representatives, to be laid before their respective bodies at the next session of Congress.

REPORT ON THE RAILWAY SYSTEM.

The Committee on the Railway System submitted the following report:

WHEREAS, We recognize the railways of the country as an effectual means of developing its agricultural resources, and as having an interest, common and inseparable, with the country through which they pass; and,

WHEREAS, We have in times past fostered and aided them by liberal charters and concessions, made by public and private parties, and still desire to encourage further development of the railway system; therefore,

Resolved, That a fair degree of reciprocity would suggest that corporations having a common interest and bublic aid, should, in their turn, endeavor to subserve the interest of the country through which they pass, by charging fair rates of freights, and by the equitable and just treatment of all localities along their lines.

Resolved, That, on the contrary, railroad corporations in many instances have been exorbitant in their charges, have discriminated unjustly between localities, and have failed to respond to the generous grants of powers and moneys that have been given them by our National and State Governments.

Resolved, That the system adopted and now practiced in the building of railroads, viz: The soliciting of stock subscriptions from individuals, corporations, and counties, and after receiving these subsidies to depress the value of said stock by forcing it upon the market and depreciating its value to such an extent as to enable a few speculators to secure control of the road, thereby depriving those who aid in its construction of all voice in its management; increasing the cost four or five times above the amount it would have cost if those managing it in the outset had had the foresight to have the funds on hand at the start to build and equip said road; then requiring the producer and shipper to pay dividends upon the fictitious cost by charging excessive freight and passenger tariffs—operates most injuriously to the best interests of the farming class, and calls loudly for reform and restraint by adequate legislation.

Resolved, That we recommend all farmers to withhold their voices and their aid from railway corporations, unless it be fully conceded and agreed that corporations so aided are subject to regulation by the power incorporating them, and will not, after receiving the advantages conferred by the public authority, claim the immunities of a private corporation.

Resolved, That we indorse and will support the doctrine promulgated by some of our courts, that a railway corporation in receiving and exercising the State's right of eminent domain, and receiving aid raised by taxation from public authorities has thereby accepted and admitted itself to be a corporation with a public function, and subject to the power from which it has received its charter, in the limitation of its rates.

Resolved, That a railway being practically a monopoly, controlling the transportation of nearly all the country through which it passes; and that as competition, except at a few points, can not be relied upon to fix rates, therefore it becomes the duty of the State to fix reasonable maximum rates, affording a fair remuneration to the transporter, and without being an onerous charge to the producer and consumer.

Resolved, That, inasmuch as Belgium has succeeded in regulating the rates upon railways by Government lines, we ask an investigation of the proposition to control the rates upon existing railways by trunk lines built and controlled by the States authorities, and run at fixed uniform and cheap rates.

Resolved, That the consolidation of parallel lines of railway is contrary to public policy, and should be prohibited by law.

Resolved, That wherever a railway corporation owns or controls a line or lines in two or more States, it is the right and duty of the General Government to regulate the rates of freight and fare upon such lines, under the constitutional power to regulate commerce between the States.

Resolved, That we commend the thorough organization of the farmers of the country in local, county, and State organizations, for the purpose of reforming the great abuses and dealing out equal and exact justice to all men.

The foregoing report and resolutions were discussed together. Professor Brown, of Indiana; Dr. A. C. Stevenson, of Indiana; Mr. Flagg, of Illinois; Major Milliken, of Ohio; Mr. Papin, of South Carolina; Mr. Marlin, of Indiana; General Duke, of Virginia; Mr. Dalton, of Illinois; Colonel Anthony, of Kansas; Colonel Younger, of California; General Jackson, of Tennessee; Mr. Williams, of Indiana; Mr. Taylor, of Indiana; and Colonel Langdon, of Alabama, participated in the debate, which was characterized by great clearness and temperance of statement.

THE AGRICULTURAL COLLEGE LAND GRANT BILL.

A committee previously appointed to discuss the subject of the Agricultural Colleges, and the manner in which they have been conducted, submitted a majority report, embodying the following resolutions:

Resolved, That the body here assembled for the promotion of agriculture approve and indorse the efforts now being made to secure additional aid from Congress in behalf of the colleges established, in consequence of the land grant of 1862, in order to promote the liberal and practical education of the industrial classes in the several pursuits and professions of life.

Resolved, That the bill known as the Morrill Bill, which passed the Senate by a large majority, with the amendment thereto which passed the House of Representatives by a large majority, shows the liberal spirit of Congress in behalf of scientific, practical education, and an increasing interest in that kind of education which pertains to the application of science to the practical arts of life.

Resolved, That a committee from this body be appointed to memorialize Congress on this subject, and otherwise promote it in any manner as they may think best.

Mr. Marlin, of Indiana, opposed the adoption of the report, because he did not want the public lands squandered in that direction. He thought the Congress would probably adopt the recommendation of the report, but he did not think the people would approve their action. It is just as much of a steal to give the lands to the agricultural colleges as it is to give them to railroad monopolies or rings. These agricultural colleges were raising up a class of kid-gloved farmers, who looked with scorn upon the hardy tillers of the soil, and refused to acknowledge them on the street wherever they met.

Dr. Daniel Reid, of Missouri, one of the committee, ably defended the resolutions and the report, giving the history of legislation in connection with the subject under consideration. He further gave the opinions of eminent scholars and scientific men upon the importance of action in the direction indicated by the resolutions. We must have the application of science to the industrial arts to fully arrive at the extent of our capabilities.

PRO AND CON.

At this point a minority of the Committee delivered a report adverse to the adoption of the resolution.

Colonel Anthony, of Kansas, said the action of Congress

upon this matter was not in answer to any demand from the people. The men who represented the colleges at Washington last winter were not farmers, and were never connected with or interested in their caucuses. At the last meeting of the Congress an attempt had been made to commit the meeting to the same resolutions at the last hour of the session. Discussion was staved off on this report last year, and the Congress refused to pass the resolutions, thanks to the noble efforts of Dr. J. A. Warder, of Ohio. Will the gentlemen who preceded me tell me where are the fruits of this tree, which has cost the people ten million dollars' worth of public lands. Are they in the State of Missouri? Are they in the State of Ohio, where Senator Patterson was chosen President of an Agricultural College? The gentleman wanted the Congress to consider this question seriously. The Agricultural Colleges in this country have not been a success. The professors in them all, with one exception, have dinned in our ears that classical education is the intent of the act upon this subject. Mr. Davis, in his seat in Congress, charged Mr. Morrill with fraud in this matter, and that under the name of Agricultural Colleges, another attempt is being made to rob us of our lands. These gentlemen claim that it is a generous paternal movement on the part of the government to educate poor agriculturists' sons. It was to so educate all sons that they may become agriculturists. The intention was that these colleges should be to agriculture what the theological seminary is to the pulpit; what the medical college is to the medical profession, and what the blacksmith shop is to the apprentice. Have we any such Agricultural Colleges?

Dr. Reid rejoined that he was utterly amazed at the statements he had heard made. Does the gentleman know that these colleges are the growth of years? Does he expect perfection at once? It is utterly impossible. Eminent mechanics and agriculturists of the country say we must have another class of education for the people of the country. We have never received a quarter of the ten millions of acres of lands as charged by the gentleman who has just taken his seat. Some of the colleges contemplated have not even been commenced. In our State we have a successful institute in operation with by far the larger class of students in agriculture who throw aside classical and scientific education. In the matter of grape culture alone we have done more already than the whole cost of the institution. The first year two of our young men went from the college immediately into positions of superintendents of grape yards. The demand for scientific agricultural education is not of this country alone, but of the whole world. Let not the Congress stamp with disapproval such education. It is not intended to take one acre of the public domain from actual settlers, nor will it be done. Dr. Reid hoped the Congress would remember that the subject of Agricultural Colleges was yet in its infancy, and great results could not be immediately expected.

On of motion of A. C. Stevenson, of Indiana, the further consideration of this subject was indefinitely postponed.

THE ELECTION OF OFFICERS, ETC.

The Committee on Nominations reported for President, General W. H. Jackson of Tennessee; for Secretary, Charles W. Greene, of Tennessee; for Treasurer, Solomon Meredith, of Indiana. At the request of General Meredith, Mr. Poole, of Indiana, was placed in nomination for Treasurer, instead of himself.

On motion, the President was directed to cast the vote of

the Congress for the nominees reported by the Committee, which prevailed, and they were declared elected.

The list of States was then called, and the several delegations nominated their Vice-Presidents, and they were confirmed by the Congress as follows: Alabama, C. C. Langdon, Mobile; California, Col. C. C. Younger, San Jose; Colorado, W. M. Byers, Denver; Georgia, O. H. Jones, Atlanta; Illinois, A. M. Garland, Springfield; Indiana, General Solomon Meredith, Cambridge City; Kansas, J. K. Hudson, Wyandotte; Kentucky, Dr. R. J. Spurr, Lexington; Minnesota, Hon. William S. King, Minneapolis; Missouri, Hon. Norman J. Colman, St. Louis; Mississippi, Dr. M. W. Phillips, Oxford; Nebraska, Governor Robert Furnas, Lincoln; Ohio, J. M. Millikin, Hamilton; Pennsylvania, Hon. A. Boyd Hamilton, Harrisburg; South Carolina, Winborn Lawton, Charleston; Tennessee, C. W. Charlton, Knoxville; Vermont, O. S. Bliss, Georgia; Virginia, Colonel H. E. Peyton, Waterford; West Virginia, H. S. Walker, Charleston; Wisconsin, Eli Stilson, Oshkosh.

In the debate upon the selection of the place for the next Congress, Atlanta, Georgia, Charleston, South Carolina, Lincoln, Nebraska, and Columbus, Ohio, were put in nomination. After a short discussion, from which it was evident that nearly all of the members from the North-west were favorable to Atlanta, it was so elected, and the second Wednesday in May, 1874, was adopted as the time of meeting.

CHAPTER XXIX.

THE NORTH-WESTERN FARMERS' CONVENTION AT CHICAGO.

THE CALL, ATTENDANCE, AND ORGANIZATION.

On October 22d and 23d, 1873, a Convention composed of about three hundred delegates from Illinois, Wisconsin, Iowa, New York, Indiana, Nebraska, Minnesota, and Canada, was held in McCormick's Hall, Chicago, assembled at the call of the Illinois State Farmers' Association. Mr. James M. Allen, of Illinois, was elected to preside, and Mr. S. M. Smith and Mr. S. T. K. Prime were chosen Secretaries. All speeches were limited, by resolution, to ten minutes.

Mr. Flagg, President of the Illinois State Farmers' Association, read a communication from the Senate Transportation Committee, then about to hold a sitting at St. Louis, expressing their desire to confer with any delegates whom the Chicago Convention might appoint.

Mr. Norton, of Nebraska, offered a resolution, which was adopted, providing for the appointment of a committee of three citizens of Illinois, to report to the Convention the effect upon producers and shippers, of the legislation on railroads in Illinois, and whether they advise similar legislation in all the States. Messrs. M. B. Loyd, L. F. Ross and M. M. Hooton, were afterward selected as the Committee.

THE QUESTION OF GOVERMENTAL AID.

Mr. Caffeen, of Illinois, offered the following resolutions, and advocated them with force and spirit:

Resolved, That the first duty of the people is to subject all transportation companies or corporations to the restraints of law.

Resolved, That it is their next duty to urge the making of a ship-canal from the Atlantic seaboard, by the way of the lakes and the Illinois and Mississippi rivers, to deep water in the Gulf of Mexico, by the National Government.

Resolved, That it is their next duty to obtain the assistance of our Federal Government by an advance of credit, for the purpose of building a double-track freight railroad from near the line of the Kansas & Nebraska, as near an air line as possible, to New York city.

In the discussion which ensued upon the resolutions, Mr. Wright, of Wisconsin, was in favor of the water route proposed, but was opposed to the General Government undertaking to build it. Seventy-five thousand dollars a year failed to keep the bar at the mouth of the Mississippi dredged. A canal could be built making a way clear to the ocean from New Orleans, at a cost of $8,000,000, and that would give an outlet for the West by way of the Mississippi, reducing the freight to Liverpool twenty cents a hundred. If the railroads added five cents per hundred to their rates, it would be equivalent to laying a tax upon the farmers of $50,000,000 a year. He was in favor of the scheme, and also of the Niagara route, but did not care to leave the work to the government. They must elect men to Congress who would do the people justice. Ten millions of white men were being robbed every day out of half their earnings by these monopolies.

Mr. Perry believed the government should do the work, and take charge of it, and then we could elect honest men to take charge of the works.

Busy Bees.

Mr. Bishop, of Illinois, wanted present relief. He did not object to being kept "busy as a bee," but was tired of working fifteen hours a day. If they waited for ship canals there would not be many of them left. He wanted the extension of patents to cease, and thought we should have a lower tariff.

Mr. Lockhardt, of Illinois, was opposed to the government going into the canal-building business.

Mr. Flagg wanted the government to do whatever it could do better than private parties. The Erie Canal was better managed than the Erie Railroad, and the Michigan Canal was run better than some railroads. The question was, which of the routes would give the most relief for the least money? There was the Kanawha and the Niagara Canals schemes. Each had its favorite. The Convention should choose something, and then urge it upon Congress.

Mr. Dixon, of Iowa, argued that water transportation was slow. Railroads could be built and run cheaper than canals. They should bring railroads down to hard pan, and then they would have cheaper transportation. He gave instances of discrimination in Iowa. What we want is immediate relief.

On motion, the resolutions and substitutes were referred to the Committee on Resolutions.

HON. W. C. FLAGG'S ADDRESS ON THE REGULATION OF RAILROADS.

When the subject of State legislation to control the rates of transportation came on, Mr. Flagg addressed the Convention at length, substantially as follows:

In their original conception and execution, railroads were private property; built upon private land, or by special permission of the people through whose land they run. This kind of a road might justly claim to be exempt from all government regulations, except police regulation, so long as it did not offer itself to do the business of a common carrier; if it would do only the business of the persons owning the road; would undertake no public function, and would not exercise the power of eminent domain conferred upon it by the sovereign power. This is the kind of railway that attorneys ought to be talking about, when they deny the right of government to interfere with railway management. But railways of that kind were few and unimportant. Government generally was requested by the railways themselves to interfere in the inception of their enterprise, to the extent, at least, of giving certain privileges to a corporation, including the right to condemn and use the land of others. This was done through a charter granted by the Legislature, under a general or special law. In this country most of the railway charters were granted by or under a State law; by special act or under general laws; but a few lines have been chartered through the Territories by act of Congress.

By these charters, the State transferred, or attempted to transfer, its right of eminent domain to the railway company, so that it may go and take possession of such lands as it may need, on the alleged ground of its being for the public use; and also the town, county, or township may vote subsidies to the railway company, on the ground that such donation will be for the public benefit. The railway was then vested with a public function. The State had given it privileges which it had no right to give, or else the railroad company was no longer a private company, and owes special duties to the public.

Any one conveying for hire becomes a public carrier.

The railway was a common carrier, and a good deal more. In the nature of the câse, it was its duty to make a special point of serving the public, even if the highest attainable profits were not realized. The company had, it was true, a private duty to its stockholders of paying the rate of interest that is reasonable in permanent and not fluctuating investments. But besides this, it owed the duty of cheap rates and large business, so as to build up the country through which it passes.

The common carrier could limit his business. The railway company was in duty bound to find railway service, at least to the capacity of the average freight and passengers offered.

The common carrier was liable to have his rates of fares and freight fixed or limited by law. They might say to the railway: "If you don't want to carry passengers for three cents per mile, you can sell out to some one who will, or tear up your track and let another company see if they can not serve the public at reasonable rates." The Dartmouth College decision was referred to. Railway lawyers told us that a railway is a private corporation; that a charter of a private corporation is an unlimited contract between the State and the corporation; that the Constitution of the United States forbids a State from passing any "law impairing the obligation of contracts;" that a law fixing reasonable maximum rates by our State Legislature was an impairing of the charter contracts existing between the State of Illinois and many or most of the railroads in it, and therefore unconstitutional. All of which was based upon the Dartmouth College case. But the railway received and used privileges which the State had no right to confer upon private corporations, and therefore had admitted itself, by its own solicitation and acts, to be at least a corporation with a public function; and in no wise in a condition analogous to that of Dartmouth College. Then it was by no means an unquestioned doctrine whether all charters, even of private companies, are contracts. It was a most dangerous doctrine. It implied that whoever can buy or steal a bill through the Legislature shall be protected in his iniquity by that "contract" forever after. In any event, the railway was reduced to this dilemma; either the State had conferred upon it, and it had exercised, privileges to which it is not entitled, and is a trespass upon the rights and property of others, or else it had admitted its obligation to serve the public and the public welfare, and is subject to regulation as a common carrier, perhaps, in either case.

Another class of roads were not only chartered, but received a grant. The Union Pacific had received immense donations of this kind. The Illinois Central and other western roads had been similarly assisted. In all these cases, the right of government to control, and the obligations of railway companies to serve the public, were correspondingly increased.

Government intervention was practically sought in all of these kind of roads. Difficulties and disputes arose only in reference to the chartered and subsidised roads. Where private gain was antagonistic to public welfare, something must be done to cure the avariciousness. They had conspiracies against the welfare of the people in other shapes, but in none so mighty as that of the railways. He wished to notice the confused conceptions that have existed as to the nature of railways and railway service. With all the changes that the railroad had brought about, they could not appreciate what they might accomplish in the future. Before fifty years had passed, narrow-guage or horse-railways might occupy the principal country roads; and thus most farm houses would have railway access. The railroads of the country were its highways, that must carry its travel and its commerce. This was what the Constitution of Illinois meant, when it declares the railways of the State public highways—free to all persons. The people, after a little disastrous experimenting, forty years ago, resolved to leave the management of railways, their building and operating, to private corporations, with more or less regulating, and this had caused the function of railways to be lost sight of. The necessity of protecting the rights of travelers and shippers was not appreciated. Feeble attempts had been made in the beginning to fix maximum rates, but the prevailing idea had always been to rely upon competition.

But that was a delusion, and as a rule a railroad had a practical monopoly of the country through which it passes. "There are many cases," said John Stuart Mill, "in which the agency of whatever nature, by which a service is performed, is certain from the nature of the case, to be virtually alone; in which a practical monopoly, with all the power it confers of taxing the community, can not be prevented from existing.

"The community need some other security for the performance of the service of corporations than the interests of the managers; and it is the part of government either to subject the business to reasonable conditions for the general advantage, or to retain such power over it that the profits of the monopoly may at least be obtained for the public. This applied to a railway. There were always practical monopolies, but the government which concedes such monopoly to a private company, does much as if it allowed an individual or association to levy any tax they choose. To make the concession for a limited time is as justifiable as the principle which justifies patents for inventions; but the State should fix a maximum of rates."

Mr. Mill, although a free-trader in the broadest sense of the term, yet recognized a class of companies needing government control.

Mr. Frederick Hill was quoted to sustain the same opinion. All who had studied the subject would agree with Mr. Adams, when he said, in his speech in behalf of the Massachusetts railroad commissioners: "That while the result of ordinary competition is to reduce and equalize prices, the result of railroad competition is to produce local irregularities, and arbitrarily raise and depress prices."

They had had, for instance, a railroad system of some sort in Illinois for about twenty years. The amount of service had wonderfully increased, and rogues had learned how to acquire railways at low prices. Figures were given to show that, notwithstanding the increase in their business, the rates of some roads had materially increased.

In September, 1873, nine different roads, radiating from St. Louis eastward, were charging, in violation of law, 4.69 cents per mile for passengers, or more than fifty-five per cent. more than they were twenty years ago.

Combination between rival lines had destroyed competition, except that occasional cutting of rates made fluctuations that could only be taken advantage of by a few shippers. Railroads were practically regulated, not by competition but by combination.

This regulation meant that the railroad managers are feudal lords, and the people are their serfs; that every car of produce that passes over the New York Central road must pay a heavy toll for right of transit to Vanderbilt, the robber and baron of modern feudalism; that the shipper must truckle to railroad officials for special favors, and skulk and avoid the farmers' movement, when they knew it was right, for fear they would compromise their pecuniary interests.

Dissatisfied with the results of this kind of regulation, the people ask governmental interference and regulation thereby.

This might be national by act of Congress, which has power to regulate commerce among the several States. Or this regulation might be done by State power, confined, of course, to the limits of that State. Or the roads might be placed under the control of a board of commissioners. Or by owning all or a portion of the roads and operating them at cheap fixed rates.

The people preferred a law to which those who were aggrieved might appeal, such as laws fixing maximum rates of fare and freight, and punishing their violation. Instances of the operations of railroad laws in several States were given. Thus far, in Illinois, the legislation was faulty, but there was a more determined effort in that direction because the constitution necessitates action, and the people have ratified that section by a large majority.

The ignorance of legislation and the difficulty of the subject, had caused the lack of success in passing laws of this character. The men in the Legislature who worked for railroad rings always got the best of the honest but not posted members. The circumstances surrounding one road were very different from those affecting another. It was about as difficult to adjust a railroad tariff as it is a protective tariff, and many are not inclined to do it for the same reason. Charles Francis Adams regarded relief under this head as hopeless. The parliamentary committee of 1872 considered that legal maximum rates afforded little real protection, since they are always fixed so high that it was, or became sooner or later, the interest of the companies to carry at lower rates. But the speaker thought that a uniform maximum passenger rate of three cents per mile would relieve the public and prevent a good deal of extortion, without much, if at all, diminishing the gross receipts of the roads. He had known a relatively better business to follow such a course. If the Illinois Central were legalized to carry at three cent a mile, it would be for its benefit. The rates on freight, especially on local business, were far above a reasonable maximum rate. They were, before the first of July, 4.72 cents per ton per mile, and 2.16 cents for through rates, so that as a temporary recourse they should have legislation giving reasonable maximum rates on freight. They wanted the cheapest rates obtainable. Any thing which added to the cost of transportation aggravates the tax, and any thing which reduces it, removes one more burden from hnman toil. "It was not enough," says Drake, "that there should be free movement for thought; free movement for the people themselves was equally as important." Travel increased as its cost diminished; whatever, therefore, operated as a tax on locomotion is inconsistent with the highest principles of State policy.

There was a need for something more flexible than statute law that can adapt rates to different conditions and classes of railways. This suggested the function of Railway Commissioners assigned to our new board, of making up schedules of maximum rates for each road. This he thought was the best thing possible under the present circumstances, but its sucess was not yet assured. They were hampered by a pro rata requirement that compels them and the companies to fix rates according to distance, whereas the expense of carriage depends upon many other considerations. But they had a chance to ascertain what was a fair compensation, and not a gross extortion. But the great difficulty they had to encounter was insufficient and vicious legislation, and the limitation of their power by State laws. There was no proper legislation regarding reasonable maximum rates; none concerning railways as public highways. There was a disposition already to find fault with the commissioners, but it was unjust. They were making the most of the laws that were given them. But the limitations of State lines would be a difficulty of a permanent character. The Illinois commissioners wanted cheap freights to the seaboard, but they were powerless. Indiana, Ohio, and New York are in the way. National legislation or regulation is required.

But the problem would increase in difficulty when the whole nation must be legislated for, or when the commissioners appointed by government attempt to fix uniform rates for the Central Pacific and the Old Colony railroads. It was deemed by many an impossible task.

This suggested the theory of the government ownership of roads, now advocated a good deal in England, and in this country by Mr. Andrews, Prof. Amasa Walker, and others.

Mr. Hill, whom the speaker quoted, argues that State ownership will alone give the advantages of competition, because amalgamations and agreements are soon made by private companies, and State ownership alone furnishes a steady opponent to combination. The example of Belgium was cited in confirmation of the soundness of the principle. Mr. Hill was of the opinion that State control furnishes the only approximation to free trade in railway service. Prof. Walker was quoted as advocating the idea that the United States Government should buy or take possession of all the roads of the country, under the right of eminent domain. As the roads would save the interest on the expenditure, he holds it would involve really but little expense to the government. Charles Francis Adams was in favor of the country's owning a part of the lines, and running them so as to compete with and lower the rates of the others.

Regulations of our existing through rates by improving and increasing the water ways of the country was a favorite idea in many quarters. A ship canal at Niagara, a canal connection of the Ohio and James rivers, a canal connection of the Tennessee and Savannah rivers, the improvement of the mouth of the Mississippi, are among the most prominent; and in regulating commerce a part of the year, it was likely they could be made effective. But water evaporates and freezes up; iron rails do not, and he looked to them as the future carriers even of cheap freights. Mr. Adams had said that steam locomotion abolished the Mississippi. But it did not, until freight could be carried by rail for one mill per ton per mile. But rivers, and lakes, and canals had lost their prestige, and railways alone, he thought, could regulate railways.

Regulation was again sought by dividing, practically, the road and the rolling stock; making one company owner of the road, and perhaps of the motive power, and another owner of the cars carrying the freight and passengers, thus securing competition of different transportation companies on the same road. The various "colored" lines, were they not perverted in the hands of rings within the railway corporations, would speedily become something of this kind, if they had the right of travel over all roads.

The speaker, after the above general history of experience concerning railway regulations, said he wished to give a few impressions of his own, as to what was desirable and best.

First. He would favor a general system of national highways, limited at present to three north and south, and four east and west; railways generally distributed and connecting the principal centres of business. They should be constructed as fast as the States through which they pass can assume the expense.

At present the great need was for a new northern freight route from Omaha to the seaboard. No entirely new route to the east had been built for fifteen years, and yet the local railways of the northwest, feeding these through routes, have at least trebled their mileage. Hence the demand made at Chicago and at New York for increased facilities; and this line, in some shape, would be built before many years. The commerce of the Mississippi was controlled by monopolies, and it would not be long before the southern trade would be compelled to ask for transportation not controlled by single companies, but by government.

There was not the present demand for north and south lines that will exist when emigration has measurably filled up the country. Then would come the more natural exchange of products between different latitudes,—sugar for wheat, and cotton for corn; and the north and south would do the carrying trade. The seven roads suggested would have a mileage of 8,000 miles, and would intersect about twenty-five States. These States would own, or at least control, the bonds issued to build their respective proportion of these roads, and the whole system be managed by national laws.

He would like to see the State have the power to build such roads as might, if they desired, connect them with these main arteries.

The power ought to be vested in every town, city, and county, to build tram, horse, and steam railways, just as they would other roads and thoroughfares. In other words, carry to its legitimate conclusion the principle that a railway is a highway, and just as much to be made and controlled by public authority as our public roads.

In conclusion, the speaker drew a glowing picture of the future under just and equitable legislation, and exhorted the convention to work that the end might soon be attained. There were strong objections to governmental interference, but he believed a happy medium was attainable.

MR. HOOTON ON RAILROAD ABUSES.

Mr. M. M. Hooton then took up the subject of railroads, and said:

Certain great questions, relating to the finance of the world, and more especially of the north-western States of America, seem to be pressing with unusual force at this time for a correct solution. The present money panic is but the voice of justice, demanding, in unmistakable language, that the laws of equity and fairness shall not be violated, and wherein they have been infringed that just retribution shall be made.

The natural forces, always at work in a well-regulated community, make ultimate redress for great wrongs inevitable, in one way or another. Hence, when a government and people have permitted greedy speculation to corrupt all the channels of trade, and oppress the great mass of the people for the enrichment and aggrandizement

Harvest Scene.

of the few, as has been the case in this country for the last twenty years, the exercise of ordinary prudence should induce them to prepare to receive the punishment which must come sooner or later.

I have said, the forces which make the punishment inevitable, are always at work. In order that we may see more clearly how they work, it will be necessary for us to take into consideration the varied relations of the occupations and interests of the people. These are all represented and comprehended in two great classes, which we shall denominate productive and non-productive. And as we Americans estimate every thing in dollars and cents, we will, for the purposes of this work, call them investments.

The productive investments are those which *create* and *increase* the aggregate wealth of the country. The non-productive investments are those which are devoted to the manipulation of industrial products.

These two classes of investment, when properly balanced, are alike essential to the constitution of a healthy and vigorous political society. But when this healthy balance is lost, the result can only be detrimental. To illustrate more fully the relation of these two classes of investments, and how one may affect the other, we will, figuratively, establish a new community, so small in numbers as to make our estimates and illustrations easy of comprehension by all. Twenty families go into a country where they engage in all the pursuits of civilized society. Ten of them, with a capital of $100,000, engage in non-producing enterprises. They lend money, establish banks, build telegraphs, railroads, establish insurance companies, etc. The other ten, with a like capital, engage in the productive industries. They improve farms, raise wheat, corn, and cattle. They manufacture all kinds of machinery, etc. They dig the ore from the ground, and convert it first into iron, then into steel, and then again into implements of industry. At the end of each year, it is found that with their utmost industry and economy they have been able to increase the aggregate wealth of the entire community three per cent. on both kinds of investments. This income was derived from industry and fair dealing under laws that bore equally upon all.

But it is a long lane that has no turning. In the course of years, the non-producers, having more leisure time, get into mischief, as idle hands are sure to do. They so influence the government as to get laws made which give them an advantage. They raise the rates of interest, and expand and inflate all their sources of income. Not satisfied with this increased income on their legitimate investment, they issue false certificates of bank, railroad, and telegraph stocks to an equal amount. They now demand, and, by skillful manipulation of Congress, the Legislature, and the courts, collect ten per cent. on both true and false investments. The general prosperity of the country is unchanged.

The creation of new wealth amounts to three per cent. But one-half of the community receives ten per cent. on their real values, and ten per cent. on a like amount of false certificates of value, making their income equivalent to twenty per cent. on their real investment. Under these circumstances what must be the condition of the other half of the community? They have received their three per cent. on the one hand, but on the other they have paid out enough to raise the income of the non-producers from three per cent., and are therefore losers to the amount of seventeen per cent. on their whole wealth. The question naturally arises how long would it require for the producers to become bankrupt, and their entire capital to be transferred to the non-producers? A little over five years would accomplish this result.

General bankruptcy of the industrial classes or repudiation must follow. But these are not the only resulting evils, for, during these years of rampant speculation, many new enterprises have been put on foot. The money of the country is diverted from the legitimate channels of trade, and invested in railroads and telegraphs through uninhabited regions of country, where the investment can not be expected to pay for many years.

To supply this demand for ready cash, the banks have advanced all the money in their vaults on false and true certificates, which in time of a panic can not be realized upon. Money becomes scarce for legitimate trade, and depositors attempt to withdraw their money from the banks. A "run" begins, and the banks must fail, bringing disaster to all concerned. This is but a picture of what has been transacted in this country in the last few years. The non-producers have so manipulated the government as to get from it vast subsidies and monopolies, which have been used, not for the public good, but to corrupt our Legislatures and Congress. Not being satisfied with a fair income on their investments, they have watered their stock in many instances to more than double the real value; they have diverted the money of the country from its legitimate function; the crops of the country can not be moved at remunerative prices. Witness the corn burned for fuel in Iowa, and the pork sold in Illinois for three and three and one-half cents per pound.

At Three Cents a Pound.

The industrial classes have recently discovered the injustice of this procedure, and will no longer pay rates on these fraudulent investments. They have come to their "bottom dollar," and are led to inquire what has become of the price of all their toil. They have discovered that they are now, and have been for years, paying rates on the railroads alone of near $800,000,000 above their real cost, and still a larger sum more than they ought to have cost. This being so, who will be surprised at the statement that these frauds cover billions of dollars, held for private gain at the expense of the industries of the country? The labor of this country can and will pay these rates no longer. They now call on all the powers of government to protect them from the injustice thus put upon them.

The result is what the bankers and public journals call "a want, great want, of confidence." Confidence in what? Simply this: That the producers of this country will be stupid enough to go on paying ten or fifteen per cent. on fraudulent certificates and bonds in which there was never one dollar invested. "Only this, and nothing more." This is a big confidence game, but it won't win any longer. The result is, that capitalists will no longer invest in these "bogus" securities, and the banks that have advanced largely on them will be compelled to break. This is just as it should be. There is no way out of the difficulty but to wholly purge our stock market and finance of every dollar of these false stocks, or to reduce the aggregate value of the real and false by the amount of the false. This implies the breaking of many banks, brokers, and dealers, as well as many innocent laboring men, but it can not be avoided. To continue the present state of things, is only to defer the inevitable retribution, and make it worse when it does come. It is this state of affairs which has swept Jay Cooke & Co. from the boards, and shaken to its foundation nearly every bank in the country. We may well fear that the worst of the crisis has not yet passed. The struggles of the financial cormorants that have amassed millions through these frauds will be terrible before they can be made to disgorge $2,000,000,000; and to remove these false stocks from the business of the country will necessarily cause a great commotion. But it must be done before we can have a solid basis of finance.

But this terrible ordeal once passed, a great reward may be expected for all pains. Money will cease to go to the Northern Pacific or any other railroad that will not pay interest on the investment. It will cease to be hoarded for speculation in fancy stocks. The money of the country will be used in legitimate trade. It will be sufficiently abundant to enable dealers to pay fair prices for agricultural products.

When we have passed through this crisis, we may be expected to enter upon an era of prosperity scarcely equaled in our history. But before this good time can be fully realized, the voters must see to it that every office-holder, whose hands are tarnished with monopolies, Credit Mobiliers, salary-grab, back pay or forward pay, is finally retired to private life or the penitentiary. Reforms necessarily move slowly when the officers of the government may be bought and sold like cattle in the open market.

In conclusion, I wish to call the attention of the Convention to a term just now becoming very popular in connection with railroad incomes. All parties agree that the owners of these roads are entitled to a "reasonable" income on their real investments. The chief difficulty seems to be in determining the basis of reasonableness. It is plain, from what has been said in regard to the relations of productive and non-productive investments, that, as the producers of the country must pay the income on the non-productive investments, that any rate which exceeds the producer's rate of income must be unreasonable.

Therefore, if, when the country is specially unprosperous, and the industrial interests suffer loss, the capitalists' rates of income on cash investments become so that he suffers loss in sympathy with the general adversity, he has no right to complain.

This is the only true basis of reasonableness, the adoption of which—in my opinion—can save a nation from financial convulsions. It is claimed that the legal rate of interest should be accepted as reasonable. But it is plain that this may be too high or too low, as it is entirely arbitrary, and has, therefore, none of the elements of reasonableness in it.

THE RESOLUTIONS AND THEIR CONSIDERATION.

The Committee on Resolutions reported the following preamble and resolutions:

It is the duty of every government to protect its people. But capital, directed by unscrupulous minds, reaps the profits of their labor. Men of great wealth revel in luxury, while those who earn the money are destitute of many of the comforts of life. Our State Legislatures have made laws depriving us of our land, for which we have a title from the General Government, for the benefit of railroad companies, because it seemed for the public good. Subsidies have been granted them, and Congress has, with a lavish hand, given them public lands—the people's inheritance; and the result is extortion and oppression. Therefore, be it

"Pay as you go." Live in the old house till the farm is all paid for.

Resolved, By this Convention that we most respectfully but earnestly request Congress, without needless delay, to pass a maximum freight and passage law regulating traffic between the States, and our Legislatures a law regulating it within the States; and we hereby protest against the further granting of any subsidies whatever to private corporations of any kind.

Resolved, That experience has proved that freight by water is the cheapest, and we most respectfully ask that Congress, in order to relieve us of our burdens, speedily take measures to open water routes from the Mississippi to the seaboard.

Resolved, That to lessen the burdens of transportation is, as far as possible, to do without transportation, and therefore we ask and urge our people to do all in their power to create and sustain by their patronage home manufactures.

Resolved, That we hail with pleasure the prospect of the early completion of the double-track Continental Freight Railway from the city of New York to Omaha, which promises that grain shall be transported over said railway at a cost not exceeding eight mills per ton per mile.

Resolved, That debt should ever be held as one of our greatest enemies; that it deprives us of manliness, and in a measure makes us slaves; that to live within our means, however small, and to pay as we go, will contribute to our success. Recognizing the fact that the people are in earnest, we would urge them to free themselves of this curse, so that, if a final struggle must come between the people and monopoly, our houses may be in order, and we the better able to withstand it.

Resolved, That no one industry can be protected by legislation, except at the expense of all other industries, and that we are opposed to all special legislation.

Resolved, That we recommend the thorough organization of the farmers of the country in local, county, and State organizations, for the purpose of reforming the great abuses now existing, and dealing out equal justice to all men.

Considerable discussion arose on the adoption of the resolutions. The preamble and first resolution were adopted without remarks.

The transportation clause was the occasion of a spirited debate, in which Mr. Morton, of Nebraska, Mr. H. C. Wheeler, of Illinois, Mr. Beman, of Iowa, and other delegates participated. The debate showed the Convention to be divided in opinion in respect to this question. Finally, a substitute, as follows, was adopted:

We demand the construction of railroads, and the improvement of water communications, between the interior and seaboard, the same to be owned and operated by the General Government, for the purpose of affording cheap and ample transportation, and to protect the people from the exactions of monopolies.

The third resolution, relating to home manufactures, was carried.

The fourth resolution, relating to the double-track continental freight railroad from New York to Omaha, was considered. A substitute was offered that it is imperatively necessary that the people obtain from the National Government assistance for building a double-track freight railroad from near the line of the Kansas & Nebraska, as nearly in air-line as possible, to the city of New York. The substitute was again read, put, and laid on the table. The fourth or original resolution was then put, and lost by a unanimous vote, and the substitute carried. The fifth, the sixth, and the last resolutions were carried unanimously.

Mr. Lawrence, of Illinois, offered two resolutions recommending the State Farmers' Association of Illinois to furnish such information to the Railway Commissioners as will warrant the prosecution of suits against the defaulting companies, and advising the farmers of other States to obtain a similar law from their Legislatures. The resolutions were adopted.

Mr. F. C. Capreol, of Canada, President of the Huron and Ontario Ship Canal, in an elaborate address presented the merits of the great scheme for water communication between the ocean and the West, by which sea-going vessels of 1,200 tons burden might pass directly to the upper lake ports. He stated that the construction of the canal would lessen the length of route by some 800 miles, and increase the value of grain ten per cent. a bushel. He showed that almost all the benefits arising from such a canal would go to the Western agriculturists; the only profit accruing to the Canadians would be the toll charged for passing vessels.

On motion, Mr. Capreol was requested to present his plans for cheap transportation in such form that they may be incorporated in the printed proceedings of the Convention.

PORK TO BE HELD FOR A RISE.

After a short address from Rev. W. R. Alger, of Massachusetts, Mr. Hunter, of Illinois, offered the following resolution, which, after a spirited but principally one-sided debate, was adopted:

Resolved, That this Convention recommend to the farmers of the North-west that, in order to carry out in a practical manner the spirit and the letter of co-operation, they will withhold from the market their live products until the price shall reach such a figure that the producer shall receive the legitimate fruits of his labor; and we consider that $5.00 per 100 pounds, gross, is a just and fair price, both to producer and consumer.

Held for $5.00 per 100.

REPORT ON THE ILLINOIS RAILROAD LAW.

The Committee on Railway Legislation submitted the following report, which was adopted:

The committee appointed to report to the Convention the effect upon producers and shippers of the legislation on railways in Illinois, and whether they advise similar legislation in all the States, have had the subject under consideration, and would report that its cost of transportation has not yet been reduced to the extent that effect has not yet been such as its friends contemplated; that the was expected when the law was first passed; but when the railroads of the State are compelled to a strict observance of the same, it is believed that favorable results will follow. Your committee repectfully represent, on the advisory portion of the resolution, that they are not yet prepared to advise other States, but believe that the people of the other States in the Union would be benefited by the passage of a law similar to the law of Illinois, or a better one if they can.

It was moved that when the Convention adjourn, it be *sine die*. Mr. Boone, of Jo Daviess County, Ill., said they could not afford to adjourn *sine die*. The producing classes sustain the same relations in modern society as serfs did in the days of history. This was to be considered as an agricultural congress. He proposed an adjournment for one year, to the same time and place.

An adjournment, subject to the call of the President of the Illinois State Farmers' Association, was then proposed, and adopted.

CHAPTER XXX.

BIOGRAPHICAL SKETCH OF WILLIAM SAUNDERS.

ONE OF THE FATHERS OF THE PATRONS OF HUSBANDRY.

William Saunders has been termed the father of the Order of Patrons of Husbandry. He was one of the originators of the ideas upon which the Order is founded. He wrote the preamble to the Constitution of the National Grange, and enunciated the principles upon which the organization is based. Although he never took the field as an organizer of Granges, not being personally calculated for that work, nevertheless, he has allowed no opportunity to pass of asserting the importance of the organization and the good that might be accomplished through its means.

His standing throughout the entire country as a working horticulturist and landscape gardener, the importance of his experiments, and the elucidation, through his writings, of various subjects connected with practical horticulture, have placed him at the head of his profession. His retiring manners never allowed him to place himself conspicuously before the public, and yet no person can converse with, or listen to, him for five minutes without being aware that his is a master mind, which works only to bring out results. Hence, all who know him, either personally or by reputation, have felt that if he recommended the Order of Patrons of Husbandry, that organization could not be very far wrong; and it is acknowledged that, without his influence and aid, it would have been difficult to establish the Order in the confidence of the agricultural masses—if, indeed, it could have continued to exist at all.

EARLY CAREER.

Mr. Saunders was born at St. Andrews, Fifeshire, Scotland, in December of 1822, and was educated in that city of universities. After leaving college, in his sixteenth year, he was articled as an apprentice to a gardener, and has followed that business, in its various branches, up to the present time. After serving out his apprenticeship, he engaged as a journeyman, working under first-class instructors, both in Scotland and England, and ultimately attaining the responsible management of an important establishment.

Early in 1848, Mr. Saunders left London for New York. His letters of introduction immediately secured him employment in his profession. He was, for some time, employed as overseer of the extensive farm and garden of John Hopkins, Esq., of Baltimore, Md., where he introduced important improvements. He erected a cold grapery, three hundred feet in length; formed flower gardens, artificial lakes, and other landscape adornments; introduced thorough draining on the farm, fall plowing of the clayey soils, and deep plowing of all. Finishing his work there, he was next employed in laying out the grounds of Thomas Winans, of Baltimore. From thence he went to Germantown, Pa., and devoted himself exclusively to landscape gardening, the laying out of cemeteries and extensive public and private grounds being among his specialties.

In treating cemeteries, Mr. Saunders introduced a system

of combining the effect of landscape gardening with the more utilitarian purposes of the grounds. In the arrangement of the grounds of suburban and country residences, he introduced the planting of useful fruit-bearing trees, as being ornamental objects as well. In order to study the habits, forms, and outlines of the various fruit trees, he visited orchards in many parts of the country. Mr. Saunders also combined garden architecture with other professional duties—among other things, introducing the now common mode of building glass greenhouses with fixed roofs, instead of the older mode of sliding sashes.

An early, devoted attention to foreign grape culture induced the study of mildew and its causes. In this he was led to the conclusion, which he afterward demonstrated as fact, that this mildew was mainly produced by injudicious ventilation. As a remedy, he advocated the admission of air from the top only, and built many houses without any other means of ventilation—none being provided at the bottom.

LITERARY LABORS.

In 1850, Mr. Saunders, in a paper written for *Hovey's Magazine*, showed the principles governing plant growth in propagating from cuttings—that of keeping the bottoms of the cuttings from thirty to forty degrees Fahrenheit warmer than the buds exposed above the surface—thus exciting the root-forming process, while bud-growth was retarded. This paper was widely copied in European horticultural journals. The practice thus recommended is now universally followed. A suggestion that the rooting of cuttings was in a great measure dependent upon the amount of starch contained in them was, twenty years later, demonstrated as fact by the investigations of German physiologists.

While engaged as a landscape gardener, Mr. Saunders' attention was early called to the lack of, and necessity for, proper ornamentation in the grounds surrounding the public schools, seminaries, and colleges of the country. He has long and urgently advocated, both by precept and example, this great necessity. The growth of the public taste and effort in this direction is largely due to his efforts.

Mr. Saunders has, first and last, furnished much practical matter for the rural press. He was a frequent contributor to *Hovey's Magazine of Horticulture* and the *Horticulturist*, and furnished, for several years, a comprehensive monthly calendar of operations for the vegetable garden, orchard, forcing houses, and the conservatory, in the last named journal. Besides writing much on landscape gardening, in architectural and horticultural journals, he has also edited and adapted various foreign works on horticulture and landscape gardening for publication in this country. He also edited, for some years, the *Farmer and Gardener*, of Philadelphia; in addition to which, his labors on other periodicals have been considerable.

CONNECTION WITH THE AGRICULTURAL DEPARTMENT.

Immediately after the battle of Gettysburg, he was intrusted, by the Governors of various States, to lay out the Soldiers' National Cemetery at that place, being the first cemetery of the kind formed during or immediately after the war.

While practicing landscape gardening, the services of Mr Saunders were in great demand, involving so much travel, and so great demands upon his time, that, his health giving way, he was obliged to abandon active labor in this direction.

Shortly after the organization of the Department of Agriculture, at Washington, Mr. Saunders undertook, temporarily, the superintendence of the gardens of this department, but resigned the position after a few months' service. He subsequently undertook the work again, under a permanent arrangement. Since the Autumn of 1862, he has been retained as Superintendent of the grounds, and has constantly labored for their extension, securing, in 1864, the grounds now occupied by the Department, and furnishing the designs for laying out and ornamenting the grounds, including the terraces, conservatories, etc. He has regularly furnished his quota to the reports, besides contributing many other articles for its pages on landscape gardening, etc.

FUTURE PROJECTS.

One of the important endeavors which, for years past, has especially engaged the attention of Mr. Saunders, is to procure for the Department of Agriculture, a complete collection of economic plants, both native and foreign. Another is to plant and form a complete arboretum, representing every tree and shrub that is hardy, from all quarters of the globe, in the latitude of Washington. Both of these great enterprises are fully under way, and the collections, even now, are the most complete in the country, that of St. Louis' most liberal citizen, Mr. Shaw, coming next.

Another noteworthy project for which Mr. Saunders is especially solicitous, is to secure, for the Department, sufficient land to plant a specimen of every fruit-bearing tree, shrub, and vine that can be procured. This, if it can be carried out, will greatly assist correct pomological nomenclature, and also prove, in many other respects, of inestimable value to the fruit-producing interests of the country at large. Mr. Saunders, since his connection with the Department, has been indefatigable in introducing and disseminating a large number of useful plants. Some of these have not proved valuable; many have not realized the full expectation that was hoped for; but enough has been done to satisfy the most skeptical that the effort in this direction is of the greatest importance to the nation. It requires time to acclimatize these exotics, and constant attention to become acquainted with the mode of culture necessary for them. It is a work that only the Government can properly carry out, and, while his efforts in this and other directions are fully appreciated by the people of the country, it is hoped the Government will take no steps calculated to disappoint the wishes of the agricultural masses in respect to these matters.

CHAPTER XXXI.

BIOGRAPHICAL SKETCH OF GEN. W. H. JACKSON.

EARLY LIFE.

William H. Jackson was born in Paris, Henry Co., Tenn., Dec. 1st, 1835. His father, Dr. A. Jackson, and his mother, Mary W. Hunt, both natives of Virginia, were married in 1829, and removed to West Tennessee in 1830. The only surviving children of this marriage were Wm. H. and Howell E. Jackson, the latter now an eminent lawyer of Memphis, Tenn.

The subject of this sketch was reared amid good and wholesome precepts in the home circle, and sound instruction in the school and church. He gained fast friends for his high spirit and the zeal with which he espoused the cause of the weak or younger children in his schoolboy days. His school broils all originated in his fervor in defending the weak against the strong. Naturally of a sanguine temperament, it required the severe military training of West Point, where he graduated, to subdue this fiery spirit. The future of his manhood was early foreshadowed in the impetuous youth, noted more for energy of action than intensity of application. His fondness for field sports often conflicted with the strict discharge of the duty required in his early school days.

AT WEST POINT AND IN THE ARMY.

In the spring of 1852, being at that time a member of the senior class of the West Tennessee College at Jackson, he received the appointment of cadet at West Point. This change brought about higher aspirations, stronger efforts, and new associations. In 1856, he graduated with the very large class of that year, his standing being highly creditable.

After enjoying at home the usual furlough of graduated cadets, he reported, in the autumn of 1856, to the cavalry school of instruction, at Carlisle, Pa., to Colonel Charles May, of Mexican war fame. He remained there one year, and, in the fall of 1857, as second Lieutenant, he joined his regiment of Mounted Rifles, in the United States Army, then stationed at various points in Texas and New Mexico. Lieutenant Jackson was on this service under Col. W. W. Loring from 1857 to the spring of 1861, giving full scope for adventures in following Indian trails, and in the pleasures of the chase.

During this time he was frequently complimented, not only from the headquarters of his regiment, but also from general headquarters, for persistence in duty and gallantry in action.

WAR BREAKS OUT.

At the commencement of the Civil War, he was operating against the Apaches in the vicinity of Fort Staunton, New Mexico. In the breaking up of old relations incident to the struggle between the North and South, our then young cavalry officer was actuated by motives which, from the stand-point of that day, were most honorable. His parents, relatives, and dearest friends were all Southerners; and, while separating with regret from companions in arms who

GEN. W. H. JACKSON,
President National Agricultural Congress.

had with him stood the brunt of many an Indian onslaught, or had participated with him in the fierce attack on savage hordes, without hesitation he decided to go with his native State in the conflict. Many of us now feel that the mere accident of birth has more to do in shaping our destinies than we might before have realized. The past has been fought out, and the honest and earnest men of North and South alike are again united in fostering the true aims and integrity of the reunited nation, and in developing the resources of the country.

In pursuance of the resolve to aid his native State, Lieutenant Jackson tendered his resignation, turned over to the proper officer of the United States Army every cent of government funds and every description of public property in his possession, and, in company with Col. Crittenden, of Kentucky, made his way into Texas, ran the blockade at Galveston, arrived in New Orleans, sent in the tender of his services through Major Longstreet, to the Confederate Government, and was at once commissioned captain of artillery by the governor of Tennessee.

After performing various duties, he was assigned at New Madrid, in 1861, to the command of a battery of light artillery. At the battle of Belmont, his battery having been disabled, Captain Jackson, by order of his general, led an infantry charge against a portion of the United States troops and was wounded in the side with a Minie ball, which he still carries—a striking reminiscence of the horrors of war. After recovering from what at the time was supposed to be a mortal wound, he was promoted to a colonelcy, and assigned to the command of the Sixth Tennessee and First Mississippi Cavalry, operating in West Tennessee and Northern Mississippi.

At the taking of Holly Springs, Col. Jackson, for gallant

conduct, was promoted brigadier-general, and in command of cavalry took part in all the various movements of Generals Hardee, Polk, and Joe Johnston, commanding the cavalry on the left wing in the memorable Georgia campaign.

HIS PART IN THE WAR.

General Jackson is a true gentleman, urbane, self sacrificing, and forbearing to his fellows. He is also a strict disciplinarian, and his command was noted for their dash and daring in the field. While in battle he was ever foremost, his high natural sense of honor, intensified by his early associations and military training, ever led him to exercise a chivalrous forbearance and clemency to those whom the fate of war threw into his power.

While engaged in the service of the South, from what to him seemed an imperative duty, he exercised no feeling of personal hostility to the people of the North, to whom he accorded the same sense of right to battle for principle as he claimed for himself. If all had been actuated by the same humane feelings, how much bitterness would have been smoothed over, and how much misery and suffering would have been obviated. His strong personal attachment to his many old chums in the Federal army, perhaps, aided his strong sense in conducting his share of the struggle upon principles of civilized usage, and with as little severity and harshness as possible.

Among the services performed, was his engagement with the dashing Kilpatrick, at Lovejoys' Station, leading with Forrest the Confederate advance into Tennessee, and covering the retreat of Hood. For this he was recommended for promotion to a division, and was assigned to the command of Forrest's old division, with the Texas brigade added. With this fine command, he operated until the close of the war, when he was assigned by General Dick Taylor, on the part of the Confederates, and General Dennis, of the United States Army, as Commissioner for the parole of troops, at Gainesville, Ala., and Columbus, Miss.

AFTER THE WAR.

The war closed, and with the same resolute purpose that had always actuated his life, General Jackson engaged in agriculture. Taking charge of his father's planting interest, he managed two farms, organizing a mixed force of white and colored laborers, and superintending their work with judgment and profit, thus cheerfully exchanging the excitement of the camp for the quietude of the farm. He went into the new service with ardent, energetic purpose, bringing to bear a quick and observant mind in the new field of employment, which has gained for him a distinction in agriculture not inferior to the fame which he earned for himself in the profession of arms. For three or four years he thus superintended the culture of cotton in West Tennessee. The life of this gentleman since the war has amply disproved the paragraph contained in one of General Sherman's letters to General Grant, at the close of the war, assigning a reason why liberal terms should be granted on surrender: "For," said he, "if we do not pursue this course, such men as Forrest, Mosby, and Red Jackson [the subject of this sketch], who know not, or care not, for danger and its consequences, will break off in command of guerrilla parties, and give the country great trouble."

In December, 1868, he married Miss Selene Harding, the daughter of General W. G. Harding, of Belle Meade, near

Nashville, Tennessee, one of the most eminent agriculturists and stock raisers of Tennessee. For this happy change of life, habits, and taste, he is indebted to the *Lost Cause*, to his connection with the Methodist Episcopal Church, and to his marriage, and his consequent intimate association with his father-in-law, one of the most extensive and successful farmers of Tennessee.

THE WARRIOR AS A FARMER.

This rare opportunity General Jackson fully improved, and this improvement, with his enthusiasm in all enterprises inaugurated for the advancement of agriculture, and the elevation of the farmer to his proper position, has been so appreciated that he now fills the offices of President of the National Agricultural Congress, President of the Farmers' Association of Tennessee, President of the Bureau of Agriculture of the State, and President of the Executive Board of the "*Rural Sun* Publishing Company," a weekly journal devoted to Southern agriculture. He is also Master of the Heart of Oak Grange of Patrons of Husbandry at Nashville, Tennessee.

Since the close of the war, General Jackson has been one of the foremost men in the South in all that tends to elevate the profession, and to unite the North and South as one fraternity, in order that the delvers of the soil might realize their full importance as a great factor in the scale of national power.

The connection of this gentleman with the Farmers' Movement is already a matter of history. It is due to him here, however, to say that, at the meeting of the National Agricultural Congress, at St. Louis, in 1872, he was tendered the presidency of the National Agricultural Congress, but declined, preferring that the office should go to the North-west. His name as Vice-President for Tennessee, and also his election to the presidency of the association at the second annual meeting at Indianapolis, in 1873, have been given elsewhere in this work, in the history of the Farmers' Movement.

General Jackson has always been firm in the belief (so frequently reiterated in this work as the writer's own opinion) that co-operation, to be successful, must be through the unity in one parent society of every association in the land.

One of the mottoes of General Jackson is, "*Festina Lente,*" which might be translated for the benefit of railroad monopolies, "Go slow up grade." Its literal translation, "Make haste slowly," is applicable to his efforts is this Movement. A convincing debater, a pleasant orator, a will strong for his conviction of right, he does not hold the plow and look back, but drives a steady team straight to the landmark, laying his furrow true and even, and without skips or turn-furrows. This is his conception of "*Festina Lente.*"

CHAPTER XXXII.

BIOGRAPHICAL SKETCH OF JOHN DAVIS.

EARLY PIONEER LIFE.

The subject of this sketch was born in a log cabin, fifteen miles south of Springfield, Illinois, in the year 1826. When three years of age, his father, Mr. Joseph Davis, removed to Macon County, Illinois, near Decatur, where he still resides.

This removal took place during the Black Hawk war, when settlements in central Illinois were few and far between, when Chicago was a mere trading village, and the whole northern portion of Illinois was an untilled and wild prairie region, except here and there, where a few hardy pioneers had formed settlements. Indians were plenty and on the war path. Troops and prairie scouts were actively engaged in guarding the sparse settlements, or pursuing the savages. Mills were situated at wide intervals, and the sufferings of the hardy settlers were such as to leave a vivid remembrance of those old days.

The winter of 1830–31 will long be remembered by the pioneers of central and southern Illinois, as the winter of deep snows. During two terrible storms in December, the snow fell to the depth of three feet over the surface, and drifted to great heights, covering fences, corn-fields, small stacks, and even the cabins of the settlers. Live stock and wild animals died in great numbers, and the ingenuity and endurance of men were taxed to the utmost to save their families and teams from perishing from cold and famine.

Among these hardy frontiersmen, none were more conspicuous for spirit and enterprise than good old Joe Davis, of Macon. When a neighbor was to be assisted, or help was wanted in any direction, he was always "to the fore," with his heavy ox team.

GRINDING AT THE HORSE MILL.

At last the pioneer father became possessed of a mill, where was ground the grain brought from a radius of over thirty miles, this method giving entire satisfaction in that primitive age. Pay was taken in kind, one-sixth of the corn and one-seventh of the wheat being the rule. But, then, there were few monopolies.

In due time, young John was promoted from driving the plow to driving the mill, and as principal miller became a somewhat important personage in the rising community. Always earnest and studious, when the day's work was done he would seize the "Life of Marion," or some other work of similar kind, and read aloud to those whose business kept them at the mill, and who, seated around the blazing log-heap in the ample fire-place, were wont to regard the fluent and earnest youth with admiration, his elocutionary powers often eliciting such remarks as this: "I'd give my best hoss if my Jim could read like the miller."

The mother of Mr. Davis was a woman of strong will and moral character, who accomplished much good in moulding the characters of the rough young men always found growing up in frontier settlements. Many a man, now past his prime, thanks "Aunt Sally" for the advice and moral influ-

COL. A. B. SMEDLEY,

Master of the State Grange of Iowa.

JOHN DAVIS,

President of the Farmer's Co-Operative Associa-

ence that saved him from strong drink, and, perhaps, a drunkard's grave.

Mr. Davis' father was a stock-farmer, breeding horses, mules, cattle, and swine, and selling the same for breeding purposes, as well as for food. The subject of our sketch continued working at the farm until reaching his twentieth year, acquiring that strength, nerve, and constitution that were to enable him, in after life, to study and store his mind with the knowledge that makes the cultured man. It is this early culture that has, more than any thing else, perhaps, given him the practical ability for which he is remarkable.

GETTING AN EDUCATION AND START IN LIFE.

At nineteen, Mr. Davis left the farm and set about getting an education, spending two years as a student and clerk in a drug store at Springfield, Illinois, and attending the academy of Professor Esterbrook. From thence he went to Jacksonville, and entered Illinois College. After leaving college, he became one of Professor Turner's agents in introducing the growth of the Osage orange on the prairies. This connection continued three or four years, leading to a close intimacy which was never sundered. Their minds worked in perfect accord in relation to education to the industries. The general ideas with the early agitators, on this subject, to use Mr. Davis' words, were, "To discard the obsolete and useless branches of education, and to adopt the modern and practical subjects in their stead."

In May, 1851, Mr. Davis was married to Miss Martha Ann Powell, of Wisconsin, daughter of Rev. Joseph Powell, and sister to Major J. W. Powell, who is now widely known as the explorer of the Colorado River. About 1853, Mr.

Davis and Major Powell entered into business relations with the lamented C. R. Overman, then of Fulton County, Illinois, and started a branch nursery in Macon County, under the firm name of "Davis & Powell." This relationship was mutually pleasant to all the parties, and lasted for several years.

While engaged as a nurseryman—a business which he continued, on a limited scale, after the termination of the partnership above named—Mr. Davis made himself a most comfortable home, about five miles east of Decatur, where he reared a family of six boys and three girls, devoting himself, on his home farm, to the raising of fruit and stock.

During his whole life, Mr. Davis has been an indefatigable planter of trees, and has found it pay. Several places which he has improved for sale have brought more money than other places naturally as good, with better buildings, but lacking orchards and shade.

"WESTWARD, HO!"

At length, a growing family induced Mr. Davis, in 1869, to visit Kansas, for the purpose of securing homes for his children; and he is now engaged in improving a farm of four hundred and eighty acres, near Junction City, Davis County, old Fort Riley being in full view from his premises. His entire family removed to their new home in Kansas, where they are all now permanently located, in 1872.

Mr. Davis is a good speaker and a forcible writer, and in his new home he could not long remain in obscurity. In January, 1873, at the invitation of President Dennison, of the State Agricultural College, he delivered an address on the "Transportation of American Products," which was favorably noticed by the press.

PRESENT PROMINENCE AND LABORS.

In March, 1873, Mr. Davis became President of the newly-formed Agricultural Society of Davis County, and went as a delegate, in company with Mr. John K. Wright, to the Farmers' State Convention, held on the 26th and 27th of the same month, at Topeka. He was elected President of the Convention, and, at the organization of the State Farmers' Association, was chosen President of that body.

Thus this earnest and untiring worker was happily harnessed into the traces in this young State, to help roll forward the car of progress.

He has been an indefatigable worker in the cause of industrial education in Kansas, pitting himself fearlessly against the sectarian cliques who sought to gain control of the Agricultural College of that State, to the exclusion of agriculture and mechanics.

One of his most characteristic efforts was an open letter, on the subject of such education, to the Governor of the State, published in the *Kansas Farmer*, early in 1873. This drew out some able criticisms from the editor of that journal, and an attack upon Mr. Davis by Rev. L. Sternberg. The discussion was sharp, spirited, and interesting, and has accomplished its full quota of good in moulding public opinion on the subject of industrial education in Kansas. It has also assisted in bringing Mr. Davis prominently before the people of the West, as an able and fearless champion of their rights.

CHAPTER XXXIII.

BIOGRAPHICAL SKETCH OF HON. W. C. FLAGG.

PARENTAGE AND EDUCATION.

Willard Cutting Flagg was born September 16, 1829, on the farm where he now resides, in what was then known as Paddock's Settlement, Madison County, Illinois. He is the son of Gershom Flagg and Jane Paddock, both natives of, and early emigrants from, Vermont.

Attending the local school and doing the usual work of a farmer's boy until 1844, he thereafter spent the winters at a first-class English and classical high-school in St. Louis, Missouri, until 1850, when he entered Yale College as freshman, graduating in course in 1854, and taking the rank of an "oration man" in scholarship. He was awarded two prizes in English Composition in the sophomore year. In the junior year he took the Yale Literary Gold Medal for English Composition, and was chosen one of the five editors of the Yale Literary Magazine for senior year.

After graduating, he returned home and commenced work upon the farm, continuing, however, to intersperse a good deal of reading and some magazine writing with his labors. On the 13th of February, 1856, he married Miss Sarah Smith, of St. Louis, Missouri. Entering into the political canvass of that year, in support of Fremont and the Republican ticket, he wrote earnestly for the political press. In 1857, after the death of his father, he devoted himself exclusively to farming, and in 1858 and succeeding years, besides building, planting, and fencing fields, old and new, he commenced orchard planting. During the next ten years, he planted about one hundred acres of orchard, principally apple, but also comprising a good many peach and other fruit trees, besides a pretty extensive collection of experimental varieties of nearly all sorts of fruits.

CONNECTION WITH ILLINOIS HORTICULTURAL SOCIETY.

In 1860, as a member of the Republican State Central Committee and the County Committee, he took an active part in politics, and wrote some political pamphlets.

In 1861 he was elected Secretary of the Illinois State Horticultural Society, a position which he held until 1869, bringing to this position an untiring industry, and a large and varied experience. The volumes of that society attracted the attention of horticulturists all over the country. In this position he continued until 1869, most of the time serving without compensation, when the Society most reluctantly accepted his resignation, and, in appreciation of his earnest and self-sacrificing labors in its behalf, unanimously elected him their President for 1871.

In 1862, Mr. Flagg introduced into Madison County, Illinois, a herd of Devon cattle, having previously bred grades of this stock, and now has a herd of about twenty "pure bred," besides grades. The same year he was appointed United States Collector of the Twelfth District of Illinois, a position which he held until January, 1869, when he resigned it in order to take his seat in the State Senate, to which he was elected from the counties of Madison and St. Clair, in 1868.

In 1864, he published a pamphlet on the Agricultural College question, then beginning to awaken a renewed interest in our State, and joined with other friends of the movement in opposing the attempt to divide the agricultural and mechanical grant between the existing colleges.

In 1867, he was appointed one of the first Board of Trustees of the Illinois Industrial University, and elected Corresponding Secretary of the Board, a position which he has held since that time.

LEGISLATIVE CAREER.

In 1868, Mr. Flagg was nominated and elected State Senator from the counties of Madison and St. Clair, and served in the sessions of 1869 and 1871, the special sessions of 1871 and the adjourned session of 1872, during which period he had an opportunity, in connection with his fellow-members from that locality, of breaking down the Wiggins' Ferry monopoly at East St. Louis. He voted, though unsuccessfully, against the infamous Lake Front Bill and the "Grab Law" of 1869, by which the railroads combined to rob Chicago of her frontage to Lake Michigan.

In the session of 1871, as Chairman of the Committee on Education, he reported a revision of the school law, and introduced the clause for the study of the elements of the natural sciences as a requirement in the qualification of teachers, and as a possible study for pupils. In both sessions his attention was called to the railway question. His opinions on the subject are briefly expressed in an address before the literary societies of Shurtleff College, in June, 1869.

"The association of capital in this country," said Mr.

Flagg, "as well as others, is going on rapidly in partial opposition to the organization of labor, and often with bad effects on the State. Capital, in the hands of a few, is organized with facility, handled rapidly, and used unscrupulously. It may do more mischief in a democracy than elsewhere in corrupting persons in power. 'In democracies,' said De Tocqueville, 'statesmen are poor, and have their fortunes to make.' It is inimical to the virtue of a democracy in aggregating wealth in the hands of men who are uneducated, immoral, and extravagant; who bring upon us the vices and corrupting influences of an aristocracy, without its culture or its vices.

"These evils, though general in the case of associated capital, are more peculiarly and specially the result of our railway corporations. They ask, and often by fraud obtain, unwarrantable franchises. They are unscrupulous in extortion when they have the opportunity, and truckling under competition; they consolidate and water stock, and compel the traveling public to pay twenty-five per cent on the real capital under the guise of eight or ten on the nominal capital; they violate even the rule of honor among thieves, and stockholder cheats stockholder in the election of directors to get control of the management."

In an address on "Our Railways and Our Farmers," delivered before the Pike County, Illinois, Farmers' Convention, in 1872, these views were elaborated and supplemented with other matter.

AGRICULTURAL EDUCATION FROM A SCHOLAR'S STAND-POINT.

In 1870, in an address on "the Education of the Farmer," before the St. Clair County, Illinois, Farmers' and Fruit-

Growers' Association, he gave his views upon agricultural education, taking the ground, in common with other practical minds "that the young men most earnest in getting an education, although farmers' sons, look forward to other pursuits than farming as the goal of their desires. These are evidently neither of them necessary results; but they must affect our theory and practice of agricultural education.

"Those of us who have gone through the prescribed drill of our college courses have generally formed the habit of getting our knowledge by the study of text-books, rather than by original research, or even by the accurate observation of things. We have formed sedentary habits. We would rather read up Allen on the 'points' of the shorthorn than go to the field and examine the animal. In other words, whilst the farmer's is an active and practical life, we have been educated to, and formed the habits of, a literary and sedentary life.

"The education of the farmer, and probably that of all men engaged in active pursuits, should be conducted with a view to avoid it. So far as possible, text-books should be used mainly for reference, and 'object-teaching' substituted. Botany should be studied by dissection of the plant in the class-room, or by rambles in the fields and forests. Chemistry should be taught, as it now is getting to be, by immediate resort to the laboratory. If breeds of animals be the topic, the lecturer should have them at hand, and take his class to study their points; if pruning, the students should go to the orchard and see the work done, and help do it; if varieties of fruit, the fruit itself, or casts of it, should be at hand, and the tree that bears them in the experimental or specimen orchard."

EDITORIAL CONNECTIONS AND FURTHER HONORS.

In 1869, Mr. Flagg became editorially connected with *Hearth and Home*, as its western correspondent, and since 1872 has edited the horticultural department of the *Prairie Farmer*. In 1872, at the meeting of Farmers' Clubs, held in Kewanee, Illinois, he was appointed on the State Central Committee, and in pursuance of the duties assigned him, and in association with Mr. S. M. Smith, General L. F. Ross, and others, aided in calling the Bloomington Convention, at which the Illinois State Farmers' Association was organized, and of which association Mr. Flagg is now President.

At the late biennial meeting of the American Pomological Society, held at Boston, Mr. Flagg was unanimously elected Secretary for the ensuing two years.

Such, in brief, are a portion of the life and services of one who unites to high culture a most practical view of that which interests men in every-day life. Always willing to acknowledge a wrong, but strong in his convictions of what constitutes right, as he himself acknowledges, his education had tended to lead astray from rural life; nevertheless, his honest mind has always kept him in the ranks of the people battling for right, although his wealth, inherited as well as earned, has never made him feel the need of labor to supply either the necessities or elegancies of life.

CHAPTER XXXIV.

THE PEOPLE VERSUS RAILWAY MONOPOLIES.

BY HON. W. C. FLAGG, PRESIDENT ILLINOIS STATE FARMERS' ASSOCIATION.

A GREAT PUBLIC DANGER.

During the last fifteen years, there has grown up in America a distrust, which, at first felt by a few, merged into the fear and finally into the denunciation of railway corporations by a large majority of the increasing number who, for any considerable time, have been subjected to the extortionate rates, the deliberate violation of moral and legal obligations, and the corrupting influence in public and private station that have characterized our railway monopolies. Admitting freely, to begin upon, that railway managers and owners are not necessarily nor *per se* worse than other men, it must be just as frankly stated that railway corporations, as such, have proved one of the worst influences in our State and national affairs.

Henry C. Carey, the political economist, was one of the few who early saw the danger. Writing to the Hon. L. Sherwood, in 1867, he said: "Nearly twenty years have passed since, without having the smallest personal interest in the question, I spent two years in the effort to free New Jersey from the tyranny that had been there established," alluding to the railroad monopoly of New Jersey. In his

"Social Science," published in 1858, speaking of the political power of railway corporations in Great Britain, he says: "So it is even now in these United States; railroad companies are already controlling the legislation of many of the States, the day for general combination having not yet arrived; but there are many evidences of its near approach. When it shall arrive it will furnish new proof to the fact, that, of all goverments, the most exhausting and oppressive is that of the transporters."

PRIVATE CORPORATIONS GOVERNING STATES.

Geo. P. Marsh, alike eminent in the annals of diplomacy and of philology, in a note to his "Man and Nature" expressed himself as follows, in 1862: "I shall harm no honest man by endeavoring, as I have often done elsewhere, to excite the attention of conscientious and thinking men to the dangers which threaten the great moral and even political interests of christendom, from the unscrupulousness of the private associations that now control the monetary affairs, and regulate the transit of persons and property in almost every civilized country. More than one American State is literally governed by unprincipled corporations, which not only defy the legislative power, but have, too often, corrupted even the administration of justice.

* * * * *

"The example of the American States shows that private corporations—whose rule of action is the interest of the association, not the conscience of the individual—though composed of ultra-democratic elements, may become most dangerous enemies to national liberty, to the moral interests of the commonwealth, to the purity of legislation and of judicial action, and to the sacredness of private rights."

Hon. WILLARD C. FLAGG,
President Illinois State Farmers' Association.

These words of warning were unheard by a nation entering upon a struggle with the other and greater vested wrong of slavery; and it was not until after the war for the Union closed, during which time the chartering and construction of railways went briskly on, that such men as Lorenzo Sherwood, Josiah Quincy, and the younger Charles Francis Adams could have an attentive hearing.

RAILWAY CORPORATIONS DEFIANT.

By this time railway corporations had grown bold and defiant. Fisk, Gould, Vanderbilt, and Drew warred among themselves, and were more or less afraid of one another; but they evidently regarded the New York legislature and judiciary as their tools. Their armed minions, like the following of mediævel lords, broke the peace and one another's heads with impunity. In other quarters, it was reported that the Pennsylvania, New Jersey, Maryland, and several southern legislatures and State goverments were the facile tools of other corporations. The Union Pacific and its Credit Mobilier ring invaded the halls of Congress, and brought scandal upon national as well as State governments. The so-called "Farmer's Movement" did not begin an hour too soon.

Attempts are made to falsify the issue, and to assume that this is a war of farmers against railroads—a class pitted against a useful invention—but they who make this attempt and the assumption lack either clear heads or fair minds. It is the eternal warfare of popular rights against privilege, in a new shape—a conflict just as irrepressible and inevitable in its results, as that other conflict which absorbed the energies and sacrificed the youthful life of the nation for four years.

I shall attempt to state the case of the people in this controversy by the affirmation of a few propositions that I think no unprejudiced person will deny.

RAILWAYS THE PUBLIC HIGHWAYS.

Railways are the highways of the country, and year by year absorb the business of transportation from earth roads, canals, rivers, and lakes, unless their charges are exorbitant. They took the business of the common road immediately on their completion, except for short distances; and it is only lately, when the charges of transportation by rail became prohibitory, that we hear again of wagons being brought into use for distances of fifty to one hundred miles. The Erie Canal carries less flour from Buffalo eastward by far than the railways competing with it.

"In 1861," says *Harper's Magazine* for November, 1873, "the canals of New York transported 2,144,373 tons of Western products, and the three trunk railroads, the New York Central, Erie, and Pennsylvania railroads, 905,521. In 1871, the canals carried only 1,863,868 tons, and the railroads 3,057,168. The Grand Trunk, of Canada, and the Baltimore and Ohio railroads must add about 40 per cent. to the latter amount." "Steam," says Charles Francis Adams, "abolishes the Mississippi River."

In 1872, St. Louis received 2,838,364 tons of freight by railroad, against 863,919 by river, and shipped 1,204,604 tons by rail, against 805,282 by river. The lakes still carry a large part of the grain, shipped from Chicago, but not of the flour.

Every-where transportation by rail seems to successfully compete, if it will, with transportation by any other method. In other words, year by year the railroads of our country replace the old-fashioned turnpike or highway and its wagons, and even the natural and artificial water ways of the country to an extent that makes them even now, and yet more, prospectively, the great thoroughfares of the country.

Now, if our county, town, or other municipal authorities, when a road was to be established, were in the habit of giving over to some person, or persons, not public officers, the privilege of building such road, with the right to condemn the land of persons through whose farms the road passed, and of remunerating himself by putting up turnpike gates and charging whatever toll he pleased of travelers, they would be doing what many of our legislatures have been doing for years with railways, and would be taken to task as not protecting the public interest. It would be claimed that public travel and trade were such a public necessity that they should be blocked just as little as practicable by hig' es; and hence, that the man who would build and keep the turnpike in order for the lowest toll, or perhaps the public authorities themselves, should take charge of the road.

HIGHWAYS OF TRANSPORTATION SHOULD BE GOVERNED BY THE PUBLIC AUTHORITIES.

This brings me to my second proposition which is this: That the highways of our transportation and travel should so far be controlled by the public authorities as to furnish transportation of persons and property at the lowest rate practicable. This is readily seen and admitted when we talk of the wagon roads from our farms to the nearest market; it is not less true of the longer railroads to the more distant market. Cheap transportation makes cheap food, not only in Illinois, but in Georgia and Massachusetts.

It makes fuel cheap not only in Pennsylvania, but in Connecticut. It distributes those necessaries of life all over the land, and gives equal advantages to all sections. It permits the free movement of the people one among another, so that a more general and continuous commingling of blood, of habits, and ideas ensues.

We admit the proposition of carrying at cost also when the matter of postal carriage comes up. We admit and approve the principle that the general government should take the risk of carrying the mails, based on the idea that such carriage shall be nearly or quite self-supporting.

But the proposition can be put in more general and equally forcible terms, and I do it, using the language of our present minister to Italy, George P. Marsh, as written ten years ago ("Man and Nature," page 54): "It is, theoretically, the duty of government to provide all those public facilities of intercommunication and commerce which are essential to the prosperity of civilized commonwealths, but which individual means are inadequate to furnish, and for the due administration of which individual guaranties are insufficient. Hence, public roads, canals, railroads, postal communications, the circulating mediums of exchange, whether metallic or representative, armies, navies, being all matters in which the nation at large has a vastly deeper interest than any private association can have, ought legitimately to be constructed and provided for by that which is the visible personification and embodiment of the nation, namely, its legislative head."

ACTUAL COST OF CARRYING PASSENGERS.

This intervention of the public authorities I justify by a third proposition, viz.: That the cost of railway transportation is, or may be, far below the charge now collected from the producer and consumer. To show this, let us see how cheaply passengers and freight have been carried, and, again, how much they are charged under existing management.

Take, first, passenger rates. We have the statement of the Pennsylvania Company, for 1872, that it costs that Company 1.837 cents to carry a passenger one mile. The same statement admits a charge of 2.45 cents per mile, or thirty-three and one-third per cent. above cost. I have no means of testing the accuracy of this report, or ascertaining whether the items of cost are legitimate, but I presume that, considering the fact that the Pennsylvania Company includes a large number of short lines, in somewhat remote and comparatively sparsely settled districts, that it is probable there are many roads whose transportation costs less to the railway company and more to the shipper. Examining the report of the State Engineer of New York, I find that, assuming cost of maintenance of roadway (including taxes), cost of repairs and machinery, and cost of operating the roads, to be the items of cost, that, in 1872, it cost, according to the returns given, an average of 1.645 cents per passenger per mile in New York, while the charge was 2.3801 cents, or nearly forty-five per cent. in advance of cost.

These are about all the attainable figures of *cost* to railway companies, excepting that we know that, in England, passengers have been carried at .42 of a cent per mile in first-class carriages, not only without loss, but with a loss of only one-half of one per cent. in the dividends, and in another case at .54 of a cent absolutely without loss, even in the dividends.

TRANSPORTATION RATES IN EUROPE AND THE UNITED STATES.

Compare these figures, now, with what the public is required to pay. In Belgium, where we find the cheapest known rates of regular passenger traffic, we find that, on railroads costing one hundred and six thousand dollars per mile, the charge for first-class rates is one dollar and fifty-eight cents per hundred miles, or 1.58 cents per mile. This seems to be a partial result of the fact that the government there owns and operates forty-two per cent of the railroads.

The charge is 2.52 in Italy, 3.12 in Prussia and Austria, and finally, and greatest of European rates, in the United Kingdom, where competition has been relied on, the Englishman, traveling on a road costing one hundred and seventy-five thousand dollars per mile, pays 4.50 cents per mile for first-class rates.

In Massachusetts the average rates for 1872 were 2.426 cents per mile; in New York, 2.3801 cents; in Ohio, 3.18; and in Illinois, as nearly as I can make it out, 3.43 for through rates, and 3.95 for local, or 3.75 for both. These are the averages of large and populous States, in which, and through which the current of travel flows broad and strong; and which, consequently, give the more favorable charges for railroad travel, although even these are far above cost.

But here is a table of prices "adopted," we are told, but not by whom, from St. Louis to the different cities of the country. You can reach Boston at 2.3 cents per mile, Quebec at 2.6, and Lynchburg, Va., at 2.7. To New Orleans, Atchison, Cairo, Chicago, and Memphis you must pay 4 cents; to Fort Scott, 4.6, and to San Francisco, 4.8 cents per mile, over a road built by government gratuities, granted, it was supposed, in the interest of the people. Over the same road you can reach Sacramento, one hundred and thirty-eight miles nearer than San Francisco, by paying a like sum, or more than 5 cents a mile; while it will cost you 5.8 cents per mile to reach Denver, and the extortionate charge of 6 cents per mile to go to Salt Lake, on a railroad given by the government.

Thus much for passenger rates. Let us now look at freight rates, which is a more important question. The men who need cheap food, cheap clothing, and cheap fuel, are less interested in travel than in keeping the wolf from the door. They ought to travel, but they can not. Bread, clothing, and fuel they must have.

WHAT FREIGHTS COST, AND WHAT IS CHARGED.

Going back to the Pennsylvania Company, we find it admits being able to carry freight, in 1872, at .886 of a cent per ton per mile, but charged 1.4163 cents, an advance of nearly sixty per cent. over the actual cost. The Syracuse, Binghampton, and New York admits carrying at a cost of .75 of a cent; the Lake Shore and Michigan Southern at .95, and the Erie Railway at .98, according to the New York report.

The actual cost of carrying coal on the Providence and Worcester Railroad, according to the report of the Massachusetts Railroad Commissioners, was six mills per ton per mile. The Syracuse, Binghampton, and New York Railway carried freight, through 1862, at a cost of .41 of a cent per ton per mile, and in England coal has been carried at an actual cost of .32 of a cent per ton per mile.

This is what has been done and can be done again, with due economy in management, but the *charge* that must be paid by the shipper or consignee is a very different affair.

The lowest average of freight charges for 1872 that I find credited to any extensive system of roads, is that of the Pennsylvania Company, given already at 1.4163 cents per ton per mile. The average amount received on the New York roads was 1.6645 cents; on the Massachusetts roads (for local freights), 2.81; on the Ohio roads, 2.55; and on the Illinois roads, 2.16 for through freights, and 4.72 for local freights, so far as I am able to figure averages from the Illinois Railway Commissioners' reports. The lowest of these rates leaves a wide possible margin of profits, and in some cases we can say how much.

When the Syracuse, Binghampton, and New York Railway carried, at a cost of .75 of a cent per ton per mile, it received 1.42 cents, or an advance of nearly ninety per cent.; when it carried at a cost of .41, it received 1.26 cents, or an advance of more than two hundred per cent. The Providence and Worcester, carrying at an actual cost of six mills per ton per mile, received from coal consumers an advance of over two hundred and thirty-six per cent. on cost, or about two cents per ton per mile. These wide margins are shown, it will be noticed, from what we, with our western experience, would call very reasonable local rates; and some would be glad to get as favorable rates, even on long hauls.

WESTERN EXPERIENCE.

If we examine into our western experience, we find that still more extortionate charges are made. Taking the cheapest freights known to our western commerce—grain in bulk, shipped from Chicago to New York by rail—we find, from figures given by the *Railroad Gazette*, of Chicago, that the average rate on fourth-class freight for nine years, beginning with 1864 and ending with 1872, was seventy-two cents per hundred pounds, or, calling the distance one thousand miles, 1.44 cents per ton per mile.

This is about the average charge on all the freights on the compartively local routes of the Pennsylvania Central, and is forty-three cents, and more, on every bushel of wheat. First-class freights, to the same point, averaged, during this nine years, one dollar and eighty-seven cents per hundred pounds, or nearly 3.38 cents per ton per mile. From St. Louis, so far as I can ascertain, the average rates have been rather less favorable.

In 1872, the rail rate from Chicago to New York, on fourth-class freight, was, according to the *Railroad Gazette*, fifty-eight and two-thirds cents per hundred pounds—1.17 cents per ton per mile—or a little over thirty-five cents per bushel of sixty pounds. Supposing this freight to have been carried at a cost of six mills per ton per mile, it would amount to thirty cents per hundred, or eighteen cents per bushel, a difference of seventeen cents per bushel; and on the two hundred million bushels we may suppose to have been shipped from the West, and to have been affected in cost of transportation and in price, this would amount to thirty-six million dollars, drawn from the pockets of producer and consumer.

EXCESSIVE CHARGES IN TENNESSEE AND IOWA.

These overcharges, however, are moderate compared with the local charges made at non-competing points, when no "contract" is made. Here the charge, in many cases, is limited and fixed, not with any reference to the cost of transportation by rail, but by the inability of the shipper or consignee to do better. A Tennessee farmer writes the *Prairie Farmer* that he is charged seven cents a bushel on corn, transported by the car load, twenty-six miles to Nashville. This is nine cents per ton per mile, or at least nine times the cost.

Suel Foster, of Muscatine, Iowa, a gentleman well and favorably known among our Iowa fruit growers, was charged the same or a higher rate for three times the distance. On bulky and cheap products, such as corn in a productive season, hay, oats, etc., the rates are often, in many places, prohibitory.

According to Poor, there were carried in the United States, in 1872, not less than two hundred million tons of freight, at a charge to the producer and consumer, in round numbers, of three hundred and forty million dollars. Assuming this freight to have been carried at the moderate charge of fifty per cent above cost, the railway companies levied a tax for transportation of more than one hundred and twelve million dollars, on the people of the United States, over and above the necessity of the case.

Transportation is simply a necessary evil in the case of freight. It adds nothing to the feeding power of grain, the warming power of coal, or the clothing capacity of cotton; and all charges levied for profit, over and above a fair rate of interest on the amount actually invested in transportation, is contrary to the public interest, and, in many localities, crushes out enterprise and prosperity.

SELF-INTEREST THE RAILWAY RULE OF ACTION.

Not only, however, is the railway an expensive necessity, which farmers near a market learn to discard, although it could serve them also to mutual advantage, but the railway corporation is, in many instances, a capricious master. Having a practical monopoly of the business of the country through which it runs, except at competing points, it illustrates the truth above stated, by Mr. Marsh, that its *interest* is its rule of action. We might add that self-interest is its *highest* rule of action; for, in many cases, the capriciousness of officials, their individual piques or private profit, have been allowed to interfere with the true policy of the best interests of the railway company.

In any event, the relative prosperity of communities of traders and manufacturers, established at different stations along the company's line, is made, for one reason or another, a secondary and trivial consideration. The result of this is what is known as "unjust discrimination," whereby one community is impoverished and its business men bankrupted, or driven away at a loss, its real estate depreciated, and its agriculture diminished, while another is unduly favored and prosperous, though, of course, not in an equal ratio. The misfortune of one community is never correspondingly to the advantage of another, however close its rivalry.

EVILS OF UNJUST DISCRIMINATION.

The evils of unjust discrimination are not fully recognized, because we do not clearly see what they have *prevented.* We see and understand the ruin of the enterprising manufacturer, who has established a desirable business in a country town, and is then driven from it by the superior "special rates" granted by the same road to his competitor in business at a competing station. But we do not know the amount of business that this short-sighted policy of the railway company has prevented from coming to the same town—the general distrust and fear of engaging in important enterprises that it excites in every community similarly situated. Hence, the anxiety of town communities having one railway, to add another, on the supposition—often a false one—that they will thus have competition in carrying, and relief.

Unjust discrimination is also a demoralizing evil. It tempts those who fear it to bribe officials, to court favors, and use other undue influences, injurious to their own self-respect and that of the railway employes. It begets the un-republican vices of fawning, subservience, and venality.

RAILWAY INTERFERENCE WITH LEGISLATION.

Another evil, that seems to be the special fruit of railway corporations in the United States, is improper interference with legislation and other functions of government. As has been already noticed, it is a widely-spread belief that railway corporations control, or have controlled, the legislation of several States, and have tampered with executive and even judicial officers. Unfortunately, there are many reasons for the suspicion, and the fact is not denied. Other corporations have been by no means immaculate, but railway corporations, for some cause, lend themselves more readily than any other to the base uses of soulless and conscienceless power. Some say it is in self-defense, but an examination of the facts disproves that statement, or shows it to be, at most, but partially true.

The railway corporation invades the halls of legislation, seeking, first, special privileges, that shall give it the advantage in the race for gain over individuals; then exemption from its responsibilities, the prevention of the extension of its privileges to its rivals, and the addition of new privileges and gifts to its own existing privileges.

There has hardly been a State of the Union in which the attempt has not been made, by railway corporations, to influence railway legislation. The legislature of New York, and the judiciary and bar of New York City, have been disgraced by the machinations of Fisk, Gould, Drew, Vanderbilt, Field, Barnard, and others. New Jersey, under the less neutralized influence of the Camden and Amboy and its successors, and Pennsylvania, under the guidance of the Pennsylvania Central, have been largely controlled and directed by railway influence. Maryland, Alabama, California, and other States, have also felt the hand of iron under the velvet glove of railway corruption; and the annals of Congress already teem with railway schemes, and "committees of investigation," of which the devices and derelictions of "railroad men" are a prominent feature.

THE BEGINNING OF THE END.

The experience of the last twelve months has proved, however, the virtue inherent in the people; that the boldness and effrontery of railway corporations have reached a point beyond which they can not go; and that railway corporations must surrender a part of their assumed prerogatives, or fare worse. New Jersey has so far got out of the control of railway influence as to pass a general railroad law. Pennsylvania has formed a new Constitution, in which railway corporations receive special attention. California, under the lead of her gallant governor, Booth, rebels *en masse* against her railway despotism. The day of deliverance seems near at hand, when railway as well as other corporations shall be held to a direct responsibility to government; when the rates for the transportation of persons and property shall be based on the correct business theory of "large sales and small profits;" when all who trade or travel shall be treated with the same impartiality that the patrons of the post-office receive; and when men who give or take bribes in legislation shall not be held worthy of place, either as railway officials, or as representatives of the people and of their interests.

CHAPTER XXXV.

RAILWAY LEGISLATION AT HOME AND ABROAD.

CONTRIBUTED BY J. W. MIDGLEY, ESQ., CHICAGO, PRESIDENT'S SECRETARY NORTH-WESTERN RAILWAY.*

The science of transportation has become a popular study. Agitation has made it so. Always interesting to a few, it has recently excited many, whose zeal has, perchance, outrun their knowledge. Impatiently, they have told all they know, and more, about the railway system. That system is not faultless; neither has its giant growth been wholly natural. But when men not yet grown old recall the America of their youth—before the locomotive created a way over the trackless West—they can hardly regard its inroads in the light of unmitigated evils.

Every country has its bane. Europe is dwarfed by landed aristocracy, military despotism, and superstition, forms of oppression here unknown. But are we quite exempt? Have we not a legislature in every State that can offset the advantage? And are not its specifics the inevitable panacea prescribed for every ill, real or fancied? Like the credulous patient who resorts to the one patent medicine

*** The three chapters next following present the "Railroad Side" of course, and with signal ability, as the careful reader will perceive.**

for every ailment, the "free and enlightened," on the first symptom, cry out for legislation as the unfailing remedy.

The disposition to "regulate" the railways is not a new manifestation. It began with the inception of the system. Through all the years intervening, wherever railways have been run, legislative control has been variously threatened. In England, the results of these experiments are recounted in more than a score of ponderous reports to Parliament, in which are embodied the experiences of continental Europe; and it is significant that each Royal Commission, after unwearied labor and exhaustive research, unanimously reported against legislative interference with the railways. Perhaps an ambition to succeed where older countries have invariably failed, whets our appetite for coercive legislation. Of one thing we can rest assured, that our statute books will never again be clear of some attempt to regulate the railways; and as the repeal of each ineffectual measure will only give place to new experiments, with a view to profit by the lessons of history, an epitome of railway legislation is herewith presented. The experience of Great Britain is particularized, because railways there originated, and now, as in all periods, their system most closely resembles our own.

The first railway charter was granted in 1801, for the construction of a railway from Wyandsworth to Croydon. It empowered the company to adjust their tariff within the maximum rate of 6d. per ton per mile for merchandise, and 4d. for coal, flour, iron, and corn. All persons were privileged to use the railway at the prescribed rates, with horses, cattle, and carriages, subject to the regulations of the company. Authority was given the company to acquire the right of way on payment of compensation. At each subsequent session new railways were chartered for the transportation of goods at maximum rates.

The acts provided only for horse power. But the advantages of steam locomotion were so urgently represented by George Stephenson that, in 1823, Parliament amended the charter of the Stockton & Wadington Railway, granted two years before, giving power to use steam-engines. In view of the fact that no feature of railway management is so objectionable as discrimination in favor of through freight, it is noteworthy that, in order to prevent this becoming a coal line to shipping ports, a clause was inserted in its charter limiting the charge for hauling coal to Stockton for shipping purposes to ½d. per ton per mile, whereas the rate allowed for all transportation of local traffic was continued at 4d. It was believed such a low rate would entirely stop the through trade; yet, not only did it prove profitable, but it established a precedent in favor of lower rates for large quantities of the same through freight that has since been a source of increasing complaint.

Ten years afterward, on the passage of the Liverpool & Manchester Railway Act, in addition to the maximum rate clause, another was inserted that if the dividend should exceed ten per cent., an abatement should be made from the maximum tonnage rates of five per cent. on the amount thereof for each one per cent. which the company might divide over and above a dividend of ten per cent. on its capital.

Although owning the roads, railway companies were not originally intended to have a monopoly or preferential use of the means of communication on their lines. Provision was made enabling all persons to use the road as canals are used. So long as cattle and horses supplied the motive power this was practicable, but the application of steam created a revolution in transportation. It was found impracticable for any or every man to run his own cars; and in order to insure a profit, the *companies were forced to monopolize* the conduct of the lines and become common carriers.

Considerable stress has recently been laid upon the public character of the first railways, and the original charters have been quoted to show that they were not designed to be monopolies. The people are reminded that they still have the right to run their own cars upon the several railroads. Let us consider the feasibility of the plan. A man goos into the Lake Shore Railway office, at Chicago, and says: "I want to start a daily train for New York, at 11 A. M;" another, "I want to start a train at 3 o'clock;" and a third wants to start one at 5 o'clock. "Very well, gentlemen," remarks the officer; "start them as you wish." But the man whose train leaves at 11 o'clock will find that he has not patronage enough to pay expenses, and the one who selected 3 o'clock will fare little better, while the 5 o'clock train is crowded. Why? Simply because to start at 11 or 3 o'clock breaks into a day, whereas 5 o'clock is at the close of office hours, is the most convenient time, and, perforce, *monopolizes* the travel. The 11 and 3 o'clock men then demand that their trains shall be started at 5 o'clock. And they are denied, simply because a railway track is not like an old turnpike road, where vehicles turn out to allow others to pass. The train going at a fixed time has the right of way, and, to prevent collision, becomes a monopoly. Were every one allowed common use of the single track, in the manner of a highway—to start out at their pleasure—some one's car that could not get out of the way would be getting run into continually. This certain result was so apparent to a select committee of the House of Commons, appointed in 1840 to investigate the subject, that they concluded the public right to run their own cars on the railways was, practically, a dead letter for three sufficient reasons: "(1.) Because no provisions had been made for insuring to independent trains and engines access to stations and watering places along the lines. (2.) Because the rates for toll limited by the act were almost always so high as to make it difficult for independent persons to work at a profit. (3.) Because the necessity of placing the running of all trains under the complete control of one head interposed numerous difficulties in the way of independent traders." To which conclusions the committee sensibly added: "That, however, improvidently Parliament may, in the first instance, have granted to the railway companies such extensive powers, it is now advisable to interfere with them as little as possible."

Complaints against the railways still being persistently urged, in 1844 another Select Committee, after giving the question a more thorough consideration than it had hitherto received, observed that "the complaint of monopoly urged against railways was an indication of the benefits they had conferred on the country, as it was not by force of special privileges bestowed upon them, but by superior accommodation and cheapness, that they had acquired the command of traveling in their district; that railway enterprise should be encouraged; that the *country still afforded great scope for the extension of the railway system; that Parliament should take no step which would induce so much as a reasonable suspicion of its good faith with regard to the integrity of privileges already executed, because one of the elements of encouragement to future undertakings was just and equitable dealings with those already established.*" The foregoing italicised words, taken from the Parliamentary Blue Book of 1867, page 11, are as pertinent as though written yesterday for the infatuated people of Illinois to ponder over to-day. Disastrous will it be alike for us and the too-confiding foreigners, whose money rendered the West habitable, if the admonitions of recorded experience are blindly disregarded.

In the earlier days the cars of one company were not transferred to the tracks of another; consequently the expense and inconvenience of making the change were very great, to obviate which, a railway clearing-house was established in London by voluntary association of the companies, and was afterward recognized by Parlimentary Act of Incorporation, in 1850. One delegate from each company constituted a committee who were empowered to recover all balances due from the companies.

It was about this time that the tendency to consolidate became alarming. The first railways were very short lines. The one extending from London to Liverpool was owned by three separate companies; disagreements between the several managements were frequent, to the great inconvenience of the public. When, therefore, the interests of both the companies and the public suggested unity of management, Parliament freely bestowed authority to consolidate.

As the localities increased in population, additional railroads were constructed, creating such active competition that the stronger companies found it expedient to buy up their rivals. This "offensive and defensive" policy aroused public hostility, because it deprived the people of competition—their only hope of protection from monopoly. Parliament was importuned to restrict amalgamation. Various expedients were suggested. The one finally adopted empowered Parliament to determine *the conditions* upon which the future consolidations should be made. But the principle thus laid down was practically ignored. Consolidations continued to be made whenever the interests of corporations drew them together. Failing, therefore, to prevent them, Parliament sought to insure such advantages as would induce the companies to remain separate. Inability to secure good running arrangements with connecting lines was the great disadvantage under which the separate lines labored. This difficulty the most stringent legislation failed to remove. No legal enactment could impel the roads to work as harmoniously as single ownership: and the result was that the route managed by one directory possessed advantages over that composed of several disjointed lines separately owned. Still the public would not accept the situation; and, so recently as last year, a Royal Commission, appointed to investigate the subject, made their report in a blue book, containing over one thousand pages, in which the present system of railway management throughout Europe is comprehensively reviewed. The evidence of some fifty experts, and several unprejudiced witnesses is given *verbatim;* the experiences of France, Belgium, Austria, and Prussia are succinctly stated; and the conclusions arrived at are summed up by the Commissioners, in a statement of which the opening words are an index of the whole: "Past amalgamations have not brought with them the evils which were anticipated."

The policy of the French Government averted consolidation by preventing the construction of more railways than would adequately accommodate the districts. Thus, while in France there was only one mile of railway open to twenty-six square miles of country, in England there was one to about six miles of territory. The result was that railways in France were assured all the business they could handle.

In Belgium, many of the lines were constructed by the State and leased to individuals, who are guaranteed the same protection assured in France.

In Prussia, competing lines are not allowed until thirty

years after the opening of a railway. There, and in Austria, concessions are granted by the Emperor, and the State undertakes the construction of many of the railways.

It will thus be seen that a comparison of the continental systems are of little practical use to us; while the English railroads, being conducted on the same general principles as our own, are especially deserving of study.

The history of American railways is a familiar story. They have grown up within the memory of men still in their prime. When inaugurated, the system was one of complete freedom. Every facility for the construction of railways, and every inducement to invest in them, was lavishly extended. Doubtless, no other policy would have fostered the system. Without them, the great West would still have been a wilderness, and the populous East the scattered home of a straggling people. Vast outlays of money wrought the wondrous transformation. Such incalculable wealth no new country ever possessed. It had to be drawn from abroad, and superior inducements were necessary to bring it here. Confiding in our integrity, and believing our contracts valid, the unsuspecting capitalists built our railways, reclaimed the waste places, and caused "the wilderness to blossom as the rose."

To enumerate the incessant attempts at railway legislation in this country, would be a desultory task. Measures innumerable have been discussed. The one most frequently urged is the *pro rata* or equal mileage plan; yet no theory is more easily refuted. In the older States, it seems buried beyond the probability of resurrection; but in the inland States, where its application would be most disastrous, it still has stubborn adherents.

The principle of charging for each class of passengers and freight in proportion to the distance carried, sounds very plausible; but a select committee of the British Parliament, after thoroughly investigating the question, last year, came to the deliberate conclusion, and so reported to Parliament, that "to impose equal mileage on the companies would be to deprive the public of the benefit of much of the competition which now exists, or has existed; to raise the charges on the public in many cases where the companies now find it to their interest to lower them; and to perpetuate monopoly in carriage, trade, and manufacture, in favor of those routes and places which are nearest or least expensive, where the varying charges of the companies now create competition. And it will be found that the supporters of equal mileage, when pressed, often really mean, not that the rates they themselves pay are too high, but that the rates which others pay are too low.

"Pressed by these difficulties, the proposers of equal mileage have admitted that there must be numerous exceptions; *e. g.*, where there is sea competition; where low rates for long distances will bring a profit; or where the article carried at a low rate is a necessary, such as coal. It is scarcely necessary to observe that such exceptions as these, while inadequate to meet all the various cases, destroy the value of equal mileage as a principle, or the possibility of applying it as a general rule."

Ohio has particularly distinguished herself in special enactments; with what success may be inferred from the State Railroad Commissioner's report in 1870. Speaking of the nine different tariffs prescribed for the transportation of passengers and freight, he pronounces these intended benefits "the most fruitful source of complaint;" and of one existing law, the Commissioner further remarked, that its strict enforcement would compel "some companies ultimately to suspend business, prohibit the transportation of certain articles by rail, and compel their transportation below actual cost."

Despite the admonitions of history, the demands for aggressive legislation increased in fierceness, until, under the uncontrollable pressure of the "Farmer's Movement," they culminated in the Illinois law against discrimination. In the clamor for its passage, the calm voice of experience was unheeded. Under the shadow of the Capitol an angry assemblage dictated the provisions of a proscriptive law. In vain a few independent members strove to stem the torrent. Their appeals were drowned in the turbulent roar. "Down with the monopolies" was the popular cry. To such a pitch were the unthinking people wrought, that, in some sections, the man who would have dared to extenuate the railroads would have been lynched. The outgrowth of *this spirit* is the Illinois law to prevent discrimination.

Dispassionately regarded, does it not seem like a mockery of justice? The corporations were impeached with "high crimes and misdemeanors," yet no opportunity was given them to put in a defense. The avenues to public attention were closed against them. No influential journal dared to espouse their cause, or accord them a fair hearing. The warnings of men whose counsel directed the investment of surplus capital were scouted and suppressed, while flaming head lines announced the incendiary declamations of lily-handed demagogues suddenly become "hard-fisted patrons of husbandry." And this monopoly of public attention was an outcry against monopoly!

The Illinois railroad law is an anomaly. It is entitled, "An Act to prevent unjust discriminations," etc., while its application countenances unjust and prohibits just discriminations. This construction of it is easily indicated, which is not a pleasing reflection for the Solons who sought to render impossible what their handiwork makes quite possible. The third section tolerates the wrong. It was the one most wrangled over, and was the joint product of both Houses. It was thrown out as a soothing concession to the "poor farmer." Carried into effect, he will find it allows discriminations in favor of one who can ship a large quantity—giving a man an advantage over his neighbor proportionate to his means; or, in other words, creating a privileged class, of which wealth is the distinctive trait. True, there are conditions under which it is perfectly sound and proper that a discrimination should be made when large amounts are shipped; but as to the articles whose transportation chiefly interests farmers, viz.: grain, cattle, and lumber, it is clearly meant to legalize preferential advantages to the one man merely because he has great possessions. The articles enumerated are carried by the car load, and the charge should be so made; then the man who ships one hundred car loads will have to pay the same price per car load as the man that ships but ten. Otherwise, the small dealer has not an equal chance in the market. If a man can ship one hundred car loads for five dollars less than the man who can only ship ten, the former can afford to do his business for five dollars per car less profit, which might leave no margin to the small shipper. Should both have to buy from the same producer, the man of small means is unable to compete against his rich neighbor. Granted that men of large means always have the advantage over those less favored, the wrong consists in authorizing railroad companies to widen the difference, by giving a preference to the rich man who does not need it. This unjust principle the law specially countenances, working injustice to the poor man by placing the control of the market for grain, lumber, and stock within the grasp of a favored few, and thus creating the worst form of monopoly.

For instance, Alexander or Sullivant, or any large shipper, having secured a special rate for fifty or one hundred car loads, may go to his poorer neighbors, who wish to ship but a few car loads each, and say: "Look here, I've got a rebate of ten dollars per car; I can ship that much cheaper than you can; now, you give me five dollars per car, and I will ship your freight along with mine at my special rate." The small shippers accept the offer, because thereby they gain five dollars per car; but, in the name of justice, why should they be compelled to pay a tax to their richer neighbor? Under such a law, are the days of feudalism gone by? Surely, if there is a statute that ought to be blotted out by any means known to freemen, it is one that prostrates the poor man under the heel of the rich.

Circumstances and conditions, however, daily arise, under which it is eminently fair to all that discrimination for the quantity shipped should be allowed. It is one of the first principles of commercial law. The man who buys a hogshead of sugar gets it at a cheaper rate than the man who buys only one pound. If the principle is sound, should it not equally apply to transportation? The dealer who can give a train load of freight to a railroad company is certainly entitled to a lower rate than the man who merely offers half a car load, *provided the distance carried is the same*; were the full cargo destined to a point only three or four miles distant, and the half car load three hundred miles, the case would be reversed, because transportation can be conducted one hundred miles much cheaper, per mile, than for ten miles, provided all other things are equal.

The further west we go the less travel and freighting is seen. The first twenty-five miles or more out of Chicago the passenger cars of the North-western, Burlington, Alton, and Rock Island Roads are crowded. Thereafter, the passengers thin out and cars are dropped off, but the cost of hauling the lighter trains, per mile, is only a trifle less than on the heavy "runs." Yet, despite this indisputable fact, the present law compels Illinois railway companies to carry passengers at the same price on branches of their road, where there is seldom one car load and never more than two, as upon their main or through lines, where, on account of there being more passengers, they can well be carried at less cost per passenger. This forces railway companies to *extort* from main line passengers compensation for work done for branch patrons. And this results from a law enacted to prevent extortion!

Reference is often made to the two-cent-per-mile rate on the New York Central Railroad. That line is dotted with populous cities its entire length, which yield it such an enormous travel that the company can afford to take passengers at a much lower rate than any western railroad can. The same reason enables leading Chicago railroads to carry passengers at less cost on their main lines than upon their branches. Trains are sometimes discontinued on these branch roads because, at the rate of fare usually charged, it does not pay to run the trains, whereas, if the people would pay what they could afford rather than not have the accommodation, the trains could be profitably run. Should this pernicious principle of the law be sustained, the companies will be compelled to run a lesser number of trains on their branch roads, and thus incommode the people; for it is plain, people must go without what they are not willing to pay for.

The second clause of our criticism charges that the law prohibits just discrimination. The Act says: "It shall not be deemed a sufficient excuse or justification of such discrimination that the point is one at which there exists competition with any other road or means of transportation." This dismisses the idea that there is such a thing as just discrimination. Is it a correct view? The rate on corn from Springfield to Chicago, we will say, is fifteen cents per bushel; to carry out the illustration, suppose that four cents per bushel is the profit over and above the actual expense

Homestead on the River.

of transporting the grain, and that this amount is only just enough to pay a reasonable return upon the company's investment. Further south on the same line, at St. Louis, there is a powerful competition—the Mississippi River, down which lumber from Minnesota, and grain, are floated to New Orleans. The river fixes the rate at which transportation shall be done. Having no expensive track to lay and maintain, the steamboats with their capacious barges can move cheaper than any railroad can, but not so cheap as to leave no profit whatever to the railroad if it carries freight at the rate thus fixed by the river. Is it not clearly better for the people of Springfield, or any intermediate station, that the company should take the produce and merchandise from St. Louis to Chicago at a profit of one cent or even one-half cent per bushel (provided that is the largest profit the rate fixed by the river will allow), and thus be enabled to do the local business a trifle cheaper than it would otherwise be forced to demand, if the whole burden of paying the interest on the cost of the road were thrown upon the local business? Were all the traffic of the several roads to be done on the low basis of the river rates, the railroads could not be maintained; nor would any one have been rash enough to build our railroads had they expected to do all the business at the prices fixed by the river. It was just because there was no navigable river running across the State that the prairie was almost unoccupied until the railroads were built. If the companies are not to be permitted to get from the river business whatever profit they can, under existing circumstances, there seems no other way than to forego that business, and let the local business pay all the expenses of the road. This statement is likely to call out the query: "How is it, if you can afford to do a particular item of business at a low rate, you can not afford to do all at the same price?" Precisely for the same reason that a farmer can not afford to have a bad crop on every acre of his land; though it would not seriously affect him to have a bad crop on one acre, if there were many acres of good crops; and he would generally prefer to have a bad crop on the one acre rather than have no crop at all.

The law discriminates in another way that is flagrantly

unjust. It annihilates legitimate competition by taking the business from north and south lines having their termini in Illinois, and gives it wholly to east and west lines terminating in Ohio and Indiana. To illustrate: the Illinois Central, between Chicago and Cairo, is crossed by eight lines having through Eastern connections. From their points of junction with the Central to the State line is an average of, perhaps, sixteen miles. These lines can comply with the Illinois law until they cross the border, where they can make the rate as low as they please, while the Central, being amenable to the pro rata law its entire length of seven hundred and seven miles in Illinois, is unable to take a pound of freight from any competing point. Moreover, it is quite possible for the Toledo, Wabash & Western Railroad, extending from Toledo to the Mississippi, to take the business of Decatur at a less rate than that of Springfield as far as the State line, then make the balance in favor of Springfield on the rate between the State line and Toledo. Conditions might arise under which the company would be justified in taking advantage of the law; for it should never be forgotten that commercial laws are as positive and binding as physical laws. Each navigable river is as much a fact controlling railroad companies commercially as are the laws of gravitation and other natural forces facts that have to be considered in determining how trains can be hauled.

One other objectionable feature. Congress interdicts the interposition of any obstruction to commerce between States. A bridge can not be thrown across the Mississippi or Ohio until government has located it where its existence will not obstruct navigation. Yet this law plainly violates that principle. It instructs the Railroad Commissioners to prepare pro rata schedules of rates, and force their adoption upon the companies. Illinois is in the direct line of the world's highway. The rich products of China and Japan have been diverted from their former channel around the Cape of Good Hope, and are daily being carried over the Pacific Railroads en route to the Atlantic, and beyond. The rate upon these cargoes of tea is made in Yokohama. Each of the companies forming the through line accept their *pro rata* of the through rate. Shall this magnificent traffic, for which empires long and desperately fought, be halted at the Mississippi River, and be made to pay toll as three men at Springfield shall dictate? Or is it too palpably absurd that the commerce between the Old and New Worlds should be regulated from the Illinois State House?

Other reasons, good and sufficient, might be advanced; but from those cited it will be evident that the law, in its present shape, is impracticable, unwarrantable, and unjust, and can not be productive of aught but harm.

What is a reasonable rate? Two generations have tried to settle this question, and failed. Their successors have now attacked it with somewhat dubious prospects. Yet the problem is not a poser. Were law makers to approach it as students do geometry, the correct solution would soon be reached. In that art are axioms whose truth is self-evident. Accepting these without cavil, and applying the rules that follow, the most difficult problems are worked out. The same principles govern the science of transportation and solve its intricacies. Until this truth is recognized, satisfactory results never will be reached. At present, the monopolist and anti-monopolist occupy different stand-points. Although regarding the same matter, they see only the side nearest each other. The one views it from the top of his wheat-stack, and the other from the treasurer's office. Then the political umpires step in and increase the trouble. Their efforts have had the one merit of persistency. It matters not how wretched their failures, renewed attempts are made. Experience, however, has developed considerations that must be admitted in determining what is a reasonable rate. Let us note a few:

Every railroad undertaking involves two sorts of expenditures; investments, which includes the cost of the roadway, rolling stock, depots, etc.; and expenditures, which cover outlays for labor and material consumed in the daily service of transportation or in maintaining the property. No one will deny that the charges should be made to yield a remunerative return upon the investment over and above all working and incidental expenses. Ordinary foresight dictates that the receipts should so far exceed expenses as to induce capital to make the necessary investments. This excess is commonly designated as a certain per centage on the investment, a fixed interest on the borrowed principal, and dividends, fluctuating with prosperity, on the contributed part, represented by shares. No other result is satisfactory, either to the owners or patrons of the road. But the benefits of a good, well-managed railroad accrue more directly to the community than to the stockholders.

Every railroad is worth what it would cost to replace it, and upon that valuation the company are entitled to a fair return. In sparsely settled localities this policy might establish rates deemed exorbitant. But is it not a fact, too often lost sight of, that it costs just as much to construct a railway across a new territory as it does through a densely populated district? It may cost more. The iron, material, and supplies have to be transported so much further; and the capital which furnished them commands interest upon its outlay as imperatively as if expended where the return would be surer and more speedy. In the nature of things, therefore, the rates exacted must be gauged to yield the necessary return. So long as the charges are such as to render transportation by rail preferable to any other mode, they are reasonable. If any one is assured that existing rates are too high, the liberty to build a rival line is free to all. There is no monopoly in this country of the right to construct railways.

The actual cost of operating the road should be ascertained. Experts only could perform the task. Novices would not think of one-half the items of expense. This statement the history of railway legislation confirms.

Has American legislation ever considered the question of *speed* while framing *pro rata* and non-discriminating laws? Yet, it is a well-established law of railroad economics that *speed* is the essence of expense. The recognized rule is, that the cost of transportation increases as the square of the velocity. Thus, a speed of ten miles per hour would be equal to one hundred, twenty to four hundred, and fifty to two thousand five hundred. In all enactments hitherto perpetrated or threatened, this startling difference in the cost of moving trains, being as $16 to $4 between an express and an ordinary accommodation train, has been wholly ignored, doubtless never thought of.

This principle was recognized by the British Parliament when, in 1844, being urged to protect the poorest classes, they required all railway companies, one-third of whose gross earnings were divided from passengers, to run one train daily, each way, upon which passengers should be carried at 1d. per mile, *at a rate not less than twelve miles an hour*. The slow rate for third-class trains is still maintained, although express trains average forty miles an hour, including stops. In addition to this just recognition of speed as one item of expense, Parliament excepted the earnings of these slow trains from taxation.

Motive power is another leading item of expense. This is largely dependent upon the character of the route. If fuel is abundant, the operating expenses are correspondingly reduced. But if, as in the case of the North-western and Milwaukee & St. Paul, there is scarcely a coal mine or a forest within reach of their far-extending systems, their cost per mile run is considerably increased, and should be taken into account in adjusting rates. Other roads again have heavy grades, up which engines of the largest capacity can not haul more than ten or fifteen cars at a time, while the same engines on other lines could easily draw fifty or sixty car loads.

A still more apparent consideration is, that the facilities provided are only partially used. The current of eastward trade largely exceeds their running in the opposite direction, and it sets most heavily eastward when the return flow is the slightest, and *vice versa*. Empty cars, therefore, abound each way. This disproportion is so great that, upon a leading trunk line, of the track and rolling stock there is frequently employed about sixty per cent. in one direction, and twenty per cent. in the opposite. The waste of expenditure becomes an extra charge upon the freight actually carried; and the drawback will continue until wise measures shall tend more equally to diffuse the trade currents and balance their volume in opposite directions. For, it should be borne in mind that, whether a freight engine runs with a full or a partial load, the items of expense are the same.

Expenses are lessened when the volume of freight increases. This is a fundamental principle of cheap transportation. To forward a single letter, by special messenger, to California would cost hundreds of dollars; but, deposited in the government mails, three cents pays for its transportation. This cheap service is possible, because simultaneously a like service is performed for the thousands of other patrons. Freight transportation is subject to the same law. Is any one stupid enough to murmur because the government carries one man's letters to San Francisco for three cents, while another is charged as much for having a letter carried four or five miles? What matters it how cheap another man's letter is carried so long as mine is taken at a reasonable rate? And if the rule holds good in regard to letters, why should it not embrace parcels and packages, etc.? The principle is so plain, when applied to postal service, that no word of complaint against its discrimination is ever heard; but when applied to property transportation, which is subject to precisely the same law, what a fearful commotion is raised!

CHAPTER XXXVI.

CONCERNING RATES AND GOVERNMENTAL RAILWAYS.

CONTINUATION OF CONTRIBUTED ARTICLE, BY J. W. MIDGLEY, ESQ., CHICAGO.

Much as we claim to be in advance of the "old country," in the recognition of the fundamental principles of cheap transportation, we are still far behind. This deplorable condition is begotten of that selfish determination not to let others get the "start." The grievous bubbles which stump orators and the country press are inflating are not novelties. They were pricked years ago in Europe. Inequality of charges is one of them. Parliament disposed of it in the Railway Clauses Consolidation Act, by declaring it "expedient that the companies should be enabled to vary the tolls upon the railways so as to accommodate them to the circumstances of the traffic," and pronounced it lawful for the companies "from time to time to alter or vary the tolls, either upon the whole or any particular portions of their railways, *as they shall think fit.*" The people still harboring the belief that unequal rates were unreasonable, a Royal Commission, comprising Lord Stanley, Robt. Lowe, Chancellor of the Exchequer, Sir Rowland Hill, Postmaster-General, Mr. Ayrton, Commissioner of Public Works, and ten other influential members, investigated the subject in all its bearings, and reported that "inequality of charge in respect of distance, besides being a necessary consequence of competition, is an essential element in the conveying trade; that is to say, the principle which governs a railway company in fixing the rate is that of creating a traffic by charging such a sum for conveyance as will induce the produce of one district to compete with another in a common market. The power of granting special rates permits a development of trade which would not otherwise exist; and it is abundantly evident that a large portion of the trade of the country, at the present

"Speed, Comfort, Safety."

time, has been created by, and is continued on the faith of, special rates." And they dismissed the suggestion of interference by adding: "The condition under which such rates are granted are so numerous that no special law could be framed to regulate them."

Their comprehensive view of the question was sustained by the Court of Common Pleas, which distinctly recognized the right of a company to charge unequal rates. In the case of Ransome *v.* Eastern Counties Railway, the court held that a company may charge different rates for transportation where the expenses thereof are different; and, as the Commission remarked, in citing this decision: "As the expense of starting a train is the same for a large or small distance, this may be fairly taken into account and justify an inequality in the rates of carriage between different places."

To load a freight car consumes twenty-four hours, and to unload it and get it into use again a corresponding period. Freight trains usually run about ten miles an hour, including stops, and a car carries about ten tons of freight. Suppose the rate 2c per ton per mile, and the distance to be hauled ten miles, the time consumed would be forty-nine hours, and the compensation for the service $2.00, or 96c per day. But were the car sent on a continuous run of 1,000 miles at the same rate, it would occupy 148 hours, and would yield the company $32.50 per day. The illustration conveys its own comments.

If each local station could make up a train of freight, the case might be different; but such condition is not possible, only at terminal points. For instance, Joliet is much nearer Chicago than is Rock Island, and would, apparently, be entitled to better rates. Yet its business costs a mere trifle less. The train of empty cars leave Chicago, the required number are dropped off at Joliet and other way stations, and, at Rock Island, the return trip is commenced, upon which the cars left off to be loaded are picked up. Meantime, these cars have been standing idle, during which time they have earned nothing; and, as cars earn money only when in motion, a reasonable rate, to insure a profitable return, must be sufficiently large to balance the unemployed time.

The unauthorized statement that rates have been steadily increased throughout the State of Illinois, during the past few years, is maliciously untrue. The tendency has been continually downward, as the following comparative statement of the average earnings per ton per mile will show:

	Lake Shore & Mich. Southern Railway.	Mich. Central Railway.	Chicago, Burlington & Quincy Railway.	Chicago & North-west'n Railway.
1868 - -	$2\frac{43}{100}$ cts.	$2\frac{45}{100}$ cts.	$3\frac{20}{100}$ cts.	$3\frac{13}{100}$ cts.
1869 - - -	$2\frac{34}{100}$ "	$2\frac{9}{100}$ "	$3\frac{1}{100}$ "	$3\frac{9}{100}$ "
1870 - -	$1\frac{50}{100}$ "	$1\frac{98}{100}$ "	$2\frac{77}{100}$ "	$2\frac{87}{100}$ "
1871 - - -	$1\frac{32}{100}$ "	$1\frac{51}{100}$ "	$2\frac{31}{100}$ "	$2\frac{67}{100}$ "
1872 - -	$1\frac{37}{100}$ "	$1\frac{56}{100}$ "	$2\frac{19}{100}$ "	$2\frac{35}{100}$ "

In flat contradiction of popular statements is the fact that the cost of transportation has steadily decreased, notwithstanding the "watering" of stock. Thus, in 1863, the New York Central Railroad carried 312,000,000 tons at a cost of $2\frac{40}{100}$ cents per ton per mile, and the Erie 404,000,000 tons at $2\frac{9}{100}$. In 1872 the earnings for transporting 1,020,000,-000 tons over the Central, were $1\frac{69}{100}$ per ton per mile, and on the Erie $1\frac{52}{100}$ for 950,000,000 tons. Meantime, the stock and certificates of the former road had, in the same period, increased from $23,631,000 to $89,428,000, while the "stock, bonds, and debt" of the latter had increased from $40,000, 000 to $118,000,000. These figures, which are absolutely correct and can not lie, conclusively annihilate one of the most pretentious and favorite accusations of the anti-railroad agitator. It follows, therefore, that the adjustment of rates is seriously affected by two conditions: 1. Economy in original outlay. 2. Economy in current expenditures.

The people are responsible for the magnitude of these items. It is a notorious fact that exorbitant prices are extorted for right of way. As soon as it becomes known that a railway is to be run through a certain district, several times the antecedent value of the selected land is demanded, and generally awarded by commissioners; and if any additional legislation is required, the companies have to pay for it. Our Legislatures are not exceptions. Some years ago it was estimated that Parliamentary contests and concessions had cost the British railway companies $350,000,000. These expenses are mainly incurred in averting threatened legislation. This single item absorbs a very considerable portion of the profits. Political cormorants long since discovered it, and worry the funds out of the companies. Then there are numerous lines projected by speculators, with no view to public benefit, but originated simply to prey upon existing companies by forcing the latter to purchase them. Effete politicians and glutted lawyers also bleed the companies profusely; but it all eventually comes out of the "dear people" in the form of rates. The money must be had, and the public have to advance it.

These remarks apply specially to the compensation awarded for injuries. No observer of current events will question the assertion that railway companies are "salted" whenever a petit jury gets a chance at them. In such cases the juries are like the Donnybrook Irishman, who could not resist the temptation of whacking every head within reach of his shillaleh, his best friends sharing his most willing attentions. It may be "fun" for the time being, but who pays for it in the end? Every outrageous verdict—such as have become common-place exceptions—means sufficiently increased rates to pay the costs. The press urges the people to pursue this vindictive policy, and readily have they responded. It matters not how flimsy the pretext, the verdict in every Western State is a foregone, heavy conclusion.

In agitating for reform, the people forget that it must begin with themselves. It is the maddest folly to demand cheap rates, and yet force the railroads into excessive expenses; and it is the baldest falsehood propagated by the press to say that the courts are corrupted into acquitting the companies. The outrageous verdicts recorded in almost every county in the West prove its falsity and burlesque justice. Long since the corporations have ceased to trust in appeals to juries, such as are commonly impaneled. For what man competent to weigh evidence does not evade the jury box if he can?

These questions intrude themselves in determining what is a reasonable rate. The companies are mulcted upon every opportunity, and the numerous depletions necessitate the imposition of high rates.

The people complain of being overtaxed. Then, why do they create the necessity? However flatly the leaders of the anti-railroad agitation may deny that their misguided action has precipitated the existing crisis, it is none the less a fact. Their threatening attitude destroyed confidence in American securities. Why should a foreign capitalist invest in a Western railroad in whose management the owners are told they shall have no voice? Practically, the farmers of Illinois, Iowa, and Wisconsin say to the capitalists, "Come, and build us railroads; then we will run them, and you shan't put in a word." The moneyed men are not such fools. They are independent; we are not. They can live without us; but can we thrive without their help? They gave us the start. Have we enough to carry us through? The vast territory west of the Alleghanies is comparatively undeveloped. There is ample room for millions more of industrious men. How can they be induced to come? What agency has made the country inhabitable? What has shortened distances and lengthened life by saving time? What has enabled us to compass in one day what consumed a season in the time of our fathers? *The steam-engine.* Who now shall run it? Shall experts, who comprehend the laws of motion, or shall it be left to men whose primal qualification is that they can distinguish a short-horn from a Galloway?

Ignorance and folly never exalted a nation. Certain

would be our downfall if passion were to displace experience. Misguided and rash attempts have been often made to decree a schedule of rates, but the statesmen conceded their inability, and were wisely willing to let those who had grown up with the system, and mastered its principles, decide what is a reasonable rate.

Forced to admit the failure of legislation, "the dissatisfied" demand that government shall purchase the railways. Perhaps the corporations would not seriously object, for it is very probable they would be the greatest gainers by the transfer. Is it at all likely that government officials of the stripe we now have would possess superior fitness for railway management? Economy is our pressing want. Is it a distinguishing trait of the Caseys, Murphys, Butlers, *et al?* The proposition premises that the State would lease the railroads. In that event the lessees would have to be responsible parties, who could give ample security. This would necessitate their being either stock companies or wealthy capitalists. In either case, they might be inexperienced in railroad affairs, which would doubtless cause the control to fall upon the old working force, thereby increasing the number of salaries and adding materially to the necessary operating expenses of the lines.

Besides, the lessees would incur risks. Should the net earnings exceed the rent, the surplus would afford a tolerably good dividend upon their comparatively small investment; but should the results be reversed, they would have no dividend whatever. Therefore, it is certain the lessees would accept the risk only at a rental insuring them against loss, but so low as not to reimburse the State for the outlay in purchase. Neither is it likely the lessees would cramp their operations by agreeing to reduce rates, irrespective of the course their own interests would dictate; consequently, they would be in no better condition to reduce than are the present directors.

This experiment has been tried in Europe. It has worked successfully in Belgium. That kingdom is densely populated, and comprises a total area much less than half of any single Western State. They have all the railroads the country needs. Only small branch lines, or "by-ways," as they are termed, will be built. The same limitations apply to Great Britain and France. The State can easily build these little side-lines. Our country does not afford a parallel case. Does any reformer wish to see the government undertake the construction of a trunk line across half a dozen States? What a chance for jobs and fat contracts! One Credit Mobilier operation should satisfy us.

As owner of so vast a property, the government would be obliged to employ a retinue of skilled officers to supervise it, and see that the lessees maintained it properly. The importance of their duties would command large salaries, which, considering the number needed, would draw heavily upon the receipts from the lessees. The economy of the plan is, therefore, open to considerable doubt. Another possibility might arise. However admirably the terms of the lessees should be drawn, in view of the great political influence the companies could wield, these conditions might be modified. Common interest would dictate that their political power should be ranged on the side of the government; and, when the millions of railroad employees are taken into consideration, this view of the question becomes alarming and sufficient of itself to defeat the scheme.

The subject carries us still further. Railway enterprise has extended to numerous accompanying undertakings—to car shops and locomotive works, to stations, warehouses, docks, harbors, vessels, transit steamers, bridges, and other subsidiary enterprises, dependent upon and incorporated with the railways. The government, if it purchased the railways, would be obliged to include these subsidiary connections.

Government ownership would discourage further construction, as tending to diminish the public revenue, or they might be made a charge upon the several States. In any event, it would quench the spirit of enterprise on the part of the individuals, which, exercised as at present, is our best protection against monopoly.

Financially considered, who could estimate the depressing effect upon our national securities were the government to enter the market annually as a borrower of say $100,000,000, for the purchase of doubtful property? Viewed in this light, the scheme does not promise well to the State, as a financial transaction; and, we take it, there is no disposition to cheapen transportation at the expense of the public treasury.

This subject has been thoroughly considered in England, and the last Royal Commission appointed for that purpose thus summed up their report: "We are of opinion that it is inexpedient, at present, to subvert the policy which has hitherto been adopted of leaving the construction and management of railways to the free enterprise of the people;" adding, in the case of Ireland, where are many unprofitable lines, "that, as the railway companies have the best opportunities of judging whether rates can be reduced so as to be recuperative within a reasonable time, they should be left free to carry out such experiments at their own risk."

CHAPTER XXXVII.

THE BENEFITS CONFERRED BY RAILROADS.

CONTINUATION OF CONTRIBUTED ARTICLE, BY J. W. MIDGLEY, ESQ., CHICAGO.

The feeling against railroads has been so intense as to ignore their beneficial effects. Yet these are not insignificant. Perhaps they can best be estimated by imagining our condition were we suddenly to be thrown back to the state of locomotion existing forty years ago. Such return would render personal travel intolerable, would suspend business, and collapse thousands of enterprises originated and made prosperous by railway facilities.

With our fathers, a journey of three hundred miles was an event in a lifetime, and was not undertaken until a man had made his will. It is now easily, luxuriously, and expeditiously accomplished. Safety and speed are incomparable benefits. Strange though it may seem in view of the numerous startling accidents, the number of persons killed or injured on all the railways in Great Britain and Ireland is less than the number killed or injured by ordinary vehicles in London alone. The cost of traveling is also diminished fully one-half.

The untold benefits of safety, cheapness, and speed apply

still more to the transportation of freight. The old-time wagons never averaged more than three or four miles an hour; now, light, valuable packages are carried on express trains at the rate of thirty miles an hour. It might also be deemed worthy of recognition that the railways have done more toward the defense of the country than all other works, by affording rapid and effective means of concentrating men and supplies in case of necessity. Then, to a degree not easily estimated, they have contributed to the spread of mor-

The Rural Toilers of Forty Years ago.

ality and the diffusion of knowledge, by their liberal concessions to delegates attending conventions, and the half fare permits given to clergymen.

One might almost have the temerity to inquire how the farmers, Grangers, and anti-monopolists could assemble to discuss their grinding wrongs (?) were the railways not to bring them together.

These results have been attained without expense to the public, who are the principal recipients. Western men—citizens or Grangers—have put comparatively little into the railways they would now confiscate. While demanding this, they do not remember the Illinois and Iowa of fifty years ago, when it cost them one bushel of produce to get another to the nearest market. Prairie farms could then be bought for $2.50 per acre, and that, too, at second-hand. The corn was accumulated in cribs and sold at ten cents per bushel. Subsequently, railroads were built, since which the farmers' price for corn has rarely fallen below twenty cents, while more frequently it has exceeded forty cents. Meantime, the new territory has become populated, and its products are transportated at one-tenth the former cost. All the enormous increase of wealth, unparalleled in the history of nations, was caused by the railways. Yet the men whom they have enriched fancy they are oppressed by them, and demand their subordination to the behests of fickle legislators.

In view of this clamor it might not be inopportune to enumerate the branches of industry that are created by and dependent upon the railways. They may be thus classified: 1. Construction; 2. Equipment; 3. Repairs; 4. Supplies. The first includes timber for ties, wooden bridges, and station buildings; iron for rails, spikes, iron bridges, and tools; stone for bridge piers and retaining walls, and brick and stone for shop and other important buildings. The second includes locomotives and cars of every description; the third provides for the incidental renewal of the former; the fourth embraces fuel, oil, waste, and the innumerable items of daily demand, such as account books, stationery, etc. Let any one consider that 70,000 miles of railway are in actual operation, and determine whether the supply trade created by them is material to the nation's prosperity or not.

1. Construction.—To build fifty miles of railroad re-

quires a multitude of men, whose expenditures in the vicinity of their labors equals that of a large army. All classes of the community benefit by their presence. Business receives an impetus, and depots of supplies rapidly grow into permanent towns. Stations are established along the lines, section gangs are formed, and a host of men are given profitable employment, thus adding to the taxable resources of the district. Iron, however, is the principal item. To lay one mile of single track averages about one hundred tons of rails. At that recognized proportion, the cost of iron rails alone in the roads built since 1862, based on the figures published by the American Iron and Steel Association, has been as follows:

	Miles built.	Iron per ton.	Cost of iron.
1863	1,050	$76.37½	$8,071,875
1864	738	126.00	9,298,800
1865	1,377	98.62½	12,594,412
1866	1,832	86.75	15,892,600
1867	2,227	83.12½	18,510,924
1868	3,033	78.37½	23,922,787
1869	4,999	77.25	38,617,275
1870	6,145	72.25	44,397,625
1871	7,453	70.37½	52,450,487
1872	6,427	85.12½	54,709,837
	35,159		$278,466,622

Various estimates are made of the amount of iron, other than rails, that is regularly used in railroads. Correct figures can not be obtained; but including spikes, chairs, fish-plates, locomotives, car wheels, axles, etc., it is assumed that the total of iron used in railroads would not fall short of two hundred tons to the mile, which would place the entire cost since 1863 at over $500,000,000. When it is further recited that, in 1860, the price per ton was only $48, it will be seen that the iron of the roads has cost at least $200,-

000,000 more than it would have done at the rate current in 1860. Notwithstanding this enormous advance in the cost of the main item of construction, it is susceptible of proof that the rates of transportation have steadily decreased.

The foregoing tabular statement does not include the several millions expended, during the past three years, on the first-class roads, for steel rails. Every trunk line out of Chicago makes the majority of renewals with steel, which, at $120 per ton, demands no small outlay. At each of the rail mills more than a thousand men are engaged, every one of whom owes his employment as directly to the railways as do the engineers who run the trains.

2. EQUIPMENT.—At favorable locations mammoth enterterprises have been called into existence to supply the railways with rolling stock. In several eastern cities are established locomotive works. One of these, the Baldwin, covers six entire squares in the city of Philadelphia; in prosperous times, employs five thousand men, supports twenty thousand persons, and annually turns out over $5,000,000 worth of work. Another Quaker City enterprise, the Whitney Car Wheel Factory, covers one square, supplies several railroads, and exports car wheels to Europe. In the same city a single railroad company, at one time, expended $5,000,000 for rails, engines, cars, etc. Locomotive and car works have built up Paterson, Manchester, Wilmington, Jeffersonville, and other similarly favored places. Numerous cities hold out inducements, in the certain knowledge that the possession of such vast establishments affords profitable employment to hosts of skillful men, whose earnings benefit the entire community. Bloomington gave a large bonus to secure the location of the Chicago & Alton Railroad shops, and Aurora enjoys like advantages from the

Chicago, Burlington & Quincy Railway. A blow at the corporation falls with crushing effect upon these subsidiary enterprises. The recent panic illustrated this truism. In its fall the mighty oak carries down with it the clinging vine.

3. Repairs.—Rails and other constituent parts of a railway wear out. If a company is not allowed margin enough to maintain its property in good condition, the public experience the discomfort and inconvenience of a rough, poor road. If otherwise, the enterprises that were advantaged by the first outlay share in the profit of replenishing the road.

4. Supplies.—Nearly every branch of industry is benefited by the operation of railroads. Several find them their best customers. An extensive list might be given, but the instances already cited will suffice to show that we are truly a dependent people. Of what avail is it that our farmer can produce a thousand bushels of grain, unless there is a market for it? And, going still further, what advantage is gained from a bountiful supply and fair demand, unless facilities are provided to convey the products to market?

The companies sustain a mutual relation. They advantage the farmer by furnishing him the cheapest and most expeditious means of getting his produce to the consumers, and they benefit the latter by placing bread within their reach and enabling them to buy it. This view of the case may evoke a repetition of the rural cry, "The farmer pays for all." But where does he obtain the wherewithal? From the consumer. Would it better any one if the number of consumers were decreased, and the producers correspondingly increased? This must be the practical result of an onslaught on the railways. Cripple them by hostile legislation, or menace them so that capital will avoid them, and the innumerable multitude of artisans that turn out material and equipment for them will be deprived of employment and be forced to become producers. Is that what the farmers want? Capital inevitably shrinks from precarious investments. If the farmers wish to utterly destroy the value of American railroad securities in foreign markets, they can not do it more effectually than to demand the abrogation of the privileges that alone make the charters worth having. While hotly charging every grievance upon the railways, they forget that the law of supply and demand invariably regulates the price. Why should the farmers of Iowa boast they have millions of bushels of grain more than they need, and then curse the railways for the low price it commands? Have they not produced thus much more than is wanted? Why berate the New England manufacturers because they will not send boots and shoes, cottons and woolens for this surplus, when they only care to exchange for as much as they need. If men will locate so far distant from market that their products are absolutely valueless, and there raise tenfold more than they or the country can consume, even as fuel, they should blame themselves, not the railroads, for their unfortunate predicament. In this respect, the Granges might accomplish some good. Instead of exciting the farmers to rush to the State capitals and demand laws compelling railroad companies to transport produce below actual cost, they might calmly take in the situation and advise their associates to raise only marketable products. For, why should a man continually grow corn, when there is no demand for it, simply because his land is adapted for it?

Every improvement which reduces the cost of transportation benefits the producer. The application of the telegraph to railway service enables the companies to do an equal amount of business, with one-third the equipment that would be needed were the post-office or special messenger the best means of communication. This great saving in time makes it practicable to distribute cars with such facility as to meet current requirements. In so far as it economizes resources by keeping them in use, and securing equal results with less quantity, it cheapens transportation.

It is possible the progress of events will develop kindred improvements. None would rejoice more than the capitalist were a metal of such quality produced that it would never wear out, or a method of locomotion be discovered that would obviate the expense of roadways and steam-power. These now indispensable adjuncts increase the cost of moving freight, and, to that extent, benefit the workmen engaged upon them, at the expense of the shipper. Until science has overcome these drawbacks, we should content ourselves with present means of transportation, because they are the best and cheapest known.

Railways create communities. In thus developing the family idea, they bless the race by conferring advantages that are beyond the reach of an isolated few. Literature, science, art, and all the concomitant benefits of education and enlightenment are assured where there is society enough to foster them. Agriculture does not found cities. It is essentially segregating in its tendency. Farmers need large fields, and, therefore, must have scattered homesteads; whereas, manufactures and railway enterprises build up populous towns, and their location in his vicinity benefits the farmer, by creating a large supply for his products near at hand, insuring him better returns, because the cost of long transportation is saved. Railways have bridged the distance between the producers and consumers, and have brought them near together. They encourage manufactures, and, by the judicious location of their extensive shops, create cities. In the vicinity of these thriving centers, one acre is worth more than a hundred or, perhaps, (as in Chicago) a thousand were before the railways had transformed the prairie into a populous hive of industry. Why is England, to-day, the richest nation on the globe? Simply because she is one vast workshop. The same enviable result is possible here if the people are educated aright. Then they will not be duped into the belief that this continent depends upon any one class for existence. Such teaching is un-American. Yet it is the average Granger's staple utterance, albeit, it does savor of despotism and old-time feudalism. We *are* mutually dependent. The farmer can not flourish unless the citizen buys his corn, and the latter must get from him enough to supply his wants. This inexorable law prevents the creation of privileged classes.

Railways educate the people. They render industrial expositions both practicable and accessible. Excursion rates are given, placing it within the reach of the poorest to view all that science or industry can produce, or ingenuity suggest. It thus enables those living in districts most secluded to participate in all the amenities of civilized life. And, as the sharp ring of the pioneer's axe on the forest tree disturbs and causes to flee away the croaking birds and howling beasts, so the advancing head-light of the locomotive dispels the darkness of ignorance, and carries light and busy life wherever it speeds its way.

Were these benefits candidly acknowledged, they would give tone and consideration to the partial harangues of the Granger's oracles. They would then remind their impatient hearers, as one has pertinently observed, that the broad prairies of the West, being a thousand miles distant

Before the Era of Railroads.

from the eastern markets, with intervening rivers not bridged, and mountains not tunneled, had they been left to depend upon the natural highways to the sea, would yet have been comparatively unbroken; and, instead of being dotted with flourishing cities and desirable homesteads, would have remained the hunting-grounds of "Indians not taxed."

Twenty years have wrought wondrous changes. Illinois and Iowa farms were not at a premium two decades ago. The rural toilers of those days could not spare time from their drugery to brood, in conventions, over fancied wrongs. They begged and prayed for railroads. Characteristic of all, was the piteous plaint of men who, having hauled their produce by ox-teams eighty miles to Rochester, Minnesota, in reply to Jesse Hoyt's inquiry if they wanted transportation, exclaimed, "For God's sake, sir, give us a railroad! Oh, if you only would!" And their sons now threaten to fence in the roads and tear up the tracks, if the companies do not tamely submit to every legislative caprice.

In the ten years following, from 1850 to 1860, farm lands increased materially in value. In Ohio the increase per acre was $13.18; in Indiana, $11.10; in Illinois, $11.36; Michigan, $11.04; Wisconsin, $7.02; Iowa, $5.82; and Minnesota, $4.53. Meantime, the cost of the railroads, which created this increase, had been about one-half the advance in value of the farms; therefore, it would have been actual gain to the farmers had they paid the entire cost of building the roads. Carefully prepared statistics show that every additional mile of railroad to 100,000 acres of farm land yielded an average increase of $1.00 per acre.

These facts, which are uncontrovertible, and will withstand the onslaught of the most fervid anti-monopolist, are commended to the consideration of those who view the railroads only in the light of soulless enemies. As Mr. Grosvenor has clearly stated, however unprofitable the roads may have been to those whose money created them, to the farmers of the West, (who now berate them with every breath) they have been worth at least $100,000 per mile.

Ten years later, in 1870, the record showed this subsequent increase in value to be: in Ohio, $3.54 per acre; Indiana, $4.68; Michigan, $7.13; Illinois, $7.28; Iowa, $7.17; and Minnesota, $1.25.

Not alone did the rural districts share the benefits. Cities—such as Chicago, Milwaukee, and Indianapolis—were created by them. A metropolis worthy of the age and the people was built in every State, and stands, to-day, the glory, no less than the advantage, of their respective commonwealths.

In one respect only has the the result exceeded anticipation. It was not supposed, when the first charters were granted, that such a volume of traffic would be attained. Naturally, then, the expenditure that produced it should command abundant return. For a time it did, whereupon shares advanced. Then came reverses, brought about by ill-advised legislation, until railway stocks sank lower in home and foreign markets than almost any other securities. Thus capitalists suffered from the imprudence of spending their money for the public good. So late as 1867, the total market value of share property in railways in England was, according to Sir Rowland Hill's report to Parliament, from which we have drawn liberally, much lower than the original amount invested therein. Neither have the losers been consoled by public gratitude. The opposite has been their experience. They have been charged with corruption and extortion, and each failure or negligence has been eagerly pounced upon and visited with a heavy penalty. Besides being subject to State taxation, the localities through which they pass also heavily taxes them, the practical effect being that while a company, by affording profitable employment in rural districts, relieves the several villages of the expense of supporting men having no other prospect of an income, it is yet made to pay the major part of the local tax levies. In short, they have been taught, bitterly, that the justice society always accords to individuals is withheld from corporations, on the unjust assumption that the loss is distributed among too great a number to cause its being felt by any one.

The people are very jealous of their own rights, but have little regard for the rights of the railroads. They overestimate the privileges granted, and forget that the valuable concessions are denied the companies. Had this spirit been manifested at an earlier day, the flow of capital to the West would have been instantly checked. But inducements were held out, capitalists were freely invited, and their confidence gave us our 70,000 miles of operated railroad, constructed at a cost of $3,159,423,057, of which 52 per cent. is represented by stocks, and 48 per cent. in bonds or indebtedness. Upon this investment the earnings, last year, were $473,241,055, 72 per cent. of which was derived from freight, and 28 per cent. from passengers. The operating expenses were 65 per cent. of the gross earnings, leaving 35 per cent. net, out of which to pay 6.70 per cent. interest on the bonds and 3.91 per cent. dividends on the stock.

Narrowing the confines, we find that the Western States—including Ohio, Michigan, Indiana, Illinois, Wisconsin, Minnesota, Iowa, Kansas, Missouri, and Wyoming, Dakota, Colorado, and Indian Territories—with a population of 14,080,-000 souls, have 28,778 miles of railway, constructed at an average cost of $50,550 per mile. For the year ending with 1872, the gross earnings were $13.76 per head of population. The net earnings were $67,317,083, which allowed an average dividend of $2\frac{83}{100}$ per cent. on the capital stock—$724,686,046. These results are not very encouraging to investors, neither are they calculated to divert capital westward. True, there has been much extravagance and unwisdom in construction, and great recklessness and knavery in individual management; not more so, however, than is incident to the growth of every mammoth system or enterprise. In such cases history repeats itself. But, granting all and more than has ever been charged, the bright fact remains, clear and undeniable, that railroads have been the pioneers of Western civilization. They may be pushed out into new Territories before there is business enough to yield running expenses. That is the stockholders' loss—the people only gain. During such time the public can afford to be generous; but when the railroads populate the vast districts and swell the State revenues, then the cry is raised, "Down with the railroads!" and the infuriated multitude would destroy the agency that has made their homes habitable and their produce marketable.

This subject has been thoroughly discussed during the past decade. British statesmen have studied it in all its bearings, and Americans, too, have given it forced consideration. Their published reports have largely affected the tenor of this article; for it is by the far-reaching light of experience that we are best enabled to comprehend present necessities and speculate upon future possibilities. What we want is, not a continuance of random firing in the hope of a chance shot hitting the mark, but a skillful adjustment and disposition of resources within reach. What more effectual method of rendering railroad enactments inoperative could be adopted than to intrust their interpretation to men who scorn the idea of understanding the system they are to control? Why burlesque and belittle education so much as to commit our leading industry into the keeping of men whose popular qualification therefor is that they know nothing practically about it? The question is too momentous to be tampered with. Let bunglers be retired and experience come to the front. A tribunal the people will have, and are entitled to have. That claim is not in dispute. But let it be constituted with an eye to fitness. The railroads are on trial. Give them the inalienable right to challenge jurors who are foresworn to adjudge them guilty before hearing the evidence. Demagogues have incited the people to clutch at the throats of the corporations, dethrone justice, and drown her voice amid communistic cries for confiscation—clamorings that will be certain, eventually, to react upon the land-owners who were duped into inaugurating the warfare.

To obviate public jealousy and secure efficient management, the chief of the tribunal or board for the several control of railways, should be selected with exclusive regard to his fitness; and the board thus created should be placed beyond the range of political action. Being intrusted with duties demanding extraordinary qualifications, industry, and discrimination, the term of office should not be dependent upon the uncertain dictates of legislators, nor expire with every administration. Fidelity to the trusts reposed should regulate the term of service. Some such conception as this possessed the late Robert Stephenson, when, in his inaugural address as President of the British Institute of Civil Engineers, he said: "What we ask is knowledge; give us a tribunal competent to form a sound opinion; commit to that tribunal, with any restrictions you think necessary, the whole of the great questions appertaining to our system. Let it protect private interests apart from railways; let it judge of the desirability of all initiatory measures, and of all proposals for purchases, amalgamations, or other railway arrangements; delegate to it the power of enforcing such regulations and restrictions as may be thought needful to secure the rights of private persons or of the public; devolve upon it the duty of consolidating, if possible, the railway laws, and making such amendments thereto as the public interests and the property now depending on it may require; give it full delegated authority over us in any way you please: all that we ask is that it shall be a tribunal that is impartial, and that is thoroughly informed; and if impartiality and intelligence are secured we need not fear the results."

CHAPTER XXXVIII.

TRANSPORTATION AND THE MONEY KINGS.

THE QUESTION FROM ANTAGONISTIC STAND-POINTS.

The article on Railroad Transportation by Mr. Flagg, President of the Illinois Farmers' Association, which constitutes Chapter XXXIV of this work, and that by Mr. J. W. Midgley, Secretary of the President of the Chicago & North-western Railroad, which is concluded on the preceding page, will be accepted, I think, not only as able but also as candid statements from the particular stand-points of the interests whom the writers represent. Mr. Flagg, in this instance, has confined himself principally to giving actual facts and figures relating to the transportation of products, leaving the reader to draw his own conclusions from what is presented.

The treatment of the subject from the railroad stand-point, by Mr. Midgley, evinces very extensive knowledge of railroad history, both in Europe and America, and sketches the growth of the railway system from its inception in England up to the present time, the introduction of steam and the changes consequently rendered necessary in the carriage of goods, and an outline of the legislation regulating the working of the system. These, I think, have never before been presented in such shape as to bring them before the masses; and from this consideration, if no other, the article is really of great value. It is needless, of course, for me to say the facts and figures presented by both these gentlemen are undoubtedly authentic, whatever may be thought of the argument deduced therefrom; which arguments must stand or fall upon their merits before the reader.

One of the great troubles with the masses always has been—perhaps always will be—that it is difficult for them to occupy conservative ground, as between two radical stand-points. Notwithstanding what has been said to the contrary, farmers as a class, the reading ones at least, *do* occupy just this ground when they come to rely on their sober judgment. They may, it is true, be carried away for the time being by the florid eloquence or magnetism of the speaker, but the result of the second sober thought is the question, What is right in the matter? Hence, incendiarism, in whatever shape it may be presented, falls harmless for evil,—a fact not generally appreciated, except by those who know the farming class intimately well.

LEGISLATION NOT THE PANACEA FOR ALL EVILS.

For myself, I do not accede to the radical view from either stand-point. I do not believe that the railroads of the West are to blame for *all* the evils that have been heaped upon the producer. The system upon which they were carried on, the publicity given to their workings, their standing directly next to the farmer as the transporter of his products, ought to prevent this. The real grievances are the shameless frauds and unfair discriminations practiced by those great operators whose scheme was to consolidate not only the railroads, but the telegraph lines of the country into one great monopoly, and through the power of centralized capital, to buy individuals, to corrupt Legislatures, and even to make the National Government subservient to their will. This is what raised the storm of public indignation, which took what seemed the most tangible avenue through which to work reform. By common consent, the unjust discriminations of railway companies became the principal point of attack in the investment and siege of fortressed wrong.

The result, so far as regards State legislation is concerned, has injured both the railroads and the people. In Illinois, a law has been produced which, with some good features, contains also some odious ones; the most objectionable being what certainly has the appearance, at least, of unjust discrimination (in its practical workings, I mean) against certain railroads. Taken as a whole, however, the present railroad law of Illinois is undoubtedly a long step in the right direction.

In the early stages of the Farmers' Movement, as always since, I strongly disapproved of the spirit that sought to bring into direct antagonism with the transporters, the worst passions of mankind, inciting the people to imprudent or illegal acts, which were bound, before the law, to result in discomfiture. Long ago, I was in favor of a commission, to be appointed by the people and the railway managers, to discuss ways and means by which the conflicting interests might be harmonized, and a basis, at least, arrived at upon which might be founded a law equal in its operations and just to all parties. Indeed, I stated the case, as it appeared to me, and made this suggestion to two of the leading railway officials of Chicago; but, while agreeing that the view was correct and would result in good if honestly carried out, they did not believe the plan feasible in the then excited state of public opinion. Unwisely, I think; for I had then, as I still have, unwavering faith in the integrity of the masses, and their willingness to do right, when not swayed by the sophistry of demagogues. At that time, the people certainly were measurably in the hands of this class. Unfortunately, too, at that time railroad officials were bound, hand and foot, by the power of the centralized capital of Wall Street, and the Eastern cites, so that they could not, if they would, have done what their calmer judgment dictated.

The Old Bird Fairly Aroused.

WE MUST STRIKE AT THE ROOT—CORRUPTION.

I still advocate the doctrine, that the root of the evil, corruption, must be struck with the ax of reform before the monopolizing tendency of capital can be brought down. It has indeed been brought into judgment at the bar of public opinion; and this is evidence of encouraging progress. But if the people rest secure in easy confidence of victory, they may yet find their foe, as many a wily fox has been found before, strong again in its fastness, from which it "can neither be frightened, drowned, nor smoked out."

The present stronghold of monoply is the corruption of public men, culminating in demoralization as shameful as has ever disgraced the officials of any country. This demoralization is one reason why it seems impossible to secure the passage of any law by our Legislatures that shall be simple in construction, go straight to the intended point, and discourage litigation. The honest men in the Legislatures are overborne and beaten down by the majority, who are promised either power or money for their votes.

The various Legislatures may legislate to all eternity upon the maximum rate that common carriers shall charge within the borders of their States, and the result will always be a conflicting of interests that can not be identical —to cripple not only the carriers, but the people. If an honest Congress should pass general and simple laws to govern all the States, and the Supreme Court should decide in the same spirit what was right and just, as between the people of a State and the transporter (whether railroad or otherwise) carrying long distances, there might be some hope of ultimately reaching a solution of the difficulty.

Will this ever be done? Yes; when the several dominant interests of the nation elect men to represent them who are not only honest, but united in interest with those whose votes give them their places. How may this be brought about? By a consolidation of the industrial classes, as against the consolidated monopolies, who use their power against the true interests of the nation; by using the voting power direct, to secure the end sought.

ONE WAY OF ROBBING THE WEST.

The New York canals are composed of the great trunk line, the Erie Canal, and various branch or sectional lines. According to the report of the Comptroller of the State, the receipts and expenditures of the Erie Canal for 1872, were $2,760,147; the expenditures for salaries and repairs were $1,687,021; excess of revenue over expenses, $1,073,126.

Corresponding figures for the other canals of the State—their gross revenue, and the expenses for salaries and repairs, taken from the same source—may be seen in the annexed table.

Canals.	Gross revenue.	Salaries and repairs.
Champlain,	$150,644	$488,083
Oswego,	90,797	313,469
Cayuga & Seneca,	17,883	64,586
Chemung,	4,121	118,985
Chenango,	5,691	383,748
Black River,	10,839	119,479
Genesee Valley,	18,828	229,613
Oneida Lake,	——	5,710
Baldwinsville,	——	150
Oneida River,	650	——
Seneca River,	154	——
Cayuga Inlet,	300	152
Crooked Lake,	270	23,705
Total expenditures,		$1,687,681
Total gross revenue,		300,182
Excess of salaries and repairs over revenue,		$1,387,499

This table shows that only four of the lateral canals, and they among the least important, paid their own expenses. The gross net income of these four amounted to only $954.

39

Consequently, the thirteen lateral canals ran the State of New York $1,387,499 in debt, while the Erie canal netted the State $1,073,126, which money, and more, was required to support the officials of these non-paying canals. Now, where did the money come from to pay these tax-eaters? Out of the products of the West shipped through the Erie canal, and consequently out of the pockets of western farmers. This is a case in point, illustrating the effects of State legislation—in imposing a tax on the commerce of other States. True, this is nothing new; it has always been done; but attention was not called to the fact until a glut of grain in the West brought the farmers face to face with pauperism. But are the citizens of the Empire State sinners above all their fellows, that such things come to pass? No; if the people of New York governed themselves, this condition of affairs could hardly exist. They are in reality governed by a few railroad magnates, stock jobbers, and ring thieves, in the City of New York, who do not scruple to buy up legislators and judges, far and near, and whose power is felt in nearly every western State. Is it strange that the people should rise in their might to put down such giant monopolies. Is it *not* strange, on the other hand, that in fighting some of the ramifications of this mighty evil they should have committed so few excesses?

HOW THE GREAT RAILROAD CORPORATIONS CORRUPT PUBLIC MORALS.

The great railroad corporations having their headquarters in New York City, have become truly fearful engines for the demoralization of the nation. For years, New Jersey struggled in the grasp of the Camden & Amboy Railroad, really one of the hydra heads of the Pennsylvania Central. Her people have recently been in a turmoil, occasioned by the attempt of that railway corporation to take virtual possession of the State. The result was the passage of a law, in the winter of 1872–3, through whose operations the people hope no longer to belong to the "State of Camden and Amboy;" this corporation insisting upon its "vested right" to levy toll on all commodities transported through the State by rail.

State Seal of New York.

Other States are almost as truly the property of these magnates, who rule New York and Pennsylvania, as the cars which carry the various products of the country, or the locomotives which haul them. The Erie railroad spent a million and a half of dollars in neutralizing the ballot in the State of New York, through the eminent services of such "statesmen" as William M. Tweed, who is now receiving a portion of his just deserts at that compulsory resort of degenerate ruffians, Blackwell's Island.

But the Erie Railway having come to grief in the battle for supremacy, its rival, the New York Central, now virtually owns the Empire State. The New York Central means

Vanderbilt, just as much as the Erie ever meant "Jim Fisk;" and Vanderbilt seems to have no sympathy with mankind in general, except the eternal itching for money. His ostentatious gifts to religious or benevolent institutions, are like the visits of angels, "few and far between," but they sufficiently demonstrate his practical wisdom in the science of advertising. Were it not for the influence exerted by the New York Central, the Erie Canal might be made to lighten the burdens of the West, by cheapening the transportation of her products.

VANDERBILT AS A PHLEBOTOMIST.

A single instance of extortion by the New York Central will suffice. A business man of Buffalo, in the habit of buying paper by the car load in New York City, has declared that he could ship the goods *via* the New York Central, from New York City to Chicago, and thence back by the lakes to Buffalo, at a less cost than he could ship it by the Central to Buffalo direct. He could save in time by shipping direct to Buffalo; he could save in money, *via* Chicago and back. But time is money, hence it came direct; so nicely does this great railroad autocrat calculate, as with the precision of the Spanish Inquisition, to just what point he dare bleed his victim and yet keep alive the spark of life.

One of the latest of the gigantic projects which this unscrupulous old man is engaged in, is to get control of the Western Union Telegraph Line, and thus to form another monopoly which shall increase his already vast power for evil. If the Clubs, Granges, and other organizations of the farmers really were responsible for the late panic, (as they were not, except for some influence in hastening it, perhaps,) their power would not have been exercised a day too soon. If existing State Legislatures and the Forty-third Congress can not see their way clear to a retrenchment in governmental expenses, and to the casting out of corrupt officials, they will assuredly find themselves relegated to deserved obscurity, and their places will be supplied by men who realize the fact that there is something pertaining to the office of legislator besides looking sharp after "number one."

THE COMMUNISM OF CAPITAL.

The facility with which, here and there, an unscrupulous man piles up fortune after fortune upon the financial ruin of his fellows, seems inevitably to demoralize every business in a country. It is notorious that the stock operations of Wall Street are based largely upon fictitious values, and that the class of operators who control them are intensely selfish, guilty of the meanest subterfuges, often lacking education, successful by dint of cunning, and unscrupulous to the last degree. They lead astray those who have not inflexible honesty inherent in their natures. By arousing their cupidity and corrupting their morals, they work their ruin, and turn them into pliant tools of their devilish arts.

The daily peculations, defalcations, and outright thefts, that are making the business of the country more a game of chance than legitimate enterprise, nearly all have their beginning in this Gomorrah of vice—speculation in stock.

The clerk who, perhaps, may have saved up a thousand, becomes acquainted with one of the stool-pigeons of the sweat-cloth of the stock market; for this class, in common with other gamblers, use all the nefarious schemes of their brethren of the other more vulgar sweat-cloth of the gambling-houses, to "rope in" the unwary. The clerk, therefore, thinks he will "put up a margin," or "pool-in" on a high market in hopes it will go higher. Stocks fall. He covers the loss, and so on, perhaps, until his money is all lost. His cupidity being now thoroughly aroused, the regret at losing his hard-earned dollars, tempts him to borrow from his employer's till to tide himself over the point whence he is assured stocks must rise. Alas! they do not rise, and the man, at last, finds himself in disgrace as a common thief. This is only one phase of the case, and one of the least dark and sorrowful at that. Many desolate homes of the country, if it could be known, would tell tales of lost innocence and happiness, perhaps, with the husband and father an exile and a fugitive from justice, and the family, once comfortable, suffering the pangs of poverty. The author of all this misery recks little. The money-king enjoys himself with his ill-gotten wealth; sits, with slippered feet, in a gorgeous home; sips his costly wines; and, feted and feting, fares sumptuously every day.

The government may punish the puny victim whom he has destroyed; but the great robber—the Mephistopheles of Wall Street—is shielded by the power of wealth.

THE GHOULS OF WALL STREET.

There is nothing to which this class of men may be more fittingly likened than Ghouls, which feed on the putrid carcasses of dead men; for these human vultures carry their victims to swift destruction, and their families to poverty and starvation. These stock gamblers subvert the established usages of trade; break down the barriers of legitimate buying and selling; abolish the coin values of the country; create fictitious values, bulling or bearing stocks at will, until the bubble bursts; and continually involve the legitimate industries of the country in serious embarrassments, if not in ruin.

It is this class of men who hold sway in Wall Street, and thence virtually rule the country. Nay, not these brokers, themselves; they are but tools who do the bidding of the Vanderbilts, Goulds, Drews, *et id omne genus*, the real Ghouls, who fatten upon the body social and politic; and who, under a garb of sanctity or honor, sit plotting in their offices, and manipulate stocks and men to suit their own purposes.

These wretches not only can create fictitious values, but can also produce a scarcity of currency at will, backed as they are, by the powerful co-operation of banks which they largely or wholly control.

Many of these latter corporations, trading largely upon the money deposited from day to day by men in legitimate business, furnish capital to these sharks on fictitious or real security—which, it matters little. A fall of stocks is brought about, and they lock up currency. Legitimate business can not borrow, but the "lame ducks" who have securities to offer—ah, *they* can have money, at from two to five per cent. a month. And thus unscrupulous banking corporations make it pay at both ends. The last panic has been called the "rich man's panic." But look at what we see around us every day, and the misnomer is only too apparent.

The remedy is simple. Neither wealth, place, nor power, must be allowed to buy exemption from the punishment which our laws affix to crime. Law must be so administered that it shall be a terror to evil-doers of whatsoever kind, degree, or station; and the public conscience must be quickened until nothing short of this will be accepted, as well in actual practice as in sentimental theorizing.

CHAPTER XXXIX.

MONOPOLIES AND SPECIAL PRIVILEGES.

WHAT ARE MONOPOLIES?

The granting of a charter or franchise of any kind creates a monopoly. Patents are monopolies. A right to a ferry across a river is a monopoly, usually more or less restricted. A tariff which protects any given industry of the country creates a monopoly. The right to do a banking or manufacturing business in some degree constitutes a monopoly. The same is true of railroads and telegraph lines. Even the pioneers of a new country, in one respect, partake of the character of monopolists; for the after-coming settler must buy of them, or not at all.

Monopolies, as these illustrations show, are not evils necessarily. It is an abuse of the powers granted that constitutes the evil. If Congress grant extraordinary privileges to certain classes of manufacturers, in consequence of which all who buy their wares are really obliged to pay a tax on the value of the goods sold, this protection constitutes a monopoly, not necessarily objectionable, however; not at all so, indeed, if the design be to build up that manufacture, and the protection bestowed is not so large as to make the tax unjust to the nation at large. But when the industry becomes strong, and while exporting their wares to foreign ports, and underselling the markets there, and especially when they use the power of their wealth to bribe officials, in order to secure a continuance of this monopoly, then it is odious, and it becomes the right and duty of a free people to rebel against this injustice, and, through the ballot-box, hurl from office the sordid placemen who have fleeced the people by their unscrupulous deeds. As instances of monopolies of this sort, it is only necessary to mention the host of reissued patents, and the protection on iron, salt, lumber, etc.; notoriously unjust, and kept going simply by the power of the wealth of those holding the monopolies, through our members of Congress and other public men.

Interior of Farm-house in the Olden Time.

THE COMMUNISM OF PROTECTED INDUSTRIES.

Greatest of all the evils of which the American people have to complain are the various conspiracies by which the people are continually fleeced. Conspicuous among these are the combinations against the public interests based upon and originating in the system of granting special privileges, by national and State Legislatures.

The ramification of this systematized robbery of the people, through the communism of capital, now extends through every industry of the nation.

The railway companies are a company of communists who take toll from all. The iron manufacturers, able to stand alone but protected to a most scandalous extent, and who have taken untold millions from the working men of the United States, exact their toll from the railroad companies, as well as every individual in the nation. We can not even toast a piece of cheese on a wire without paying toll to these arch-conspirators. They are now so strong that individuals can not even undertake the manufacture of iron without asking their gracious leave. The immense capital at the command of the few persons concerned in this industry enables them to dictate to those entering the business what they shall and what they shall not do. If they agree to use money to keep the monopoly intact, they are taken into the communion; if not, they are crushed, just as the iron-masters of England sought to crush this and other industries in the United States while yet young and weak. This is why tariffs were originally instituted; but in these days the strong and rich are protected, and the weak and poor are made to pay for all.

EXAMPLES OF ODIOUS PROTECTION.

Salt is protected, although the poor use more than the rich, and although the manufacturers sell their surplus in foreign markets lower than they do at home. Iron is protected, although, however poor the individual, he can not cook or eat his meat without paying tribute to these iron lords, who, in reality, are able to compete with any nation on earth on equal terms. Almost every man and woman in the nation, however poor, now uses tea or coffee as one of the necessities of life, and ought to use as much, nay more, per individual, than the rich. They are obliged to pay an enormous tax for this privilege, and we have not the poor excuse to offer that it is protecting American industry.

On the other hand, the money changer buys up government bonds, upon which he pays no tax but receives interest. Depositing these again with the government, he is allowed to issue notes to nearly the amount deposited, and upon these notes he received the full interest which he may be able to grind out of the necessities of the people, besides the profits from the wear and tear of his paper currency (sometimes amounting to ten, fifteen, or twenty per cent.), and the discount thereon as compared with gold. He then uses the moneys of his depositors to speculate with. The history of commercial convulsions shows that usually it is not forthcoming when most wanted.

RAILROADS AS PROTECTED MONOPOLIES.

A railroad corporation is granted a vast area of the public domain, more than sufficient to build the road; nay, the government subsidizes it besides with a grant of large sums of money per mile. In return, and with the very moneys thus donated, the management corrupt our public men, that they may still further bind their fetters about the people.

Or, a railway is projected through a country already thickly settled. It is given the right of way, and, perhaps, subsidized to the extent of from $10,000 to $75,000 by the townships and cities through which it runs. The company has a monopoly of the carrying trade, necessarily so. In turn, it refuses to carry the property of the individuals who have helped to build the road, by discriminating unjustly against them, and making them help to pay the lesser profits or actual expenses accruing from business at competing points.

It is idle for the railroad officials to say the people are not obliged to go to them for transportation. They are obliged to do this; for there is not enough trade to pay a competing road, and, even if there were, the people have already helped to pay for the road in the subsidies they have granted. They may, indeed, carry by their own wagons, as in several instances they have sneeringly been told to do; but it must be remembered, again, that they really own rights in the roads, and that transportation by railroad, and the consequent impetus to production, has already put it out of their power to carry by wagon, as they did formerly, except at a ruinous loss.

The traveling public must travel and shippers transport on the railroads, or else not at all. Hence the obvious justice of the demand that, if the railway company discriminates unjustly against particular localities, it should be made amenable to law. It is futile to talk about vested rights. The law can grant no rights that conflict with the liberty of the subject; and, if it could, the power that made can unmake. Nevertheless, under the law, the courts only can legally decide.

VESTED RIGHTS AND POLITICIANS.

From a business point of view, railroad companies can not be expected to take lesser profits when they can make greater, nor are they more reprehensible in influencing Legislatures to their exclusive benefit, than are any other class of ring-masters. As before insisted on, the ax must be laid at the root of the evil—corruption among the law-makers themselves. If they were above bribes, or if briber and bribe-taker were promptly punished, the enormities complained of would soon be stamped out.

We must cease sending third-rate lawyers to legislate for us; men without briefs, fallen in the scale of humanity, until they become pot-house politicians, suddenly re-appearing as statesmen; unscrupulous and needy; taking to bribery as a duck does to water.

We must cease lending willing ears to glib-tongued adventurers of every sort, and begin to think for ourselves. We must cease granting rights to corporations without exacting some guarantee or fair equivalent in return. Our laws must be purged of the legal verbiage that now incumbers them,—purposely so framed, in order that they may the more readily be construed to mean something which they should not. If we would prevent trouble in the future, we must cease to grant extraordinary and exclusive privileges to railway and all other similar corporations. We must prevent the former from taking possession of our land; taxing us to build their works; rendering lands which we have bought non-paying; watering stocks at their own good will and pleasure, and then, while claiming vested rights, claiming, with all these extraordinary privileges, the rights and privileges of private citizens.

The solution of the problem is not difficult. We must claim representation in ratio to our voting strength. Farmers must represent the agricultural interests; the mechanic, mechanics; the merchant, commerce; the legal profession, law; the stock jobber, gambling, if you like; and so on through the whole category. The lawyer may plead for us; the doctor may bleed, blister, and physic us; the divine may preach and pray for us; but the integrity of a free nation does not depend upon the so-called privileged classes making our laws.

SPECIAL PRIVILEGES DANGEROUS TO THE PEOPLE AT LARGE.

Among all nations, and in all times, opposition of the masses has arisen from the granting of special privileges, which, once secured, have thereafter been used to rivet the chains and destroy the liberties of the subject. The rise and downfall of nations may be traced largely to the operation of causes thus set in motion, from the earliest historic ages down to our own day.

The old feudal barons exercised special privileges. One of them was to build castles that commanded the roads through which the traffic of a region or country must pass. From this they collected tribute, which they spent in living in affluence, and in feeding the hirelings whom they had bought to do their murders upon unoffending citizens. If a traveler tried to go around he was infringing upon their vested, or, as they were pleased to consider it, divine rights, and was incontinently "put out" with the sword.

The nobility of England also, by the same vested right, have the benefit of entail, by which the eldest son inherits the property from generation to generation, thus keeping up caste and a class who, as a rule, simply eat and drink what others produce. Fortunately for the United States, the framers of the Constitution prohibited not only this, but the unity of the Church and State. Were it not for this, we should have been to-day the least free, as really we are the worst-taxed, of any people on the face of the earth.

It is fortunate, and a consolation in our troubles, that the immense fortunes wrung from the masses must, at the death of the holder, commence disintegrating. The hoards of individuals of one generation will be spent by the next. If capital ever becomes strong enough, it will seek to alter all this. If accomplished, it will be one of the last nails in the coffin of American freedom. Liberty will go out of sight forever.

"We're going to have a Railroad!"

England, and other European nations, have their aristocracy of birth. We have that worst and most unscrupulous of all aristocracies—an aristocracy of wealth. It is composed largely of shoddyites and corruptionists; those who have grown rich out of contracts during the war, and the great manipulators of fictitious stocks. These stocks are largely represented in railway property. It required but the breaking down of a half dozen individuals to see the whole fabric dissipate and disappear as dew before the summer sun.

The ideas and efforts of this class are as essentially antagonistic to true republicanism as the Spanish Inquisition was antagonistic to human liberty. It is not strange, therefore, that leading minds in Europe predict that the United States will yet pay tribute to commerce as surely as Europe itself once did to the sword. Let but the idea of a centralized and paternal government become fixed in the mind of the nation, and carried into effect, and the thing is done.

THE FARMERS NOT INIMICAL TO RAILROADS.

Baseless as the assertion is, it has often been made, that the "Grangers" are at the bottom of all our troubles, and are responsible for our financial difficulties. The term "Granger," by the way, is used in a derisive or contemptuous sense. Some writers who have claimed to be recording history have fallen into the traps thus laid, and write learnedly of the "Grangers," apparently not knowing that the word was first applied, in contempt, to a class of politicians who who were wont to go about with rough boots and "hay-seed in their hair," supposing the farmer to be the stolid boors that a caricaturing and subsidized press sought to make them appear.

It would be a little singular if this word, originally applied in contempt, and innocently used by those who have professed to be writing in their interest, should, in the course of time, be accepted as the honorable title of those who are uniting, not to fight the railroads, but the abuses of chartered powers which go under the name of monopoly. If the railroads choose to throw themselves in the way of this gathering storm, we shall have to say, as George Stephenson said of the cow upon the railroad track, "verra awkward for the coo."

Not only the Granges, but the Farmers' Clubs, are united to resist the encroachments of consolidated monopolies.

They attacked the unjust discriminations of certain railroad companies, which, in their fancied security of power, treated the whole matter in agitation with contempt.

It is, undoubtedly, true that some railroad corporations have suffered, perhaps, to the extent of actual injustice; but had not the people suffered untold wrong? And had they not borne and forborne, until forbearance ceased to be a virtue?

If the issue had been foreseen as clearly by these corporations as it was by the writer of these lines, who long ago urged a just compromise between the people and the railroad officials, much of the gall might have been made sweet to the takers on both sides. The real trouble was that the railroad interest of the country was then firmly in the grasp of a few manipulators, who thought themselves so strongly entrenched behind the power of their immense capital, that those honorable railroad officials who would gladly have done what they thought was right were powerless to act. The battle is not principally with railroad corporations as such, but rather with the corrupting influence of subsidized and protected monopolies. The corruption that has already been sloughed off from the festering ulcer—the partial crippling of the stock gamblers achieved thus early in the contest—gives token of brighter days in the future. These will surely come, if the masses unite to overthrow every official of whatever grade who violates the trust reposed in him by the people.

CHAPTER XL.

CREDITS MOBILIER, FAST FREIGHTS, ETC.

"CREDIT MOBILIER" DEFINED.

In the French language, from which "Credit Mobilier" is derived, the term may be made to mean an innocent lending of money upon movable property, as upon chattels; but usage has really given it a more specific, limited signification. Under the empire of Napoleon III, certain of his cliques erected a system by which money was loaned, not only on real estate, but also upon personal property. This property might or might not be at the time valuable; in fact much of it was very doubtful; but, like the loans of the pawnbroker, who runs a credit mobilier shop on a small scale, if the risks were great, the interest corresponded. Money was thus lent upon enterprises, such as commercial railroads, and the like, while they were yet in embryo, and often of very uncertain outcome.

It was, in many cases, the lending of a credit upon credit for the stock of the Credit Mobilier; and the stock to which it lent its credit might be upon the market at the same time. In this case it was credit built upon credit; a row of bricks, one leaning upon the other—an inverted pyramid built upon quicksand, liable, at any time, to fall by the moving of a single brick, or to topple by the shiftings of the quicksand. Upon this system of credit built upon credit, it was that the French entered upon some of the wildest stock gambling the world has ever known. Transplanted to America, the same system found a congenial home, and made Wall Street a pandemonium—its votaries a horde of gamblers. It has well-nigh swamped the railroad system of America, covering the nation and many of our pubilcists, once in honorable repute, with a lasting disgrace.

The Stalking-horse of Swindlers.

The watered stock of a railroad may be a Credit Mobilier; the road itself may be one in the bad sense of the name; the warehouseman who issues fraudulent certificates upon grain in his elevator, is a sort of Credit Mobilier; the so-called fast transportation line that is run by a ring of railroad managers at the expense of the transporters, is a Credit Mobilier. In short, Credit Mobilier is a system of lending a fiction and getting a reality. This is one of the principal things that has ruined American credit abroad, and made the name of certain American statesmen and financiers to stink in the nostrils of all honest men.

THE GREAT CREDIT MOBILIER.

The American swindle was originally more an imitator in name than in actual organization. A charter had been issued in Pennsylvania to a company, but had not yet been used. The Credit Mobilier bought this loose charter, its stockholders and those of the Union Pacific Railway Company being identical. The railroad company had been endowed by Congress with twenty alternate sections of land per mile. The government had also agreed to loan it $16,000 for some two hundred miles, then $32,000 per mile for six hundred miles, and from thence $48,000 per mile. The Union Pacific Railway Company issued stock to the amount of $10,000,000, which stock was received by the stockholders upon the payment of five per cent. of its face value.

At this point the Credit Mobilier steps in. All the assets of the railroad company were turned over to this new company, in consideration of full paid shares of the new company's stock and its grant to build the road. In the meantime, the government had been induced to allow its first mortgage bonds to become second mortgage bonds; whereupon the Union Pacific Railroad Company issued first mortgage bonds, which, of course, took precedence as a loan, and the government lien immediately became virtually worthless, since the new mortgage bonds amounted to the entire value of the road. The proceeds of this shameless transaction went to swell the ill-gotten hoards of the rascals who devised it, and the *innocent* Congressmen who helped to engineer the scheme. The Credit Mobilier had nothing to pay, except the mere cost of construction, the bonded debt of the road exceeding by $40,000,000 the cost of building the road. Is it strange that shares with which Congressmen were allowed to load up at $100 each, could not be purchased for less than $300 or $400? How nicely the film of decency, in charging these incorruptible Congressmen several months interest, was laid over; this interest having accrued while these shares were being held by Oakes Ames, to see where he could "put them to do the most good," in his own language; or, in plain words, to see whom he could buy the most cheaply.

It will be seen that an original share of Union Pacific stock, upon which was paid $5.00, became $100 Credit Mobilier, paying dividends to the Legislators with whom it was placed to do good amounting to three or four times its nominal value. And yet these honorables stalk majestically abroad, as though they had never been smirched with the filth of this swindling transaction!

Hon. D. C. Cloud, in his "Monopolies and the People," in speaking of the Central Pacific Railroad, from Ogden to Sacramento, says: "Taking the character of the route as given, with the facilities for building the road, and it is not probable that the actual cost of construction averaged more than $30,000 per mile, or $57,000,000 for the whole line. Taking the highest rate, as given, viz., $50,000, and applying it to the whole road, the entire cost would be $94,000,000.

"To aid in the construction of this road the government issued subsidy bonds at the rate of $48,000 per mile for three hundred miles; $32,000 per mile for nine hundred and four miles, and $16,000 for the balance of the main road and branches. The funded debt of the companies owning and operating the road (not including the debts of the branches), after deducting the amount of bonds they received from the government, to-wit: $65,000,000, is, as is shown by their own report, $93,000,000. How much their floating debt amounts to we can not tell. The stock on this road can not cover one-tenth of the amount of their debts. The companies report a paid up capital stock of $91,028,-190."

Mr. Cloud makes the total investment in the road from paid up capital, bonds from government, and funded debt to be $294,028,190. Per contra: Actual cost of construction, $94,000,000; balance, $155,028,190.

If we deduct from 37,500,000 acres of land at $1.25 per acre, or $46,875,000, the balance against the road would be the nice little sum of $108,153,190. Mr. Cloud then says: "Thus, after placing the land received from the government to the credit of the road, still a small balance of more than $108,000,000 has disappeared, and the companies are not able to pay the interest on the government bonds. The reports of these companies show, for the year 1871, that the net earnings of their roads (over and above all expenses, including taxes, repairs, damages to property and persons, cost of snow sheds, and all other items of expense) amounted to about $9,000,000; and yet, because these companies asked it, Congress released them from the payment of the interest on the subsidy bonds." This action of Congress was an outrage. Truly, other "statesmen" than Boss Tweed should be looking through the bars of a prison to-day. While we are taking railroads to task on general principles, let us not forget those in high places who have enabled railroads to fleece the people.

SMALLER CREDIT MOBILIER ASSOCIATIONS.

The Chicago, Rock Island & Pacific Railroad Company is five hundred and forty-four miles long; that is, in Illinois, from Chicago to Rock Island, one hundred and eighty-four miles, and from thence to Davenport and Omaha three hundred and sixty miles. The total reported cost of the road was $28,496,899, or $52,384 per mile. The official figures show that the Illinois portion of this road cost less than $30,000 per mile, and the Iowa division still less. In round numbers, if one estimate the road, including the Rock Island bridge, at $30,000 per mile, it will give $15,320,000, the difference between which sum and the reported cost of the road will represent the watered stock, $13,176,896. Add to this the value of the lands granted to the Iowa portion of the road, 550,000 acres, and the country and municipal aid, said to have been $500,000 more, and it would seem to have been a very pretty little speculation indeed.

This is a specimen of the way in which the people have been swindled time and again. If public indignation should ever reach that point where it should insist upon a thorough searching out such abuses as these, and a restitution should be ordered, the proceeds would pay the national debt. And why not? It would be the people of the United States who would even then pay the debt; for the money was fleeced from them—though it must be acknowledged they were, in some cases, willing lambs to these wool gatherers.

The Springfield, Clinton & Gilman (Illinois) Railroad, which the courts have recently placed in the hands of a receiver, is said also to have been dallying with this Delilah of watered stock. The Indiana, Bloomington & Western road is just now, as we write, being investigated. Indeed, if the examination ever be made searching, the roads that have not "covered back" will pretty certainly be found the exceptions, and not the rule.

The object in all this is to enable a few individuals of New York, Boston, Philadelphia, etc., (but principally Wall Street, New York, for here the whole horde have their headquarters) to amass colossal fortunes. If Mr. Brown, or Jones, or Smith, or the three combined, control a road costing a given sum, and can, by adroit manipulation, declare dividends on twice or thrice that sum, they issue stock under one pretense or another to that amount. Then the stock is made to pay no dividends, with the object of forcing the

The Water Sprite—Farmer's Daughter.

stock as low as possible; or, in other words, they "bear" the market in order to get control of more stock. This accomplished, up goes the stock again, dividends are again declared, even if the money has to be borrowed to pay them with. The stock is again watered; and so the process goes on, cheating the *bona fide* shareholders, robbing the people who are forced to patronize the road, and outraging every instinct of common decency and justice that should govern business transactions between man and man.

WHEELS WITHIN WHEELS.

It must not be supposed, however, that while these great railroad magnates are thus making money the lesser ones are working hard for nothing. There are "Blue Lines," "White Lines," "Star Lines," "Fast Freights," "Dispatch Companies," and the like, to whom franchises have been granted by virtue of which their cars have the precedence in point of speed and time. The shipper wants cars; the railroad company has none, but the dispatch company has. The freight must go, and go it does at the advanced rates charged by the dispatch company. Here is a wheel within a wheel—another Credit Mobilier. Certain managers, stockholders, and outside parties constitute the dispatch company. If they sacrifice the interests of the road, they console themselves with the reflection that the stock dividends must not be too large, else the people at large will grumble; dividends must be kept down to a *normal* figure. The people think it a pity that the railroad company can not provide cars. The members of the ring know it does not want to do so. They propose to enrich themselves, while that other few are doing the same thing by the manipulation of stocks, the people being made to pay for all. Farmers may grumble, shippers protest, merchants threaten; they swing the scythe, and prepare to cut into the tallest grass they can find—they make hay while the sun shines.

In the summer of 1873, there was a conflict between the Pullman Palace Car Company and certain railroad companies. The railroad companies claimed that the Pullman Company would rent a whole section to an individual, by which that individual would occupy the room originally designed for four. They paid the railroad company for the single passenger only, while the railroad company claimed they should receive pay for the space occupied, one reason given being that the cars were far heavier than ordinary first-class coaches, and that it was injustice to the stockholders. The probability is that nothing more will be heard of this litigation. If thoroughly probed, it is quite probable that it would appear that not a few of our railroad managers are interested in the receipts arising from this species of transportation; or., in other words, that they have been leasing to themselves privileges which belong only to the stockholders, and not to the officers of the road.

So with express companies. The ramifications are so wide and intricate that to get at the gist of the matter would require that the whole system of transportation be renovated—a consummation earnestly wished for by some of the more conscientious railroad men to-day. But this can not be done in a single State, without its reacting unjustly on that State. It can not be done by a community of States, until the penalty for dishonorable action be sharply defined, and made swift and certain. When once the tap root of this tree of evil is struck, then may we hope to see the beginning of the end.

WATERED STOCK.

There were 70,178 miles of railroad in operation in January, 1873, in the United States, and the total cost of these roads, as reported by themselves, is $3,436,638,749, or an average of about $48,970 per mile. Besides this great sum there have been put on the market railroad bonds for the additional amount of $2,800,000,000, forming an immense aggregate of $6,236,638,749, equal to nearly $88,872 per mile.

We have heretofore shown how stocks are watered. Allowing these figures to be correct, the difference between the cost, as reported by themselves, and $6,236,638,749, would be about $2,800,000,000. Mr. Cloud, however, from an actual examination of the cost, as reported by the engineers of the various roads, puts the actual cost at $35,000 per mile, or a total of $2,456,230,000. According to these figures, the *actual* total of watered stock would be $3,780,-408,747.

Cornelius Vanderbilt, of the New York Central, and "Colonel" Scott, of the Pennsylvania Railroad, represent about $1,400,000,000 of this stock, and a handful of men, comparatively, control almost the entire amount. These are the men who control market values, and by a stroke of the pen in their offices, cause to be flashed along the wires what the farmer of the West shall receive for his grain, by commanding the superintendents of these roads to put up the tariff five or ten cents per bushel.

In their strongholds, entrenched behind the power of their ill-gotten wealth, they control the government of States, and under the present system of election, could make a President of the United States, by buying up a majority of the Presidential Electors; that is, allowing the price of these men to be about that of the modern Congressmen.

CHAPTER XLI.

GOVERNMENTAL OWNERSHIP OF RAILWAYS.

ITS CORRUPTING POWER.

One of the most chimerical schemes, though plausible on its surface, for regulating the inter-state transportation of the country, is the proposition that government shall buy and work the railroads of the country. This idea is a great pet with those who have plundered the people of untold millions, through the sinking in their own pockets of the local aid secured in building their roads, and who have gobbled up immense tracts of land obtained through corrupt legislation, and other nefarious plunderings. If the railroads of the country with their fictitious and inflated stocks were to be turned over to government, and bonds taken therefor, what a vast debt would be created, to be added to the load now borne by a people already taxed far beyond the limits of patient endurance!

Let us imagine the situation with the scheme actually consummated: The interest on the lands must be paid; the salaries of the officials—and they must be experts—must be paid; the system must be extended; the wear and tear must be made good; machinery, buildings, and the thousand and one etceteras, which none but a railroad expert can even name, must be provided for; defalcations and peculations would constantly occur; there could be no rigid economy practiced; the whole railway system would soon fall into confusion; and worst of all, there would be a centralization of power in the hands of the government, such as would imperil, and probably subvert, the whole fabric of American liberty.

THE COST OF RAILROADS IN THE UNITED STATES.

The figures involved in the proposition of governmental purchase, etc., are really stupendous. According to Poor's Manual for 1873, there were in operation, the year previous, in the United States, 57,323 miles of road. These are represented as earning, net, 5.20 per cent. on the cost of the roads, and 3.21 per cent. on the capital stock; but, while some roads earned nothing or actually ran their owners in debt, other paid large dividends, and all of them paid large salaries to officials; we do not say larger than the same class of men could command in other business, and certainly not larger than government would have to pay the same or similar class. Even if the roads were as economically run as at present, no relief would be obtained, for the interest on this vast sum must come out of the people at last.

The net earnings of the 57,323 miles of railroad in the United States were, according to Poor's Manual, $165,000,-000; the cost of the roads is represented by the sum of $3,173,076,923. The following table will show the nominal stock of some of the principal roads of the country, the dividends paid, and their general indebtedness:

	Nominal capital stock.	Dividend, per ct.	General debt.
MASSACHUSETTS.			
Boston & Albany, ...	$19,664,100	10	$3,567,560
NEW YORK.			
N. Y. Central & H. R., new, .	$89,425,300	8	$16,497,387
Erie, ...	86,536,910	7	28,912,301

	Nominal Capital stock.	Dividend, per ct.	General debt.
NEW JERSEY.			
Central New Jersey, . . .	$20,000,000	10	$12,267,104
United Companies, ...	18,990,400	10	16,660,705
PENNSYLVANIA.			
Delaware, Lack. & West., . .	$20,000,000	10	$9,633,545
Pennsylvania R. R. . . .	53,271,937	10	33,039,846
MARYLAND.			
Baltimore & Ohio, ...	$16,704,762	9	$12,456,637
OHIO.			
Cleveland, Columbus, Cincinnati & Indianapolis, . .	$14,991,275	7	$3,375,000
Lake Shore & Mich. S., . . .	50,000,000	8	28,820,219
Fort Wayne, ...	22,214,286	7	13,638,230
MICHIGAN.			
M. H. & Ontonagon, . . .	$2,306,600	10	$4,750,000
Michigan Central, ...	17,987,048	8	6,591,233
INDIANA.			
Ohio & Mississippi, ...	$24,030,000	7	$10,440,752
Terre Haute & Indiana, . .	1,988,150	12	1,042,429
ILLINOIS.			
Chicago & Alton, ...	$11,353,300	10	$4,451,000
Chicago, Burlington & Quincy,	18,649,910	9	12,034,750
Chicago & North-western, . .	35,878,644	7	20,988,300
Chicago & Rock Island, . . .	18,990,000	8	8,098,000
Illinois Central, ...	25,483,890	10	19,439,847
WISCONSIN.			
Milwaukee & St. Paul, . .	$26,225,144	7	$27,465,500
IOWA.			
Burlington & Missouri River,	$7,397,673	6	$7,947,235
MISSOURI.			
St Louis & Iron Mountain, .	$10,000,000	3	$5,461,000
St. L., Kan. City & North., .	24,000,000	2	6,000,000

WATERED STOCK.—NEW YORK CENTRAL.

As an instance of what the people would have to pay in case the government should buy the railroads of the United States, let us take the New York Central and Hudson River Railroads, which affords a prominent example of watered stock.

Two years ago, Mr. Rufus Hatch, a broker of Broad Street, New York, issued a number of circulars in relation

Farm Scene.—The First Snow.

to railroads, which, it is fair to presume, were intended for speculative purposes. In his first circular, he said that, at that time, 1871, there were 50,000 miles of railroads in the United States; the cost of which exceeded $2,000,000,-000. The earning of these roads exceeded $400,000,000 annually, or eleven dollars per head for the entire population of the country. This would give the average cost, per mile, at $50,000, from the railroad stand-point.

Just how the New York Central was manipulated to pay dividends on a large and fictitious capital, we propose to let

Mr. Hatch show. He states that Mr. Vanderbuilt, getting control of this important line, was not slow in seeing the great advantage that would accrue to himself in levying tolls, from his own conscientious stand-point, upon every pound of freight passing over his line. But, to keep pace with the modern theory of business, he must water, and re-water the stock.

As soon as they were fairly in his grasp, he commenced a series of waterings that have only been exceeded by the manipulations of the Union and Central Pacific.

The first act in this great drama was the doubling, in 1867, of the capital stock, then $7,000,000, of the Hudson River Railroad. Upon this stock, only fifty per cent. was called up; the transaction, consequently, netted the modest sum of $3,500,000. Taught by such instruction, Mr. Vanderbuilt, in 1868, declared a script dividend of eighty per cent. upon the share capital of the Central Railroad, then $28,730,000. This dividend produced $23,036,000! But these vast sums by no means satisfied the maw of this financial agent. He contrived the union of the two roads, and made it the pretext for another stock dividend of twenty-seven per cent. on the Central, which produced, with a small addition thereto of alleged surplus earnings, the sum of $8,524,400. At the same time, a dividend was declared upon the share capital, increased at the time to $16,020,800, of the Hudson River. This dividend produced the sum of $13,623,800.

How it Figures up.—The following is a statement of the several waterings: First watering of Hudson River, $3,500,000; first watering of New York Central, $23,036,-000; second watering of Hudson River, $13,623,800; second watering of New York Central, $8,524,400. Grand total, $48,684,200.

The present share capital of the consolidated roads, including the script dividend, is $90,000,000. The waterings of Mr. Vanderbuilt, consequently, exceed the capital actually paid in, by $7,368,400!

The length of the New York Central & Hudson River Railroad is given at four hundred and forty-two miles. This being the divisor for the total of watered stock, $48,684,200, would give the sum of $110,145 per mile of watered stock, for the whole length of the line.

Is it strange that this Vanderbilt should have his fortune variously estimated at from $70,000,000 to $100,000,000? Who have been made to pay for it? The people of the West have paid a large share of it, in dividends upon this and other watered stock which this moneyed tyrant has grasped. Will the people consent that the government shall buy this road, and put so much cash in the hands of this unscrupulous man? Would not this self-styled "Commodore" be glad, now that he has one foot in the grave, to shift his sins of oppression upon the government, so that his heirs might show clean hands with this ill-gotten wealth? This is but one instance of watered stock. There have been others still worse, but none probably where the proceeds have so largely gone to swell the hoards of one individual.

Would the people like to follow out this plan with each and every other road in the country? Would they like to supplement these with the telegraph lines added; with the vast schemes of corruption and jobbery, that must naturally grow out of this governmental control of railroads and telegraph lines; and with the vast horde of employees who would be obliged to hold their votes at the behest of the official who had the distribution of this immense patronage? The answer, we apprehend, is not difficult.

CENTRAL PACIFIC STOCK.

The Central Pacific road is reported to have cost $120,432,717. Its length is 881 miles. Its cost, therefore, at that rate, would be $136,700 per mile. Mr. Cloud, the author of "Monopolies and the People," says that information obtained through reliable channels induces the belief that it cost less than $50,000 per mile, and less than $50,000,000 for the whole road. He says: "The company represent a capital stock $54,283,190, and a funded debt $82,208,000. They also report the liabilities of the road at $136,491,190, being more than $80,000,000 above the actual cost, and $16,000,000 more than the reported cost. The stock of this company was watered to so great an extent that, to pay the interest on the funded debt and declare a dividend on the stock, and pay operating expenses and other contingencies, the road must earn at least fifty per cent. per annum."

Are the public, therefore, defrauded or not in this road? If so, how is it by virtue of vested rights that they so cheat the people?

May roads absorbing vast grants of land, and heavily subsidized, as in the case of the Union and Central Pacific roads, now make charges that will allow high dividends upon stock fraudulently obtained? If so, where is the justice in sending the petty swindlers of our cities to the Bridewells, or in consigning the common forger to the penitentiary? Has this fictitious wealth already become so omnipotent in this once free land that the people are powerless to help themselves? It would almost seem so.

Is it not time that not only the farmers, but also every other industrial class in the country, were banded together in one vast brotherhood; to put a stop to these crimes, these robberies forever; to assert their rights at the ballot-box, and hurl from power those who have so shamefully betrayed them; to insist that laws be enacted to bring to the bar of justice, not only those who have betrayed the trusts confided to them by the people, but also the swindlers themselves who have so shamefully obtained the public money by false pretenses?

GOVERNMENT PURCHASE OF RAILROADS A FALLACY.

The railroads operated in the United States are reported as costing, in round numbers, almost three billions five hundred millions of dollars ($3,500,000,000). Many of them are operated with tolerable honesty; the majority, however,

The Capitol at Washington.

are now so consolidated that they are manipulated by comparatively a few individuals, who, at "their own sweet will," can virtually say, from their offices, what shall be received by the farmer for his grain. Lately, however, they have seen that the movement among the masses is acquiring so much strength and developing so much practical wisdom, that they fear it greatly; they see that we are looking squarely to where the trouble lies. They would, therefore, willingly sell to the government their franchises and so-called vested rights, knowing full well that, by skillful maneuvering, they could still control, by the hard cash it would place in their hands, power and position in these roads.

If the government should possess itself of our vast system of railroads, with all the varied industries that cluster around it, and the added interests of telegraph lines (for one must follow the other), we should have from 25,000 to 30,000 men out of every 1,000,000 inhabitants, whose votes would be directly controllable by the influence of Executive dictation and patronage. The centralization of power in the government is even now so great that the screws can be applied with telling effect when deemed necessary; and many and grievous have been the complaints on this point during the last twenty years.. There is no administration, however pure, that ought to be trusted with so great a power. Certainly, we dare not increase that power now. The civilized world stands aghast at the corruption and frauds practiced at the seat of government, wherein both Republicans and Democrats seem to have struck hands together, and wherein even those who had heretofore been supposed to be irreproachable have come out with characters so besmirched that even the pity of a sorrowing people could not cover the iniquity.

This centralization of power and the corruption of wealth have carried many a once proud nation down into the grave of effete slavery, and barbarians have roamed where once civilization dwelt. It behooves America to profit by these dread examples in time.

CHAPTER XLII.

BIOGRAPHICAL SKETCH OF COL. A. B. SMEDLEY.

OUTLINE OF A USEFUL CAREER.

Colonel A. B. Smedley, the present Master of the State Grange of Iowa, whose portrait is given on page 379, was born in Jefferson County, New York, in 1825. During his boyhood, he was constantly employed in such practical duties of the farm as usually falls to the lot of boys so reared. Later he studied mechanics, and became a master machinist.

In 1849 Mr. Smedley emigrated to Wisconsin, where he remained until the breaking out of the war. In 1862 he entered the United States service, showing the same zeal and fidelity that have always been his chief characteristics.

At the close of the war, in 1865, he retired from the service, and in 1868 removed to his present home at Cresco, Howard County, Iowa, where he actively engaged in horticulture, making a specialty of the raising of fruit, a pursuit in which he was always an enthusiast.

In whatever sphere of activity and usefulness this earnest and able man has moved, he never failed to gain the good will and fellowship of those who learned to know him intimately. Always a reformer, earnestly laboring for the advancement of the industrial masses, in all movements for the elevation and improvement of the workingmen of the country, these classes have constantly found in him a firm and true friend, whose counsel was always tempered with calm judgment, which easily sifted the false from the real.

AS A PATRON OF HUSBANDRY.

In the Order of Patrons of Husbandry, therefore, it is not strange that he easily saw the means for carrying out his favorite idea, namely, a citizenship in which the laboring men of the country should be so educated and enlightened that corruption or wrong-doing should be all but impossible.

His own Subordinate Grange was among the first and most successful in the State; and to his careful study of the work in hand, and his firm and temperate discipline and counsel, is due much of the credit for the wonderful growth and success of the Order in Iowa.

At the third annual session of the State Grange, a vacancy occurring in that body, Colonel Smedley was almost unanimously elected as Master. At the fourth annual session, when the regular election was held, the members of the State Grange showed their appreciation of his earnest zeal and ability by giving him two hundred and thirty-seven out of two hundred and sixty-eight votes on the first ballot, and thereafter making his election unanimous.

Colonel Smedley is said to have given the *unwritten work* and the laws and usages of the Order of Patrons of Husbandry more careful study than almost any other individual in the country. Bringing to the task a full and abiding faith in the integrity and usefulness of the Order as a means of ameliorating the condition of his fellows, he has labored in that organization with indefatigable industry and conspicuous ability, to the end that no legitimate means should remain unemployed to render success certain. As evidence that the efforts of himself and his co-laborers have not been in vain, and as incentive to the faithful spirits now holding the "tug oar" in other States, Iowa may justly and proudly point to her muster-roll of Granges, numbering nearly a quarter of the entire list of the United States.

CHAPTER XLIII.

BIOGRAPHICAL SKETCH OF DUDLEY W. ADAMS.

YOUTH AND EMIGRATION WESTWARD.

The subject of this sketch was born at Winchester, Mass., on the 30th of November, 1831. Like many of the now prominent men of the nation, he passed his childhood and grew up to man's estate in a section where farming means the tillage of a soil never rich, and whose natural productions are rather rocks and stones than rank herbage and generous crops. But if the soil of the New England States is not celebrated for its agricultural wealth, the constant labor necessary to gain daily bread has taught her sons lessons of persistent industry and self-reliance that are simply invaluable.

It is not those reared in the lap of luxury, and who take to their studies as a fashionable dandy does to dress, as a mere superficial adornment, that furnish the country her statesmen or her master minds in trade and finance. On the contrary, it is those who thirst for knowledge; who incessantly employ the brain, whether at labor or actual study; who train their mind habitually, in working out ideas, to grasp, connectedly, whatever subject may present itself. Many of the brightest names and strongest characters in American history were self-made men; and such, if imbued with sympathy for their fellows, and a willingness to labor for their well-being, are the real noblemen of nature.

Sooner or later, in the revolution of the wheel of time, this class come to the front, and are truly appreciated.

When young Adams was four years of age, his father died, and he was thus left to the care of one of the most self-sacrificing of mothers, who spared no pains to lead the young mind in the paths of honor, probity, and religion. His time, until sixteen years of age, was spent as that of many New England boys is, in assisting in the work of a rocky farm, attending the district school and church, and engaging in the innocent frolics incident to such life. In time the district school was exchanged for the village academy, and to this early training is undoubtedly due the practical workings, later in life, of a mind always studious and eager for knowledge, and fostered and directed by the judicious care of a devoted mother. From the age of seventeen until his majority, he continued to work steadily on the farm during the summer months, teaching school in the winter, and pursuing his studies in the spring and autumn.

His majority attained, Mr. Adams found that incessant labor and study had seriously affected his constitution; he was threatened, in fact, with that dire scourge of New England, consumption.

Carefully weighing the chances between an early death if he remained in his native hills, and the possibility of regaining his health in some other locality, he quickly decided to emigrate to the then Eldorado, the West, and at once made his way into north-eastern Iowa. Here, in 1852, he located on a tract of wild land, which, under his skillful hand, was soon transformed into an excellent farm, on which he has ever since resided. That the choice of a location was sagaciously made, has since been fully demonstrated. The flourishing village of Waukon has since grown up around it.

SERVICES IN BEHALF OF AGRICULTURE.

While working hard to improve his farm, Mr. Adams never lost sight of the necessity of organization for the promotion of agriculture. At the age of twenty-two he was elected President of the Allamakee County Agricultural Society, one of the youngest incumbents on record in connection with such an office; and since that time he has been connected almost constantly with the Society in some capacity, either as Secretary, member of the Executive Committee, or other responsible position.

Mr. Adams was never a believer in the dogma that fruit could not be successfully grown in the West. After the terrible winter of 1856, he still had faith in the ultimate success of fruit culture. In spite of the discouragements of climate, and the still more discouraging advice of friends, he gave much of his time and energies to this engaging pursuit. It is not strange, therefore, that Mr. Adams now looks back with some pride to his efforts in this direction, as one of the useful labors of his life.

At the age of thirty-six, Mr. Adams was chosen Secretary of the Iowa Horticultural Society, in a manner highly complimentary to himself, although other business prevented his attendance at that session of the Society. This position he held until the winter of 1872–3, when his other official duties made it necessary that he should decline a re-election. That the office was worthily bestowed and honorably gained is evidenced by the fact that, in 1871, Mr. Adams exhibited at the Iowa State Fair one hundred varieties of apples of his own growth, of such uniform beauty and excellence as to receive the highest award of the Society. This was in the same year that his State received so high commendations at the exhibition before the American Pomological Society.

EARLY STRUGGLES AND PUBLIC SERVICES.

The pioneer who makes a farm in the wilderness, with little save his own hands, must bear a skillful hand in various ways to keep the wolf from the door until something can be raised from the soil. Mr. Adams' previous education had made him conversant with the business of a surveyor; and, for years, in the intervals of farm labor, he carried a surveyor's compass in establishing corners, running lines, and laying off the farms of his pioneer neighbors, far and near. For about ten years he served his neighbors, also, in the several offices of Assessor, President of the District School Board, Township Trustee, County Supervisor, Chairman of the County Board of Supervisors, and held various other public trusts of a local nature.

At the age of thirty-two, Mr. Adams became the Republican candidate for the State Senate from his district, but was unsuccessful, the ticket being buried out of sight under the majority then given the entire Democratic ticket.

Two years later, the finances of his county having become almost hopelessly involved, he was elected a member of the Board of Supervisors for the county. This board consisted of eighteen, one from each township. Elected Chairman of the Board, he performed the duties of the office for three years, and then resigned. At the time of his election the county warrants were at a discount of fifty per cent. In two years, they were at par; and now the State of Iowa can proudly point to the fact that there is no State debt upon which the people pay taxes as interest—a fact most creditable to the exertions of her citizens in their several stations as public officers.

In the spring of 1873, the friends of Mr. Adams nominated him for governor of Iowa. This nomination was declined, not because the nominee was not as willing as heretofore to serve his fellow-citizens, but because he was at that time too deeply absorbed in the great work of his life—spreading the organization of the Order of Patrons of Husbandry. The tenets of the Order proclaim it to be non-political. Had he acceded to the wishes of his friends, the Order would have been immediately stigmatized as seeking political ends. Mr. Adams was willing to forego the prospect of gubernatorial honors, in order that he might still labor in the field of his choice, to promote the business and social welfare of the agricultural masses. These he represents as the chief executive officer of the National Grange; and truly it is a higher honor than to be a State governor.

SERVICES IN THE ORDER OF "PATRONS OF HUSBANDRY."

Early in the year 1870, Mr. Adams and two of his neighbors, having heard of the Patrons of Husbandry, called together other neighbors, and organized Waukon Grange, No. 3, of the State. Seven months later, they organized Frankville Grange, No. 4. Six months subsequently, or June 12, 1871, the State Grange was organized temporarily, and Mr. Adams was chosen Master. In December of the same year, a permanent organization was effected, and he was elected the Master for two years. This office he held until his election as Master of the National Grange, early in 1873.

In 1871, when elected to the State Grange, there were less than a dozen Granges in the State. He left it with over eight hundred working organizations. Since this time the State has fully kept pace with its previous record, its present membership showing over one hundred thousand tillers of the soil, working as a unit for their social, moral, and industrial elevation among the great brotherhood of mankind.

Since his election to the Chief Executive of the National Grange, Mr. Adams has continued untiring in his efforts for the benefit of his brethren in toil, and the spread of the Order. That he is doing more good than he possibly could have done as the governor of his State, there is no doubt; for now his field of labor is national. Those sterling patriots who have cast from them the glittering prizes of political preferment until the nation shall have become sufficiently purged of corruption, will not be forgotten by a grateful people when the political panderers of the present day shall be buried deep in oblivion, with none so mean as to do them reverence.

CHAPTER XLIV.

EDUCATION TO THE INDUSTRIES.

IMPORTANCE OF THE SUBJECT.

Education is one of the most potent factors in the advancement of the rising generation to the status which they should properly occupy. After the rudiments of a fair English education are secured, the youth who aspires to become a working man should be pushed in the acquirement of certain knowledge relating to the industry which he contemplates pursuing. The farmer's boy readily masters the art of driving horses, plowing, reaping, binding, stacking, the care of the domestic animals, etc. For this it is not necessary that he should go to school. It must be learned on the farm, just as the tradesman acquires his art under the direction of a master workman.

There is something, however, beyond all this—or, we might almost say, before it; for it underlies the economies of every trade and profession in life. What is it? The study of the sciences underlying the profession or art that is to constitute the life-work of the individual.

This subject is beginning to interest the thinking portion of the present generation; it is the lever that will move the next. The why, and not the how, is the true point to be aimed at; for proper knowledge concerning the first makes the latter easy. Chemistry is, in truth, the "corner-stone of agriculture;" nevertheless, a man may be a good chemist and yet a very poor farmer. Mathematics, as a science, underlies mechanics, and yet a knowledge of mathematics in itself would not constitute a mechanic. Nevertheless, the student who first acquires a knowledge of the principles of chemistry, will make a better farmer than he who knows nothing about it. Just so, a good mathematician would make a better and far more intelligent mechanic than he who had simply a smattering of arithmetic. What we want, then, is education to the several professions in life.

WHERE SHALL OUR CHILDREN LEARN?

We should begin in our common schools; but, instead of carrying the pupil forward in the old-time grooves, ground him thoroughly in reading, writing, and arithmetic. The first should include that much neglected study—the proper use of words; the second, the equally neglected one of facility in expressing them on paper; and the third, turning the figures we are taught to some practical account. How many of our teachers are well grounded in this practical application themselves? Very few. And yet they are the persons who are supposed to have become especially fitted for imparting such instruction.

They have been educated in an undeviating groove, and are only fitted to mould the youth in the same inflexible line. We elect County and State Superintendents of Schools; but they, too, have been formed in the same groove. One thing too many of them have learned, namely, that there is money in a change or exchange of text-books for the schools; and this knowledge many of these officials are forward enough to turn to practical account. After he

Off to School.

leaves school, the child finds that he is just getting ready to acquire an education—just getting ready to learn somewhat of things. Many of our teachers do, indeed, endeavor to follow the divine precept; the conscientious portion of them do try to "train up a child in the way he should go," forgetting, however, to apply it from a Socratian stand-point, equally important, "To teach a child in youth that which he is to follow in age." From the common schools, some

What has made Industrial Education possible.

of the pupils go to college. Here again there is the same groove, "the classics" dominating all else. Whatever the life-work of the student is to be, a certain routine must apply to all; and after spending years of mental trial, the young man or woman finds, at last, that the real education that is to fit him or her to battle with life must now commence through self-culture.

HOW SHALL WE BEGIN?

Begin from the start, by instructing the pupil WHY this thing or that proposition is so; *why* addition, multiplication, and division, are all there really is of arithmetic; *why* the rivers, constantly flowing into the sea, never increase its volume; *why* chemistry is the corner-stone of agriculture, and mathematics the foundation upon which mechanics rest. The fact is, the so-called higher education is an artificial affair, contrived originally for a class—the learned professions. Hence, the vast army of toiling workers who, to-day, are hungering for that certain knowledge that would enable them, through the exercise of mind upon matter, to properly lay hold of that Archimedian lever—an intelligent and diversified industry.

One of the first things for the masses to understand is that education is not incompatible with labor; on the contrary, indeed, that the better educated a man is the more intelligently he can perform the ordinary duties of life. There is a right and a wrong way to do every thing, from hod-carrying to the most intricate sculpture; from plowing the furrows that are to receive the seed to building the stack or rick of grain that shall turn rain, resist the wind, and keep its contents intact.

How many artisans, through education to their art, can claim to be really master-workmen, and able to command the highest wages of the craft? Scarcely one in a hundred.

FARMERS AS CRAFTSMEN.

How many farmers are really excellent plowmen, understanding the niceties of turning sod, stubble, or fallow, and the proper management of the furrow-slices, through the various gradations of sand and loams to stiff clay? How many farmers can build a stack of hay or grain so that it shall preserve its proper shape in settling, and in its contour present the greatest resistance to the influence of the weather? Not one in fifty even of managing farmers properly know what good plowing really is in its various details. Not one in a hundred can build a series of stacks, either of hay or grain, similar in size and shape, and superior in their structure. Why is this so? The answer is simple. They have never been taught why furrows laid at different angles exert different influences; why the mold-board and share of one plow is made different from another; why, in building a stack, the proportions should be after exact rules, the whole bearing definite relations to the quantity of material to be used, etc.

These are among the most common processes of the farm, and yet but little of their philosophy, so to speak, is known by the majority of farmers. There are many others equally important and equally neglected. If the merchant, the manufacturer, or the tradesman manifested the same indifference in their several industries, they would all, sooner or later, be involved in a common bankruptcy. That farmers are not is due to the fact that nature is constantly working for them, even while they are sleeping, and that drafts on her storehouse are always honored to the full extent of her ability.

EXPERIENCE A THOROUGH TEACHER.

Of the details of mechanics I know but little, except as to the repairs of farm machinery in a rough way. An experience in working the soil for a third of a century, during which time I have constantly educated myself to the various details of agriculture, by reading and experiment, has shown me that the farmer never ceases to learn while life lasts. The trouble is that many do not begin to educate themselves until many important years of their working life are past.

Experience, that thorough but costly teacher, eventually shows them how little they really know, and how much they have yet to learn. The theorizing of gentlemen ruralists and mere scholars has disgusted them with book-farming.

Availing themselves at length of such works as they can find, containing the practical labors of adepts in the art, they discover most important unexplored fields before them, almost appalling in their extent, except to the mind trained to study. Carefully considering the details of the art, they finally decide upon the specialty which they will follow, and thenceforward they devote themselves chiefly to stock-breeding or stock-feeding; the cultivation of the cereals, or of hay; orcharding; the raising of vegetables or of seeds; floriculture, or the like,—according as their position and location will warrant, and their previous education will allow. It takes years and successive and grave mistakes before the knowledge is gained which will enable them economically to blend these specialtes with the succession and relation of crops necessary to keep up the fertility of their farms. A few are successful, and leave their farms better than they found them, but vastly more exhaust their soil and their energies in a perpetual struggle for the necessities of life.

To obviate this difficulty, and lead the coming generation to a proper education of their faculties, education to the industries was proposed and agitated, upon the basis of endowment, by national aid, of industrial schools for the better training of youth to these pursuits.

THE CLASSICS AND AGRICULTURE.

Unfortunately, many of these colleges have slid into the old-time ruts of classical education, although a few have made progress in the right direction, and public opinion is forcing still others reluctantly toward technical education. Those in the West which have made the most uniform progress are those belonging to the States of Michigan and Iowa. In Illinois and Kansas the people are steadily working to infuse a spirit of practical effort into the fossils, or worse, who have mismanaged these institutions. It is one of the legitimate provinces of the Farmers' Movement to see that these colleges are made what they were intended to be—schools where the application of practical science might aid the student to be a better farmer or artisan than he otherwise would be, and not mere easy-chairs for college dons, retired clergymen, decayed politicians, or theoretical farmers.

At the East, the agricultural schools that have shown the greatest progress are those of Amherst, Massachusetts, and Cornell University, New York. In the South few of these schools have been established for a sufficient length of time to enable a fair judgment to be made of their usefulness; but, so far, most of them appear to be actuated by an earnest desire to make their system of training as thoroughly practical in their nature as possible.

While it was never supposed by practical men that these colleges would be able, all at once, to accomplish the end sought, still less, however, was it expected that Industrial Colleges were to adopt the curriculum, essentially, of the average literary college, with simply enough varnish of agriculture and mechanics to enable them to annex the endowment of the nation and of the States where situated. Yet to-day such is the fact with the majority of them. This is altogether wrong, and a gross perversion of the endowment granted by Congress for a very different purpose, as will be apparent to the reader who carefully examines the act in question, given in full in Chapter XLVI.

CHAPTER XLV.

POPULAR AGITATION ON INDUSTRIAL EDUCATION.

A WANT LONG FELT.

The necessity has long been recognized among our more advanced thinkers of some system of education that should be to the industrial classes what the schools of law, medicine, and theology are to those professional classes. In the West this need was especially felt, and such men as Professor J. B. Turner, Bronson Murray, John Gage, Smiley Shepherd, John Davis, and other educators, were engaged in preparing the public mind therefor for over thirty years. The feeling on this subject led to the calling of a convention in 1851, at Greenville, Ill., at which this important question was fully discussed. Two of the resolutions there adopted were as follows:

Resolved, That, as the representatives of the industrial classes, including all cultivators of the soil, artizans, mechanics, and merchants, we desire the same privileges and advantages for ourselves, our fellows, and our posterity, in each of our several pursuits and callings, as our professional brethren enjoy in theirs; and we admit that it is our own fault that we do not also enjoy them.

Resolved, That, in our opinion, the institutions originally and primarily designed to meet the wants of the professional classes, as such, can not, in the nature of things, meet ours, any more than the institutions we desire to establish for ourselves could meet theirs.

The next resolution provided that immediate steps be taken for the establishment of a university, expressly to meet the wants of each and all the industrial classes in the State. It was also recommended to found high schools, lyceums, institutes, etc., in each county, on similar principles, so soon as it might be found practical to do so.

At this Convention Prof. Turner, in an exhaustive address, unfolded an elaborate plan for the establishment of a State University, which was subsequently made the ground-work upon which the act of endowment by the United States, and the law regulating the Industrial University of Illinois, were founded.

INDUSTRIAL LEAGUE AND FURTHER AGITATION.

A second Convention was held at Springfield, Ill., June 8, 1852. On this occasion there was a prolonged controversy, forced upon the Convention by the representatives of a few of the old classical and theological colleges, who had been admitted by courtesy to participate in the debate. As is usual with many of this class, they consumed the greater part of the time without making much, if any, impression for good on the minds of their auditors.

These advocates of the colleges just named desired to be themselves made the custodians of, and instruments through which, the funds of the State should be applied to the education of the industrial classes. This the representatives of these classes then and since, in all their Conventions, have unanimously and steadfastly opposed. It was still fought for after the law of Congress endowed a more practical system of colleges; and when the masses thought they had finally beaten the scholiasts, and had secured the fund to the uses of those for whom it was intended, they soon found that their foe had only been beaten off to come up again in another form.

A third Convention was held at Chicago, November 24th, 1852, at which it was resolved to establish an Industrial League of the State of Illinois, which was subsequently

"Pegging Away."

chartered by the Legislature. The League was empowered to raise a fund to defray various expenses: as, first, to disseminate information, both written and printed; second, to keep up concert of action among the friends of the industrial classes; and, third, to employ lecturers to address citizens in all parts of the State.

At this Convention much important business was transacted; many helpful methods and useful aims were presented and many interesting ideas elaborated. Prof. J. B.

Turner was appointed Principal Director of the League, and John Gage, Bronson Murray, Dr. L. S. Pennington, J. T. Little, and Wm. A. Rennel, Associate Directors. The Convention was harmonious throughout, the members having wisely decided to exclude those professional educators who had no practical knowledge of the wants of the industrial classes.

The most noteworthy action of this Convention, however, was the passage of a resolution to memorialize Congress for the purpose of obtaining a grant of public lands to establish and endow Industrial Colleges in each and every State of the Union. Thus was finally brought forth a definite plan of action, which immediately took firm hold of many leading minds throughout the country, consolidating, in valuable degree, persistent and unselfish efforts which had previously been more or less scattered.

A fourth Convention was held at Springfield, Ill., on the 4th of January, 1853, at which the duties of the members and terms of office of officers of the League were fixed. Nevertheless, the important business of this Convention was the preparation of a memorial, this time to the Legislature, setting forth, in the strongest light, facts, figures, and arguments, to show the great need of a thorough and systematic education of the masses to the industries they would follow in after life. The following extracts from this memorial will show the animus and tenor of the work:

MEMORIAL TO THE ILLINOIS LEGISLATURE.

We need the same thorough and practical application of knowledge to our pursuits that the learned professions enjoy in theirs, through their universities, and their literature, schools, and libraries, that have grown out of them. For, even though knowledge may exist, it is perfectly powerless until properly applied; and we have not the means of applying it. What sort of generals and soldiers would all our national science (and art) make, if we had no military academies to take that knowledge and apply it directly, and specifically to military life?

Are our classic universities, our law, medicine, and divinity schools, adapted to make good generals and warriors? Just as well as they are to make farmers and mechanics, and no better. Is the defense, then, of our resources of more actual consequence than their production? Why, then, should the State care for the one and neglect the other?

It was shown that only one in two hundred and sixty of the population of the State were, in 1853, engaged in professional life, and not one in two hundred in the Union, generally; and that a great proportion, even of these, never enjoyed the advantages of classical and professional schools. Further, there were, in the United States, two hundred and twenty-five principal universities, colleges, and seminaries, schools, etc., devoted to the interest of the professional classes, besides many smaller ones, while there was not a single one, with liberal endowments, designed for the liberal, and practical education of the industrial classes.

It said: "No West Point, as yet, beams upon the horizon of hope; true, as yet, our boundless resources keep us, like the children of Japhet emigrating from the Ark, from the miserable degradation and want of older empires; but the resources themselves lie all undeveloped in some directions, wasted and misapplied in others, and rapidly vanishing away as centuries roll onward, under the unskillfulness that directs them. We, the members of the industrial classes, are still compelled to work empirically and blindly, without needful books, schools, or means, by the slow process of that individual experience that lives and dies with the man. Our professional brethren, through their universities, schools, teachers, and libraries, combine and cencentrate the practical experience of ages into each man's life. We need the same. . . . .

"We seek no novelties. We desire no new principles. We only wish to apply to the great interest of the common school and the industrial classes precisely the same principles of mental discipline and thorough scientific, practical instruction, in their pursuits and interests, which are now applied to the professional and military classes. . . .

"We would, therefore, respectfully petition the honorable Senate and House of Representatives of the State of Illinois, that they present a united memorial to the Congress now assembled at Washington, to appropriate to each State in the Union an amount of public lands, not less in value than five hundred thousand dollars, for the liberal endowment of a system of Industrial Universities, one in each State in the Union, to co-operate with each other, and with the Smithsonian Institute at Washington; for the more liberal and practical education of our industrial classes, and their teachers, in their various pursuits; for the production of knowledge and literature needful in those pursuits, and developing, to the fullest and most perfect extent, the resources of our soil, and our arts, the virtue and intelligence of our people, and the true glory of our common country."

They further petitioned that the Executive and Legislatures of all other States be invited to co-operate in the enterprise, and that a copy of the memorial be forwarded by the governor of Illinois to the governors and senators of the several States.

A similar memorial, but addressed directly to Congress, had been presented to the Convention by the Committee, of which Governor French was the Chairman, which was accepted, and forwarded to Washington.

The merits of the plan suggested by the Convention were fully and widely discussed by the State Legislature, then in session. The result was the passage, by a unanimous vote in both Houses, of the following resolutions.

THE LEGISLATIVE RESOLUTIONS.

Resolutions of the General Assembly of the State of Illinois, relative to the establishment of industrial universities, and for the encouragement of practical and general education among the people. Unanimously adopted.

WHEREAS, The spirit and progress of the age and country demand the culture of the highest order of intellectual attainment in theoretical and industrial science; and,

WHEREAS, It is impossible that our commerce and prosperity will continue to increase without calling in requisition all the elements of internal thrift arising from the labors of the farmer, the mechanic, and the manufacturer, by every fostering effort within the reach of the government; and,

WHEREAS, A system of industrial universities, liberally endowed, in each State of the Union, co-operative with each other, and with the Smithsonian Institution at Washington, would develop a more liberal and practical education among the people; tend the more to intellectualize the rising generation, and eminently conduce to the virtue, intelligence, and true glory of our common country; therefore, be it

Resolved, By the House of Representatives, the Senate concurring herein, that our Senators in Congress be instructed, and our Representatives be requested, to use their best exertions to procure the passage of a law of Congress, donating to each State in the Union an amount of public lands not less in value than five hundred thousand dollars, for the liberal endowment of a system of industrial universities, one in each State in the Union, to co-operate with each other, and with the Smithsonian Institute at Washington, for the more liberal and practical education of our industrial classes, and their teachers; a liberal and varied education, adapted to the manifold want of a practical and enterprising people; and a provision for such educational facilities, being in manifest concurrence with the intimations of the popular will, it urgently demands the united efforts of our national strength.

Resolved, That the Governor is hereby authorized to forward a copy of the foregoing resolutions to our Senators and Representatives in Congress, and to the Executive and Legislature of each of our sister States, inviting them to co-operate with us in this meritorious enterprise.

This resolution was signed by the Speaker of the House of Representatives, John Reynolds, and the Speaker of the Senate, G. Koerner; and, on the eighth of February, 1853, was approved by the Governor, J. A. Matteson, and attested by Alexander Starne, Secretary of State. It was then duly forwarded to Washington.

LEADING UTTERANCES OF TWENTY YEARS AGO.

To show the animus of the press and the people of twenty years ago, upon this subject, the following extracts, relating to the movement in various States, will prove interesting, as historical records at least.

The *New York Tribune*, of February 26, 1853, said: "Here is the principle contended for by the friends of practical education abundantly confirmed, with a plan for its immediate realization. And it is worthy of note, that one of the most extensive of public-land (or new) States proposes a magnificent donation of public lands to each of the States, in furtherance of this idea. Whether that precise form of aid to the project is most judicious, and likely to be effective, we will not here consider. Suffice it that the Legislature of Illinois has taken a noble step forward, in a most liberal and patriotic spirit, for which its members will be heartily thanked by thousands throughout the Union. We feel that this step has materially hastened the coming of scientific and practical education for all who desire, and are willing to work for it. It can not come too soon."

Governor Hunt, of New York, in his annual message to the Legislature of that State, used the following language: "Much interest has been manifested for some years past in favor of creating an institution for the advancement of agricultural science, and of knowledge in mechanical arts. The views in favor of this measure, expressed in my last annual communication, remain unchanged. My impressions are still favorable to the plan of combining in one college two distinct departments for instructions in agriculture and mechanical sciences. I would respectfully recommend that a sufficient portion of the proceeds of the next sale of lands for taxes be appropriated to the erection of an institution, which shall stand as a lasting memorial of our munificence, and contribute to the diffusion of intelligence among the producing classes, during all future time."

Hon. Marshall P. Wilder, of Boston, in advocating this system of education before the Berkshire Agricultural Society of Massachusetts, held that: "For want of knowledge, millions of dollars are now annually lost by the Commonwealth, by the mis-application of capital and labor industry.

. . . .

On these points we want a system of experiments directed by scientific knowledge. Are they not important to our farmers? Neither the agricultural papers, periodicals, or societies, or any other agents now in operation, are deemed sufficient for all that are desirable. We plead that the means and advantages of a professional education should be placed within the reach of our farmers. This would not only be one of the most important steps ever taken by the Commonwealth for its permanent advancement and prosperity, but would add another wreath to her renown for the protection of our industry and elevation of her sons."

Rev. Dr. Hitchcock, President of Amherst College, while advocating the endowments of such institutions, before the Massachusetts Board of Agriculture (1851), testified as follows: "I have been a lecturer on chemistry for twenty years. I have tried a great many experiments in that time, but I do not know of any experiments so delicate or so difficult as the farmer is trying every week. The experiments of the laboratory are not to be compared to them. You have a half dozen sciences which are concerned in the operation of a farm. There is to be a delicate balancing of all these, as every farmer knows. To suppose that a man is going to be able, without any knowledge of these sciences, to make improvements in agriculture by haphazard experiments, is, it seems to me, absurd."

THE ALBANY, NEW YORK, CONVENTION ON AGRICULTURAL EDUCATION.

A general Convention on the subject of a national system of practical university education, was held at Albany, January 26, 1853. This Convention was numerously attended by some of the most illustrious men of the country, including many distinguished educators, scientists, and divines. A committee of twenty-one was appointed to report a plan of action. Among these appear the names of President Wayland, of Brown University; Bishop Potter, of Pennsylvania; Washington Irving; Governor Hunt and Senator Dix, of New York; President Hitchcock, of Amherst College; Professors Webster, Dewey, Henry, and Bache; Professor Mitchell, of Cincinnati; Professor Pierce, of Cambridge, etc.

Rev. Dr. Kennedy spoke of "the want that had long been

felt for institutions different from those already established." Professor C. S. Henry insisted that "the welfare of our country was, in a great degree, dependent upon what should be done in regard to the proposed university." Rev. Ray Palmer said "there was lack of opportunity for scientific men to perfect themselves in their various pursuits, and desired that this want should be supplied to all parts of the country."

Rev. Dr. Wykoff considered that the first *desideratum* to the establishment of the institution was a conviction of its importance. When the souls of men are fired up, the money will not be wanting. He believed that the proper spirit was abroad—a feeling that would redound to the honor and benefit of the people, and that the work would be done. The enterprise was one for the masses. It would open the path of knowledge for all the youth in the land; and, from the common school to the highest university, he would like to see our educational institutions thrown open to all.

Professor Henry said that he should bid the enterprise "God speed!" He deprecated the idea of attempting to establish a university at a moderate outlay. "One fitted for the wants of this country should throw open its lecture rooms freely, to all who might wish to avail themselves of their advantages. It should be the complete development of the principle which lies at the foundation of our common schools." Rev. President Wayland expressed the belief that "such an establishment in New York would be an example, which, he believed, would be followed in other States. A university with a thousand students would abundantly sustain itself; and he thought the needed expense would not be so great as some gentlemen anticipated."

Did these gentlemen know any thing about the subject of practical education in America?

THE VOICE OF AGRICULTURE.

Said the lamented Downing, the father of rural art in this country, in the last number which he edited of the *Horticulturist:* "The leaven for the necessity for education among

The Farmer's Boys.

the industrial classes begin to work, we are happy to perceive, in many parts of the country." Speaking of the plan of Professor Turner, he said: "It is not often that the weak points of an ordinary collegiate education are so clearly exposed, and the necessity of workingmen's universities so plainly demonstrated." This was in July, 1853. Before the article was published this pre-eminent disciple of his art was lost in the ill-fated steamer Henry Clay.

An editorial in the *North American* (the oldest paper in Philadelphia) on education and agriculture, said to be written by Judge Conrad, said: "To secure the diffusion and practical application of agricultural science, it seems necessary that it should be interwoven with general education, and its acquisition made an object of early pride and animated ambition." . . . . . "The triumph of a republic can only be successfully achieved and permanently enjoyed by a people the mass of whom are an enlightened yeomanry, the proprietors of the land they till, too independent to be bought, too enlightened to be cheated, and too powerful to be crushed."

Said Dr. Lee, the talented editor of the *Southern Cultivator*, the leading monthly periodical of the southern planting interest, published at Augusta, Georgia, in reply to a letter inquiring for some practical agricultural school for the sons of the planters (which letter he published as a "fair sample of scores of similar letters received every month"): "There is not a good agricultural school in the United States. The truth is, the American people have yet to commence the study of agriculture as the combination of many sciences. Agriculture is the most profound and extensive profession that the progress of society and the accumulation of knowledge have developed. This is why the popular mind is so long in grasping it. Whether we consider the solid earth under our feet, the invisible atmosphere which we breathe, the wonderful growth and decay of all plants and animals; or, the light, the heat, the cold, the electricity of heaven,—

we contemplate but the elements of rural science. The careful investigation of the laws that govern all ponderable and unponderable agents is the first step in the young farmer's education. To facilitate his studies, he needs, as he preeminently deserves, a more comprehensive school than this country now affords."

CHAPTER XLVI.

CONGRESSIONAL ACTION ON INDUSTRIAL EDUCATION.

HOW THE AGRICULTURAL BILL BECAME A LAW.

From the time of the general awakening on the subject of Industrial Education, as noticed in the last chapter, the discussion of the subject was kept prominently before the people of the United States. This eventuated in the introduction of several bills into Congress, most of which fell still-born. One of them, however, successfully ran the gauntlet of Congressional opposition, only to be strangled in the very last stages of law-making. The following is a brief summary of the matter.

On the 14th of December, 1857, a bill was introduced into the House of Representatives by Hon. Justin S. Morrill, of Vermont, who was at that time Chairman of the Committee on Agriculture, to appropriate a portion of the public land to the several States for the purpose of founding colleges for the advancement of agricultural and mechanical education. Great opposition was manifested to the bill at once, and, instead of being referred to the Committee on Agriculture, where it should legitimately have gone, it was referred to that on Public Lands. There it was held four months, when the Chairman of that Committee, Mr. Cobb, of Alabama, reported upon it adversely. Notwithstanding this, the subject was earnestly discussed by the House, and the bill finally passed by a small majority. The Senate reached it in the winter of 1859, when it was strongly advocated by Senators Wade, Harlan, and Stuart, and as

The Rural Home.

determinedly opposed by Senators Davis, Mason, and Pugh. Subsequently, it was passed by a majority of two and went to the President, Mr. Buchanan, who, with great alacrity, returned it with his veto.

The same bill was again introduced into the Senate in 1862, by Mr. Wade, was favorably reported by Mr. Harlan, and was passed on the 10th of June, by the decisive vote of thirty-two to seven. From thence the bill went to the House where, on the 17th of June, it was passed by the equally decisive vote of ninety to twenty-five. It was approved by President Lincoln, and on the second day of July became a law.

So much has been said and argued by the various minds who have endeavored to interpret this law, that it will not be out of place here to give this bill, and the amendment to the fifth section in full, so that every reader of this work may judge for himself what was the true intent and meaning of this act for the education of the masses to industrial pursuits.

TEXT OF THE ACT OF CONGRESS.

AN ACT donating Public Lands, to the several States and Territories which may provide Colleges for the benefit of Agriculture and the Mechanic Arts.

Be it enacted by the Senate and House of Representatives of the United States of America, in Congress assembled, That there be granted to the several States, for the purposes hereinafter mentioned, an amount of public land, to be apportioned to each State, in quantity equal to 30,000 acres for each Senator and Representative in Congress to which the States are respectively entitled by the apportionment under the census of 1860: *Provided,* That no mineral lands shall be selected or purchased under the provisions of this act.

§ 2. *And be it further enacted,* That the land aforesaid, after being surveyed, shall be apportioned to the several States in sections or sub-divisions of sections not less than one quarter of a section; and whenever there are public lands in a State, subject to sale at private entry, at one dollar and twenty-five cents per acre, the quantity to which said State shall be entitled, shall be selected from such lands, within the limits of such state; and the Secretary of the Interior is hereby directed to issue to each of the States, in which there is not the quantity of public lands subject to sale at private entry, at one dollar and twenty-five cents per acre, to which said State may be entitled under the provisions of this act, land scrip to the amount in acres for the deficiency of its distributive share; said scrip to be sold by said States, and the proceeds thereof applied to the uses and purposes prescribed in this act, and for no other use and purpose whatsoever: *Provided*, That in no case shall any State to which land scrip may thus be issued, be allowed to locate the same within the limits of any other State, or of any Territories of the United States; but their assignees may thus locate said land scrip, upon any of the unappropriated lands of the United States subject to sale at private entry, at one dollar and twenty-five cents or less per acre. *And provided further*, That not more than one million acres shall be located by such assignees in any one of the States. *And provided further*, That no such locations shall be made before one year from the passage of this act.

§ 3. *And be it further enacted*, That all the expenses of management, sperintendence, and taxes from date of selection of said lands previous to their sales, and all expenses incurred in the management and disbursement of the moneys which may be received therefrom, shall be paid by the States to which they may belong, out of the treasury of said States, so that the entire proceeds of the sale of said lands shall be applied, without any diminution whatever, to the purposes hereinafter mentioned.

§ 4. *And be it further enacted*, That all moneys derived from the sale of lands aforesaid, by the States to which the lands are apportioned, and from the sales of land scrip hereinbefore provided for, shall be invested in stocks of the United States, or of the States, or some other safe stocks, yielding not less than five per cent. upon the par value of said stocks; and that the money so invested shall constitute a perpetual fund, the capital of which shall remain forever undiminished (except so far as may be provided in section fifth of this act), and the interest of which shall be inviolably appropriated by each State, which may take and claim the benefit of this act, to the endowment, support and maintenance of, at least, one college, where the leading object shall be, without excluding other scientific and classical studies, and including military tactics, to teach such branches of learning as are related to agriculture and the mechanic arts, in such manner as the Legislatures of the States may respectively prescribe, in order to promote the liberal and practical education of the industrial classes in the several pursuits and professions in life.

§ 5. *And be it further enacted*, That the grant of land and scrip hereby authorized, shall be made on the following conditions, to which, as well as to the provisions hereinbefore contained, the previous assent of the several States shall be signified by legislative acts:

First—If any portion of the fund invested, as provided by the foregoing section, or any portion of the interest thereon, shall, by any action, or contingency, be diminished or lost, it shall be replaced by the State to which it belongs, so that the capital of the fund shall remain forever undiminished; and the annual interest shall be regularly applied without diminution to the purposes mentioned in the fourth section of this act, except that a sum, not exceeding ten per centum upon the amount received by any State under the provisions of this act, may be expended for the purchase of lands for sites or experimental farms, whenever authorized by the respective Legislatures of said States.

Second—No portion of said fund, nor the interest thereon, shall be applied, directly or indirectly, under any pretense whatever, to the purchase, erection, preservation, or repair of any building or buildings.

Third—Any State which may take and claim the benefit of the provisions of this act, shall provide, within five years, at least not less than one college, as prescribed in the fourth section of this act, or the grant to such State shall cease; and said State shall be bound to pay the United States the amount received of any lands previously sold, and that the title to purchasers under the State shall be valid.

Fourth—An annual report shall be made regarding the progress of each college, recording any improvements and experiments made, with their cost and results, and such other matters, including State industrial and economical statistics, as may be supposed useful; one copy of which shall be transmitted by mail free, by each, to all the other colleges which may be endowed under the provisions of this act, and also one copy to the Secretary of the Interior.

Fifth—When lands shall be selected from those which have been raised to double the minimum price in consequence of railroad grants, they shall be computed to the States at the *maximum price, and the number of acres proportionally diminished.*

Sixth—No State, while in a condition of rebellion or insurrection against the government of the United States, shall be entitled to the benefits of this act.

Seventh. No state shall be entitled to the benefits of this act, unless it shall express its acceptance thereof by its legislature within two years from the date of the approval by the President.

§ 6. *And be it further enacted,* That land scrip issued under the provision of this act, shall not be subject to location until after the first day of January, 1863.

§ 7. *And be it further enacted,* That land officers shall receive the same fee for locating land scrip issued under the provisions of this act, as is now allowed for the location of military bounty land warrants under existing laws. *Provided,* Their maximum compensation shall not be thereby increased.

§ 8. *And be it further enacted,* That the Governors of the several States to which scrip shall be issued under this act, shall be required to report annually to Congress all sales made of such scrip until the whole shall be disposed of, the amount received for the same, and what appropriation has been made of the proceeds.

Approved July 2, 1862.

THE AMENDMENT TO THIS ACT.

AN ACT to amend the fifth section of an act entitled "An act donating public lands to the several States and Territories which may provide Colleges for the benefit of Agriculture and the Mechanic Arts," approved July two, eighteen hundred and sixty-two, so as to extend the time within which the provisions of said act shall be accepted and such colleges established.

Be it enacted by the Senate and House of Representatives of the United States of America, in Congress assembled, That the time in which the several States may comply with the provisions of the act of July two, eighteen hundred and sixty-two, entitled "An act donating public lands to the several States and Territories which may provide colleges for the benefit of agriculture and the mechanic arts," is hereby extended so that the acceptance of the benefits of said act may be expressed within three years from the passage of this act, and the colleges required by the said act may be provided within five years from the date of the filing of such acceptance with the commissioner of the general land office. *Provided,* That when any Territory shall become a State, and be admitted into the Union, such new State shall be entitled to the benefits of the said act of July two, eighteen hundred and sixty-two, by expressing the acceptance therein required within three years from the date of its admission into the Union, and providing the college or colleges within five years after such acceptance, as prescribed in this act. *Provided, further,* That any State which has heretofore expressed its acceptance of the act herein referred to, shall have the period of five years within which to provide at least one college, as described in the fourth section of said act, after the time for providing said college, according to the act of July second, eighteen hundred and sixty-two, shall have expired.

Approved July 23, 1866.

DISTRIBUTION OF THE LANDS TO THE SEVERAL STATES.

The following table, from the Report of the Department of Agriculture, for 1867, shows the number of acres which should fall to each State under the law, with other facts of value for future reference:

States.	No. of Senators and Rep'tives.	Acres in Scrip.	Date of acceptance.	Date of establishment.	Designation and location of College.
Alabama	8	240,000	....	....	
Arkansas	5	150,000	....	....	
California	5	150,000	March 31, 1866	March 31, 1866	Agricultural, Mining, and Mechanic Arts College.
Connecticut	6	180,000	June 24, 1863	June 24, 1863	Sheffield Scientific School of Yale College, New Haven.
Delaware	3	90,000	Feb. 17, 1867	March 14, 1867	Delaware State College, Newark.
Florida	3	90,000	....	....	
Georgia	9	270,000	....	....	
Illinois	16	480,000	Jan. 25, 1867	Feb. 28, 1867	Illinois Industrial University, Urbana, Champaign County.
Indiana	13	390,000	March 6, 1865	....	Indiana Agricultural College.
Iowa	8	240,000	Sept. 11, 1862	March 29, 1866	State Agricultural College and Farm, Ames, Story County.
Kansas	3	90,000	Feb. 8, 1863	Feb. 16, 1863	State Agricultural College, Manhattan.

STATES.	No. of Senators and Rep'tives.	Acres in Scrip.	Date of acceptance.	Date of establishment.	Designation and location of College.
Kentucky	11	330,000	Jan. 27, 1863	Feb. 22, 1865	Agricultural and Mechanical College (Kentucky University), Lexington.
Louisiana	7	210,000	....	....	
Maine	7	210,000	March 25, 1863	Feb. 25, 1865 ———, 1856	State College of Agricultural and Mechanic Arts, Orono.
Maryland	7	210,000	Jan. 24, 1864	....	State Agricultural College, Hyattsville.
Massachusetts	12	360,000	———, 1863	April 10, 1861 April 29, 1863	Massachusetts Institute of Technology, Boston. Massachusetts Agricultural College, Amherst.
Michigan	8	240,000	Feb. 25, 1863	March 18, 1863	State Agricultural College, Lansing.
Minnesota	4	120,000	March 2, 1865	January, 1868	Agricultural College of Minnesota, with State University, St. Paul.
Mississippi	7	210,000	....	....	
Missouri	11	330,000	....	....	
Nebraska	3	90,000	....	....	
Nevada	3	90,000	March 9, 1865	....	
New Hampshire	5	150,000	July 9, 1863	July 9, 1866	New Hampshire College of Agriculture (Dartmouth College), Hanover.
New Jersey	7	210,000	March 21, 1863	April 4, 1864	Rutgers' Scientific School and Rutgers' College, New Brunswick.
New York	33	990,000	May 14, 1863	April 27, 1865	Cornell University, Ithaca.
North Carolina	9	270,000	....	....	
Ohio	21	630,000	April 13, 1865	....	
Oregon	3	90,000	October 9, 1862	....	
Pennsylvania	26	780,000	May 1, 1863	April 13, 1854	Agricultural College of Pennsylvania, Center County.
Rhode Island	4	120,000	Jan. 23, 1863	....	Scientific School of Brown University, Providence.
South Carolina	6	180,000	....	....	
Tennessee	10	300,000	....	....	
Texas	6	180,000	....	....	
Vermont	5	150,000	Nov. 11, 1863	Nov. 22, 1864	University of Vermont and State Agricultural College, Burlington.
Virginia	10	300,000	....	....	
West Virginia	5	150,000	Oct. 3, 1863	Feb. 7, 1867	Agricultural College of West Virginia, Morgantown.
Wisconsin	8	240,000	April 2, 1862	April 12, 1866	University of Wisconsin (College of Arts), Madison.
Total	317	9,510,000			

From the foregoing table it will be seen that a large majority of the States have, nominally at least, availed themselves of the benefits of the act of Congress. It is greatly to be regretted that the measures contemplated by the framers of the law have been, in many cases, carried out so imperfectly, or not at all.

CHAPTER XLVII.

AGRICULTURAL COLLEGE EDUCATION.

ITS SCOPE AND AIM.

It is a fair presumption that Agricultural Schools were intended to benefit the present as well as the future farmer. To secure either of these ends, constant series of experiments must be carried on. The professors, also, should be men of more than ordinarily broad and comprehensive minds and acute faculties, for the reason that they have not simply one science to deal with, but many. It is their province to investigate as well as to teach. They should be working professors, who in the field can elucidate what they have taught in the halls or laboratory. If this combination of faculties can not always be found, then the working professors must take the students just where the theoretical one left them; and this, day by day. The farm is the laboratory where problems propounded in the halls must be worked out. The soil is nature's great laboratory where the elements are formed into grass, timber, grain, vegetables, fruits, fibers, and flowers. So also the animals of the farm are laboratories for the conversion of grass, grain, vegetables, etc., into flesh for the sustenance of man.

Agriculture consists primarily of chemical changes and transformations which result in elaborating from the elements, through the medium of the soil, all the varied and wonderful vegetable wealth that clothes the earth, from the minute lichen upon the bare rock to the giant monarch of the forest which slowly accumulates its structure through decades of centuries. The farmer assists nature in these transformations, by such mechanical means as he may be able to employ. Scientific agriculture should go still further. It should teach *why* certain conditions were necessary and how produced. This is what makes the difference between the farmer and agriculturist. The farmer knows how, by mechanical effort, under favorable influences, he may produce crops. The agriculturist seeks to know why certain causes produce favorable or unfavorable results, in order that he may increase the one or guard against the other. This knowledge has made a Colling, a Bakewell, a Buel, a Meehan, and many other self-educated men. They, however, bear no greater proportion to the masses than the great oak does to the various trees of the forest. We need this class of minds in our agricultural colleges, to develop the practical application of science to agriculture.

ONE GREAT MISTAKE.

One of the great mistakes which has been made in carrying out the details of this "new education" consists in attempting to cover too much ground, either by making the agricultural schools a part and parcel of a great university course already provided, or seeking to erect those newly founded into great universities. The agriculturist wants to know something of many things, but it is folly to suppose that, in order to acquire this certain knowledge, he must follow out the science relating to a co-ordinate study in its most abstruse bearings or minuter details.

A single example will illustrate our meaning. Of the commoner insects there are between two hundred and three hundred varieties noxious or beneficial to vegetation. The farmer should be conversant with these, and should learn their history and habits, the means for the destruction of the first and the manner of increasing and protecting the second, etc. Under the old system, the student must learn all about the infinite orders, families, and sub-families that compose insect life, in order to acquire what he wants. To follow out this idea, life would be too short to get even a "smattering of agriculture," and hence the disrepute into which the system has fallen.

If, on the other hand, these insects, destructive or beneficial to vegetation, were thoroughly classified, and their history and habits presented as far as known, with natural specimens properly arranged in cases, the student would soon acquire a correct knowledge of all that would be necessary for him to know of entomology. Similar principles should govern the other sciences—at least in the case of the student of two, three, or four years. The knowledge in the various sciences pertaining to agriculture should be condensed, so that the student expecting soon to return to the farm might work directly towards the end sought; while his "chum," who is aiming to make scientific pursuits his profession for life, either as a teacher or writer, might climb and explore science after science at will. The farmer, of course, though less profoundly versed in mere technics, might still keep pace with the new discoveries in his profession by a judicious system of reading.

PRACTICAL EDUCATION TO AGRICULTURE.

The ability of a business man is demonstrated by his success in performing a given piece of work himself, or in hiring and managing the proper workmen to carry out the details, the principal himself knowing, when finished, whether it be well or illy done. More failures are made in life for want of a proper education to business, than from any other known cause. If there be any science in a man's or woman's occupation (and there is science even in turning a spade full of earth), he or she will be successful, with due industry, just in proportion as the principles of this science are understood. The merchant generally acquires his knowledge of the laws underlying his profession after he leaves his clerkship, and too often through gross mistakes, which, leading to failure, make him begin anew. It is, therefore, the province of mercantile schools and business colleges so to instruct the student that he will understand business principles and usages. So of all schools of technology. Why not, then, the same with the farmer?

The difference between practical and theoretical education is that the first begins just where the other leaves off. The practical education of the physician begins in the lecture and dissecting rooms and in the laboratory. This is continued, as he goes along, all through life, and until death overtakes him. The farmer, like the physician, has to practically educate himself, and, like the physician, never ceases to learn while life lasts.

Agricultural colleges should be so organized and equipped that the student may there investigate the useful subjects which he has no proper facilities for doing on the farm, and also examine and compare each year's experiments, and note their results.

The ordinary farmer is not able to give his children more than one, two, or three years of scientific education. In this time the student should acquire a knowledge of the nature and composition of soils, and of the economy of animal and vegetable life; should investigate the effects produced upon soils by mechanical means, such as deep and shallow, trench, and sub-soil plowing; should study the benefits of thorough drainage and other methods of working the soil; should master the principles of a proper rotation of crops; should store his mind with information relative to the application of special manures to certain crops, and the like practical details, etc., etc.

THE STUDY OF CHEMISTRY, PHYSIOLOGY, AND OTHER SPECIALTIES.

The agricultural student will also need some knowledge of the chemical changes which soils undergo through various agencies other than the disintegration of rocks; as, for instance, the effects of a top-dressing of mulch or manure as compared with a similar application that is plowed under, and where one would be beneficial and the other hurtful; and

The Stock-breeder's Museum.

the certain effects of fall and spring plowing on different soils—when and where to be practiced, andwhen not. As a stock breeder, he will need to acquaint himself with the different breeds of horses, cattle, sheep, swine, etc.; the results of their various crosses and grades; their adaptability to various uses and conditions; their diseases and the proper remedies therefor; the proper methods of breeding, rearing, sheltering, and fitting them for market; and with farm structures, fences and fencing materials. In vegetable economy the student should understand as much as possible of the nature and growth of plants; their botanical characteristics, including variation and varieties; the adaptability of various plants to certain climates, with the proper means for acclimatization, etc., etc. He should study entomology, so far as it concerns insects beneficial or injurious to vegetation, and mineralogy and geology so far as they relate to soil." So with other subjects. The student should pursue them to the bounds within which they pertain to his profession, but no further than this, if he wishes to put to practical every-day use on the farm simply the knowledge he has acquired.

Feeding the Lamb.

The education of girls should differ from that of boys in its practical bearing. This is really one of the most vital questions of the day. Girls should be educated with reference to their duties as wives and mothers as well as to the economics of the household. They should be well versed in pomology, floriculture, bee-keeping, the care of poultry, and other light and suitable branches of agriculture. They should understand the chemical and other changes which milk undergoes during its manufacture into butter and cheese. They should understand structural botany, vegetable physiology, and the various other studies that would enable them in after life to become true counselors and partners in all that pertains to farm life.

PRACTICAL EDUCATION NEED NOT BE RESTRICTED OR SORDID.

A *practical* education, then, is what the farmer needs. But need it, therefore, be an ignoble, sordid training, whose only end is to fit him the better to grapple with the ever-recurring problems of dollars and cents? By no means. On the contrary, it should be, and it may be, such as shall expand his faculties and ennoble his whole being, lifting him up to a plane of intelligence where he can behold, with appreciative eye, the miracles which Nature's hand is working out on every side; where he must first wonder, then by degrees begin to understand and perpetually admire; and where, if of a devout mind, he will soon learn to "look from Nature up to Nature's God."

"Nature's Miracles on Every Side."

Is this the kind of education which our farmers' sons and daughters are being furnished, in most of our common schools, to-day? Let us examine this point. How many are there who know the power which water has exerted in the earth's history, and still exerts upon the farm every day? that by its action all our stratified rocks were formed? that to its solvent power and chemical action we owe our useful minerals and our metallic deposits? that it is the great mechanical power in nature? that it has moved mountains and filled valleys through its glacial action? or that through its agency our most fertile soils have been deposited over vast areas?

Again, how many know that the sun is the real, moving life-power upon the earth, and that through the action of its rays upon water we have dew, clouds, fogs, rain, snow, and frost? How many know that the crystalline rocks at the earth's surface contain a greater quantity of water than all the seas and rivers of the globe; that if the conditions surrounding us should change so that the earth would absorb only four thousandths of one per cent. of water more than it now contains, the ocean would disappear, and we should lose not only our moisture, but the atmosphere itself? How many comprehend that it is the sun, after all, which is the great master power that moves all on earth, water being only the agent?

Now, the student in agriculture should understand, for instance, how the agency of water is exerted for the benefit of the farmer; but it is not necessary that he should know every thing which science teaches about water in all its forms and phases. Life is too short for such all-embracing investigations.

Truly, we live in a realm of wonders. Nature's silent operations on the farm are a succession of miracles, until we understand the laws by which she works. Then they become to our wondering minds as simple as they are beautiful, even in their vastness and complexity. The number of tons of water raised by an acre of corn, during its summer's growth, is simply marvelous. How many farmers understand the processes by which it is accomplished, or can realize the immense measure of force and energy expended by nature in producing his twenty to fifty bushels of corn per acre? How many appreciate the important fact that it is in his power to assist nature in economizing a portion of this vast force, by enabling her to produce ten, twenty, thirty bushels more of grain per acre than his land now yields? Hardly one in a thousand; and why? Simply because they have never been educated to their calling—have never been taught to use their senses aright; to store their minds with useful, expansive knowledge; or to reason from cause to effect, and from effect back to cause.

"IN THE SWEAT OF THY BROW."

Since ninety-nine out of every one hundred men and women have to earn their living by actual labor, is it not better that they know something about that business in its several departments, rather than to know all about some one particular department? It is this knowing something of many things that makes the practical man; the knowing all about some one or two special things, the scholar. This knowledge comes slowly, as gray hairs grow, to a thinking man. What we want is to hasten the ripening of this practical knowledge among the masses, through schools especially devoted to the departments of science relating to agriculture and other industrial pursuits.

A man may be a good chemist and botanist; may understand the anatomy and structure of animals, with their diseases and the remedies necessary to their cure; may understand the nature and composition of soils—all these without being a farmer; nevertheless, if a farmer, he can not have studied the several branches in their bearings upon agriculture without being a much better one therefor. Afterward, if he chooses to make a specialty of any one of the sciences, what should hinder? He has the foundation to work on, if he so desire. On the other hand, those whose means might allow them to spend a longer time would necessarily want a different curriculum. To the one class of students the classics would not be beneficial; to the other, they would be necessary, as enabling them to pursue their higher studies more surely.

I believe the time is coming when our industrial schools and agricultural colleges will begin to educate just where the other schools leave off; that is, if the student comes for from one to four years, with an ordinary English education to begin with, he will be pushed in those branches that will make it possible for him as an agriculturist, to comprehend science enough to enable him to work understandingly, and still pursue his studies by a course of reading thereafter. Meanwhile, the life student in agriculture having time, brains, and means to take a higher and wider range, will climb from science to science, and become in turn a teacher to others.

It is for some such system as this that the life-long workers in organizing Education to the Industries have been insisting. Have they succeeded? Only in a measure. But let us be thankful for what we have gained, and still press forward.

By the system that I have outlined there will be trained an army of students, who, when they have finished their education, instead of despising the labors of the farm, will glory in the fulfillment of the great command—far less a curse than blessing—which says, "In the sweat of thy brow shalt thou eat thy bread." Theirs, also, will be the power to gain a juster appreciation of the power and majesty of nature in her manifold workings; a boon denied to those whose aspirations rise no higher than the mere drudgery of labor, where all are the abject slaves of toil, and the whole of life consists of one dull, ever-recurring routine of eating, drinking, working, and sleeping.

THE FUTURE OF INDUSTRIAL EDUCATION.

While it is altogether right for the people to demand that the schools specially endowed for education to the industries shall accomplish some good to the present generation, and to the masses in that immediately succeeding ours, and while they not only ask, but continue to insist upon this, they will not deny as high educational facilities to the Agricultural Colleges as exist anywhere else on the broad earth. They do well not to compromise the claim that this new education, which advanced educators and the press have said would revolutionize the world, shall be carried out faithfully to its legitimate results.

The future of industrial education must be that the student shall be made as thorough as possible, in the rudiments that shall best assist him in after life to earn his broad, by the application of certain knowledge pertaining to the particular industry which he follows. The accomplishment of this end must be one of the persistent objects aimed at in the movement now in progress to disenthrall the masses from the power of monopolies.

Since the act of Congress granting lands for the endowment of Agricultural Colleges, we have seen the persistence with which existing colleges have sought to absorb this fund, that the power might remain with themselves. They have told wild stories that science, if not tempered with the old dogmas, would overturn society and bring the earth back again to the darkness of paganism, forgetting that true science conflicts with no law that is capable of demonstration, but only attacks and demolishes the weak dogmas of mere theorists. They have stated that scientists were infidels, when the fact is that the true scientist is nearly always a firm, unwavering believer in the One Great Cause, the Supreme Ruler of the Universe, fashioning its materials through the operation of uniform, undeviating law, directing its infinity of operations, and controlling all things "in the heavens above and the earth beneath, and the water that is under the earth."

CHAPTER XLVIII.

BIOGRAPHICAL SKETCH OF PROF. J. B. TURNER.

EARLY STRUGGLES.

The mere politician lives upon the excitement of public life, and the spoils of office. The feats of the warrior are blazoned over the land, as though he was something to be worshiped. To his memory lofty monuments are erected, which ultimately crumble to dust, or are demolished by the chance of war, or accident. The real benefactors of their race too often live only in the green memories of their fellows.

JONATHAN BALDWIN TURNER, the "wheel-horse of Industrial Education," like many other of our best men, was born on a farm, and reared to a practical familiarity with the routine of daily toil. In his youth, inured to patient effort, and the exacting labors of the farm, he acquired those habits of self-denial and self-reliance that have since enabled him to successfully battle with the world, and acquire a wide-spread and powerful influence for good among his fellow-men.

At college, where he educated himself by the results of his own labor, he early gained high distinction as a classical scholar, but especially excelled in mathematics. He soon ranked with the very foremost among the students as a writer and thinker. His determined energy, originality of mind, and vigorous thought, thus early gave promise of his useful and illustrious future.

Professor J. B. Turner.

PROFESSOR AT ILLINOIS COLLEGE.

Leaving college, he became a teacher; endearing himself to his associates by his uniform courtesy and earnestness; making fast friends, whose love and respect he retains to this day, in addition to many substantial testimonials of their fraternal and lasting regard.

But his energies were not destined to be spent among the hills of his beloved New England. The love of a pioneer life, contracted in youth, led him, in 1832, to emigrate to Illinois, where he was soon chosen one of the professors of Illinois College; in which position he continued for fifteen years, when, at length, his incessant labors, and the controversy of opinions respecting practical education and freedom of thought, undermined his health, and he was compelled to resign his professorship.

Those of his many friends who were conversant with his clear perception and logical mind urged him to undertake the law as a profession; but Providence had a broader field and nobler work in reserve for him as an educator of the masses at large. His honest mind was constantly revolving some project by which he could ameliorate the condition of his fellows, scattered, as yet, at wide intervals over the broad and luxuriant prairies of Illinois. His instincts, fortunately for the children of the State, led him back to the labors of the farm. Since that time he has been steadily engaged in the various duties of his farm, garden, orchard, and vineyard.

As early as 1833, he lectured in various towns of the State, to awaken an interest in education through the founding of common schools, urging, with all the strength of his mind, the necessity of a permanent system while yet the

State was in its infancy. To his utterance of these forcible truths, the people of Illinois are largely indebted for the comprehensive system of common schools that is now the pride of the State, and the power which has carried it forward, and made its men and women foremost in the land in resisting the encroachments of tyranny, of whatsoever kind.

THE INTRODUCER OF THE OSAGE ORANGE FOR HEDGE PURPOSES.

Thus engaged, he traversed, day by day, these broad prairies that wanted only timber to make them the paradise of the farmer. Not a habitation was to be seen except at long intervals, when some skirt of timber enabled the hardy pioneer to procure logs for his cabin, and rails for his first corn-patch. Dug-outs, cabins built of sod, were a make-shift then unknown. It required the still greater lack of timber of the country then called the "Great American Desert," but now the fertile fields and smiling homesteads of Kansas and Nebraska, to suggest this idea.

Thus journeying from town to town in the good cause of education, his practical mind was ever asking the question: "What can public schools do for families thus situated?" Schools could not flourish without compact settlements; settlements could not be organized without something to fence fields with. The "no-fence" law was not then in vogue, and the herding of cattle away from the fields of grain was not yet practiced. Mr. Turner at once set himself to experimenting, and, after spending an immense amount of time and trouble, fixed upon the Osage Orange as the plant that could be most easily made available for hedging purposes. To this he adhered with all the tenacity of his nature, through good and evil fortune, till at length "Turner's folly," as the unbelieving had christened it, became a great fact. Some of those same scoffers immediately set about dividing the honor of introducing it. But that honor belongs to Professor Turner alone. It is a pleasant fact to chronicle, that this, and other labors, have secured Mr. Turner an ample fortune for enjoyment in his old age.

THE EDUCATOR AS AN INVENTOR.

One of the leading ideas in Mr. Turner's mind was that, if anywhere in the world, the prairies, where in many localities a furrow might be turned, during a day's march, without the plow striking even a pebble—that here the crops might be worked almost exclusively without that tiresome hand-work so laboriously performed in less favored countries. It early occurred to him that corn might be planted by machinery; and that it might be cultivated by other machinery, allowing the operator to ride.

In working out these ideas, he secured some of the first patents for machines for planting, weeding, and cultivating crops. By essays and lectures upon these matters, and by his own practical efforts as an inventor, he probably did more to illustrate the feasibility of the now universal system of cultivation than any other one man in the West. It was he, in fact, who conceived the idea of many of the implements now in use, which other persons have perfected and reaped the profit from.

HIS CONTRIBUTIONS TO SCIENCE.

These have been voluminous for a life-long worker, who earned with his hands his daily bread. They have been mainly contributed through the agricultural press, by means of essays, lectures, papers written for various scientific societies, and the transactions of State agricultural and horticultural societies. They are of inestimable value to the student or practical man desirous of exploring the mysteries of science.

His lectures and essays on "Practical Education" have been published in various periodicals both East and West; that "On the Three Great Races of Men, the White, the Yellow, and the Black," published in book-form. The discourses "On Microscopic Insects;" "On Matter, Force, and Spirit;" "On the Ocean Currents and Open Sea at the Poles;" and his remarks on tornadoes, delivered at the anniversaries of the Illinois Natural History Society, during his presidency of the same, from 1858 to 1862; his premium essay "On Cultivation of Crops;" and papers "On Industrial Education,"—are all published in the third, fourth, and fifth volumes of the Illinois State Agricultural Society Transactions.

"An Essay on the Forces that promote Vegetable Growth," read before the Illinois Horticultural Society, was published in the fifth volume of their Transactions. "The Discourse on Climate," delivered before the Illinois Industrial University, together with his address at the laying of the corner-stone of their new university buildings, was published in the Fourth Annual Report of that University.

These discourses cover an immense range and variety of topics and subjects. They suggest many varied and original lines of thought for our consideration, not found in any other book or books whatever; and whatever errors or defects may attach to them, they could hardly fail to lift the reader into a new and higher region of thought and action and enterprise than even most of our more minute specialists in science have as yet attained.

These writings have attracted the attention and admiration of some of the profoundest minds of the age; they teem with vigor of thought, minuteness of detail, and scientific erudition, and yet are so simple in their language, and so plain in their minuteness, that the ordinary comprehension can readily understand them.

ADVOCACY OF A NATIONAL BUREAU OF AGRICULTURE, ETC.

Professor Turner labored long and earnestly for the establishment of an Agricultural Bureau at the national seat of government. He delivered many public addresses in advocacy of this measure, in which he urged the vital importance of the establishment of some such department. He showed that it had been urged upon Congress by almost every president and statesman from Washington down; and urged the farmers to give their representatives to understand that there must be no further delay of decisive action. The agitation on this subject at last resulted in the formation of the Department of Agriculture at Washington. This has been productive of some good out of a mass of corruption, but, like Industrial Education as carried out in Professor Turner's own State, has not borne just exactly such fruit as he expected.

Another project which early enlisted Professor Turner's efforts was the establishment of a permanent State Society for holding fairs; and the formation of what eventually became the Illinois State Board of Agriculture, is due, in no small degree, to his exertions. In one of his earlier addresses he thus eulogizes them, and points the finger of scorn at the mere politician. "Think of our county fairs, our State fairs, our world's fairs; their congregated millions, the immensity of their products, the variety and perfection of their processes and arts, the increase of their moral and mental power, so great already that we can hardly fence politicians out of our show-grounds, although we offer no premium for the stock or breed. Then think that all this has been achieved by a class of men who centuries ago were the mere serfs of the soil; bought and sold with the cattle; tortured, or hung, or burnt at the base bidding of some haughty lord."

CHAMPIONSHIP OF LIBERAL EDUCATION TO THE INDUSTRIES.

In a preceding chapter we have traced Professor Turner's hand in the development of a system of education to the industries. It will not be out of place here to show still more fully his sentiments relating to this education, the one dear subject next his heart. He saw the bill whose history we have given elsewhere, now up, now down, tossed from one house of Congress to another as a foot-ball, until at last it was vetoed by a vacillating and recreant president.

While Senator Douglas lay dying in Chicago, Professor Turner, entirely ignorant of the fact was busy at his own desk, in Jacksonville, Illinois, writing and preparing manuscript, at the Senator's request, relating to a new bill which Mr. Douglas proposed to press forward at the next Congress with all the zeal and power for which this eminent statesman was noted. Alas! too soon the word came that this giant intellect had passed away just when the nation most needed its staunch support.

Professor Turner always held, as he does now, that the mind can be so disciplined in the several professions and industrial pursuits of life as to bear the full fruition of the education so bestowed; and this was his doctrine at a time when agricultural education was classed as among the absurdities. On this subject Mr. Douglas was in full accord with him, and early declared: "This educational scheme of his is the most democratic scheme of education ever proposed to the mind of man." Later, the leading press of England expressed the opinion that, if fully carried out, it would revolutionize the world.

It is a grievous spectacle to see so much of the magnificent endowments allotted to the agricultural colleges frittered away in the old time-worn collegiate courses, absolutely stolen by scholiasts who have no sympathy in common with the industrial masses, and who merely provide food and material for the drones of society.

"Where," says Professor Turner, in one of his pamphlets, with characteristic directness and force, "where did Socrates and Cincinnatus, and Washington, and Franklin, and Sherman, and Kossuth, and Downing, and Hugh Miller, and a host of worthies too numerous to mention, get their education except from their connection with the practical pursuits of life? Where all other men have gotten theirs, so far as it has proved itself of any practical use to themselves or the world. If all our divines had been trained at West Point, all our lawyers, physicians, and generals at Andover or Princeton, would there have been either the same energy of effort and success, or the same discipline of mind in these professions? Skill and a proper knowledge of projectiles—the chain-shot and the bomb-shell—would hardly make a divine; nor familiarity with the folios of the Fathers have achieved the conquest of the empire of the Montezumas.

"So far as discipline of mind is concerned, the greater part of it is procured, in all professions, not at their several schools, however excellent, but by enforced habits of reading, thought, and reflection in connection with the pursuits in after life, and if not so acquired, it is never acquired at all."

Such were the sentiments, and such the massive logic, of the man who was opposed by many politicians of both parties, whose interest it is to keep the masses ignorant; opposed by that class of scholiasts who conceive that high education is only for the few aristocrats of mere wealth; opposed, also, by various classes of citizens, including even farmers and mechanics, who believed his scheme of education Utopian. In Illinois, bigotry and mismanagement have sadly squandered the means and dwarfed the fruit of the industrial education scheme; but we have the satisfaction of seeing in some of the other States, and especially in the neighboring ones of Michigan and Iowa, this beneficent system growing and developing year by year towards the high standard of its projectors' ideal hopes.

PERSONAL SIMPLICITY, AND THE GREATNESS OF HIS WORK.

The early life of Professor Turner was one of poverty and privation. Thus he early learned the value of economy. In later life he continued to practice a prudent economy from choice. But economy with his nature did not carry meanness. He is generous and noble in his instructions. Believing extravagance the great and growing folly of his countrymen, he continues to this day, although in the possession of an ample fortune, to practice the utmost simplicity in his dress consistent with the proper usages of society.

Desiring no public position or office or power, except the power he has exercised for good in his day and generation;

working daily in his green old age on his farm; his children settled comfortably in life,—he awards a generous hospitality to those of his many friends who may visit him at his home. His declining years solaced by a knowledge that he has ever sought to benefit mankind, he looks back with satisfaction upon his efforts in the various means which he has used to do good to his country and its people, through the discussion of the numberless questions which he has treated—the natural sciences, internal improvements, industrial education, the tariff, finance, etc. He may well be proud, if his modesty would allow, of the praise bestowed upon him by Daniel Webster while Secretary of State. Mr. Webster pronounced an earlier essay by Professor Turner on the currency question "one of the ablest papers he had ever read." His definition of liberty was: "That liberty is the right of every sentient being to a sphere of action and enjoyment suited to that capacity of action and enjoyment which God has given each individual creature." This has been universally admired and accepted by many political writers as the most comprehensive and accurate definition of liberty in the English language.

CHAPTER XLIX.

WHAT THE GROUNDSWELL HAS ACCOMPLISHED.

THE GOOD WORK IN CALIFORNIA.

In California the Granges have done noble work toward disenthralling the people from the power of some of the combinations and rings that heretofore have held the industrial interests in their grasp. In the fight for political regeneration, they have exercised their power (though not as an organization), against monopolies, and with decided success. The brilliant and convincing arguments of Governor Booth (lately elevated to the United States Senate) contributed much toward the triumph of popular rights. The entering wedge has found a lodgment in that State that will, it is believed, rend the gnarled stump of corruption there. Large amounts of money have already been saved to the members of the Clubs and Granges, and the farmers of the State have been brought into closer brotherhood. The fraternal feeling thus engendered is constantly making clearer the fact, so often demonstrated, that in co-operation toward a given end lies the power of the masses for good. That an organization so young as is the Grange in California should have accomplished so great good, seems truly surprising, until we reflect how great was the necessity for action there. It speaks well for the intelligence of the people of the State, that they should have worked so practically and harmoniously toward the end sought.

IN OTHER WESTERN STATES.

Kansas wheels into line with her Clubs and Granges, Nebraska following close after. Iowa, with her grand consolidation of Granges, striking blows as with a pile-driver, already sounds in the ears of monopolies the knell that betokens a speedy funeral. Minnesota and Wisconsin, with her Clubs and Granges, are marching shoulder to shoulder in the battle for human rights. Illinois, strong in her amalgamated organization, is in the fore front of the fray. Her sturdy shout rings out clear with every stroke of the axe at the root of the upas tree of monopoly. Michigan, Indiana, and Ohio, though feeling less the evils that are experienced elsewhere, are working manfully for the good cause.

Every-where the jealousies that at first seemed to exist between the secret and open organizations are gradually giving way to the knowledge that, in the work in hand, there must be no faltering nor looking back; that each have their legitimate sphere of action; and that each, however many there may be, is necessary to the other.

As the flint against the steel elicits sparks, so the friction of mind against mind, at the Club and Grange meetings, is developing not simply good debaters, but even orators whose eloquent utterances have power to stir the masses to noble efforts.

To have been assured of this it was only necessary to have attended the convention at Decatur, of the Illinois Farmers' Association, December 15, 1873, when for four days, holding three long sessions each day, full delegations from the Clubs and Granges of every County in the State save one were present The work of this representative body of men, together with the work and resolutions of the Iowa State Grange, and the Illinois State Grange, which met the week previously—the first in Des Moines, Iowa, and the latter at Bloomington, Illinois—will serve to show the animus and earnestness of the men engaged in the movement.

ACTION OF THE IOWA STATE GRANGE, DECEMBER, 1873.

The resolutions passed by these three great conventions are important in many respects. The platform of the Iowa Patrons of Husbandry, was confined principally to the inner workings of the order. It recommends the establishment of a circulating library, in connection with the Subordinate Granges, a step of the greatest importance, and productive of vast good as a means of still further educating the members in social and intellectual life. It is also easy of accomplishment, since the only obstacle is a financial one that may be easily overcome. A committee was also appointed to arrange for the establishment of a newspaper, to be strictly educational in its character—an organ of the Order, which should be the mentor and teacher of each Grange.

The Iowa Patrons also expressed themselves strongly as to the necessity of a modification of the school laws, that they might be more efficiently carried out in practical education through efficient teachers. While doing this, they emphatically urge the continued education of the farmers after the school days are over. Hence, the necessity of libraries to which all may have access. The Patrons fully acknowledge the importance of the common schools, the

Agricultural Colleges, and the Press, as the great levers of progress, in making mankind and womankind thoroughly humane and enlightened.

One very significant resolution of the Iowa State Grange is: "That we specially urge upon our brethren the duties of fraternal arbitration in settlement of all difficulties without resort to legal tribunals."

The address of the Master of the Iowa State Grange contains the following precepts which the Executive Committee were instructed to publish in a circular for the use of the brethren and others:

First, the family relation or social phase—as represented in the the Subordinate Grange. The needs of farmers in this direction are plainly apparent to all. The Grange gives that social culture so much needed in our isolated condition. In the Grange room we meet to strenghten those social ties without which life is shorn of those enjoyments which vitalize existence and make labor become ennobling and honorable. The American people, and more especially those of us who follow agriculture as a profession or calling, pay too little regard to the social enjoyments. Coming into a new country, strangers to each other, urged on by the absolute necessity of making from the soil, homes and a standing in the community, we put all of our lives into the material work before us, forgetting that any life purely material in its character must be practically a failure. The Order of the Patrons of Husbandry aims to meet this want, and our past though short experience has shown us that in this direction alone it is worth infinitely more than it has cost.

The second phase of our work is the intellectual and educational one. No organization in the world has ever before opened such a field of opportunity for the men and women who avail themselves of its benefits. In the Grange room we learn how to compare methods; we teach each other the best way of arriving at results. Measures of both private and public interest receive that full and careful attention which is so much needed. Under the old system, each individual drew his knowledge and conclusions from his limited sphere of thought and observation. Here a fund of thought and study is brought into the common store, and ALL, according to their capacity, receive the full measure of benefit. As one instance of the good coming to us in this connection, it is estimated that among members of the Order in our State, nine out of every ten cases of dispute which, under the old system, would be litigated in the courts, are settled in subordinate Grange by friendly and fraternal arbitration. I do not suppose our friends of the legal profession will consider this a creditable feature, but, on the whole, I think we shall be able to stand it.

There is no computing the amount of knowledge which this educational feature of our work has brought to our members. The remark is made by business men outside the gate, "How much more the farmers know of business than they did two years ago."

Questions of a public nature receive their full share of attention, and our relations to each other, and to the government, are day by day becoming better and more clearly understood. To women, these two first phases of our work already have, and are destined to bring rich blessings. Nowhere else does woman meet her brothers on terms of absolute equality. Here her field of thought and action is only limited by the measure of her capacity. She may enter into the consideration of every question, and by her quick and fine intuitive reasoning, stimulate and help forward her slower and more plodding brother. I have at times been deeply touched at the expressions of thankfulness coming from a full heart from women, who fully appreciate the good which is coming to them through their connection with the Order; and I feel thankful to our founders, who were wise enough to incorporate this feature in our fundamental law.

Finally, we come to the material, or business phase of our work. One mistake sometimes made, is in supposing that the saving of money in buying and selling is the chief aim of the order. Persons who take this view of the objects and purposes of the Patrons, utterly fail to comprehend the scope and genius of the institution.

Such persons will do better to turn their energies and thoughts in the direction of acquiring money outside the gates of the Order.

The saving of money, the learning how to buy and sell, and to use the results of accumulated industry to the best advantage, is a part, but ONLY A PART, of the work of the Order. Co-operation in buying and selling has long been conceded by thinking men as the true secret of business success.

WHAT THE ILLINOIS STATE GRANGE BELIEVES.

The Illinois Patrons, at their annual session at Bloomington, December, 1873, asserted that they regard the various organizations with entire cordiality, and earnestly invite their fraternal co-operation. They put their opinions strongly on record concerning the denudation of forests, in its relation to meteorological changes, and the consequent changes of atmospheric conditions; denounced the infamous salary grab; and accepted as a compliment the opprobrium sought to be cast upon the Farmers' Movement by ascribing to it the late panic in stocks, and otherwise, in the centers of speculation, even though involving the legitimate business interests of the country in temporary disaster.

On the question of the power of Congress to regulate inter-state commerce, the Illinois State Grange declares the right of Congress so to do, and approves the recent action in this direction. The entire inadequacy of the present system of transportation is pointed out, the improvement of natural channels, and the opening of new railroad routes is demanded, not, however, to be constructed by government except as a last resort. The resolutions conclude with a strong denunciation of the civil service system of our government as now administered.

Is there any thing revolutionary in this? Does it look like an expression of views from the stand-point of "communism." Is there any "red republicanism" in all this? Are the

Patrons "immersed up to their throats in partisan politics?" If so, it is concealed with a Machiavelian subtlety, which would prove the "Patrons" worthy pupils of that class of journalists who have so accused them. On the contrary, is not the entire absence either of partisan politics or political action of any kind, except the broad ground upon which all may unite who truly love their country, commendable?

ACTION OF THE ILLINOIS STATE FARMERS' ASSOCIATION.

As distinguished from the action of the two representative bodies of men composing the Grangers just noticed, the Illinois Farmers' Association, at their second annual meeting at Decatur, Illinois, took strong political ground. This organization is composed of delegates from both Clubs and Granges, but more largely of the former. The Patrons, however, did not attend under the auspices of the Granges, but as individuals representing constituencies. This body did not hesitate to express themselves emphatically upon the live political issues of the day, much to the disgust of both the revolutionary and monopolist organs, who, in the early days of the association, set themselves up as its mentors, and who have since sought by every means to guide its course. Various party "organs," too, fancy they see hand-writings on the wall that are particularly unpleasant.

Some of the latter are particularly anxious that the farmers should know that they themselves did not start the movement, but a lot of broken-down Washington politicians—the only grain of truth in which bushel of chaff is that the Order of Patrons of Husbandry was established *at* Washington. This organization, however, represents only one of the three great elements in the Farmers' Movement.

If the farmers were the stolid set that this class of journalists suppose, all this tirade might be well. But those who for years have been trying to stem the tide of corruption, and nullify the insane blindness of too grasping monopolists, will not accept the arbitrary dogma that they are controlled by a body of Washington politicians.

WHAT THE ILLINOIS FARMERS DID ASSERT.

The Illinois Farmers' Association, at its formation, did not organize a political party. It has, however, managed to succeed in placing representative farmers in various offices in a majority of the counties of the State. The Granges, on the other hand, have steadily kept themselves aloof from politics, and there is no present appearance that they will ever change their course, notwithstanding the efforts of certain journals to force them so to do by covert sneers and open vituperation. The leading minds of the Order know well that such a course would destroy its influence in other directions. Its power is potent because exercised in an educational and business way. The Illinois Patrons are among the most conservative of the Order, from the fact, perhaps, that there is another distinct body in the State who may and do exert political power.

One of the great features of the Order of Patrons is, that their educational facilities will insure, at the proper time, the casting of the ballots of the fraternity in accordance with law and order, and against the usurpation of unjust power of any kind. Conservative men have always held that the only proper way for freemen to right political wrong is at the ballot-box. It is difficult to see how this is to be done without taking political action. For this reason, the Farmers' Association have now wisely resolved to cut loose from all partisan politics, standing firmly upon the broad and sound platform of principles, not men. To show the feeling that actuated this body of men, I give the text of the resolutions that were stigmatized as a mass of "stupidly-framed rhetoric." Each reader of the Groundswell may

Saturday Afternoon.

thus judge for himself of the animus of their critics, who should be marked as having written themselves down the enemies of all popular reform.

WHEREAS, Through the departure from the primary principles of our Government as promulgated by its founders, and through the imprudent exercise of that highest prerogative of the freeman—the right of suffrage—we, the farmers of Illinois, in common with the wealth and food-producers of these United States, have, by our past action, acquiesced in a system of class legislation which makes the great majority slavishly subservient to a small minority; and,

WHEREAS, This condition is clearly traceable to the fostering protection which has been accorded by our legislative bodies, both State and National, to the financial, mercantile, manufacturing, and transporting interests, enabling them to accumulate an undue proportion of the national wealth, and encouraging them in the exercise of the corrupting, lobby influences which have become inseparable from our legislative system; therefore,

Resolved, That the preservation of our national life imperatively demands that every American voter should attend with care to all primary nominations and elections, so as to insure the election of competent and honest men to all offices in the gift of the people.

Resolved, That the past record of the old political parties of this country is such as to forfeit the confidence and respect of the people, and that we are, therefore, absolved from all allegiance to them, and will act no longer with them.

Resolved, That we demand the unconditional repeal of the salary grab law, the repeal to be retroactive in its action, and this without a restoration of the franking privilege.

Resolved, That we do not recognize any necessity that public officers should receive extravagant salaries to the end that they may conform to the demand of expensive and fashionable tastes, which, in their very nature, are antagonistic to republican principles, and we demand a reduction of official salaries.

Resolved, That we demand the immediate reform of abuses in the civil service, through which the patronage of the government is dispensed as a reward for partisan service rather than with regard to the public necessities.

Resolved, That we are in favor of improving and perfecting the navigation of our lakes and rivers and water connections, as soon as it can possibly be done.

Resolved, That we are opposed to a protective tariff.

Resolved, That we deprecate any further grants of public lands or loans of the public credit; and of National, State, or local subscriptions in aid of corporations.

Resolved, That we favor the repeal of our National Banking Law, and believe that the Government should supply a legal tender currency directly from the Treasury, interchangeable, at the option of holder, with Government bonds bearing the lowest possible rate of interest.

Resolved, That we hold that our patent laws are too often made to subserve the interest of monopolists, and should be carefully revised and restricted.

Resolved, That the existing railway legislation of this State should be sustained and enforced until thoroughly tested before the courts.

Resolved, That we oppose any legislation by Congress, under the plea of regulating commerce between the States, which shall deprive the people of their present controlling influence through State legislation.

Resolved, That the right of the legislature to regulate and control the railroads of the State must be vindicated, established, and maintained as an essential attribute of State government; and that those holding the doctrine that railroad charters are contracts in the sense that they are not subject to legislative supervision and control have no just appreciation of the necessary powers and rights of a free government; and we will agree to no truce, and submit to no compromise, short of complete vindication and re-establishment of the supremacy of the State government in its rights, through its legislature, to supervise and control the railroads of the State in such manner as the public interest shall demand.

Resolved, That we uncompromisingly condemn the practice of our public officials in receiving free passes from railroad managers.

Resolved, That we demand a reduction of all public expenditures, to the end that taxation may be reduced to the lowest possible limit.

Resolved, That we condemn the action of our legislature in adjourning the regular session, thereby practically defeating the provision of the constitution providing biennial sessions.

Resolved, That since a large number of plow manufacturers of the West have thrown down the gauntlet, we take it up, and recommend to the farmers of this State to patronize none of said manufacturers until they will sell to us direct, at wholesale rates.

CHAPTER L.

THE ORDER OF PATRONS OF INDUSTRY.

ITS ORGANIZATION AND RAPID GROWTH.

Differing in sphere, yet very similar to the organization of Patrons of Husbandry in other essential respects, this new Order aims to associate together the working men and women of our towns and cities in bonds of fraternity. The organization was effected in New York City, by various working men, of several States, in August, 1873; and, already, its lodges are numbered by hundreds.* The emblem of the Order is a circular saw, around which are grouped the implements used in the various mechanical industries.

In the short time since its organization, it has met with unqualified success, which would seem to give assurance that it will soon become one of the most useful and powerful organizations in the United States.

Its grand object, as stated in one of its circulars, is not only the general improvement of the laboring classes, but to increase the wealth, and general happiness, and prosperity of the country. It is founded upon the axioms, that the laborer is worthy of his living; that individual happiness depends upon general prosperity; and that the wealth of a country depends upon the general intelligence and mental culture of the laboring classes. The best mode of securing

"Lots of Fun."

Picking Apples.

One of the Pets.

Back of the Barn.

Nooning in the Shade.

A Sly Little Customer.

A Page for the Little Folks.

a diffusion of knowledge, with a view to its application for the increase of the power and prosperity of the laboring classes, is, therefore, one of the most important questions that can be propounded. Its objects are thus further explained in a circular issued by the Order:

AIMS, ADVANTAGES, AND METHODS OF THE ORDER.

Clubs [of workingmen] for mutual instruction and friendly interchange of ideas seem to lose their interest as soon as the first excitement of organization is past. The incentive to the formation of these societies results from the recognition of the well-known principle, that *unity of action* is necessary to secure success; but to encourage and maintain progressive success, this unity must be made solid and permanent, not trivial and spasmodic. When we reflect upon the fact that certain associations have stood the test of ages—many centuries—as, for example, the Masonic Order—we may well pause and ask, "In what does their permanency consist?" We can find but one satisfactory answer to this question, and that is, in their ritual, secrecy, fraternity, and mutual benefits.

If, then, these are the efficient elements of extension, permanency, and success, why not employ them for the dissemination of useful knowledge, and a more general and effective organization of communities engaged in laboring pursuits?

And this we propose, not only for their benefit, but also for the increase of national wealth and power. If these are available accessories for the permanent organization of workingmen—all other means having failed—why not adopt them? If a *secret* organization of workingmen, with an appropriate and impressive ceremony of initiation, will secure fraternity, unity, efficiency, discipline, and permanency—as the projectors of this Order believe—all intelligent citizens, and especially those engaged in laboring pursuits, will approve and sustain our enterprise, and extend to the Patrons of Industry their unqualified approval and support. Women are admitted into our Order, as well as young persons, of both sexes, over the ages of fifteen and eighteen, respectively.

Young men are constantly being attracted to the cities from the country; leaving behind them the most certain sources of comfortable competence, for precarious competition in channels already overflowing. There are undoubtedly good and sufficient reasons for this migratory tendency: a want of attractions for the mind, and the absence of organization and *esprit du corps* in rural pursuits. All of these should join the Patrons of Industry.

We solicit the co-operation of woman, because of a conviction that, without her aid, success will be less certain and decided.

Much might be said in this connection, but every husband and brother knows that where he can be accompanied by his wife or sister no lessons will be learned but those of purity and truth.

The novelty of this organization and the manner it proposes of introducing a system of co-operation, not only in financial, but in political affairs, has hitherto prevented the originators from calling public attention to its work, but the great favor with which it has been received, prompts to a bolder action—satisfied that the noble purposes to which the Order is dedicated, will command the respect and serious attention of all.

We ignore all religious discussions in the Order. We do not solicit the patronage of any sect, association, or individual, upon any grounds whatever, except upon the intrinsic merits of the Order. It needs no such patronage, and would not be what it is, if it did.

Its objects, as already indicated, are to advance the condition of those who labor; to elevate and dignify the occupation of workingmen and women; and to protect its members against the numerous combinations by which their interests are injuriously affected. There is no association that secures so many advantages to its members as this.

The Order of the Patrons of Industry will accomplish a thorough and systematic organization among workingmen throughout the United States, and will secure among them intimate social relations, and acquaintance with each other, for the advancement and elevation of their pursuits, with an appreciation and protection of their true interest.

By such means, may be accomplished that which exists throughout the country in all other vocations, and among all other classes, combined co-operative association, for individual improvement and common benefit, and for the purification of our State and National Legislatures.

In the meetings of this Order, all but members are excluded, and there is in its proceedings a symbolized ritual, pleasing, beautiful, and appropriate, which is designed not only to charm the fancy, but to cultivate and enlarge the mind and purify the heart, having, at the same time, strict adaptation to rural pursuits. It is an Order in which all persons will find innocent recreation and valuable instruction, pecuniary profit and mutual protection. It is, in truth, a need long felt and now required. The secrecy of the ritual and proceedings of the Order has been adopted chiefly for the purpose of accomplishing desired efficiency, extension and unity, and to secure among its members in the internal working of the Order confidence, harmony, and security.

Among other advantages which may be derived from the Order can be mentioned systematic arrangements for procuring and disseminating, in the most expeditious manner, information relative to labor, demand and supply, prices, and markets, and transportation throughout the country; and for the establishment of depots for the purchase of special or general products of the country; and for the purpose of procuring help at home or from abroad, and situations for persons seeking employment; and for detecting and exposing those that are unworthy, and for protecting, by all available means, the laboring interest from fraud and deception of any kind.

It is desired that every Lodge shall be in intimate relation with its neighboring Lodges, and these with the State Lodge, and the State Lodge in unity with the National Lodge. Valuable information and benefits enjoyed by one are communicated to all. The old style of workingmen's clubs, like the old style of machinery, were very good in their day, but they are of the past, and too far behind all other enterprise in the progress of civilization. Hence the necessity for this new Order.

DEGREES, OFFICERS, ETC.

The local lodges are composed as follows: First Degree, Apprentice; Second Degree, Laborer; Third Degree, Journeyman. These are the degrees for males. The corresponding degrees for females are: First Degree, Apprentice; Second Degree, Maiden; Third Degree, Matron. The State lodges are composed of Master Workmen of local lodges and their wives who have taken the third degree, or their proxies. The National Lodge is composed of Master Workmen of State lodges, and their wives who have taken the third degree, or of their proxies.

The officers of the various lodges consist of and rank as follows: Master Workman, Workman, Helper, Laborer, Secretary, Treasurer, Lodge Keeper, Watchman, Stewardess, and Workwoman.

The ritual, like that of the Patrons of Husbandry, is simple in its character, and devoid of the ceremony that so marks many of the old-time secret orders. The expenses also are light and within the reach of any working man. Unlike Trades' Unions, this organization is not confined to any particular industry, but here all can meet on the common ground of universal brotherhood.

This, then, with the Farmers' Clubs and Granges, would seem to furnish three sides of a perfect square. The figure may be rendered perfect by a co-operation of these three great industrial associations of America. Herein, again, may be typified the integrity of the square, containing as it does the social, the intellectual, the moral, and the political. Herein, it is believed, no drones can enter. The true parallelograms forming the square are the producers of food and the producers of manufactured articles. Herein, it is hoped, the farmers and the artisans may clasp hands, that with consolidated force they may work towards a common goal, upon which shall be inscribed in letters of gold, "Unity of purpose for NATIONAL PROSPERITY."

CONSTITUTION AND BY-LAWS OF THE ORDER.

The Constitution of the Order first names the officers of the various lodges as already noticed. The remaining portion is as follows:

All officers shall be chosen by vote. There shall be an Executive Council composed of the Master, Secretary, and Treasurer of the

National Lodge; and they shall act with full power for the National Lodge when the latter is not in session. They shall have full power to appoint members of the Order as Deputies to organize Lodges, and shall remove them at their discretion.

Local Lodges shall meet at least once in each month. State Lodges shall meet at least once in each year. The National Lodge shall meet annually. Special meetings may be called at any time by the Master Workman of each Lodge.

All laws, rituals, etc., or changes of the same, shall be made by the National Lodge.

Any person of the age of eighteen years (males), or fifteen years (females), is eligible and entitled to membership after due examination. Every application must be accompanied by the fee of membership; if rejected, the money will be refunded. All applications must be certified by a member in good standing, and the character of the applicant will be carefully inquired into by a committee appointed by the Master Workman. If the report of these is satisfactory, they will be balloted for. Three negative ballots will be required to reject an applicant.

The initiation fee for males shall be two dollars, and for females one dollar. The dues shall not be less than ten cents monthly, from each member.

Eight men and two women may be accepted to organize a Local Lodge. All charters issue directly from the National Lodge.

Ten Local Lodges may constitute a State Lodge. The expenses of the State Lodges shall be assessed upon the Local Lodges *pro rata*, according to the membership, and the expenses of the National Lodge shall be assessed in a like manner upon the State Lodges. A charter fee of $16 shall accompany each application and be paid into the treasury of the National Lodge. The funds of the National Lodge shall be appropriated by ballot of said Lodge.

The Executive Council shall appoint a General Purchasing Agent, who shall give bonds for his fidelity. He shall have charge of all arrangements for purchasing, between the producers and consumers, of all sorts of commodities. Any member or members of the Order may purchase any article they may wish, through the Master Workman of their Local Lodge, upon payment of the amount required on the price list. Such payment must be made in advance, with a written order, endorsed by the Master Workman, and bearing the seal of the said Lodge. Each Lodge shall keep a seal, an impress or copy of which shall first be filed with the General Purchasing Agent. Price lists shall be issued by the Executive Council, giving the reduced price—less the agent's profit—of each article, as agreed to by those who sell to Patrons, at first prices: such lists shall be kept by each Master Workman, and shall never be disclosed to any person outside of the fellowship of the Order.

The duties and obligations of the officers of the National, the State, and the Local Lodges, shall be known only to the members of the Order.

There are no oaths used by this Order. Members are obligated upon their sacred honor and written pledge, never to disclose any thing connected with the organization. Each Lodge cares for the sick, afflicted, or destitute, in its membership.

As no real or lasting benefit can accrue to the working men of the United States without political action, the Patrons of Industry will aim to correct, at the ballot box, the evils of special and class legislation under which we are common sufferers and victims. The votes of the Patrons of Industry will be cast for honest men, and we can find them in our own Order. We shall not need to go outside of it for honesty and ability to fitly represent us in our State Legislatures or in the National Congress. Men of all shades of political and religious opinions can meet on one common ground and act in political concert; for we will ignore party organizations if such do not give us justice, and form our own party, whose basis shall be justice to those who labor for their bread.

Unworthy members, against whom charges of unfaithfulness to the interests of the Order may be proven, shall be expelled by the Master Workman.

BY-LAWS. ARTICLE 1. The seventh day of August, the birthday of the Patrons of Industry, shall be celebrated as the anniversary of the Order.

ART. 2. Not less than the representation of twenty States present at any meeting of the National Lodge shall constitute a quorum.

ART. 3. At the annual meeting of each State Lodge it may elect a proxy to represent the State Lodge in the National Lodge in case of the inability of the Master Workman to attend, but such proxy shall not thereby be entitled to the third degree.

ART. 4. Questions of administration and jurisprudence arising in and between State Lodges, and appeals from the action and decision thereof, shall be referred to the Master Workman and Executive Council of the National Lodge, whose decision shall be respected and obeyed until overruled by action of the National Lodge.

ART. 5. It shall be the duty of the Master Workman to preside at meetings of the National Lodge; to see that officers and members of committees properly perform their respective duties; to see that the Constitution, By-laws, and resolutions of the National Lodge and the usages of the Order are observed and obeyed; to sign all drafts drawn upon the treasury; and, generally, to perform all duties pertaining to such office.

ART. 6. It shall be the duty of the Secretary to keep a record of all proceedings of the National Lodge, to keep a just and true account of all moneys received and paid out by him, to countersign all drafts upon the treasury, to conduct the correspondence of the National Lodge, and, generally, to act as the administrative officer of the National Lodge, under the direction of the Master Workman and the Executive Council.

It shall be his duty, at least once each month, to deposit with the Fiscal Agency holding the funds of the National Lodge all moneys that may have come into his hands, and forward a duplicate receipt therefor to the Treasurer, and to make a full report of all transactions to the National Lodge at each annual session.

It shall be his further duty to procure a monthly report from the Fiscal Agency with whom the funds of the National Lodge are deposited, of all moneys received and paid out by them during each month, and send a copy of such report to the Executive Council and the Master Workman of the National Lodge.

ART. 7. It shall be the duty of the Treasurer to issue all drafts upon the Fiscal Agency of the Order, said drafts having been previously signed by the Master Workman and countersigned by the Secretary of the National Lodge.

He shall report monthly to the Master Workman of the National Lodge through the office of the Secretary, a statement of all receipts of deposits made by him, and of all drafts or checks signed by him during the previous month.

He shall report to the National Lodge at each annual session, a statement of all receipts of deposits made by him, and of all drafts or checks signed by him since his last annual report.

ART. 8. It shall be the duty of the Executive Council to exercise a general supervision of the affairs of the Order during the recess of the National Lodge; to instruct the Secretary in regard to printing and disbursements, and to place in his hands a contingent fund; to decide all questions and appeals referred to them by the officers and members of State Lodges; and to lay before the National Lodge at each session a report of all such questions and appeals, and their decisions thereon.

ART. 9. No compensation for time and service shall be given the Master Workman, Secretary, Treasurer, and Executive Council, except actual expenses.

Whenever General or Special Deputies are appointed by the Master Workman of the National Lodge, said Deputies shall receive only such compensation for time and services as is stated in Section 2, of this article: *Provided,* In no case shall pay from the National Lodge be given General Deputies in any State after the formation of its State Lodge.

SEC. 2. General or Special Deputies are entitled to a fee of one dollar, besides traveling expenses, for organizing Local Lodges.

ART. 10. The financial existence of Local Lodges shall date from the first day of January, first day of April, first day of July, and first day of October, subsequent to the day of their organization, from which date their first quarter shall commence.

State Lodges shall date their financial existence three months after the first day of January, first of April, first of July, and first of October immediately following their organization.

ART. 11. Each State Lodge shall be entitled to send one representative, who shall be a Master Workman thereof, or his proxy, to all meetings of the National Lodge. He shall receive mileage at the rate of five cents per mile both ways, computed by the nearest practicable route, to be paid as follows: The Master and Secretary of the National Lodge shall give such representative an order for the amount on the Treasurer of the State Lodge which he represents, and this order shall be receivable by the National Lodge in payment of State dues.

ART. 12. The ritual and secret word of the Order may be altered by the Executive Council whenever, in their judgment, such alterations may be necessary for the interests of the Order.

The Executive Council is composed of the Master Workman, Secretary, and Treasurer of the National Lodge, and they shall act with full power for the National Lodge when the National Lodge is not in session.

THE ORDER LAW-ABIDING, AND BENEVOLENT.

There is every reason to believe that the Patrons of Industry will always be found as law-abiding as the most conservative of their enemies could possibly desire; and that, in case any attempt should ever be made by those inimical to the integrity of the Government and the rights of property, to trample down, or cripple by violence the just rights of any class of citizens of the United States, none would be found more ready to throw the weight of their influence in the scale of law ond order, than the Patrons of Husbandry and its kindred society, the Patrons of Industry. This has been repeatedly asserted, and in the most emphatic terms.

The primary feature of this order, like that of the Patrons of Husbandry, is to so educate its members that intelligent thought, moral deportment, and a conscientious performance of duty shall be the rule and guide of their action. Therein, and therein only, lies the true road to permanent prosperity for any nation.

THE END.

www.ingramcontent.com/pod-product-compliance
Lightning Source LLC
LaVergne TN
LVHW021230110826
845150LV00002B/292

* 9 7 8 1 4 2 5 5 6 3 0 6 6 *